AF324073

Understanding Contexts of Business in Western Asia

Land of Bazaars and High-Tech Booms

New Teaching Resources for Management in a Globalised World

Print ISSN: 2661-4774
Online ISSN: 2661 4782

Series Editor: Professor Léo-Paul Dana

The classic economic view of internationalisation was based on the theory of competitive advantage, and over the years, internationalisation was seen in various lights, as an expansion option. With the reduction of trade barriers, however, many local small enterprises face major international competitors in formerly protected domestic markets. Today, competitiveness in the global marketplace is no longer an option; it has become a necessity as the acceleration towards globalisation offers unprecedented challenges and opportunities.

This book series will bring together textbooks, monographs, edited collections and handbooks useful to postgraduates and researchers in the age of globalisation. Relevant topics include, but are not limited to: research methods, culture, entrepreneurship, globalisation, immigration, migrants, public policy, self-employment, sustainability, technological advances, emerging markets, demographic shifts, and innovation.

Published:

Vol. 4 *Understanding Contexts of Business in Western Asia:*
Land of Bazaars and High-Tech Booms
edited by Léo-Paul Dana, Aidin Salamzadeh, Veland Ramadani and Ramo Palalić

Vol. 3 *The Entrepreneur's Field Guide: The 3 Day Startup Method*
by Andrew Zimbroff and Cam Houser

Vol. 2 *Entrepreneurial Finance: A Definitive Guide*
by Vincenzo Butticè, Massimo Gaetano Colombo, Annalisa Croce, Massimiliano Guerini, Giancarlo Giudici and Francesca Tenca

Vol. 1 *Qualitative Methodologies and Data Collection Methods:*
Toward Increased Rigour in Management Research
by Edward Groenland and Léo-Paul Dana

New Teaching Resources for Management in a Globalised World

Volume 4

Understanding Contexts of Business in Western Asia

Land of Bazaars and High-Tech Booms

Editors

Léo-Paul Dana
Dalhousie University, Canada

Aidin Salamzadeh
University of Tehran, Iran

Veland Ramadani
South East European University, North Macedonia

Ramo Palalić
Sultan Qaboos University, Oman

World Scientific

NEW JERSEY · LONDON · SINGAPORE · BEIJING · SHANGHAI · HONG KONG · TAIPEI · CHENNAI · TOKYO

Published by

World Scientific Publishing Co. Pte. Ltd.

5 Toh Tuck Link, Singapore 596224

USA office: 27 Warren Street, Suite 401-402, Hackensack, NJ 07601

UK office: 57 Shelton Street, Covent Garden, London WC2H 9HE

Library of Congress Cataloging-in-Publication Data
Names: Dana, Leo Paul, editor. | Salamzadeh, Aidin, editor. |
    Ramadani, Veland, editor. | Palalić, Ramo, editor.
Title: Understanding contexts of business in Western Asia : land of bazaars and high-tech booms /
    editors Léo-Paul Dana, Dalhousie University, Canada, Aidin Salamzadeh,
    University of Tehran, Iran, Veland Ramadani, South East European University,
    North Macedonia, Ramo Palalić, International University of Sarajevo, Bosnia and Herzegovina.
Description: Hackensack, NJ : World Scientific Publishing, [2022] |
    Series: New teaching resources for management in a globalised world, 2661-4774 ; volume 4 |
    Includes bibliographical references and index.
Identifiers: LCCN 2021037431 | ISBN 9789811229688 (hardcover) |
    ISBN 9789811229695 (ebook for institutions) | ISBN 9789811229701 (ebook individuals)
Subjects: LCSH: Business--Middle East. | Bazaars (Markets)--Middle East. |
    Entrepreneurship--Middle East.
Classification: LCC HF5230.A3 U56 2022 | DDC 338.0956--dc23
LC record available at https://lccn.loc.gov/2021037431

British Library Cataloguing-in-Publication Data
A catalogue record for this book is available from the British Library.

For any available supplementary material, please visit
https://www.worldscientific.com/worldscibooks/10.1142/12082#t=suppl

Desk Editors: Poornima Harikrishnan/Lai Ann

Typeset by Diacritech Technologies Pvt. Ltd.
Chennai - 600106, India

Thank you Michelle for inspiring us

_{vii}

Foreword from International Business

Not one size fits all. Yet, some books teach business with minimal focus on the context for business. In reality, firms – large and small – are highly affected by the context in which they operate; yet, context is not uniformly conceptualised, theorised and operationalised by scholars of business and management. While most theories have come from developed countries with bountiful contexts, the diverse contexts of Western Asia are little understood. Religious factors are profoundly dominant in Western Asia, and businesses in this diverse area operate with considerations that are rarely considered in research. This book reveals a variety of schools of thought that have moulded several business models and mechanisms, which are, to some extent, different from the context of Western economies.

Valuable insights on marketplace phenomena result from careful observation, thoughtful interpretation and articulate expression. I am so pleased to see that these criteria have been met by the contributors of this book. Indeed, their work represents well-informed conclusions and sound advice. This book is a valuable reading for academics, practitioners, as well as public policymakers.

S. Tamer Cavusgil
Callaway Professorial Chair
Executive Director
and
Center for International Business Education and Research
Georgia State University
Atlanta, Georgia, USA

Foreword from Political Science

Western Asia is not a region most people in the world associate with vibrant economies, business opportunities or thriving commerce. Instead, for much of the last century, it has been tragically known as a region in conflict: conflict between the Cold War superpowers, conflict between religious communities and even branches of Islam, and of course the conflict between Israel and the Palestinians and their Arab allies, which has led both to the creation of a Palestinian refugee diaspora and to the destruction of centuries-old Jewish communities throughout the Arab world. Yet, it has not always been thus. In the Middle Ages, before European hegemony, Western Asia was the linchpin of a vast trading network spanning from Europe to the Pacific.[1] Even in the 19th century, Western travellers marvelled at the vibrancy of the region's markets and its peoples' rich entrepreneurial culture. Early in the age of aviation, it promised to become again a transport hub for intercontinental travel. Whereas today the region is best known as the centre of the world's oil production, it also boasts a wide variety of other exports and potential exports, including spices, fabrics, fruit and luxury goods. Western Asia also features rich, varied cultural traditions, and it continues to produce numerous highly educated, professionally driven people, many of whom sadly must seek their fortune outside the region.

In this innovative volume, the editors bring together a comprehensive survey of the opportunities for business and entrepreneurship in the countries of the region, from Iran to Georgia. The contributors to this collection read Western Asia against the grain, critiquing the dominant popular and scholarly narratives of violence, economic stagnation and oil dependence. The authors see the potential of this region, taken as a whole, as well as the distinctive business traditions, political environments and regulatory challenges facing each country. While Israel is clearly in an economic class by itself, and its entrepreneurial dynamism has been captured in the now

---

[1] Abu-Lughod, Janet L. (1989), *Before European Hegemony: the World System A.D. 1250–1350*, New York: Oxford University Press.

widely recognised concept of "Start-up Nation", the business panorama elsewhere in the region is by no means as gloomy as many people believe. A particularly encouraging sign for the future is that governments all over Western Asia are becoming aware of the need to invest in human capital, diversify exports and re-examine regulatory structures that impede entrepreneurship. While it would be premature to suggest that the region is heading for a Japan-style economic miracle that allows it to catch up to the Global North within a few decades, the chapters in this volume demonstrate the region's potential to achieve robust development. In particular, business in the region is characterised by dense networks of trust and sociability, which have the potential to facilitate the development of commerce in ways different from, but no less effective than, the organisational and technological achievements of Global North countries.

As the place where the three main monotheistic religions were born, Western Asia has been home to thriving Muslim, Christian and Jewish communities for centuries. Without exaggerating the extent to which either harmony or equality was actually attained, the coexistence and sometimes cooperation of these communities helped structure the economic life of the region, yielding both ethnic specialisation and networks of regional and long-distance trade. In the Ottoman Empire, Armenians, Jews and Greeks played a strong role in the empire's later economic development.[2] In Persian bazaars, distinct community structures promoted trust and accountability. There is no denying that in the last century Western Asia has become tragically known for intercommunal violence and ethnic cleansing. The genocide of the Ottoman Armenians is the most extreme example, but other groups have experienced mass killings as well, including the Kurds of Iraq and many communities in Syria since the onset of the current rebellion against the Assad regime. The creation of Israel led to the mass flight of Mandatory Palestine's Arab population, many of whom remain stateless residents of the West Bank, Gaza and several countries more than 70 years later.

What is perhaps less known is that the Arab–Israeli conflict also led, first, to the expulsion of Jews from Jordanian-controlled areas of the West Bank and East Jerusalem, and later to the expulsion and flight of nearly all the Arab world's Jewish communities, many of whom had contributed substantially to the economic and social development of their countries. The Egyptian Jewish communities of Tel Aviv, Rome and Montreal are

---

[2] Barkey, Karen (2008), *Empire of Difference: The Ottomans in Comparative Perspective*, Cambridge: Cambridge University Press.

examples of the new diasporas formed in this process. Meanwhile, the region's Christian population, which came under pressure in mainly Islamic states, has declined gradually and at times precipitously for decades. Yet while it may be too late to recreate the region's full religious diversity at the local level, it still exists at the pan-regional level, as well as in connections to ethnic diasporas outside the region. As the pieces in this collection demonstrate, the distinctive business traditions, specialisations and networks of the many ethnic and faith communities that populate Western Asia constitute a potential source of strength and development, particularly if the political conflicts that still hold the region in their grip could be resolved. In this regard, the recent burst of diplomacy that resulted in new peace treaties between Israel and several Arab states, including Bahrain and the United Arab Emirates, represents a hopeful sign that the imperative to achieve economic progress may yet overcome the desire to resolve old disputes by force.

A particular strength of this collection is the systematic manner in which the contributions explore the link between government policy and business. Governments greatly affect the environment for business, and those open to multiculturalism benefit from a society in which persons of various ethnicities contribute to the economy through their links with members of their communities elsewhere in the region and the world. As a post-Soviet scholar, I am very familiar with the ways in which historical legacies that are beyond the control of contemporary actors interact with the decisions of policymakers to create unexpected outcomes. Likewise, as the book in hand demonstrates, a society's economic success rests on both its intrinsic, exogenously given strengths, and on the ways in which government policy potentiates or fails to potentiates those strengths. With the right combination of government policies, there is every reason to believe that the people of Western Asia are just as prepared as any in the world to achieve the prosperity to which their drive, commercial acumen and historically developed trading networks entitle them to aspire.

Matthew Light
Munk School of Global Affairs & Public Policy
University of Toronto, Canada

Greeting from Michael Brecher

I wish you great success with this new publication…
The Middle East should continue to be a fascinating focus of your scholarship and intellectual interest in the decades ahead.

With all good wishes,
Michael Brecher
Professor
McGill University, Canada

Contents

Preface

L. Dudley Stamp[3] – the Sir Ernest Cassel Reader in Economic Geography at the University of London – referred to Western Asia as "The Near East." At the time, this was the commonly used expression used to describe this area of Asia, relatively near to Europe. Of course, the Near East is east of Europe, but for a reader in New Zealand, Western Asia is rather far, and to the west. To avoid the ethnocentricity of the term Near East, this book simply uses the term Western Asia.

Geography here has influenced history and culture, and impacts business today. I agree with Stamp that "Afghanistan is in a very crucial position, lying between Russian Central Asia and India… (1939, p. 418)", and that "The old Turkish Empire extended its influence over a very large portion of the globe and over still larger portions when one remembers that the old Sultan of Turkey was also the Caliph or the head of the Mohammedan religion. The modern Turks have divorced politics from religion" (p. 420). Elsewhere in Western Asia, religion is entrenched in politics and affects the environment for business.

My fascination with Asia began at Expo 67 – the 1967 World's Fair, in Montreal, Canada – where I would spend hours exploring the pavilions of Asian nations. Among the most impressive was that of Iran; while waiting in the long queue, my mother told me I should pay special attention because this was the land from which her grandfather had come. Once inside, I greatly enjoyed learning about Persian culture. With a fascinating history, Iran is a place where one can find a variety of old bazaars in each of its cities, some of which have origins in the Achaemenid Empire.

Other pavilions that I found amazing included those of Burma (today's Myanmar), Ceylon (now Sri Lanka), China, India, Israel, Japan, Korea and Thailand. I was overwhelmed by the diversity of Asia.

The idea to put together a book about Asia was first given to me in Copenhagen. It was November 1996 and I was presenting an

---

[3] Stamp, L. Dudley (1939), *A Commercial Geography*, London: Longmans, Green and Co., p. 418.

invited faculty seminar at the Asia Research Centre of the Institute of International Economics and Management, at Copenhagen Business School. Subsequently, I wrote several related books[4] and also compiled my five-volume collection published by SAGE.[5]

The present publication is completely different as it brings together, from various countries, prominent academics who are experts on Western Asia, and together we join forces to give the reader a taste of this vast region, its people, cultures, religions and how all these create a context for business. Western Asia is an amazing place; the wheel was developed here, and this is the birthplace of agriculture and writing. Christianity, Islam, Judaism and Zoroastrianism (Mazdayasna), trace their origins to Western Asia. Jews and Muslims are equally indigenous to this region. Zoroastrianism, with the belief in the deity Ahura Mazdā, is among the earliest religions in this region; Zoroastrians reformed early polytheism by Persians.

The bazaar is originally a Persian phenomenon, which was introduced thousands of years ago. This phenomenon was further developed by Muslims, after the emergence of Islam. However, Christians and especially Jews – among the most successful persons in business in Western Asia – also added some of their traditions to this phenomenon. Jews have the reputation for being among the most reliable businesspersons in Iranian bazaars, such as the Grand Bazaar in Tehran and the *Yahoudi Bazaar* (Jewish Bazaar) in Kermanshah, the largest Kurdish-speaking city in Iran.

Across Western Asia, cultural, linguistic and religious factors are still profoundly dominant, and they affect the context for business. A reminder of Islam's early days is the privileged social status accorded to self-employed merchants and artisans. This is not surprising, given the

---

[4] Dana, Léo-Paul (1999), *Entrepreneurship in Pacific Asia: Past Present & Future*, Singapore, New Jersey, London and Hong Kong: World Scientific, Dana, Léo-Paul (2000), *Economies of the Eastern Mediterranean Region: Economic Miracles in the Making*, Singapore, New Jersey, London and Hong Kong: World Scientific; Dana, Léo-Paul (2002), *When Economies Change Paths: Models of Transition in China, the Central Asian Republics, Myanmar, and the Nations of Former Indochine Française*, Singapore, New Jersey, London and Hong Kong: World Scientific; Dana, Léo-Paul (2007), *Asian Models of Entrepreneurship – From the Indian Union and the Kingdom of Nepal to the Japanese Archipelago: Context, Policy and Practice*, New Jersey, London, Singapore, Beijing, Shanghai, Hong Kong, Taipei and Chennai: World Scientific; Dana, Léo-Paul (2014), *Asian Models of Entrepreneurship – From the Indian Union and Nepal to the Japanese Archipelago: Context, Policy and Practice*, 2nd edition, New Jersey, London, Singapore, Beijing, Shanghai, Hong Kong, Taipei & Chennai: World Scientific.

[5] Dana, Léo-Paul, ed. (2015), *Asian Entrepreneurship*, 5-volume collection, London: Sage.

environment in which Islam developed. Muhammad was personally impressed by the camel caravan voyages of traders, and on several occasions, he travelled with them in his youth. He spent over a decade in caravan trading, covering a wide territory from the Mediterranean to the Indian Ocean. His first wife Khadija was a successful merchant whom he worked for and later worked with.

The bazaar is still closely inter-linked with Islam. During the fasting month of Ramadan, a question that often arises is, "Are you fasting?" During negotiations, there are frequent references to religion.

Tradition dictates that Muslims should pray five times a day: before sunrise, at noon, during the mid-afternoon, at sunset and at dusk. As traders bargain vividly, behind their voices one can often hear muezzins calling people to pray, from the minarets of mosques that serve as public address systems. This custom stems from Bilal, Muhammad's Black companion, who called followers to prayer in Medina.

Even among secular Muslims, it is common to mention Allah during leisure conversations, business negotiations and even simple greetings. I recall one time when I was checking in for a flight and requested a seat in the "No Smoking" section of the aeroplane, the agent at Trans World Airlines (TWA) responded, *insha Allah*. If God wanted I would be seated in the "No Smoking" section, but my personal preference seemed irrelevant to the agent checking me in that day. I had no power.

When examining the social structure of the bazaar economy, the relations among the players within it, their organisation and their economic principles, it is useful to consider the power structure involved. In Islam, religion and law are one. Traditionally, the leader of an Islamic community exercises three political powers: executive, legislative and judiciary; in addition, he is considered a religious leader.

The early caliphs, including Abu Bakr, Ali, Omar and Othman, were considered to be successors to Muhammad, the prophet of God. They were regents, judges, military chiefs and religious leaders all in one. According to Ibn Khaldoun, the political and religious leader has the responsibility to protect the religion as well as the direction of the people. Interestingly, such principles survived into the present century.

More striking is the fact that principles of bazaar economics have survived, and these dominate business transactions, often unconsciously. Business in the bazaar economy has traditionally focused on people, relationships and networks. This is in sharp contrast with the West's firm-type economy, where the focus has been on the product, rather than on the individual selling it.

Exhibit P.1   Selling sheep at a Thursday market; photo © 2021 by Léo-Paul Dana

While there are overall similarities across countries, chapters in this volume make it evident that Western Asia is also vast with contrasts. The region has modern cities and traditional markets in which prices are negotiated (see P.1).

A rugged country with fertile valleys, Afghanistan is home to many subsistence farmers; transportation infrastructure is little developed here and pack animals are helpful for transporting goods. Likewise, camels are used as beasts of burden in Syria. In contrast to these food producers, the 34 islands that make up Bahrain import most of their food. Likewise, Qatar has limited vegetation. Kuwait pumps water from deep under its desert and also desalinates water from the sea.

Following military conquest by the Romans in 70 AD, Jews were for centuries a nation without a country. Likewise, Armenia fell to the Romans in 114 AD. Like the Jews, Armenians spread to many lands and earned a reputation for being successful in business. The Armenians form a distinct genetic cluster and are a culturally isolated population[6]; they have long conducted business with – but did not mingle with – other ethnic groups. Exhibit P.2 features an Armenian community centre in Canada.

---

[6] Haber, Marc, Massimo Mezzavilla, Yali Xue, David Comas, Paolo Gasparini, Pierre Zalloua and Chris Tyler-Smith (2016), "Genetic Evidence for an Origin of the Armenians from Bronze Age Mixing of Multiple Populations," *European Journal of Human Genetics* 24, pp. 931–936.

Exhibit P.2   Armenian community centre – formerly the Young Israel of St. Laurent –
in Ville St. Laurent, Quebec, Canada; photo © 2021 by Léo-Paul Dana

Among notable Armenian entrepreneurs in Western Asia was Ivan
Mirzoev, who worked in the silk trade and the fishing sector before establishing the first successful oil-drilling operation in Azerbaijan in 1871.
Thanks to him, czarist Russia (that controlled this region) became the
world's largest producer of crude oil.[7] During the 20th century, Armenian
and Jewish states were reinstated. Israel has a Jewish majority, with equal
rights for Armenians, Bahai, Druze, Christians, Muslims and others.

This volume includes a chapter about every country in this very
diverse region, including Armenia, Azerbaijan and Georgia, formerly communist constituents of the Union of Soviet Socialist Republics; Bahrain,
a former British protectorate, which Abercrombie[8] referred to as the hub
of the Persian Gulf and Midas of oil; Iraq, where the Organisation of the
Petroleum Exporting Countries (OPEC) was born in 1960; Israel, which
Senor and Singer[9] called Start-up Nation; Jordan, carved out of British

---

[7] Daintith, Terence (2010), *Finders Keepers? How the Law of Capture Shaped the World Oil
Industry,* Washington, DC and London: RFF Press.

[8] Abercrombie, Thomas J. (1979), "Bahrain: Hub of the Persian Gulf," *National Geographic*
156 (3), pp. 300–329.

[9] Senor, Dan, and Saul Singer (2009), *Start-up Nation: The Story of Israel's Economic Miracle,*
New York: Grand Central Publishing.

Palestine in 1921[10]; Lebanon, where according to mythology Venus met Adonis[11]; Oman, a sultanate that Azzi[12] described as once ruling the East African sea trade; Saudi Arabia, the birthplace of Islam; and Yemen, where slavery was legal until 1962. Although Cyprus is a member of the European Union, the island of Cyprus is included in this book as the United Nations Statistics Division considers it to be in Western Asia.

Julie Ziskind and Annika Brack[13] of the World Economic Forum wrote, "Only a short flight separates Tel Aviv from many European capitals, but the seaside city's leadership on innovation and its bustling start-up culture can make it seem worlds away. Ranked sixth in the world by Start-Up Genome's Start-Up Ecosystem Rankings in 2019, Israel has been recognized internationally as the start-up nation... How does this tiny nation manage to be so creative? And if some of these factors are specific to its unique culture, is there anything Europe can replicate?"

Asians study in the West and many migrate. They understand the West and how to do business there. Exhibit P.3 features an Iranian retailer in California. In contrast, relatively few Westerners go to study in or immigrate to Asia. The purpose of this volume is to provide readers an introduction to the context of business in Western Asia.

We are living a paradigm shift and timing has perhaps never been better than now, to seek an understanding of, and plan business with, Western Asia. In September 1970, news headlines around the world focused on terrorism in Western Asia (Exhibit P.4). Henry Luce III[14] wrote, "world disorder never seemed closer than last week during the Middle East hijackings, when a small band of fanatics terrorized hundreds of people, blew up four planes and held the world at bay... The great drama, of course, was played out on the dusty plain north-east of Amman... The situation was hardly more stable in Amman, where Palestinian commandos and Jordanian troops were battling in the streets..." (1970, p. 7).

---

[10] For details, see: Friedman, Isaiah (2012), *Miscalculations by the British and the Rise of Moslem Nationalism: 1918–1925*, New Brunswick, New Jersey and London: Transaction Publishers.

[11] Ellis, William S. (1970), "Lebanon: Little Bible Land in the Crossfire of History," *National Geographic* 137 (2), pp. 240–275.

[12] Azzi, Robert (1973), "Oman, Land of Frankincense and Oil," *National Geographic* 143 (2), pp. 205–229.

[13] Ziskind, Julie, and Annika Brack (2019), From Israel's 'start-up nation', 4 Lessons in Innovation, (Retrieved from https://www.weforum.org/agenda/2019/09/israel-start-up-nation-innovation)

[14] Luce III, Henry (1970), "Letter from the Publisher," *Time* 96 (12), p. 7.

Exhibit P.3 Iranian shop in Los Angeles; photo © 2021 by Léo-Paul Dana

Indeed, on 6 September 1970, a secular, Palestinian, Marxist-Leninist organisation – the Popular Front for the Liberation of Palestine – hijacked three passenger jets, a Pan Am Boeing 747, a Swissair Douglas DC-8 and a TWA Boeing 707. Hijackers also tried but failed to hijack an El Al flight;

Exhibit P.4   1970 headline; photo © 2021 by Léo-Paul Dana

a hijacker, Leila Khaled, was held in custody in London. On 9 September, a British Overseas Airways Corporation (BOAC) Vickers VC10 flying from Mumbai, then known as Bombay, to London via Bahrain and Beirut was also hijacked by the Popular Front for the Liberation of Palestine and all aboard were held hostage until the release of the Leila Khaled. The Popular Front for the Liberation of Palestine blew up the Pan Am jumbo-jet in Cairo and the BOAC, Swissair and TWA jets, in Jordan. And that's the way it was in September 1970. Readers may recall "that's the way it was" was the signature sign-off of Walter Leland Cronkite (1916–2009) who was CBS Evening News anchorman at the time (from 1962 to 1981).

Fifty years later, news from Western Asia was quite different when headlines announced that on 15 September 2020, Bahrain, Israel, United Arab Emirates and the United States signed the Abraham Accords Peace Agreement promising cooperation in facing common challenges, and direct ties between the populations of Bahrain, Israel and the United Arab Emirates. As well as contributing to international business, this is a positive and important step towards enhancing regional stability, security and peace. Welcome to the NEW Western Asia, and enjoy!

Léo-Paul Dana

Acknowledgements

Every chapter has been peer-reviewed by at least two referees who provided valuable feedback on manuscripts. This input contributed to the rigour of chapters. We wish to thank all the members of the Editorial Board; names are listed in alphabetical order below.

Zoltan ACS	Editor, *Small Business Economics*
Kholoud AL-KHALDI	Deputy Director, International Labour Organisation
Mohammed AL-QASSABI	Researcher, Public Authority for Social Insurance, Oman
Yasser AL-SALEH	Researcher, The Public Authority for Applied Education and Training of Kuwait
Abeer ALKHWALDI	Mutah University, Jordan
Ilan ALON	Professor of International Business, University of Agder
Yochanan ALTMAN	Editor, *European Management Review*
Alistair ANDERSON	Distinguished Professor, Lancaster University and Editor, *Entrepreneurship & Regional Development*
David B. AUDRETSCH	Distinguished Professor, Ameritech Chair of Economic Development, Indiana University and Visiting Professor, King Saud University, Saudi Arabia
Peter BAMBERGER	Editor, *Academy of Management Discoveries*
Mané BEGLARYAN	American University of Armenia

(continued)

Ezzeddine BEN MOHAMED	University of Sfax
Héla BEN SOLTANE	University of Ha'il, Saudia Arabia
Ahmed BENANI	Head, International Observatory for Palestinian Affairs, Switzerland
Sergio CARVALHO	Dalhousie University
Gözde Inal CAVLAN	European University of Lefke, Northern Cyprus
Mustafa Fedai ÇAVUŞ	Osmaniye Korkut Ata Üniversitesi, Turkey
Helene Balslev CLAUSEN	Department of Culture and Learning, Aalborg University, Denmark
David CRAWFORD	Director of International Studies and International Business & Professor, Department of Sociology and Anthropology, Fairfield University, Fairfield, Connecticut, USA
Laure DIKMEN	Researcher, IAE de Poitiers
Pavlos DIMITRATOS	Research Professor, University of Glasgow
Amir EMAMI	Kharazmi University, Iran
Hamid ETEMAD	Professor, McGill University
Marvin GOLDMAN	Curator, New York
Zeevik GREENBERG	Researcher, Tel Hai College
Abdulsattar Abdullah HAMAD	Tikrit University College of Science, Iraq
Avi HEINRICH	Consultant, Haifa
Elahe HOSSEINI	Researcher, Yazd University, Iran
Kevin IBEH	Pro Vice-Chancellor (International) at Birkbeck, University of London
Hiroko KAWAMORITA	Ondokuz Mayis University, Turkey
Tuğberk KAYA	Cyprus International University, Northern Cyprus

(continued)

Shad KHAN	University of Buraimi, Oman
Ivan H. LIGHT	Professor *Emeritus,* UCLA
Sébastien LINDEN	Managing Partner, Linden & Swift, Grenoble
Nick LITSARDOPOULOS	Kingston University, UK
George LODORFOS	Professor & Dean, Leeds Business School
Esra MEMILI	University of North Carolina at Greensboro
Ehud MENIPAZ	Dean, School of Industrial Engineering & Management, Ben Gurion University
Orly C. MERON	The Interdisciplinary Department of Social Sciences, Bar-Ilan University
Sachi Nandan MOHANTY	ICFAI Foundation for Higher Education, Hyderabad
Kanellos Panagiotis NIKOLOPOULOS	Nikolopouleio School of Foreign Languages and Vocational Studies
Salar Alizad POURSAEIDI	Iran University of Science and Technology
Mohammad Rezaur RAZZAK	Sultan Qaboos University, Muscat, Oman
Abira REIZER	Associate Professor, Ariel University
Shahamak REZAEI	Roskilde University, Denmark
Ognjen RIĐIĆ	Associate Professor, International University of Sarajevo
Steffen ROTH	Professor of Management, La Rochelle Business School and Adjunct Professor of Economic Sociology, University of Turku
Mohammad Mahdi ROUNAGHI	Researcher, Islamic Azad University, Mashhad, Iran
Omar SHABAN	Founder and Director, PalThink for Strategic Studies, Palestine
David SMALLBONE	Professor, Kingston University, UK

(continued)

Ioannis SOLOMOU	Head of the Media and Public Relations Department, Press and Information Office, Ministry of Interior, Cyprus
Christophe STEPHAN	Montpellier Business School
Mosab I. TABASH	Director, Al Ain University, UAE
Shlomo Y. TARBA	Editor, *British Journal* of *Management*
Ron TUNINGA	Vice-President Academic Affairs, Wittenborg University of Applied Sciences
Jan VANG	Professor, University of Southern Denmark
Jonathan WARNER	Professor of Economics, *Emeritus,* Quest University Canada
Nagi George Selim ZEIDAN	Historian and author, Lebanon

As well, we would also like to thank the families who invited us into their homes and shared much knowledge (see Exhibit A.1).

Exhibit A.1   Inviting us to lunch

About the Editors

Léo-Paul Dana is a Professor at Montpellier Business School and at Dalhousie University. He is associated with the Chaire ETI at Sorbonne Business School. He is also Visiting Professor at Kingston University and an Adjunct Professor at Auckland University of Technology. A graduate of McGill University and HEC-Montreal, he has served as Marie Curie Fellow at Princeton University and Visiting Professor at INSEAD. He has published extensively in a variety of journals.

Aidin Salamzadeh is an Assistant Professor at the University of Tehran. His interests are startups, new venture creation and entrepreneurship. Aidin serves as an associate editor in *Revista de Gestão, Innovation & Management Review* (Emerald), *Entrepreneurial Business and Economics Review, Journal of Women's Entrepreneurship and Education* as well as an editorial advisory in *The Bottom Line* (Emerald). Besides, he is a reviewer in numerous distinguished international journals. Aidin is a member of the European SPES Forum, the Asian Academy of Management, and Ondokuz Mayis University.

Veland Ramadani is a Professor at the Faculty of Business and Economics, South East European University, the Republic of North Macedonia. His research interests include entrepreneurship, small business management, family businesses and venture capital investments. He authored or co-authored around 140 research articles and produced 27 books (11 authored, 16 edited). Dr. Ramadani is a co-Editor of *Journal of Enterprising Communities: People and Places in the Global Economy* (JEC). He serves as a member of Supervisory Board of the Development Bank of North Macedonia. Dr. Ramadani received the Award for Excellence 2016 – Outstanding Paper by Emerald Group Publishing. His last book is *Entrepreneurial Family Businesses*, published by Springer.

Ramo Palalić teaches at Sultan Qaboos University, in Oman. His research is in the area of entrepreneurship, leadership and management. Dr Palalić has authored and co-authored many articles in globally recognised journals like *Management Decision, International Journal of Entrepreneurial Behavior & Research, International Entrepreneurship and Management Journal* and alike. Additionally, he has co-authored/co-edited several books and many book chapters in the field of business and entrepreneurship published with internationally prominent publishers (Springer, World Scientific). Moreover, Dr. Palalić is serving as the reviewer/editor board member in several well-established international journals. Apart from his research, he was involved in business projects in the areas of entrepreneurial leadership and marketing management, in private and public organisations.

https://doi.org/10.1142/9789811229695_fmatter

About the Contributors

Ali Ahmadi studied MBA in strategy at the Industrial Management Institute of Tehran and is currently a PhD candidate in strategy at Queen's University in Kingston, Canada. Ali is interested in strategic management and innovation in high-velocity contexts. Coming from a mechanical engineering background, he is interested in technology and emergent business models and their consequences for market turbulence.

Mohammed Alarifi holds an MBA from Imam Mohammad Ibn Saud Islamic University, Riyadh, KSA. He also achieved his Bachelor's Degree in Business Administration from Imam Mohammad Ibn Saud Islamic University, Riyadh, KSA. He has experience in both private and public sectors. He worked as a Teaching Assistant at Al-Jouf University, Al-Jouf, Saudi Arabia, and as a procurement category specialist in a food manufacturing company in Riyadh, Saudi Arabia.

Wassim J. Aloulou is an Associate Professor at the College of Economics and Administrative Sciences at Imam Mohammad Ibn Saudi Islamic University, Riyadh, KSA. He received his PhD in Management Sciences from the University of Pierre Mendes, France Grenoble 2, France, and from the Faculté des Sciences Economiques et de Gestion de Sfax, Tunisia, in 2008. He teaches graduate and undergraduate courses in entrepreneurship in MBA and BBA programmes. His research interests currently focus on digital entrepreneurship, FinTech, entrepreneurial intentions and orientations of individuals and organisations. He is an editor of the *Entrepreneurship Review*, and an article editor of *Sage Open*. He has authored and co-authored multiple articles in reputable international journals, book with IGI Global and multiple book chapters (with Edward Elgar and World Scientific).

Gözde İnal Cavlan is an Associate Professor at the Department of Business Administration at the European University of Lefke, Gemikonagi, Northern Cyprus. Her research interests include mainstream, ethnic minority and women entrepreneurship, career choice and work-life balance. She has been teaching organisational behaviour, management theory and practice, international business and human resource management at undergraduate and graduate levels. She has published several book chapters on entrepreneurship topics in international books and papers in journals including *Journal of Management Development, Equality, Diversity and Inclusion Journal* and *Career Development International Journal.*

Maia Chiabrishvili is a Professor at the American University of the Middle East teaching Economics on undergraduate and graduate levels. She has extensive experience in teaching business-related subjects (different universities in Georgia); consulting on business sustainability after donor disengagement in the post-soviet states (Booz Allen Hamilton); implementation of programme defence budgeting in the Armed Forces of Georgia (Ministry of Defence, Georgia). Her research interests include education in multicultural environment and defence economics; research results are presented at international conferences and published in high-ranking journals. She is a senior reviewer for IAFOR (International Academic Forum).

Vladimir Dzenopoljac is an Associate Professor of Strategic Management and is the Director of MBA programme at the College of Business Administration, American University of the Middle East, Kuwait. He received his PhD Degree from the University of Kragujevac, Serbia, in the field of intellectual capital and value creation. He is an active researcher and published a significant number of journal articles in the area of intellectual capital, knowledge management, strategic management and entrepreneurship. Alongside his academic career, Vladimir was providing business consultancy services in the areas of strategy development and execution, business planning, and financial planning and analysis.

Luan Eshtrefi is an Associate Professor at the Keller Graduate School of Management at DeVry University in the United States. He teaches graduate courses in Business Economics and Global Perspectives on International Business. Dr. Eshtrefi has been teaching for more than 17 years at the tertiary level and has worked both in the private sector and in the public sector in multiple locations including Dubai, United Arab Emirates, where he was faculty lead in teaching Entrepreneurship and Innovation at a public university. His research interests currently focus on entrepreneurship education and international business and globalisation. He has authored and co-authored articles in international journals, books and multiple book chapters.

Hamid Etemad is a Canadian Organisational Theorist and a Professor at the Desautels Faculty of Management, McGill University. He has served as President, Vice President and Membership Chairman of the Administrative Sciences Association of Canada, as well as on the Board of Directors of the Social Science Federation of Canada.

Bella L. Galperin is Dana Professor of Management and Senior Associate Director of the TECO Energy Center for Leadership at the Sykes College of Business at the University of Tampa. Her interests include cross-cultural management, leadership, ethics, and workplace deviance – both destructive and constructive. She has published in the Journal of Business Ethics, International Journal of Human Resource Management, Leadership Quarterly, International Business Review, and other journals. She co-authored a book entitled *LEAD: Leadership effectiveness in Africa and the African diaspora.* She is an associate editor of *Journal of Managerial Psychology.*

Çolpan Karan Galperin is an artist and retired dentist who works with mediums including painting, sculpture, and photography. In her most recent series, Turkish Delights, Galperin revisits her birthplace of Turkey. After living abroad the majority of her life, she rediscovers the colours, shapes, textures, and movement amidst the chaos and paradoxes of Istanbul. Galperin is a graduate of dentistry (New York University) and visual and media arts (Université du Québec à Montréal). For more information, visit: https://bellalgalperin.wixsite.com/colpankaran

Shqipe Gërguri-Rashiti is an Associate Professor at the American University of the Middle East Kuwait – currently serving as the Dean of the College of Business Administration. Dr. Gërguri has a very diverse educational background in different international institutions, which can be a great asset for an academic, with excellent communication, decision-making, planning and organising skills with a strong touch of personal and professional integrity. She has a unique experience in living and working in diverse cultural environments worldwide. Her research interests are on female entrepreneurship, innovation, technology and strategic management based on which she has written and co-authored papers. She published research articles in several internationally recognised journals such as *International Journal of Entrepreneurship and Small Business, Journal of Enterprising Communities, Strategic Change: Briefings in Entrepreneurial Finance*, etc.

Irine Guruli is an Associate Professor in Business Administration focused on Entrepreneurship at Ilia State University. Prior to this position, since 2015 she has been working as a visiting lecturer. Since 2011, Irine has been working at the Economic Policy Research Centre (EPRC), where she currently serves as a Deputy Director. She has extensive experience in research, training, monitoring and advocacy activities. Irine is engaged in conducting research in the directions of economic policy, private sector development, SME policy and regulatory impact assessment. Irine received her PhD Degree in 2019 from Ilia State University (Dissertation topic: Entrepreneurship and SME Development in Emerging Economies – the case of Georgia). She earned her Master's Degree in Business Administration from Jönköping University, in 2017–2018 she was a PhD visiting researcher at the same university with the support of the Swedish Institute.

Vahid Jafari-Sadeghi is a Lecturer in Business Strategy in the School of Strategy and Leadership at Coventry University. Vahid holds his PhD in international entrepreneurship from the University of Turin where he has served as a post-doctoral fellow. Also, he has been a visiting research scholar at the University of Regina and contributed to different research projects with various scholars and universities. Vahid has published papers in several international journals and publications such as *Journal of Business Research, International Business Review, Journal of International Entrepreneurship, Research in International Business and Finance*, etc. He is a member of the editorial board at *British Food Journal* and acted as guest editor and reviewer for several academic journals and performed as track chair and presenter for a number of international conferences.

Ali Safar Kamel is a Postgraduate of Media Management from the University of Tehran and a lecturer in journalism at the Polytechnic University in the Kurdistan Region (Iraq). He is interested in advertising, digital marketing, magazine design and photography.

Hans-Ruediger Kaufmann completed his sponsored PhD in 1997 and worked at Manchester Metropolitan University. Later, he worked in Budapest, first as Course Director Marketing for a company affiliated with the Chartered Institute of Marketing and then as an Assistant Professor in Marketing at the International Management Centre Budapest as well as its contractual consultant. He launched his international management consultancy in 1997. At the University of Applied Sciences Liechtenstein he was the Academic Director Private Banking and, later, the Head of the Competence Centre International Management. Since October 2006 he was an Associate Professor at the University of Nicosia and was ranked Full Professor in February 2013. He has been a launching member and President (2007–2009) of the international research network on consumer behaviour, CIRCLE. He also was a launching member of and is currently Vice-President of the EuroMed Research Business Institute (EMBRI). In 2011, Rudi was elected into the Board of the American Marketing Association Global Marketing SIG as Vice-Chair Communications. He is a member of the editorial board of a variety of journals and an Associate Editor of the *World Review of Entrepreneurship, Management and Sustainable Development.*

Zeinab Khansari is an Affiliate Researcher working with the University of Regina and Ryerson University in Canada. She received her PhD degree in Chemical Engineering (Energy and Environment specialisation) from the University of Calgary and is interested in performing multidisciplinary research in the field of engineering, entrepreneurship and education. She has previously taught undergraduate and postgraduate courses at various universities in Canada and the Middle East. Dr. Zeinab is an associate member of the Institute of Chemical Engineers (AMIChemE) and EIT member of the Association of Professional Engineers and Geoscientists of Alberta (APEGA).

Sepideh Khavarinezhad is a Doctoral Research Fellow at the Università degli Studi di Torino. Her research interests are international entrepreneurship, female entrepreneurship and internationalisation. She has published papers in several international journals and publications such as *European Journal of Islamic Finance, International Journal of Applied Research in Management and Economics* and as a PhD student has some papers in the process of publishing. Sepideh is a member of editorial board/reviewer of scientific journals.

K. Rajappa Manjunath is an Associate Professor and a Research Supervisor at the Department of Management, Kuvempu University. He obtained his PhD in Stock Derivatives and Strategies for Portfolio

Performance Optimisation, his research interest includes risk management, derivatives, strategic HRM, strategic finance, entrepreneurship, etc. He has been a Research Supervisor on Masters and Doctorate research scholars since 2014. He teaches SAPM, derivatives, risk management, research methodology, and corporate communications, for Master students.

Ahsanullah Mohsen is an Assistant Professor at Kabul University, Faculty of Economics. Previously, Assistant Professor in Economics Department and Head of Research and Publication Committee at the Faculty of Economics, Kardan University. Previously, he worked as Academic Vice-chancellor at Jahan University, Kabul. He obtained Master of Science in Management and Economics from Ruhr University Bochum, Germany and a Bachelor in Business Management from Goa University, India. His works are published in IEE, Ruhr University Bochum and *Asian Journal of Technology Management*.

Mohammad Sediq Nawabzada is a Lecturer and Head of the Department of Banking and Finance, Faculty of Economics, Shaikh Zayed University, Khost, Afghanistan. He has been working here since 2011 (formerly as a teaching assistant). Mohammad Sediq Nawabzada completed his Bachelor's in Business Administration at Shaikh Zayed University in 2010 and went to Germany for Master studies in 2014. He completed his Master's in Management and Economics at Ruhr University Bochum in 2017. He currently teaches financial markets at the bachelor level. His research interest includes financial markets, financial system, risk management and commercial banking.

Kanellos-Panagiotis Nikolopoulos has 25 years of professional experience in foreign language teaching and vocational training. He codirects the family business, Nikolopouleio Schools of Foreign Languages and Vocational Studies (www.nikolopouleio.gr), which specialises in the aforementioned fields as well as in online education for Greek and overseas markets. His research interests include cross-cultural management, cosmopolitanism and entrepreneurship and global knowledge workers' social networks. He has presented workshop and conference papers at international academic conferences and has contributed journal papers and book chapters. In 2018 he won jointly with Léo-Paul Dana the *European Management Review* Best Paper Award for 2017. He is a founding member of the Entrepreneurship as Practice Research Group on Entrepreneurship (www.entrepreneurshipaspractice.com).

Giorgi Ormotsadze is a Research Fellow at the Economic Policy Research Centre (EPRC), Georgia. He has studied at Charles University in Prague and holds a Bachelor's Degree in Sociology from Tbilisi State University. He has valuable experience working for both local and international think tanks and research organisations, including the Estonian Institute of Human Rights, Baltic Journal, and Institute of International Relations Prague. Giorgi has also produced and published articles and policy papers. His research and professional interests include European integration, political and economic developments in the Baltic Sea Region, Eastern partnership and Russia's soft power.

Sayed Fatah Sadat holding an MBA from Osmania University of India and a BA in Economics from Balkh University of Afghanistan was born on 20 December 1987 in Kabul Province of Afghanistan. He is a Lecturer at the Department of Business Administration, the Faculty of Economics of Kabul University since 2017, and has also served as the Deputy Dean of the said Faculty from 2019 to 2020. He has the experience of working with Khurshid Institute of Higher Education in different capacities such as Lecturer, Head of Department and Deputy Dean of the Faculty of Economics of the said institute from 2015 to 2017.

Yashar Salamzadeh is a Senior Lecturer in Graduate School of Business at Universiti Sains Malaysia. He had published +100 research articles in international journals and conferences. Yashar has 11 years of teaching in MBA and Master of management courses in four different universities and has supervised more than 65 graduate dissertations. Yashar has developed many managerial workshops on leadership, social entrepreneurship, HRM, and business models in Iran, Turkey, Russia, Malaysia and Hungary. He has worked as a Project Manager in many international research projects. Besides being an EFQM auditor, Yashar has five years of management consultancy experience for different public and private organisations on leadership, organisational re-structuring, EFQM, culture, HRM and organisational behaviour. He also has cooperated in more than 20 international journals as an editorial board member and review board member. His interest fields include entrepreneurship, entrepreneurial universities, [digital] leadership, business models, strategic management, green business, CSR, HRM (HCM) and networked organisations.

Mugaahed Abdu Kaid Saleh is a Yemenite research scholar, he obtained his Master of Business Administration in Jawaharlal Technological

University in Hyderabad, India. He is now pursuing his PhD research at the Department of Management and Business Administration, Kuvempu University, India in the field of entrepreneurship and SMEs development. His research interests entrepreneurship and entrepreneurial empowerment among youth in underdeveloped economies.

Ekaterina Vorobeva is a doctoral candidate at Bremen International Graduate School of Social Sciences and an EU researcher at the Research Centre for East European Studies, the University of Bremen. She previously worked in several research projects on forced migration, international migration and migrant entrepreneurship in Finland and Malta. Ekaterina co-authored scientific articles and book chapters published by SAGE Business Cases, GeoJournal, British Journal of Middle Eastern Studies, Palgrave Macmillan, the University of Turku and the University of Dhaka.

Naveed Yasin is Associate Professor of Entrepreneurship at the Canadian University Dubai. He is an academic with over 10 years of experience and a history of delivering excellence internationally. He was 2015 winner of the 'Outstanding All Round Academic Award' from the Teaching & Learning Institute, in the UK. Senior Fellow of the Higher Education Academy (SFHEA), holder of Chartered Manager and Fellow status from the Chartered Management Institute (UK), and Fellow of the National Council of Entrepreneurship in Education (NCEE), Dr. Yasin has published in journals as well as textbooks.

Saad M. Zighan is an associate professor of management studies within the Faculty of Administrative and Financial Sciences at Petra University, Jordan. Saad teaches Operations Management, Supply Chain Management, and Project Management to undergraduate and graduate students. Saad has over 15 years of experience. His research interests are related to strategic operations management, dealing with operation management issues within a strategic context. He is concerned with getting things done based on developing operations activities consistent with long-term strategic intentions and contributing to organisational competitive advantage.

Section I

The Context

Chapter 1

Introduction

Léo-Paul Dana, Aidin Salamzadeh, Veland Ramadani & Ramo Palalić

Abstract: This chapter introduces this book about the contexts of Western Asia, a region that has long been important for business, including the spice trade that prompted cultural interaction among different cultures with unlike religions and resulted in the cross-fertilisation of ideas and spread of technology. The chapter provides a brief historical overview and shows how today's countries have been shaped by colonial powers.

Keywords: context, bazaar, Ottoman Empire, British Empire, mandate

Context

The purpose of this book is to help the reader understand the contexts for business in our globalised world. Based on his research at the *Institut Européen d'Administration des Affaires* (INSEAD), Laurent concluded, "Deep seated managerial assumptions are strongly shaped by national cultures and appear quite insensitive to the more transient culture of organizations" (1983, p. 75). Likewise, Huntington (1993, 1996) showed that globalisation has neither standardised societies nor produced a homogeneous world culture. Even today, regional and national cultures continue to thrive.

Among early studies to focus on the context, Dana (1995) showed that the culture of an individual influences that person's response to opportunity and is, therefore, a highly relevant explanatory variable. Likewise, Dana (1996) confirmed that individuals of different cultures view the same business opportunity differently, and that which is an opportunity for one person is not for another of a differing culture. In a similar vein, Light and Dana (2013) showed that the decision for an individual to enter or not to enter the business world is affected by cultural capital.

When people do business, the way they do so is culturally influenced and very much a function of context (Dana, 1995; 1996). Firms – large and small – are highly affected by the context in which they operate. Yet, most theories have come from developed countries with bountiful contexts and Westerners are familiar with the relevant assumptions relating to enterprise in this context.

In contrast, the diverse contexts of Asia – the world's largest continent – are less understood. Although much literature exists about Central Asia (e.g., Dana, 2002), Pacific Asia (e.g., Dana, 1999) and South Asia (e.g., Dana, 2014), knowledge about Western Asia is more limited.

In Western Asia, religious factors are profoundly dominant, and businesses in this diverse area operate with considerations that are rarely considered elsewhere. There have been Jews in this region since at least 1,000 BC, and in the 7th century Islam was created here. Jews and Muslims have very much in common and some differences too. Deshen and Zenner (1996) focus on Jews among Muslims.

Oil reserves in Western Asia are common knowledge, but there is much more than oil here. Major crops in Iran include pistachios, rice, tobacco and wheat. Coriander and cumin are believed to have originated in Persia, and today many spices continue to grow well in Iran's arid climate. Iraq grows much cotton and dates, as does Israel (see Exhibit 1.1). Among Omani exports are dates, iron ore, nuts and pomegranates. Yemen is an important exporter of fish. This book spans Western Asia, a heterogenous region that includes bazaars and high-tech booms.

Western Asia

Western Asia has long been important for business, including the spice trade that prompted cultural interaction among different cultures with unlike religions and resulted in the cross-fertilisation of ideas and spread of technology. Traces of vanilla have been found in a Bronze Age tombstone in Israel, suggesting there was already inter-continental trade about 3,600 years ago (Bower, 2018).

The concept of 'Asia' originates from the ancient civilisation of Mesopotamia and the eastern shores of the Mediterranean Sea.

In Assyrian, *asu* means 'east'. It is likely that ancient Greek entrepreneurs adopted the term from Phoenician merchants, thus designating the land to the east. That was probably between 600 and 500 BC. The Greeks cultivated relations with Asians, and trade expanded considerably. Both land and sea routes were further developed under the Romans (Dana, 1999, p. 5).

Westerners sometimes speak of an Asian model of business or management, without considering the vast diversity within this vast geographic region. Yet, business is shaped by the cultural and historical context of societies.

Among the largest empires in history and straddling Europe and Asia, the Ottoman Empire was an important player in Western Asia and greatly influenced the region. The Ottoman Empire once ruled as far east as Azerbaijan and as far south as Yemen; nearby, parts of Saudi Arabia and northern Yemen were never colonised.

When the Ottoman Empire emperor resided in the 285-room Dolmabahçe Palace (Exhibit 1.2), in Istanbul, Ottoman subjects travelled

Exhibit 1.1 Date-packing plant; photo © 2021 by Léo-Paul Dana

Exhibit 1.2   Dolmabahçe Palace; photo © 2021 by Léo-Paul Dana

Exhibit 1.3   Ottoman Bank; photo © 2021 by Léo-Paul Dana

and conducted business throughout the region. A common currency and the vast network of the Ottoman Bank (Exhibit 1.3) facilitated transactions.

Under Ottoman rule, people relocated, contributing to multiculturalism. Afyoncu (2018) emphasised peace within the Ottoman province of Damascus, which included the states of Gaza, Jerusalem and Nablus. For centuries, Christians, Jews and Muslims lived here peacefully. Exhibit 1.4 shows an Armenian convent in Israel, while Exhibit 1.5 features

Exhibit 1.4 Armenian convent in Israel; photo © 2021 by Léo-Paul Dana

Exhibit 1.5 Synagogue in Izmir; photo © 2021 by Léo-Paul Dana

a synagogue in Turkey. The Ottoman Empire was tolerant of minorities, and multiculturalism was the norm across Western Asia. Jews continue to live in Turkey and among Turkish exports to the United States are Hanukkah candles (Exhibit 1.6) for Jews to use during an annual celebration.

Once the Ottomans were conquered, the map of Western Asia changed considerably, as did demographics. In 1917, the Balfour Declaration announced the support for the establishment of a "national home for the Jewish people" in Palestine, an Ottoman region corresponding to the historical entity of Israel where Jews had lived until the conquest by the Romans in 70 AD. In 1918, the Arab Kingdom of Syria declared its independence.

Exhibit 1.6 Made in Turkey; photo © 2021 by Léo-Paul Dana

Its king was Faisal bin Hussein, a son of Hussein bin Ali, who gained British favour by co-operating against the Ottomans. In 1919, Faisal and the president of the Zionist Organisation signed the Faisal–Weizmann Agreement for Arab–Jewish Co-operation, in which Faisal accepted the Balfour Declaration. In 1920, the kingdom surrendered to France and the British subsequently offered Faisal the crown of Iraq.

According to Article 22 of *The Covenant of the League of Nations*, a system of mandates came into force, established by "advanced nations" namely France and the United Kingdom, for the administration of peoples "not yet able to stand by themselves under the strenuous conditions of the modern world" on invaded Ottoman lands. Schayegh and Arsan (2015) focused on the Middle East mandates.

In 1921, the British partitioned Mandatory Palestine into two entities: (i) Transjordan, which in 1949 became the Hashemite Kingdom of Jordan; and (ii) Mandatory Palestine, which they proposed to partition a second time in 1947. They offered the crown of Jordan to Abdullah, a brother to Faisal bin Hussein. Thus, new countries were created, and heterogeneity within each became relatively limited. As the United Kingdom carved up Ottoman lands, creating the country that became Jordan, Barclays (Exhibit 1.7) became prominent in British Mandatory Palestine. France spread its

Exhibit 1.7 Barclays Bank, scarred with war-time bullet holes; photo © 2021 by Léo-Paul Dana

language and culture to lands that would become Lebanon and Syria, and Air France made Beirut a hub[1] where passengers from its Hong Kong–Hanoi-Rangoon-Baghdad–Damascus route could transfer to either: (i) flights headed to Athens, Corfu, Naples, Marseille, Paris and London; or (ii) flights to Lydda (later known as Lod – today's TLV airport), Alexandria, Benghazi, Tripoli, Tunis, Marseille and Paris.

Structure of this Volume

This book is comprised of 14 sections. Section I begins with introductory chapters. Within this section, Chapter 2 focuses on the bazaar economy. Subsequent chapters discuss specific nations, grouped according to historical contexts. Following the 1919 signing of the Treaty of Versailles at the Paris Peace Conference, the formerly secret Sykes-Picot Agreement of 1916 became the basis of post-war boundaries: Area A, the northern part of Ottoman province of Syria became the French Mandate for Syria and the Lebanon. Land to the south became the British Mandate for Palestine, later divided between Jordan and Mandatory Palestine. Further east, the oil-rich Ottoman area of Mesopotamia became Mandatory Iraq. Therefore, countries of the Levant – an Eastern Mediterranean region (see Dana, 2000) with historically distinct culture within the broader Western Asia context – are grouped by the relatively modern historic separation of French and British territory (see also: Barr, 2011), which prompted a distinct, and long-lasting, impact on doing business.

Historically, the major trading centre of the Persian Gulf region was the port of Muscat, and up to 1861, the Omani Empire spread along the east coast of Africa and included Zanzibar and Mombasa (now in Kenya), and its influence spread east to Pakistan. Section II contains Chapter 3, which deals about Oman, until 1970 known as the Sultanate of Muscat and Oman.

---

[1] Later, Pan American Airways used Beirut as a hub where passengers travelling on PA118 from Paris and Rome would connect with flights to destinations east, including Basra, Calcutta, Bangkok, Hong Kong, Tokyo and Guam. Complementing services provided by foreign companies, in 1934, a Zionist by the name of Pinhas Ruttenberg founded Palestine Airways Limited (the Hebrew name of which was literally Land of Israel Airways Ltd), in conjunction with the Histadrut Trade Union and the Jewish Agency; this airline operated flights from Beirut (which was spelled Beyrouth in its timetable) to Haifa and Tel Aviv's Sde Dov airport, but it ceased operations when its fleet was taken over by the Royal Air Force in 1940. For a discussion of Palestine Airways, see Katz (2020).

Section III contains Chapter 4, which deals about Iran, the successor to the Persian Empire, among the largest empires in history. Carpets have been produced here for 2,500 years and the sector is still thriving (Light et al., 2013). While Persian ethnicity is a trait of most people in Iran and some in Afghanistan, the Persianate world extends to Pakistan, Tajikistan and Uzbekistan (see Dana, 2002). Persian language is spoken in Afghanistan where it is known as Dari, in Iran it is referred to as Farsi and in Tajikistan it was named Tajik.

Section IV groups successors to the Russian Empire (see Dana, 2005): Armenia (Chapter 5); Azerbaijan, home to the world's first oil pipeline – made of wood (Chapter 6); and Georgia (Chapter 7).

Section V is about the entities on the island of Cyprus, an Ottoman province until 1878, when the United Kingdom took the island as a British protectorate. The island was part of the British Empire, first under military occupation from 1914 to 1925, and then as a Crown Colony until 1960, when the island became an independent republic. In 1974, Turkish troops occupied the north of the island, creating a new entity using Turkish currency and unofficially known as the Turkish Republic of Northern Cyprus (TRNC). Today, the constituents of this island are the Republic of Cyprus (Chapter 8) and northern Cyprus (Chapter 9).

Section VI groups nations that evolved from early British protectorates. With the objective to establish a supply port to service British shipping to India, in January 1839, the British East India Company landed soldiers and occupied Aden (Willis, 2009). The opening of the Suez Canal in 1869 further contributed to the strategic importance of Aden, which thrived selling coal to ships that used this port as a hub between Europe and Asia – and which the British took as the Aden Protectorate. Aden remained among the world's busiest duty-free ports until the protectorate was disestablished in 1963. This land is now in Yemen, the subject of Chapter 10. Chapter 11 is about Bahrain, the protectorate status of which was sealed in 1880. Chapter 12 is about Kuwait, which became a British protectorate in 1899. Chapter 13 is about Qatar, which became a British protectorate in 1916.

Although some consider Afghanistan to be in central Asia, others including the Food and Agriculture Organisation of the United Nations consider Afghanistan to be in Western Asia, and it is therefore included in this book. Section VII contains Chapter 14, which deals about Afghanistan, which formerly served as a buffer between British India and the Russian Empire (Bayly, 2015). Afghanistan became independent from the United Kingdom in 1919.

Exhibit 1.8 Istanbul skyline with Galata Tower; photo © 2021 by Léo-Paul Dana

Section VIII contains Chapter 15, about Turkey, a country much smaller than the Ottoman Empire that preceded it but spanning two continents. Although in Europe, Istanbul's Galata Tower (Exhibit 1.8) is visible from Asia.

In 1920, the League of Nations proposed a mandate for Mesopotamia. It was superseded by the somewhat similar Anglo-Iraqi Treaty. The result was the Kingdom of Iraq under British Administration, the successor of which is today's Iraq, the subject of Chapter 16, in Section IX.

Along similar lines was the "French Mandate for Syria and the Lebanon". Note the word "the" in its title. As noted by Haber et al. (2010), the Maronite Church – that emerged during the tumult of Christian doctrinal evolution during Byzantine rule, nearly concurrent with the Muslim expansion and conquest of Lebanon by the Umayyad Caliphate – is the dominant Christian sect within Lebanon. To benefit the Maronite Christian community, in 1920, France carved Greater Lebanon from the Levantine territories it acquired from the Ottoman Empire. Chapter 17, which deals with Lebanon, and Chapter 18, about Syria, are in Section X, which covers territories that fell under French rule after the conquest of the Ottoman Empire. Ouahes (2018) focused on cultural imperialism to which these lands were exposed.

Colonial powers brought with them their values and institutions. The Young Men's Christian Association (YMCA) was established in London in 1844 as a refuge for Christian prayer and Bible reading. In 1928, the British High Commissioner for Mandatory Palestine laid the cornerstone for a YMCA building (Exhibit 1.9) in Jerusalem. Designed by American

Exhibit 1.9 Tower of the YMCA, Jerusalem; photo © 2021 by Léo-Paul Dana

architect Arthur Loomis Harmon of Shreve, Lamb and Harmon – designers of the 102-storey art deco Empire State Building, constructed during 1930 and 1931 – the Jerusalem YMCA was dedicated in 1933 by British general Edmund Henry Hynman Allenby, 1ˢᵗ Viscount Allenby, who had occupied Jerusalem from the Ottomans in 1917.

Section XI is about the territories of the "Occupied Enemy Territory Administration" that were taken by the British, led by Allenby. Chapter 19 is about Jordan that was carved out of Palestine in 1921 (see Friedman, 2008) and enlarged in 1950 when Jordan annexed East Jerusalem and the West Bank. Chapter 20 is about Israel and Chapter 21 is about Palestine. As observed by Hakim (2019), "A century after the victorious Allied powers distributed their spoils of victory in 1919, the world still lives with the geopolitical consequences of the mandates system established by the League of Nations" (p. 1689).

Section XII is about the successor to the Rashidun Caliphate, namely Saudi Arabia, the subject of Chapter 22. During the 7ᵗʰ century, Muhammad founded Islam in which is now Saudi Arabia. Except during the COVID-19 pandemic, Mecca receives approximately 2 million pilgrims annually – creating demand for 20,000 buses.

Section XIII is about the successor to the Trucial sheikdoms, namely the United Arab Emirates, featured in Chapter 23. With the Abraham Accords Peace Agreement, the United Arab Emirates became the first Persian Gulf nation to formally normalise its relationship with Israel; benefitting Palestine, Israel concurrently suspended plans to annex parts of the West Bank. The first ship with cargo from the United Arab Emirates to Israel arrived in October 2020, beginning a new era of international business in Western Asia. Section XIV concludes the book.

References

Afyoncu, Erhan (2018), "400 Years of Peace: Palestine under Ottoman Rule," *Daily Sabah*, May 18.

Barr, James (2011), *A Line in the Sand: Britain, France and the Struggle that Shaped the Middle East*, London: Simon & Schuster.

Bayly, Martin J. (2015), "Imperial Ontological (In)security: 'Buffer States', International Relations and the Case of Anglo-Afghan Relations, 1808–1878," *European Journal of International Relations* 21 (4), pp. 816–840.

Bower, Bruce (2018), "A Bronze Age Tomb in Israel Reveals the Earliest Known Use of Vanilla," *ScienceNews* (Retrieved from https://www. sciencenews.org/article/bronze-age-tomb-israel-reveals-earliest-known-use-vanilla?utm_source=email&utm_medium=email&utm_campaign=latest-newsletter-v2, accessed 15 February 2021)

Dana, Léo-Paul (1995), "Entrepreneurship in a Remote Sub-Arctic Community: Nome, Alaska," *Entrepreneurship: Theory & Practice,* 20 (1), Fall, pp. 55–72. Reprinted in Norris Krueger, Ed., *Entrepreneurship: Critical Perspectives on Business and Management,* Volume IV, London: Routledge, 2002, pp. 255–275.

Dana, Léo-Paul (1996), "Self-Employment in the Canadian Sub-Arctic: An Exploratory Study," *Canadian Journal of Administrative Sciences* 13 (1), pp. 65–77.

Dana, Léo-Paul (1999), *Entrepreneurship in Pacific Asia: Past Present & Future,* Singapore, London & Hong Kong: World Scientific.

Dana, Léo-Paul (2000), *Economies of the Eastern Mediterranean Region: Economic Miracles in the Making,* Singapore, London & Hong Kong: World Scientific.

Dana, Léo-Paul (2002), *When Economies Change Paths: Models of Transition in China, the Central Asian Republics, Myanmar, and the Nations of Former Indochine Française,* Singapore, London & Hong Kong: World Scientific.

Dana, Léo-Paul (2005), *When Economies Change Hands: A Survey of Entrepreneurship in the Emerging Markets of Europe from the Balkans to the Baltic States,* New York & Oxford: Routledge.

Dana, Léo-Paul (2014), *Asian Models of Entrepreneurship from the Indian Union and Nepal to the Japanese Archipelago: Context, Policy and Practice,* Second Edition, Singapore, London & Hong Kong: World Scientific.

Deshen, Shlomo, and Walter P. Zenner, eds. (1996), *Jews among Muslims: Communities in the Precolonial Middle East,* London: Palgrave Macmillan.

Friedman, Isaiah (2008), "How Trans-Jordan was Severed from the Territory of the Jewish National Home," *Journal of Israeli History* 27 (1), pp. 65–85.

Haber, Marc, Daniel E. Platt, Danielle A. Badro, Yali Xue, Mirvat El-Sibai, Maziar Ashrafian Bonab, Sonia C. Youhanna, Stephanie Saade, David F. Soria-Hernanz, Ajay Royyuru, R. Spencer Wells, Chris Tyler-Smith, Pierre A. Zalloua, and The Genographic Consortium

(2010), "Influences of History, Geography, and Religion on Genetic Structure: The Maronites in Lebanon," *European Journal of Human Genetics* 19, pp. 334–340.

Hakim, Carol (2019), "The French Mandate in Lebanon," *The American Historical Review* 124 (5), pp. 1689–1693.

Huntington, Samuel P. (1993), "The Clash of Civilization," *Foreign Affairs* 72 (3), pp. 22–49.

Huntington, Samuel P. (1996), *The Clash of Civilization and the Remaking of World Order,* New York: Simon and Schuster.

Katz, Dikla Rivlin (2020), "The Disappearance of 'Palestine Airways' from the Historical Narrative," *Israel Studies* 25 (2), pp. 49–71.

Laurent, André (1983), "A Cultural Diversity of Western Conceptions of Management," *International Studies of Management and Organization* 13 (Spring/Summer), pp. 75–96.

Light, Ivan, and Léo-Paul Dana (2013), "Boundaries of Social Capital in Entrepreneurship," *Entrepreneurship: Theory & Practice* 37 (3), pp. 603–624.

Light, Ivan, Shahamak Rezaei, and Léo-Paul Dana (2013), "Ethnic Minority Entrepreneurs in the International Carpet Trade: An Empirical Study," *International Journal of Entrepreneurship and Small Business* 18 (2), pp. 125–153.

Ouahes, Idir (2018), *Syria and Lebanon under the French Mandate: Cultural Imperialism and the Workings of Empire,* London: I. B. Tauris & Co.

Schayegh, Cyrus, and Andrew Arsan, eds. (2015), *The Routledge Handbook of the History of the Middle East Mandates,* London & New York: Routledge.

Willis, John M. (2009), "Making Yemen Indian: Rewriting the Boundaries of Imperial Arabia," *International Journal of Middle East Studies* 41 (1), pp. 23–38.

Recommended for Further Reading

Dana, Léo-Paul, and Richard W. Wright (2015), "Bazaar Economies, Modern Networks and Entrepreneurship," in Sir Cary L. Cooper, ed., *Wiley Encyclopedia of Management,* 3rd edition, Hoboken, New Jersey: John Wiley & Sons, Volume 3, Michael Morris and Don Kuratko, volume eds. pp. 15–18.

Ellis, William S., and George F. Mobley (1970), "Lebanon, Little Bible Land in the Crossfire of History," *National Geographic* 137 (2), pp. 240–275.

Geertz, Clifford (1963), *Peddlers and Princes: Social Development and Economic Change in Two Indonesian Towns,* Chicago: University of Chicago Press.

Geertz, Clifford (1978), "The Bazaar Economy: Information and Search in Peasant Marketing," *American Marketing Review* 68, pp. 28–32.

Harold, Frederick (1892), *The New Exodus,* London: C.P. Putnam's Sons.

Julius, Lyn (2018), *Uprooted: How 3000 Years of Jewish Civilization in the Arab World Vanished Overnight,* Elstree: Vallentine Mitchell.

Sayigh, Yusif A. (1962), *Entrepreneurs of Lebanon: The Role of the Business Leader in a Developing Economy,* Cambridge: Harvard University Press.

Tishby, Noa (2021), *Israel: A Simple Guide to the Most Misunderstood Country on Earth,* New York: Simon & Schuster.

Recommended Watching

An Israeli Love Story, 2017 film directed by Dan Wolman.

Promises & Betrayals: Britain and the Struggle for the Holy Land, 2002 documentary narrated by Struan Rodger, directed by Arense Kvaale, https://www.youtube.com/watch?v=Xo6YRCcajXM

Where Do We Go Now? (وهلّا لوين؟ *w halla' la wayn*, French: *Et maintenant, on va où?*), 2011 film directed by Nadine Labaki.

Chapter 2

The Bazaar Economy[1]

Léo-Paul Dana & Hamid Etemad

Abstract: The bazaar is an ancient institution that continues to thrive today, holding a complex web of carefully managed relationships – in which sellers cooperate for mutual gain. In this sense, it is very similar to today's airline sector in which United Airlines cooperates with others in the Star Alliance while giving "gold" status and related privileges to pre-ferred clients of the alliance; not all customers are treated equally. Brand loyalty is influenced by preferential treatment that is based on relation-ships. Would-be competitors in the bazaar cooperate as do airlines within an alliance, reinforcing relationship networks. This chapter discusses the structured bazaar in detail, revealing that the degree to which the struc-tured bazaar resembles the World Wide Web is striking. Managerial impli-cations are also discussed.

Keywords: Negotiation, bargaining, guilds, sliding-price system, relation-ships, Bottom of the Pyramid, transactions, competition

> *An American population expert …called on King Abdul Azziz al Saud, who told him: "You're wasting your time. There are 7 million people here." With apologies, the American said there could not be more than 3 million. "You're wrong," said the King. "There are at least 6 million."…the American insisted…no more than 4 million. At this point the King held out his hand … bazaar-style, saying "All right, five and a half."*
>
> *–Time Magazine*, May 22, 1978, p.26

---

[1] This chapter is based on Dana (2000).

Introduction

The bazaar has long been addressed in the literature. Christian (1943) emphasised the speed with which information travels in the bazaar, without the need for advertising. Passantino (1946) and Long (1952) focused on clustering of retailers selling identical products. Parsons and Smelzer (1956) described the sliding-price system of the bazaar, in which prices are not set (see Exhibit 2.1) by the vendor but rather negotiated. Geertz (1963, 1978) further legitimised the complex balance of relationships in the bazaar as a field of research.

In Western economies, culture and circumstances changed the nature of the marketplace. In many places, traditional systems were phased out and replaced by governmental and/or free-market forces. Local culture gave way to a culture of impersonal mass marketing with advertisements and frequent buyer loyalty schemes. Despite the importance of bazaars at the Bottom of the Pyramid (BoP) (Gupta and Srivastav, 2016), Western firms became more concerned with market share than with individual buyers. Many firms hired teams of lawyers (see Chapter 7 in Light and Dana, 2020) to monitor transactions – quite a contrast from the bazaar in which it was deemed preferable to monitor a relationship than monitor a transaction.

Exhibit 2.1 Prices not indicated; photo © 2021 by Léo-Paul Dana

In Western Asia, cultural values continue to emphasise personal relations, and so the bazaar continues to thrive. Whereas business in the Occident may be described as being focused on money, in the bazaar, the context of business is very much about people and their relationships. Here, much importance is given to prayer (see Exhibit 2.2) and to drinking tea or coffee and/or sharing food with members of one's networks (see Exhibit 2.3). Rather than monitoring a transaction, a person in business monitors

Exhibit 2.2 The Blue Mosque, Istanbul; photo © 2021 by Léo-Paul Dana

Exhibit 2.3 Drinking coffee with a sheikh; photo © 2021 by Léo-Paul Dana

his/her relationships. The establishment of long-term relationships makes future transactions more efficient and even pleasurable. As transaction-centred costs begin to decline, mainly due to the rise in social capital, the overall transaction costs (Williamson, 1985, 1996) begin to approach Williamsonian optimality, whereby buyer and seller feel highly satisfied with the transaction. An intangible resource decreases future transaction costs (Penrose, 1959).

Here, people believe that destiny determines who gets a particular sale. An individual will sell, *insha'Allah* – if God wants. Superstition is important and garlic is used to ward off that which is called the evil eye, as is the *khamissa* (see Exhibit 2.4). In the Iranian context, vendors believe that if they have the first profitable sale in the morning, they will have a day full of profit, and vice versa. They call it *dasht-e-aval*.

The survival of the bazaar appears to be linked to the importance of cultural beliefs and personal relationships. Understanding its dynamics is a prerequisite to succeeding in it. In Western Asia, rich cultural capital is perpetuated as children learn about business from their parents, starting at an early age. Generally, sellers in a bazaar take their children to their stores

Exhibit 2.4 Five fingers of the *khamissa*; photo © 2021 by Léo-Paul Dana

Exhibit 2.5   Participating in the family business; photo © 2021 by Léo-Paul Dana

in order to teach them how to negotiate and sell products. Thus, the bazaar is a place for future generations to acquire cultural capital including traditional negotiation skills, as well as to learn day-to-day activities necessary for business (see Exhibit 2.5).

Definitions

The West is familiar with the *firm-type economy* – an economic institution, which involves a mode of commercial activity such that industry and trade take place primarily within a set of *impersonally defined* institutions, grouping people according to organisation and specialisation (Weber, 1924). It is assumed that profit-maximising transactions will occur based on rational decision-making, rather than on the nature of personal relationships between entrepreneurs and consumers. *The focus is on impersonal transactions.* The decision space is occupied by product attributes and by services attached to them, backed by formal warranties. As a result, the buyer and the individual salesman are secondary, if not trivial, to the transaction decision. The interaction between the buyer and the product (and/or service) is deemed to be more critical than that between the buyer and the seller. Competition takes place among sellers.

These may be spread across town; they are seldom all in the same district. Segmentation refers to the market. Vendors decide the selling price of a product; this may reflect market forces, including the number of competitors and the price charged by competing firms. Items available for sale are tagged so as to identify the price requested by the vendor.

In contrast, Western Asia is home to the bazaar (*bazaar* in Persian, *souq* in Arabic and *shouq* in Hebrew).[2] Dana observed, "The bazaar is a way of life and a general mode of commercial activity such that most of the flow of commerce is fragmented into numerous transactions centred on *individuals and personal relationships*. In the bazaar, economic transactions are *not* the focus of activities; instead, the focus is on personal relationships. In this scenario, consumers do not necessarily seek the lowest price or the best quality. An individual gives business to another with whom a relationship has been established, to ensure that this person will reciprocate. Reciprocal preferential treatment reduces transaction costs" (2007, p. 19). As explained by Geertz (1963), the complex balance of credit relationships is carefully managed and the multiplicity of small-scale transactions results in a fractionalisation of risks and, therefore, of profit margins.

Dana, Etemad and Wright elaborated, "The Bazaar-type Economy is a social, cultural and economic system in which the physical clustering of vendors facilitates the consumer's comparative information search, by eliminating displacement time. Business is strongly affected by relationships and networks; relationships and preferential treatment are integral to business. Consumers are not treated equally. Different people pay unlike prices. The price paid and the level of service provided is a function of status and relationships. Products and services are personalised, and this leads to customer loyalty. Internationalisation is a function of multi-polar networks involving special relationships" (Dana et al., 2008, pp. 110–111).

The bazaar involves production as well as distribution. Furthermore, there are infinite short-term opportunities for small-scale speculation. Nevertheless, complicated bookkeeping and managerial accounting are lacking. Nevertheless, space, time, production and sales must be well managed, and personal inter-relations must be managed even more delicately. The units of interest are the entrepreneur, his micro-enterprise and his client. This establishes a personal relationship between buyer and seller. Personal conversations precede an economic transaction. Producers are

---

[2] Greeks use the word *pazari* (derived from bazaar) to refer to a market of micro-sellers.

segmented, often clustered on a street named after them, and medieval towns borrowed from structural bazaars, with streets often named for the entrepreneurs clustered on them, for example Changers' Alley (Singapore), Exchange Alley (London), Fisherman's Wharf (San Francisco), Workman Street (Montreal), *Raasteh* (Iran), *rue des Bouchers* (Strasbourg). In Rome, fashion designers have shops clustered along *via dei Condotti*.

Given the difficulty in determining the value of a product, a sliding price system is in effect in the traditional bazaar and this results in a price within the prevailing limits. Prices are negotiated, as determined by the economically oriented tension between buyers and sellers (see Exhibit 2.6). Not to negotiate would be seen as a cold-blooded and uncaring avoidance of human contact. Interaction tends to take place between the buyer and the seller, rather than between the buyer and the product. This is summarised in Table 2.1.

Historical Context

Bazaars evolved and thrived in transport-hub cities, such as Kerman and Isfahan in Iran, Damascus in Syria and Istanbul in Turkey. Many were located on ancient trade routes connecting Europe to the Chinese Empire, through the Persian Empire and the Indian sub-continent. Others served as nodes along the Sahara Desert.

The southern Silk Road started from Xian, the capital of the Middle Kingdom (currently in China). With loads of silk and other exotic Chinese products – including gunpowder, the compass, ink, paper and writing instruments – camel caravans (see Exhibit 2.7) headed out to conduct international trade. Indian spices, as well as Chinese commodities, were traded along the journey. Also profitable was the trade of finely woven fabrics and carpets in Kerman (currently in southeastern Iran) and expertly designed jewellery, ornaments, ceramics and glassworks in Isfahan, the capital of the Safavid dynasty.

Popular routes passed through population centres while avoiding mountains and deserts as well as road hazards such as organised bandits. An alternate route travelled through the Central Asian Plateau passing along the shores of the Caspian Sea, towards Asia Minor.

Grand bazaars were critically vital to the functioning of trading routes – including the Silk Road; bazaars formed an infrastructure resembling the hub-and-spoke system of today's air transportation industry. In some ways, the ancient trading caravans were similar to modern airlines: their working capital was relatively large, and they were pressed for time.

Exhibit 2.6   How Much Do You Want to Pay?; photo © 2021 by Léo-Paul Dana

Table 2.1. Economic Systems

Bazaar Economy	**Firm-Type Economy**
Focus on personal relations	Focus on impersonal transactions
Segmentation refers to producers	Segmentation refers to the market
Competition refers to the tension between buyer and seller	Competition is an activity that takes place among sellers
Prices are negotiated	Prices are indicated

Exhibit 2.7 Camels waiting; photo © 2021 by Léo-Paul Dana

Grand bazaars served as hubs, connected to each other and supplied by caravans travelling the trade routes. Smaller regional bazaars, in neighbouring towns, absorbed some of the imports brought in by caravans and supplied some of the goods sold to caravans, or bartered. Bazaars thus functioned as inventory depots for the supply chain of other regional bazaars.

In some ways, caravans resembled trade missions of modern times. The most critical aspect of ancient caravans was time. The long and arduous voyage between Xian and Rome stretched endurance beyond limits. Although the travellers stopped to re-supply along their routes and rested in organised and strategic locations, called caravanserai – literally "home of caravans" in Persian – the traders could not allow dis-organised, inefficient or poor markets to delay their schedule (Starkey, 2012). There were some small bazaars near those places where sellers used to sell their products to other sellers or buyers. The ideal bazaars – with a large functional capacity along trade routes – featured the following:

- *Efficiency:* The ideal bazaar allowed for the efficient performance of market functions – both, in terms of time, and barter supplies or gold coins, which were available in sufficient supplies only in grand bazaars.
- *Information Dissemination:* Due to arbitrage aspects of bazaars, up-to-date supply-related information could be disseminated very fast, in an environment otherwise with asymmetries of information.
- *Absorptive Capacity:* The potential buyers and/or their agents (the intermediaries) collectively had sufficient absorptive capacity to make mutually beneficial spot market transactions with a newly arrived caravan.
- *Supply:* Local suppliers were collectively able to supply caravans with food, drink, inventory and even camels for transport. A popular tea, to this day, is made from hibiscus leaves. Exhibit 2.8 shows mesh bags containing hibiscus leaves.

The bazaar was critical to the continued functioning of international caravan trade; markets enhanced the efficiency of caravans by acting as clearinghouses. The caravans were thus the predecessors of exporters and export agents, and they manifested many features of today's strategic alliances. In the absence of international law and modern international trade infrastructure, there was mutual trust and interdependence between traders.

Bazaar agents resembled modern-day importers and import agents, accumulating supplies for normal day-to-day trade, as well as bartering with the caravans. They evidently performed both functions efficiently, and reliably, with mutual respect, to the long-term benefit of all parties.

The bazaar imposed discipline. In the absence of large firms and the current facilities of modern corporations, most agents connected to a bazaar had no choice but to be entrepreneurial. They behaved in ways that

Exhibit 2.8 Hibiscus (*karkade,* in Arabic) from Sudan; photo © 2021 by Léo-Paul Dana

we now attribute to creative entrepreneurs, taking and sharing calculated risks, relying on their business network and acting on an opportunity, buying or selling as appropriate.

The supply of foodstuffs was often temporally oriented – the regulating aspect of the bazaar, balanced supplies over time, to satisfy demand throughout the year. Geographic distance contributed to the disparity between the temporal equilibrium prevailing in each regional marketplace. This impacted the state of information about overall supplies and demands. The prevailing equilibrium in a market was therefore regional and at times isolated from the overall conditions elsewhere.

Segmentation by Production

Marketing in the West has led to the sophisticated segmentation of consumers. Firms segment the market and focus on target market segments, consisting of consumers with attributes in common. In contrast, segmentation in the bazaar refers to the geographical clustering of producers, according to the specialisation of suppliers.

The bazaar economy evolved at a time of imperfect markets. Since early marketplaces were often seasonal, relying on farmers and their fresh produce, prices reflected supply and demand; they would vary significantly during any given day. In the bazaar, this made possible the efficient clearing of agricultural products, at seasonal markets. From this occasional existence arose the structured market, a stable and permanent structure for buyers and sellers to engage in trading.

Transactions ranged from small, retail sales to very large and complicated wholesale activities. In time, merchants, intermediaries and even customers found efficiency in specialisation, and this led to geographical clustering.

Thus – in contrast to the Occident, where segmentation refers to the market – in the bazaar economy, production is segmented, as are retailers. As early as the 1300s, one of the greatest Moorish explorers, namely Ibn Battouta, noted the segmentation of producers and retailers. Even today, shops still are clustered according to the goods offered therein.

Typically, a bazaar might have an area designated for clothing and another for produce; there may be a wing for gold and jewellery, another for carpets, and yet others for spices, fish, etc. Potential buyers and suppliers – of a given good or service – converge on that specific region.

High concentration in a given location is critical to efficiency, as it allows for highly efficient information processing. This includes an information search, a comparative evaluation, and decision-making.

In the absence of efficient information processing capabilities, geographically scattered markets would tax operational efficiencies. Finding and then accessing geographically scattered suppliers – as compared to having them in a concentrated area – would add to transaction costs; an information search through physical access would become more complicated and limited to one's ability.

In contrast to the Occident, where entrepreneurs spread out in order to maximise profit, entrepreneurs in the bazaar prefer to be clustered with others belonging to the same guild, buying from the same supplier and/or selling similar wares. Brotherhood is an unwritten rule of the game in such bazaars. The more people consider one person as their brother, the more they will respect him/her. There is little if any differentiation among clustered sellers. In the bazaar, there is considerable co-operation among retailers and also among wholesalers. Several entrepreneurs may share a truck, for instance, and there is a sense of belonging to a community. There is a complex balance of carefully managed credit relationships, each with a minute risk.

Contrary to Western market rules, when a bazaar vendor is failing or declares bankruptcy, others will help him/her, by means of a traditional crowdfunding technique, called *golrizan* in Persian (Salamzadeh et al., 2017). This was a well-known tradition among Zoroastrians and Jews in Persian bazaars, even before the emergence of Islam, and this is still practised.

Guilds

Organisations of employers appeared as early as the ancient Mesopotamian civilisations of Assyria and Babylon. Groups of craftsmen formed associations to safeguard their interests and to develop relationships, among members as well as between members and the state. To protect their profitability, they created barriers to entry. Simultaneously, they performed a quality control function by assuring an existing expert has sufficiently trained those future members. While examining the guild system of the Occident, it is evident that an apprentice in Western Europe was dependent on his master and subordinate to him; he was therefore expected to be submissive to the master.

In contrast, in the bazaar economy of Western Asia, the most remarkable difference between a master and an apprentice (see Exhibit 2.9) is simply a professional qualification. While the European guild focused on

Exhibit 2.9 Master and apprentice; photo © 2021 by Léo-Paul Dana

production, the focus in the bazaar is on pride in one's work and in belonging to a community. Hierarchy in the bazaar is less rigid than in the West. In traditional bazaars, sellers even invite their apprentices to their homes for dinner or sometimes provide them with living accommodation, etc. By turning from a manager to a leader, sellers will become more able to penetrate to others' hearts and thus will become more successful in their business.

Competition and Pricing

While "competition" in the firm-type economy is understood to take place between sellers; "competition" in bazaar refers to the tension between buyer and seller, rather than between sellers. Besides, lack of information results in an imperfect market, and with few exceptions, such as basic food staples, retail prices are not indicated but rather negotiations determine these. The customer first tests price levels informally, and only later begins to bargain. Often it is the buyer who proposes a price, which is eventually raised. Once a mutually satisfactory transaction has taken place, it is desirable to establish a long-term relationship. This makes future purchases more pleasurable and efficient, as less time is spent negotiating, and more can be allocated to drinking tea, for instance. Effective communication is essential, allowing a sale to be equated to pleasure, rather than work. Sometimes, a consumer sends his wife to bargain, hoping that gallantry will yield better prices.

Prices are generally firm and high in the morning. By the afternoon, vendors are often less likely to maintain high prices, especially when the effect of heat diminishes one's energy. It is a tradition to give a discount to the last customer of the day. This may be due to the recognition that consumers have a choice, and the quality of remaining stock decreases with time. Also, a vendor with remaining inventory, at the end of the day, incurs transportation and possibly storage costs; in the case of perishables, the situation is aggravated. Thus, price is a function of a variety of factors, including cost, perceived value, time, negotiating skills and circumstances.

Especially in the case of perishable foods, goods may be sold at substantially lower prices at the end of the day; merchants calculate the cost of spoilage, transportation and storage until the next market day, and this affects the willingness to sell at a reduced price. This is true not only in bazaars of Western Asia but also common in the open markets in Europe.

London, for example, has several open food markets, including Borough Market, where perishables are sold for lower prices in the afternoon. Other markets in London include Camden Market and Petticoat Lane Market (Exhibit 2.10). Petticoat Lane Market is one of the several markets in the neigbourhood of Brick Lane (Exhibit 2.11) – in former times known as Whitechapel Lane – a street linking Whitechapel with Bethnal Green, the working-class neighbourhood that served as setting of the famous sociological study *Family and Kinship in East London* (Young and Wilmott, 1957). Today the centre of London's Bangladeshi community, in the 19th century Brick Lane was the destination of many Jews from Eastern Europe; while most establishments were closed on Sundays for the Christian day of rest, the government gave Jews a dispensation to have a Sunday market – and although most Jews have relocated elsewhere, to this day buyers and sellers bargain here on Sunday.

The Modern Bazaar

A bazaar functions reasonably efficiently, largely thanks to the geographical concentration and clustering of vendors in like occupations. Nevertheless, this is not obvious to a Westerner. A comprehension of the

Exhibit 2.10 Petticoat Lane Market operating since the mid-18th century; photo © 2021 by Léo-Paul Dana

Exhibit 2.11 This chemist shop at 76 Brick Lane operated from 1939 to 1991; photo © 2021 by Léo-Paul Dana

social context of the bazaar is most helpful when trying to understand the particular way of functioning of the bazaar economy.

The structured bazaar, common across Western Asia today, allows physical concentration. Such concentration enables potential buyers and suppliers to meet efficiently at a pre-determined location. This reduces search costs and minimises disparity caused by geographic fragmentation. Thus, the bazaar reduces overall transaction costs, as all parties concerned converge on a central location.

In a bazaar, today, one can observe a distinct pattern of economic activity. A potential buyer can easily locate the designated part of the bazaar for goods/services under consideration. Once at that location, it is possible to compare the goods of several dealers, within a short span of time. This allows the shopper to develop a feel for the prevailing market conditions, including the price and supply range. As more supplies enter or exit the market over time, and as the range shifts, the potential buyer can decide when and how to take a definitive position (i.e., to buy or to defer). The structured bazaar provides vital market functions, including the following:

- *Information Dissemination.* Individuals disseminate their proprietary information regarding new products and emerging trends in supply or demand.
- *Updating.* Potential suppliers and buyers quickly update and upgrade their state of information and incorporate their new knowledge to assume a new position.
- *Temporal Equilibrium.* Some potential suppliers and buyers behave as intermediaries, and they profit from arbitrage. They engage in co-operative bargaining and negotiations, forming strategic alliances.
- *Control.* The non-committal nature of arbitrage – coupled with the bazaar-imposed sense of ethics – regulates behaviour in the bazaar, and by extension the bazaar itself. Traders are ethically bound to honour their words. The possible enforcement of collective sanctions controls both the frequency and the range of fluctuations in the bazaar.

With little variation, the style and procedures of trade, in the bazaar, reflect a particular pattern:

(i) A potential buyer inquires about supplies and prices from several suppliers, within eye-and-ear-shot of each other. This allows the person to form a reasonably informed opinion about the state of the market at the time.

(ii) When the person's initial intention is to buy, he returns to a dealer and attempts to negotiate the price, by making an offer or counter-offer.

(iii) When the initial intention is to sell to a dealer at the bazaar, a person may return to the dealer with the highest selling, to offer a wholesale transaction.

A justification is usually offered through the use of a typical negotiation ploy, for instance, "Another dealer is selling the same at this price, but I would like to do business with you, because of our past relationships." The response may be along the lines of one of the three alternatives:

(i) To ignore the counter-offer as a ploy based on what he knew of the prevailing tight range of prices and supplies (especially when the offered price is outside or close to the lower bound of the price range).

(ii) To attempt to unload his supplies with a firm counter-offer of his own by splitting the difference on the price side and conditioning it upon a larger quantity than required by the potential buyer.

(iii) To buy a quantity (as opposed to selling) at the offered price, to both impact the dynamics of that transaction and the market by signalling a readiness to sell or buy. This is a sufficiently logical behaviour to influence the decision of potential buyers, regardless of initial intentions.

Bazaar-imposed ethics oblige buyers and sellers to honour their words. This is the foundation of the concept of trust. Two outcomes are common: (i) The prospective buyer succeeds to buy at a fair price when the buyer intended to buy at close to the prevailing equilibrium price; and (ii) a new price level begins to prevail when arbitrage was the original intention in the above characterisation. The increasing possibility of intermediaries participating in a perceived imbalance in the market place allows for the virtual consummation of many transactions at prices associated with total supply and demand at each moment in time. Ongoing arbitrage – combined and enforced by bazaar-imposed discipline – accords the structured bazaar functional efficiency, even in modern times.

Managerial Implications

As explained by Dana (2007), when examining the bazaar, it is essential to understand the relationships among the players within it, their organisation and their economic principles. The bazaar is a hub of information exchange. Buyers and sellers express intentions, and an intricate network of relationships facilitates commercial activities.

To the Western manager, the economics of the bazaar may not be evident. Nevertheless, the bazaar does have its efficiency, and its principles are highly relevant in Western Asia. While competition in the Occident is understood to be competition between sellers, in the bazaar economy, competition implies a tension between buyer and seller, rather than among sellers. In the bazaar, personal relations are more important than impersonal transactions. Profitability through relations is more important than market share; both the buyer and the seller seek a relationship. Unlike Western relationship marketing, which is customer-centred, whereby a seller seeks long-term business relationships with clients (Evans and Laskin, 1994; Zineldin, 1998), the focus in the bazaar is on the relationship itself. A Westerner who approaches the bazaar, with an understanding of the bazaar belief system, is likely to succeed better than those who assume a Western orientation.

Towards Future Research

COVID-19 resulted in lock-downs (Exhibit 2.12), with grave consequences for merchants accustomed to working in the bazaar with much human contact and interaction. Despite a slowdown, bazaars bounced back to life. The bazaar was an institution of the past, and it shall also thrive in the future. Some of its features have been adapted to online commerce (Dana et al., 2004). For instance, price comparisons on online shops or online bidding platforms borrowed much from the logic of bazaar. Controversial axioms and traditions of the bazaar, which were/and still are the key success factors of merchants, some of whom have even grown into national and sometimes international entrepreneurs, are among the essential issues to be considered by future researchers. There is much opportunity studying vendors who maintain centuries-old traditions and prosper therefrom, for instance merchants who for decades, instead of competing based on the cutting-the-edge techniques and using modern marketing tools, help each other and never let their competitors leave the competitive scene! Future

Exhibit 2.12 Shops closed; photo © 2021 by Léo-Paul Dana

research might dive further into this. How could other areas benefit from the understanding of bazaar concepts?

References

Christian, John LeRoy (1943), "Burma: Where India and China Meet," *National Geographic* 84 (4), pp. 489–512.

Dana, Léo-Paul (2000), *Economies of the Eastern Mediterranean Region: Economic Miracles in the Making,* Singapore, London & Hong Kong: World Scientific.

Dana, Léo-Paul (2007), *Asian Models of Entrepreneurship from the Indian Union and the Kingdom of Nepal to the Japanese Archipelago: Context, Policy and Practice,* Singapore, London & Hong Kong: World Scientific.

Dana, Léo-Paul, Hamid Etemad, and Richard W. Wright (2004), "Back to the Future: International Entrepreneurship in the New Economy," in Marian Jones and Pavlos Dimitratos, eds., *Emerging Paradigms in International Entrepreneurship,* Cheltenham: Edward Elgar, pp. 19–36.

Dana, Léo-Paul, Hamid Etemad, and Richard W. Wright (2008), "Toward a Paradigm of Symbiotic Entrepreneurship," *International Journal of Entrepreneurship and Small Business* 5 (2), pp. 109–126.

Evans, Joel R., and Richard L. Laskin (1994), "The Relationship Marketing Process: A Conceptualization and Application," *Industrial Marketing Management* 23 (5), pp. 432–452.

Geertz, Clifford (1963), *Peddlers and Princes: Social Development and Economic Change in Two Indonesian Towns,* Chicago: University of Chicago Press.

Geertz, Clifford (1978), "The Bazaar Economy: Information and Search in Peasant Marketing," *American Marketing Review* 68, pp. 28–32.

Gupta, Shruti, and Pratish Srivastav (2016), "Despite Unethical Retail Store Practices, Consumers at the Bottom of the Pyramid Continue to be Loyal," *The International Review of Retail, Distribution and Consumer Research* 26 (1), pp. 75–94.

Light, Ivan H., and Léo-Paul Dana (2020), *Entrepreneurs and Capitalism Since Luther: Rediscovering the Moral Economy,* Lanham: Lexington Books.

Long, George W. (1952), "Indonesia Faces the Dragon," *National Geographic* 102 (3), pp. 287–328.

Parsons, Talcott, and Neil J. Smelzer (1956), *Economy and Society,* Glencoe: Free Press.

Passantino, Joseph E. (1946), "Kunming, Southwestern Gateway to China," *National Geographic* 90 (2), pp. 137–168.

Penrose, Edith T. (1959), *The Theory of the Growth of the Firm,* Oxford: Blackwell.

Salamzadeh, Aidin, Zahra Arasti, and Ghanbar Mohammadi Elyasi (2017), "Creation of ICT-based Social Start-ups in Iran: A Multiple Case Study," *Journal of Enterprising Culture* 25 (1), pp. 97–122.

Starkey, Janet (2012), "The Continuity of Social Space," in Gharipour Mohammad, ed., *The Bazaar in the Islamic City: Design, Culture, and History,* Cairo: American University in Cairo Press, pp. 115–148.

Weber, Max (1924), *The Theory of Social and Economic Organization,* New York: Free Press.

Williamson, Oliver E. (1985), *The Economic Institutions of Capitalism,* New York: Free Press.

Williamson, Oliver E. (1996), *The Mechanisms of Governance,* New York: Oxford University Press.

Young, Michael Dunlop, and Peter Wilmott (1957), *Family and Kinship in East London,* London: Routledge and Kegan Paul.

Zineldin, Mosad Amin (1998), "Towards an Ecological Collaborative Relationship Management," *European Journal of Marketing* 32 (11–12), pp. 1138–1164.

Section II

Successor to the Omani Empire

Chapter 3

The Context for Business in Oman

Naveed Yasin & Zeinab Khansari

Abstract: Once known for its rich maritime history where Sinbad the Sailor had infamously sailed his dhow to China, the Sultanate of Oman plays a crucial role across the Persian Gulf and in the Middle East. Oman has been a tax-haven nation for its residents and businesses but has enforced VAT from 16 April 2021 and is expected to introduce personal income tax from 2022; this will have an impact on existing and future businesses.

Keywords: Oman, Sinbad the Sailer, Persian Gulf, tax haven

Introduction

The Sultanate of Oman is the oldest independent country in the Arab world. It is situated in the southeastern coast of the Arabian Peninsula; see map in Exhibit 3.1. Oman is one of the seven Arab states bordering the Persian Gulf comprising Bahrain, Kuwait, Qatar, Saudi Arabia and the United Arab Emirates. Oman shares land borders with the United Arab Emirates (UAE), Yemen and Saudi Arabia. The Sultanate of Oman is an absolute monarchy, and an Islamic country, with 85.9% of the population comprising Ibadi, Sunni and Shiite Islamic doctrines of the faith; however, Ibadi Islam is the most dominant across the Sultanate of Oman.

Geographically, Oman has a strategic location that further diversifies its economy from oil and gas revenues similar to the other Gulf Cooperation Council (GCC) countries. From the north, Oman is connected to the Strait of Hormuz, which is one of the world's most important

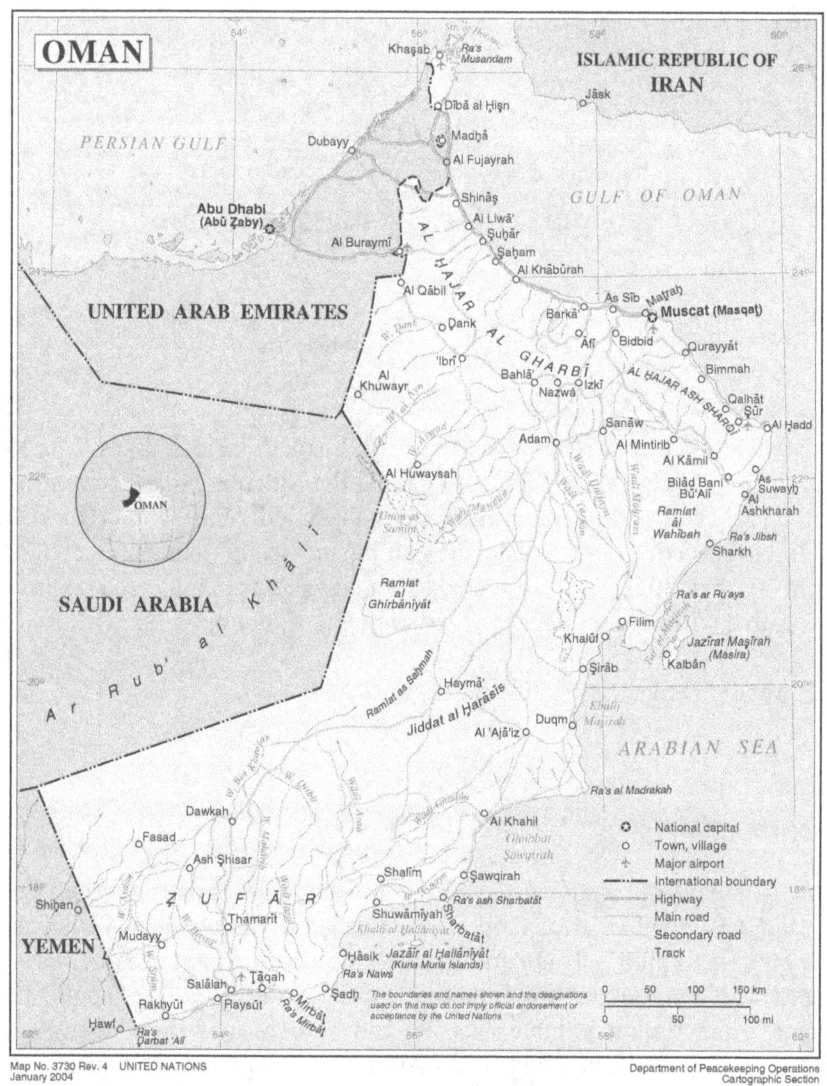

Exhibit 3.1 Map 3730 of Oman; courtesy of the United Nations

economic and geopolitical checkpoints. From the south, the port of Salalah serves the markets of southern and eastern Africa, the Persian Gulf, Red Sea and the Indian subcontinent towards the trade route between Chinese and European countries (Wright, 2007). Oman consists of 11 governorates with Muscat, the capital city, situated in the northeast of the Sultanate, followed by the second-largest city, Salalah, which is situated in the southwest of the country.

As an oil and natural gas-rich nation, Oman has a land area of 119,499 square miles and serves as a strategic transport hub. Scenery is varied (see Exhibits 3.2–3.4). The Sultanate consists of various ethnic groups comprising Arab, Baluchi, Bangladeshi, Pakistani, Sri Lankan, Indian and African ethnic communities. According to the 2014 census data, the expatriates and migrants are mostly male workers who have migrated from south Asian countries, whereas most female workers are from Indonesia, the Philippines and Sri Lanka (World Bank, 2018).

The Sultanate of Oman is a member of the GCC that was established in 1981 as a regional intergovernmental economic and political union among selective Arab states (see Dana et al., 2021). The GCC comprises Bahrain, Kuwait, Oman, Qatar, Saudi Arabia and the United Arab Emirates. Oman is a politically stable country and takes a neutral stance in regional and international conflicts (such as the Saudi–Yemen conflict, Qatar blockade and US–Iran tensions) while offering to play a mediator role to further secure peace and stability in the Gulf region.

Exhibit 3.2 Al-Dakhliyah; photo © 2021 by Hussain Al-Bahrani and Saif Al-Wahaibi, used with permission

Exhibit 3.3 Muttrah coast, Muscat; photo © 2021 by Hussain Al-Bahrani and
Saif Al-Wahaibi, used with permission

Although there are a considerable number of expatriate and migrant
workers in the Sultanate of Oman, the Omani Government has actively
introduced measures to increase the number of Omani nationals in the local
labour market. Similar policies have been utilised across most neighbouring
Gulf countries such as Saudi Arabia, Kuwait, Qatar, United Arab Emirates

Exhibit 3.4 Sur port; photo © 2021 by Hussain Al-Bahrani and Saif Al-Wahaibi, used with permission

and Bahrain. In 2017, Oman's unemployment rate was reported at 3.02%. To counteract the unemployment situation and develop the human capital of local citizens, an 'Omanisation' policy was enacted by the government in Oman to replace expatriate workers with trained Omani personnel. This initiative requires companies to reach mandated governmental goals to create employment for local citizens. Moreover, a recent study conducted by the Oxford Business Group found that Omani business leaders struggled with visa restrictions when recruiting foreigners for critical roles in their companies. According to this study, 59% cited an urgent need for reforms to local labour laws and legislative changes to promote economic growth (Khoury and Moghadam, 1995).

The Public Authority for Small and Medium Enterprises Development reported 31,916 micro-sized businesses, followed by 9,202 small-sized businesses and 3,349 medium-sized businesses in Oman. According to small and medium enterprises (SMEs) are concentrated in the capital of Muscat at 36%, followed by Al-Batinah at 15% and Al Dakhliyah at 12%. For a discussion of SMEs in Oman, see Dana et al. (2021).

Historical Context

Since the 1st century AD, Oman has been well known for being a trade and commerce sea and land hub that has played an integral role in shaping the culture of the Sultanate with trade partners from the Far East to Europe (Times of Oman, 2017). Oman's geographical location served as an important trade route for incense; famed dye; spices including nutmeg, cloves, cardamom and cinnamon; domestic camels; silk; textiles; gold; leather; carpet; pearls; pottery; lapis lazuli; timber; figurines; ebony; silver; tin; oils; grain; copper; bitumen; and sandalwood. For Oman, their strategic geographical location enabled trade from various empires such as the Phoenicians (now the area of Lebanon), Sri Lanka (formerly Ceylon) and China, Sumeria (now known as Iraq), Persia (now known as Iran), the Romans, Indus Valley civilisations (Pakistan and Northern India) and Zanzibar and East Africa. Many infamous sailors traded through Oman such as Abu Abdallah Bin Qasim Al-Amani, Vasco Da Gama, Abu Al-Hasan Al-Masudi, Ibn Battuta and Ahmad Ibn Majid. For more than 200 years, the area of Muttrah (situated in the Muscat province of Oman) has been well known for being the centre for commerce prior to the discovery of natural oil resources.

Oman has had a significant colonial presence in other nations as they once possessed the island of Zanzibar on the eastern coast of Africa. In 1781, Oman and United Kingdom (UK) signed a Treaty of Friendship, but this was followed by the division of the Omani empire and separation of the Sultanate of Oman and Muscat from the Sultanate of Zanzibar due to a succession crisis in 1856. In 1891, Oman and the capital of Muscat became a British Protectorate. Oman received its independence from Great Britain under the 1951 Treaty of Friendship, Commerce and Navigation. Until now, Oman's ruling monarchy holds close ties with the British monarchy (The National, 2020).

For many generations, the Sultanate has been ruled by the House of Al Said. In the 1970s bloodless *coup d'etat*, Sultan Qaboos Bin Said overthrew his father – Sultan Said bin Taimur. This led to the rapid reform and modernisation of the Sultanate of Oman. Following the death of Sultan Qaboos in 2020, the throne was succeeded by Sultan Haitham bin Tariq as Sultan of Oman.

As noted by Palalić et al. (2019), Oman is one of the kindest and warmest countries for foreigners, and it embraces people from neighbouring lands, welcoming them with the chance of being successful in various businesses across the country.

Context for Enterprise and Implications for Doing Business

The traditional *souq* and bazaar of Muttrah are well known for the retail of frankincense, gold and silver jewellery, spices, textiles, fruit, vegetables, dates and perfume oil.

The Oman 2020 economic vision was designed to shift the country's economic reliance from the public sector to private enterprise (Ghailani and Khan, 2004). The Late Royal Highness of Oman, Sultan Qaboos bin Said, proactively encouraged Omanis to pursue entrepreneurship and developed a 70-million Omani Rial fund to enable young men and women to develop entrepreneurship and small businesses more effectively. The government also encouraged SMEs to develop a competitive edge with incentives such as free land. Due to the issuance of the Royal Decree No. 56/2002, three free zones have been established: Salalah Free Zone, Sohar Free Zone and Al Mazyunah Free Zone. Companies established in these free zones are exempt from paying corporate taxes for up to 30 years, customs duties for goods and services, and allow 100% foreign ownership with full repatriation of capital and profits boosted by low start-up capital requirements (Thomson Reuters, 2012).

Oman has a young population with more than 60% under the age of 25 and more than 35% under the age of 15 (Ministry of National Economy [MoNE], 2010). Furthermore, despite implementing international standards within higher education institutes (HEIs) (Kawamorita et al., 2020), the number of graduates exceeds the number of available jobs in Oman (Al-Barwani and Ameen, 2009), and the graduates are recognised as unqualified by almost half of Arab CEOs. Therefore, the regional economy is a combination of parallel and interconnected factors of hydrocarbon revenue and foreign labour (Ennis, 2015). Thus, all GCC countries rely on expatriates due to their dependency on oil and gas reserves and the lack of a sufficient and skilled national workforce (Ennis, 2013). However, Oman has the least dependency on expatriate labour compared to its other neighbours, such as Qatar consists of 94% of the expatriate labour force, UAE 93%, Kuwait 80.5% and Bahrain 77.3% of expatriates. Oman's population encompasses only 59.4% of the foreign workforce (Ennis, 2015).

Until 2021, the Sultanate of Oman placed no taxes on personal income, and there were no requirements for individuals to file income tax returns (Thomson Reuters, 2012). Limited Liability Companies (LLC) are the most popular form of business incorporation in Oman in terms of registered business entities. This requires each partner to be liable only to the extent of their share in a business (Business Start-up, 2020).

The level of entrepreneurship and competitiveness of nations are evaluated by Global Entrepreneurship Monitor (GEM) and the World Economic Forum, and as such, are represented via either the Global Entrepreneurial Index (GEI) or Global Competitiveness Index (GCI) (Dana et al., 2009). The GCI consigns countries into three classifications: (1) the countries in the first group are developing the fundamental requirements including economic infrastructures, a health system and primary education, (2) the second class encompasses countries with a developed economic structure, focusing on higher education, vocational training and exploiting the domestic and foreign workforce, (3) countries in the third section have innovation-oriented economies with emerging technologies, creative products and complicated business procedures. In the MENA region (the Middle East and North African countries), Oman is in the sixth place and is ranked 39th globally, being assigned to the second classification by the GCI (Al-Harthi, 2017; Schwab, 2014; Barrichello et al., 2020).

Since 1970, Oman has seen radical improvements in the economy, education and well-being after His Majesty Sultan Qaboos Bin Said; governmental and private sectors started supporting the enterprise system to strengthen the entrepreneurial infrastructure and establish the enterprise culture. Intilaaqah is a private institute, initiated by Shell and established in 1995 to stimulate unemployed Omanis to get engaged with entrepreneurial activities, assist SME businesses, create young entrepreneurs and further diversify the hydrocarbon-dependent Omani economy. Since then, more than 7,000 Omanis have been trained by Intilaaqah of whom many now have their own successfully running businesses. Intilaaqah also provides financial support of up to one million US dollars to SMEs in the Sultanate of Oman (Al-Balushi and Anderson, 2017). Alternatively, SMEs in Oman can easily access the Al-Rafd fund, which provides approximately 250,000 US dollars with no guarantee requirement. In addition to the private support system, Riyada is a governmental support mechanism with five major initiatives: the launch of business incubators, entrepreneurs' business cards, facilitating registration for industrial land, entrepreneurs' newspaper and entrepreneurs' clubs.

Although the government-owned public sector employment is a more appealing opportunity for Omani nationals, there is evidence that most of Oman's start-up businesses are established with positive intentions and motivations rather than a forced stimulus (Salamzadeh, 2018). For instance: improvement in income, inclination towards independence, better future and building a successful business have been mentioned as the greatest inspirations for Omani entrepreneurs (Al-Balushi and Anderson, 2017). Moreover, based on survey responses from 60 entrepreneurs aged 19–40, and with different levels of education from high school diploma to master's degree, and at different stages of their business from the early stages of start-up to successful and well-developed businesses, about 63% of participants were somewhat satisfied to fully satisfied with the entrepreneurial support in Oman (Al-Balushi and Anderson, 2017).

In 2013, His Majesty, Sultan Qaboos Bin Said, the Sultan of Oman, replaced the Directorate General of Small Medium Enterprises (Riyada) with a managerial structure with some major purposes: developing and fostering the financial support and collaborative infrastructure for SMEs, promoting the culture of entrepreneurship, strengthening the sustainability and diversification of the national economy through training programmes, providing partnerships between governmental and private sectors, and providing technical support and consulting opportunities. For instance, in 2018, The National Centre for Entrepreneurship Education (NCEE) held a three-day event in collaboration with the Middle East College (Muscat, Oman) and Coventry University (England, UK) to create a new programme to encourage and appraise the entrepreneurial capacity of the Omani leadership and Omani institutions to manage change. This programme focused on providing insights into various leadership styles and changing management approaches and techniques. The participants were required to identify challenges in their organisations while being supported to address the challenges of developing practical strategies. This initiative brought business leaders and educators together on a shared platform to encourage entrepreneurial activity across the Sultanate of Oman (National Centre for Entrepreneurship in Education, 2018).

While half of Oman's population are females, Oman's cultural and religious context defines the primary role of a woman as a wife and a mother. Thus, traditional gender roles exist within Oman as women tend to give priority to their male counterparts for engagement with business, promotion and entrepreneurial activities, although they are more qualified or have the same level of academic qualifications. This hinders the full economic potential of females to be harnessed effectively for economic growth and business sustainability. On the other hand, male dominance in the business environment further hinders women's participation within the labour market (McElwee and Al-Riyami, 2003; Al-Mandhry, 2000). However, there have been considerable developments in the number of women who started businesses in Oman since the 1970s. For instance, in a qualitative study conducted by McElwee and Al-Riyami (2003), the findings revealed that most Omani female entrepreneurs started businesses to create self-employment while being supported by their families and spouses. The study also suggested that the nature of such business establishments was concentrated in the service industry and was small. Furthermore, the participants in this study suggested a lack of networks for businesswomen.

Although entrepreneurship is thriving in Oman, due to security, higher salaries, complimentary benefits and fewer working hours within governmental jobs, entrepreneurial endeavours are still overlooked and not considered as a serious job option by most Omanis (Atef and Al-Balushi, 2015; Romano and Seeger, 2014). An empirical study focussing on entrepreneurial attitudes among graduate students of Sultan Qaboos University, College of Banking and Financial Studies, Muscat College and Majan College in Oman found that although Omani graduates perceived entrepreneurship positively, their preferences for self-employment upon graduating remained relatively low (Ibrahim et al., 2017). The recent development of entrepreneurial initiatives in education mandated by the Ministry of Higher Education (MOHE) has resulted in enterprise education being embedded across all programmes at HEIs. A study conducted by Yasin et al. (2020), demonstrated improvements across all enterprising characteristics of Omani Arab female engineers at Muscat University (in partnership with Aston University and Cranfield University UK) following an entrepreneurship bootcamp course.

In comparison to the United Arab Emirates, Oman is less well known for technology-based start-up programmes, but there have been modest developments with Oman's vision for 2040 to become a hub for global technology and small- to medium-sized businesses. On the other hand, the United Arab Emirates is well known to have the largest hub for start-ups across the MENA region accounting for above 35% of the region's start-ups, whereas Oman hosts only 2% of the total share. Some of the notable tech start-ups in Oman are ClickforMeal; Genesis International, LLC; Ki-Bros Productions; Alatool Muscat; and Al-Etijahat for Design (Business Live Me, 2019).

As Oman is proactively taking steps to become a knowledge-based economy and to develop its information, communication and technology sectors (ICT sectors), Techween, Waadi Accelerator and Jasoor Venture programmes have recently emerged to support entrepreneurs with high-potential technology and to develop technical innovation within ideas and projects (Oman Technology Fund, 2020). A sovereign wealth fund of

$200 m has been pledged to fund investments in Oman's start-ups and attract global start-ups to be established in the Sultanate. This will inevitably contribute towards overcoming structural issues in the economy through youth job creation, growing the ecosystem and policy formulation (Computer Weekly, 2019).

The importance of family-owned businesses also plays an essential role in explaining the entrepreneurial landscape of the Sultanate. Recently, Oman's six family-owned businesses were ranked in the Forbes most powerful list. The list included Suhail Bahwan Group, Zubair Corporation, W.J. Towell and Co, Mohsin Haider Darwish and MB Holdings (Arabian Stories, 2020). Family firms have been critical in explaining Oman's economic success and contribution to GDP, and their significance has been described as the backbone of the economy. Many of these family firms are increasingly becoming involved in corporate social responsibility (CSR) initiatives to serve the local community (Oman Daily Observer, 2020). For example, Zubair Corporation established Zubair Small Enterprise Centres as a voluntary CSR initiative to contribute towards the strategic vision of Oman and has effectively been supporting local business start-ups through its direct support programmes, business advisory services, specialised advisory services, Tjaseer initiative and Tajribati initiatives (Zubair Small Enterprise Centre, 2020).

Social entrepreneurship has started to receive more interest for its potential to boost the role of the private sector of the Oman economy. In 2016, the CEO of Riyada emphasised the importance of the greater participation of Omanis in social entrepreneurship initiatives. He also mentioned that such initiatives needed to flourish beyond the capital of Muscat to other geographic regions. Some of the notable examples of Oman's social entrepreneurship activity have been developments in irrigation systems, recyclable materials, community lending facilities, flood prevention and youth empowerment initiatives (Times of Oman, 2016).

In 2015, Oman's high-performing entrepreneur, Mr Qais Al-Khonji, was the recipient of the Social Entrepreneur Award by Business Worldwide Magazine for his role in promoting and encouraging entrepreneurship in Oman's national school curriculum (PR Newswire, 2015). Another example of social entrepreneurial success is, with support from the W.J. Towell Group, Aisha Baabood, the executive director and founder of White Hands Centre for Assistive Technology and Rehabilitation, was able to effectively develop supportive solutions for those with disabilities by providing switches, trackballs, large keys keyboards, portable alarms, memory devices, epilepsy alarms, braille readers and magnifiers.

Towards the Future

Over the last few decades, also known as Oman's Renaissance period (Brandenburg, 2013), there have been revolutionary and fast-paced improvements in various aspects such as business, economy, education, general welfare and health in Oman. However, promoting the interrelation between education and industry, encouraging Omani females and providing accessible entrepreneurship education seem to have further accelerated the growth of entrepreneurship in Oman (Magd and McCoy, 2014). Two national committees (Main Committee and Executive Committee) have been assigned to address entrepreneurial education availability and create links between education and industry. Moreover, to enhance the graduates' enterprising skills, the Ministry of Higher Education has collaborated with the Ministry of Defence, Ministry of Manpower, Oman's Research Council and Ministry of Commerce and Industry (Oman Accreditation Council [OAC], 2006; UNESCO and Stratreal Foundation, 2013). Other vocational trainings in the fields of business and entrepreneurship such as Know About Business (KAB), Injaz and Intilaaqah are actively functioning to promote the culture of entrepreneurship in Oman further. The SANAD programme established in 2001 aims to support jobseekers within the age window of 18–40 years. To encourage Omani females, SANAD assigned special funding only for females. For instance, from 2002 to 2004, about 37% of funding was provided to females (Khan et al., 2005). In terms of financial support, Al-Rafd fund, bank loans, Intlaaqah and Riyada are a few of the Sultanate's available resources.

Even though there is a robust support system in Oman to foster the culture of entrepreneurship, diversify the economy from oil and gas revenue, fortify sustainable business development and tackle the number of graduates exceeding the available governmental positions, it seems there is still room for further actions. Based on Ennis (2015), expatriates can have a considerable impact on economic development, while Oman's limitations for foreign employments (such as visa restriction, Omanisation and not having transparent and well-established rights and regulations for expatriates) can hinder or retard the entrepreneurship prosperity and economic growth. Nevertheless, the significant attempts and impressive development in fostering entrepreneurship culture, supporting policies, prosperous diversification since 1970 and being blessed with an abundance of maritime opportunities, a bright future is ahead for conductive and fruitful entrepreneurial endeavours and prosperity in the Sultanate of Oman.

It is evident that Oman is making progress in developing commerce to fulfil its future vision of a widespread and effective business environment. Although there have been developments in Oman concerning the various strands of contemporary enterprise activities, such as entrepreneurial leadership initiatives, gender and entrepreneurship, graduate enterprise education initiatives, technology-based start-up support, and family and social business start-ups, there is a greater need to assess the effectiveness of such initiatives through empirical studies and qualitative case studies that provide further insights into the nature of such entrepreneurial activities and SME development initiatives across the Sultanate of Oman. There is limited secondary research to suggest the existence of immigrant and refugee entrepreneurial activities and the development of digital entrepreneurial financing initiatives (i.e., crowdfunding). These are the potential areas for the further growth of SMEs that could provide further vibrancy to the Sultanate of Oman's economy and its aspirational strategic visions for the future.

References

Al-Balushi, Rashid Ali, and Alistair R. Anderson (2017), "Entrepreneurship in Oman Policies and Practices," *Journal of Asia Entrepreneurship and Sustainability* 13 (4), pp. 29–47.

Al-Barwani, Thuwayba Ahmed, and Hana Ameen (2009), "Strategic Brain Drain: Implications for Higher Education in Oman," *Higher Education Policy* 22 (4), pp. 415–432.

Al-Harthi, Aisha Salim Ali (2017), "Understanding Entrepreneurship through the Experience of Omani Entrepreneurs: Implications for Entrepreneurship Education," *Journal of Developmental Entrepreneurship* 22 (1), pp. 1750001–1750021.

Al-Mandhry, Zeinab (2000), "Development of Women in the Sultanate of Oman," *Al-Markazi* 25 (5).

Arabian Stories (2020), (Retrieved from https://www.thearabianstories.com/2020/06/30/revealed-omans-six-family-owned-businesses-ranked-in-forbes-most-powerful-list/)

Atef, Tamer Mohamed, and Masooma Al-Balushi (2015), "Entrepreneurship as a Means for Restructuring Employment Patterns," *Tourism and Hospitality Research* 15 (2), pp. 73–90.

Barrichello, Alcides, Emerson Gomes dos Santos, and Rogerio Scabim Morano (2020), "Determinant and Priority Factors of Innovation for the Development of Nations," *Innovation & Management Review* 17 (3), pp. 307–320.

Brandenburg, Torsten (2013), "The Political Economy of Internationalization and Privatisation of Higher Education in the Sultanate of Oman," in Steffen Wippel, ed., *Regionalizing Oman,* Dordrecht: Springer, pp. 289–303.

Business Live ME (2019), (Retrieved from https://www.businessliveme.com/economy/small-business/top-tech-startups-in-oman/)

Business Start-up (2020), (Retrieved from https://www.businesssetup.com/om/limited-liability-company-llc-in-oman)

Computer Weekly (2019), (Retrieved from https://www.computerweekly.com/news/252470791/Inside-Omans-new-tech-startup-drive)

Dana, Léo-Paul, Mary Han, Vanessa Ratten, and Isabell M. Welpe (2009), *Handbook of Research on Asian Entrepreneurship,* Cheltenham: Edward Elgar.

Dana, Léo-Paul, Ramo Palalić, and Veland Ramadani (2021), *Entrepreneurship in the Gulf Cooperation Council Region: Evolution and Future Perspectives,* Singapore: World Scientific.

Ennis, Crystal (2013), *Rentier 2.0: Entrepreneurship Promotion and the (Re) Imagination of Political Economy in the Gulf Cooperation Council Countries.* Unpublished PhD thesis, University of Waterloo, Ontario, Canada.

Ennis, Crystal (2015), "Between Trend and Necessity: Top-Down Entrepreneurship Promotion in Oman and Qatar," *The Muslim World* 105 (1), pp. 116–138.

Ghailani, Juma S., and Sami A. Khan (2004), "Quality of Secondary Education and Labour Market Requirement," *Journal of Services Research* 4 (1), pp. 161–172.

Ibrahim, Omer Ali, Sonal Devesh, and Vaheed Ubaidullah (2017), "Implication of Attitude of Graduate Students in Oman Towards Entrepreneurship: An Empirical Study," *Journal of Global Entrepreneurship Research* 7 (8), pp. 1–17.

Kawamorita, Hiroko, Aidin Salamzadeh, Kursat Demiryurek, and Mahyar Ghajarzadeh (2020), "Entrepreneurial Universities in Times of Crisis: Case of COVID-19 Pandemic," *Journal of Entrepreneurship, Business and Economics* 8 (1), pp. 77–88.

Khan, Sami A., A. P. Ghosh, and Donald A. Myers (2005), "Women Entrepreneurship in Oman," Proceedings of the 50th World Conference of the International Council for the Small Business (ICSB), June 15–18, Washington, DC.

Khoury, Nabil F., and Valentine M. Moghadam (1995), *Gender and Development in the Arab World: Women's Economic Participation, Patterns and Policies,* London: Zed books.

Magd, Hesham A. E., and Mark P. McCoy (2014), "Entrepreneurship in Oman: Paving the Way for a Sustainable Future," *Procedia Economics and Finance* 15, pp. 1632–1640.

McElwee, Gerard, and Rahma Al-Riyami (2003), "Women Entrepreneurs in Oman: Some Barriers to Success," *Career Development International* 8 (7), pp. 1–12.

Ministry of National Economy (MoNE) (2010), "Statistical Yearbook 2010," (Retrieved from http://www.moneoman.gov.om)

The National (2020), (Retrieved from https://www.thenational.ae/ arts-culture/a-good-friend-of-my-family-and-the-uk-when-queen-elizabeth-met-sultan-qaboos-1.985414)

National Centre for Entrepreneurship in Education (2018), (Retrieved from https://ncee.org.uk/2018/12/17/omans-entrepreneurial-leaders-programme/)

Oman Accreditation Council (OAC) (2006), Accreditation vs Recognition of Programme in Oman, A Poster Developed by Oman Accreditation Council.

Oman Daily Observer (2020), (Retrieved from https://www.omanobserver. om/article/77433/Opinion/economic-impact-of-family-businesses

Oman Technology Fund (2020), (Retrieved from https://www.wamda. com/2019/10/oman-startup-opportunity)

Palalić, Ramo, Veland Ramadani, and Léo-Paul Dana (2019), "Refugee Entrepreneurship: A Case Study from the Sultanate of Oman," in Sibylle Heilbrunn, Jörg Freiling, Aki Harima, eds., *Refugee Entrepreneurship,* Cham: Palgrave Macmillan pp. 207–220. doi:10.1007/978-3-319-92534-9_14

PR Newswire (2015), (Retrieved from https://www.prnewswire.com/ news-releases/qais-al-khonji-wins-social-entrepreneur-of-the-year-oman-2015-524042071.html)

Romano, Julia Craig, and Seeger Lee (2014), "Rentierism and Reform: Youth Unemployment and Economic Policy in Oman," (Retrieved from https://cpb-us-e1.wpmucdn.com/blogs.gwu.edu/dist/6/1613/files/2018/11/Romano-Seeger-Capstone-Final-xlu6ps.pdf)

Salamzadeh, Aidin (2018), "Start-up Boom in an Emerging Market: A Niche Market Approach," in Datis Khajeheian, Wilfried Mödinger, Mike Friedrichsen, eds., *Competitiveness in Emerging Markets,* Cham: Springer, pp. 233–243.

Schwab, Klaus (2014), *The Global Competitiveness Index 2014–2015,* Geneva: World Economic Forum, pp. 3–52.

Thomson Reuters (2012), (Retrieved from https://uk.practicallaw.thomsonreuters.com/w-007-5872?transitionType=Default&contextData=(sc.Default)

Times of Oman (2016), (Retrieved from https://timesofoman.com/article/80630/oman/government/social-entrepreneurship-has-huge-potential-in-oman)

Times of Oman (2017), (Retrieved from https://timesofoman.com/article/100895/HI/This-Weekend/Oman-History-Explore-the-ancient-Omani-trading-routes

UNESCO and Stratreal Foundation (2013), "Entrepreneurship Education in the Arab States," (Retrieved from http://www.ita.gov.om/ITAPortal/Pages/Page.aspx?NID=675&PID=2494&LID=125, assessed on 3 January 2014)

World Bank (2018), (Retrieved from https://data.worldbank.org/indicator/SP.POP.TOTL?locations=OM)

Wright, Robert (2007), "Desert Town that Became a Port at Crossroads of World Trade Oman's Salalah Port has Answered a Need for a Trans-shipment Hub, but it is not all Plain Sailing for its Operators, writes Robert Wright: (Asia Edition)," *Financial Times,* p. 3. Retrieved from ABI/INFORM Global database. (Document ID: 1212220031)

Yasin, Naveed, Zeinab Khansari, and Taimur Sharif (2020), "Assessing the Enterprising Tendencies of Arab Female Undergraduate Engineering Students in The Sultanate of Oman," *Industry and Higher Education* 34 (6), pp. 429–439.

Zubair Small Enterprise Centre (2020), (Retrieved from https://zubairsec.org/who-we-are/our-profile/)

Section III

Successor to the Persian Empire

Chapter 4

The Context for Business in Iran

Sepideh Khavarinezhad & Vahid Jafari-Sadeghi

Abstract: The word "bazaar" is originally Persian and was introduced thousands of years ago in this region. A bazaar, as an integral part of the Iranian culture, was a place in which various goods were sold based on their nature. This logic was transferred to different Middle Eastern countries, and this region became the central place to use this traditionally effective and efficient marketing approach. Today, Iran is the second-largest country in the Middle East. It enjoys a dry desert climate and Mediterranean-type climate, and also cold in mountainous areas. Iran is a leader in fossil fuel production, and it has a young workforce. During the last decade, new technology-based firms have changed the business environment, and the country is experiencing a high-tech boom in different areas. Nevertheless, both traditional bazaars and the emerging markets are working simultaneously. Besides, the business environment is full of success stories of businesspersons who have made significant changes in Iran's economy.

Keywords: bazaar, fossil fuel, Persia, young workforce

Introduction

Formerly known as Persia, Iran covers 1,648,195 km^2. As depicted in the map (Exhibit 4.1), Iran's neighbours are Turkey to the northwest and Iraq to the west, Afghanistan and Pakistan to the east, and Armenia, Azerbaijan and Turkmenistan to the north. Iran is geographically located in a strategic position with access to the Persian Gulf, Gulf of Oman and the Caspian

Sea (the largest lake in the world). Besides, it is considered a highway to connect central Asia to the Middle East, which was also historically part of the Silk Road. The population of Iran is very diverse, and different ethnic groups, even with different religions including but not limited to Muslims (Shia and Sunni), Christians, Jews, Zoroastrians, Mysticists, are living in peace. This diversity is due to the country's history, which goes back to thousands of years ago when the Great Persian Empire used to rule over a large land called Persia. There is evidence of the earliest civilisations in this region, like the Saltmen, which were discovered in the Salt mines of Iran dated to more than 2,500 years ago.

Exhibit 4.1 Map 3891 of Iran; courtesy of the United Nations

The official language is Persian or Farsi, but since various ethnic groups are living in this country, people also use Turkish, Azeri, Arabic, Lori, Kurdish, Gilaki, Mazandarani, Balochi and Turkmen as primary languages. At the same time, also there are tens of local languages and accents that Iranians use. Iran is well known for its incredible history, which is distinct from the European and American history that is mostly known for its churches and palaces. In addition to mosques, churches, synagogues and palaces, there are various historical places, the world's heritage sites and technologies such as Qanat (Kariz) around the country. Persia was a cradle of science in ancient times. Several distinguished philosophers and scientists were born and grown in this country, who changed the world's scientific history. Scientists like Avicenna (father of early modern medicine), Al-Khwarizmi (creator of algorithm and algebra) and Zakariyya al-Razi (discovered ethanol/alcohol, and its refinement) are among the hundreds of well-known scientists who have changed the history of science and philosophy.

Iran is a four-season country with various lands, mountains and beaches, which make it possible for tourists to enjoy different weathers and landscapes by a less than an hour journey using a car or an aeroplane. Besides, while Iran has only around 1% of the world's population, it owns a significant percent of the world's resources. For instance, 7% of the world's mineral resources (Rahimdel and Noferesti, 2020) belongs to Iran, and it is ranked fourth and second in terms of oil and gas resources (Ahmadi et al., 2020).

Historical Context

According to available documents, the history of markets in Iran dates back several thousand years. The word bazaar in terms of lexicography can reveal more emphasis on the Iranianism of this urban element. A bazaar is a place for buying and selling and supplying all kinds of goods and products (Dana and Wright, 2015). Despite its brilliant history, over the past centuries, Iran had gone through significant ups and downs economically, politically and socially; when European societies were in the process of rapid development and progress after the early stages of the Industrial Revolution, Iran was a follower due to its particular socio-political situation and an eight-year imposed war with Iraq. Thus, the country did not develop significantly based on its development plans during the past four decades, that is, after the revolution in 1979.

Several dynasties ruled over Iran for more than 2500 years. During the Qajar period (1789–1925), rulers' incompetence and rivalry reached its peak.

Loss of important parts of Iran's territory and resources, war defeat costs, treaties and their excessive fines, neglect of human and social capital, recessionary and contractionary policies (excessive tax increases), lack of economic planning and legislation, the granting of concessions to companies and colonial countries, the establishment of Russian and British banks, and the foreign goods caused severe damage to the structure of Iran's economy (Moghadam and Salamzadeh, 2018).

Reza Shah Pahlavi subsequently ruled from 1925 until 1941 when he was forced to abdicate by the Anglo-Soviet invasion. His son Mohammad Reza Pahlavi subsequently ruled and westernised the nation, until the Iranian Revolution of 1979.

Iran's economy was manifested in the constitution after the Islamic Revolution and the Islamic Republic regime's formation, which included a picture of the Iranian-Islamic economy's general lines (Tajpour and Salamzadeh, 2019). Iran's economy, which has become a monopoly economy, was dependent on oil revenues after the entry of oil-generated wealth; it has also undergone several structural changes over the past 20 years.

Iran is ranked 18th out of the 20 outstanding economies with more than 700 billion dollars of Gross Domestic Product (GDP). Iran has around 18% of the world's natural gas resources and about 9.3% of the world's crude oil, in addition to significant reserves of copper and other mineral reserves. Iran is ranked second in the world in terms of hydrocarbon reserves such as oil and gas. Besides, it has second place in crude oil exports. Iran has a positive balance of payments, significant foreign exchange reserves, and low foreign debt. The country's policymakers have recently tried to make Iran a place for investment and domestic production for domestic consumption and export (Jafari-Sadeghi et al., 2020; Rezaei et al., 2017).

The Iranian economy had benefited considerably from the abolition of the nuclear sanctions in 2016, when the Joint Comprehensive Plan of Action (JCPOA) nuclear deal was signed (Biancone et al., 2016; Ghodsi et al., 2018; Sadeghi et al., 2019). It has led to a 27% increase in the overall exports (regarding goods and services in US dollar terms) and actual GDP growth of 12.5% in 2016/17. However, Iran's economic forecasts have been adversely affected by the United States' recent (May 2018) decision to withdraw from the JCPOA nuclear deal, which the previous US administration signed under President Obama. The EU has repeatedly reiterated its continuity to the JCPOA deal (along with Russia and China), but it has not been able to affect the US position (Sadeghi et al., 2017; 2018). Iran is a member of the Organisation of the Petroleum Exporting Countries (OPEC), the second-largest producer among the members and the fifth-largest producer in the world. Moreover, the share of foreign trade in the country's GDP is over 48% Exports are spearheaded by crude oil and petroleum products (around 70%), whereas vehicles, maise, rice and medicaments are among the main imported items. This report presents a broad picture of the Iranian economy, which concludes with a summary of the main research findings and outlines the most crucial issues for the Iranian economy in the given circumstances.

Traditional markets have played a pivotal role in the urban economy in the spatial organisation of old and historic cities. However, we have seen changes in the role, function and shape of traditional markets in recent decades. Among these changes, we can mention the changes in the uses around the market, which have been affected by the market's role, function and economy. Iranian markets, which are called Bazaars in the economic field, with their major commercial use and social and economic activities are considered a significant example of urban spaces in which social and cultural capital plays a substantial role in their economic situation. The markets in Tehran, Tabriz and Isfahan remain the main arteries of urban life and are known as the centre of socio-economic activities. These bazaars are shaped based on the bazaar economy's presumptions, which differ from the firm-type economy (Dana et al., 1999a, b). For instance, there are unwritten rules of the game (like, *Ravabet*), which are more important than written ones (like, *Zavabet*) (Rezaei, 2011; Rezaei et al., 2019). *Ravabet* deals with networks and connections, which originally shape families and then are extended to their businesses and societies. In comparison, *Zavabet* represents the formal standards and rules that are expected by each part of a relationship (Light et al., 2013; Rezaei et al., 2013). Such formal and informal institutions have thousands of years of history in the bazaar economy.

The word bazaar is very old, and it refers to a place where goods are bought and sold. This Persian word has found its way into the other languages such as Arabic, Turkish, Ottoman and some European languages, whose speakers have traded with Iran. Iranian bazaars are places where you can look around, explore people's lives and discover many cultural

Exhibit 4.2 Tabriz Bazaar; photo © 2021 by Aidin Salamzadeh

realities deeply rooted in Iranian culture. Domestic and foreign trade have led to the growth of urbanisation and the development of cities and the bazaars of large cities such as Isfahan, Tabriz, Qazvin and Shiraz.

Exhibit 4.3 Shiraz Bazaar; photo © 2021 by Aidin Salamzadeh

Such trades have also caused new queues built alongside old queues and also several caravanserais were set up side by side in the bazaars. Bazaars, as the public space of the city, have always been inextricably linked to human life.

Exhibit 4.4 Isfahan Bazaar (Naghsh-e-Jahan Square); photo © 2021 by
Aidin Salamzadeh

The most important shopping centre in the capital, called Iran's economic heart, is the "Tehran Grand Bazaar". It is a large and extensive market with unique architecture that is a relic of the Qajar era and is still an important place for buying and selling goods.

The Tehran Bazaar is a venue where many wholesalers, manufacturers, retailers, commercial warehouses and vendors gather and present their goods and products. These bazaars are successful and vibrant examples of Iranian markets that have special physical and structural characteristics with cultural, social and economic capital. Iranian Bazaars with major commercial functions as well as social and economic activities are a significant example of urban spaces in which social and cultural capital plays a significant role in their economic situation. Tehran, Tabriz and Isfahan's markets remain the main arteries of urban life and the centre of socio-economic activity. These markets are successful and vibrant examples of Iranian markets that have unique physical and structural characteristics with cultural, social and economic capital. The bazaars are social and economic capitalist urban spaces in Iran and are the manifestations of

Exhibit 4.5 Tehran; photo © 2021 by Aidin Salamzadeh

traditional Iranian architecture and urban planning, playing a role as the beating heart of each city. The city's main bazaar starts along the most important roads of the city and continues to the centre.

Context for Enterprise and Implications for Doing Business

Iran's economy is a single-product, oil-dependent economy with the highest advantage of hydrocarbon resources; it has continued to operate, in recent years, relying on the structure and system of the state economy. Due to the oil-dependent nature of Iran's economy, an important part of the country's economy is therefore affected by global developments; moreover, to some extent, the instability in the global oil market and economic sanctions imposed on the regime have influenced the national economy, and this instability has become an inherent part of the country's economy. The transition from a state-controlled and oil-based economy to a free market economy requires an improved business environment for enterprises — a prerequisite for the implementation of economic privatisation policies (Dana, 2000a). In recent years, the government has acted as the major employer in the Iranian economy and, despite extensive divestitures and privatisations under Law No. 44, it has had a dominant share in the economy and has been considered as a major player in the country's economy. Furthermore, the government is a serious competitor to the private sector (Tajpour et al., 2020).

The World Bank's annual business reports announce the business situation in the countries for the next year concerning the reforms and changes made in this regard. These reports provide the necessary information about the application of laws and regulations as well as the business environment in countries with economic policymakers along with domestic and foreign investors. These indicators for the Iranian business environment are examined in the following section.

Only 9% of the land is arable, and primitive farming methods remain prevalent. Yet, agriculture contributes to 9.5% of the total GDP, employing 17.2% of the active population. The main local crops include pistachios (Iran is considered the world's largest producer), wheat, rice, oranges, tea and cotton. Illicit cultivation of opium poppy is fairly common as well. The industrial sector employs 32% of the workforce and contributes to 35% of the total GDP (World Bank report). Iran's industry is spearheaded by the hydrocarbon industry as the country is rich in mineral resources including mainly oil (the fourth largest proved crude oil reserves in the world) and gas (the second biggest reserves in the world) as well as copper, lead, zinc, and so on. Nevertheless, Iran's crude oil production, which has risen gradually in the aftermath of the nuclear agreement, has fallen drastically since 2018 following the implementation of American sanctions on this sector and it reached the lowest level since the 1980s in July 2019 (International Energy Agency). The textile industry is the second most crucial industry

Table 4.1 Breakdown of Economic Activities by Sector

Breakdown of Economic Activity by Sector	Agriculture	Industry	Services
Employment by Sector (*in % of Total Employment*)	17.8	30.3	51.9
Value Added (*in % of GDP*)	9.5	34.9	54.4
Value Added (*Annual % Change*)	3.2	3.0	4.4

Source: World Bank, Latest Available Data. Because of Rounding, the Sum of the Percentages May Be Smaller/Greater than 100%

following the oil sector. Other significant industries include sugar refining, food processing, petrochemicals, cement and construction. Traditional handicrafts such as carpet weaving and ceramics manufacturing, silk and jewellery are also vital to the economy. Breakdown of Iran's economic activities by sector is shown in Table 4.1.

The oil industry is one of the most effective and largest industries globally, especially in Iran. In addition to being a major source of energy in today's world, oil also plays an important role in determining the level of national power and international prestige of different countries. The oil sector in the Iranian economy has been providing the main national income for many years and, in fact, this sector plays a dominant role in the country's economy. On the other hand, given that the developing countries have struggled with limited resources and unlimited needs and therefore cannot develop all economic sectors simultaneously, they must prioritise their important and key sectors. Iran's four-month export statistics show that gas condensate with more than 17% has the largest share among all the Iranian exports. In this vein, we should mention the export of Iranian carpets as the second-largest export commodity.

The history of Iranian art and industry cannot be imagined without Iranian carpets. Iranian carpet has a global reputation and has this capacity. Export of Iranian carpets to other parts of the world officially reached 5.5 thousand tons by weight in the very last year of the Pahlavi regime in 1957. Furthermore, Iranian hand-woven carpets are a manifestation of the taste, art and talent of the people of this land; such carpets have an inseparable connection with Iranian culture and spirit. Nonetheless, hand-woven carpets have always been considered as one of the most important non-oil exports of the country (Rezaei et al., 2019).

Exhibit 4.6 Persian carpet; photo © 2021 by Aidin Salamzadeh

Given the economic conditions and in order to get rid of the mono-product economy (oil-dependence), the carpet industry is of great economic importance because all the raw materials (wool, yarn, etc.) are found within the country, and there is no need to import raw materials to prevent the outflow of currency. Secondly, this industry has significant added value and forms the largest economic value among non-oil exports. Iranian carpets are now exported to 32 countries. Although traditional Iranian carpet markets such as the United States, Italy, the UAE, Lebanon and Japan are often the target markets, the significant growth in the export of Iranian carpets to three countries, Brazil, Africa and China, is also noteworthy.

Iran's carpet industry has a significant role in the country's resistant economy in terms of job creation, value-added and foreign exchange. Despite having the lowest amount of valuation, this industry is also the least expensive way to create employment. In Iran, the problems caused by the single-product economy and reliance on oil revenues have led to creating an economy that is easily affected by external factors, especially the unstable oil market. Accordingly, we can understand the importance and role of non-oil exports in the country. Among the country's non-oil exports, handmade carpets have always been in the first place and account for more than 25% of non-oil exports. Handmade carpets follow a socio-economic flow and play an essential role like other social phenomena (Salamzadeh et al. 2017).

According to the latest World Bank annual ratings, Iran is ranked 127th among 190 economies in terms of ease of doing business. Iran's rank had improved from 128 in 2018 to 127 in 2019. According to the latest report of the World Bank regarding the ease of doing business index, Iran's ranking has improved in only two sub-indices of micro-investor protection as well as the conditions and regulations for obtaining a construction license, which are 3 and 1 in 2020, respectively.

Iran's GDP is estimated at US$440 billion during the Iranian calendar year 2019/20 for a population of about 82.8 million. Iran's economy is characterised by its hydrocarbon, agricultural and service sectors as well as a noticeable governmental involvement in the manufacturing and financial services. While its economic base is relatively diversified for an oil-exporting country, economic activities and government incomes still rely on oil revenues and have, therefore, been volatile. The Iranian authorities have adopted a comprehensive strategy of market-based reforms in their 20-year economic vision document and also the sixth 5-year development plan from 2016/17 to 2021/22. The plan comprises three pillars: the development of a resilient economy, progress in science and technology and the promotion of cultural excellence. On the economic front, the development plan forecasts an annual economic growth of 8%. The reform of state-owned enterprises, financial and banking sectors, as well as the

Exhibit 4.7   Persian carpet; photo © 2021 by Aidin Salamzadeh

allocation and management of oil revenues are among the main governmental priorities during these five years.

Iran's actual GDP decreased by 6.8% in 2019/20; also, the oil sector shrank by 38.7%. Non-oil GDP grew by 1.1%, which was driven by agriculture and manufacturing as the exchange rate depreciation made domestic production more competitive. Expenditure-side components of GDP declined over 2019/20. The decline in GDP continued in Q1/2020/21; border closures and containment measures, which COVID-19 imposed in March and April, contributed to GDP reduction by 3.5% (year-on-year). It is considered a modest contraction compared to many other countries (Salamzadeh and Dana, 2021). In contrast to past recessions, services were much more impacted as a reflection of the huge impact of COVID-19 on service sectors worldwide. The main indicators of Iran's economy have been presented in Table 4.2.

Table 4.2 Main Indicators of Iran's Economy

Main Indicators	2018	2019 (e)	2020 (e)	2021 (e)	2022 (e)
GDP (*billions USD*)	435.59	583.70	610.66	651.71	685.29
GDP (*Constant Prices, Annual % Change*)	−5.4	−6.5	−5.0	3.2	1.5
GDP per Capita (*USD*)	5	7	7	7	7
General Government Gross Debt (*in % of GDP*)	40.3	44.7	45.4	40.4	39.2
Inflation Rate (*%*)	31.2	41.0	30.5	30.0	25.0
Unemployment Rate (*% of the Labour Force*)	12.0	10.7	12.2	12.4	13.1
Current Account (*billions USD*)	26.74	6.55	−3.12	1.96	4.03
Current Account (*in % of GDP*)	6.1	1.1	−0.5	0.3	0.6

Source: IMF – World Economic Outlook Database, October 2020

In the last two centuries, the world has witnessed a new socio-economic phenomenon called women's participation in the labour market (Jafari-Sadeghi, 2020; Salamzadeh and Ramadani, 2021). It has been the result of fundamental changes in the social, economic, cultural and political approaches of human societies to the issue of women and work (Boudlaie et al., 2020; Dana 2000b; Sadeghi and Biancone, 2017). In total, two-thirds of all the work in the world are done by women, who make up half of the world's population. Given this group's potential to do all kinds of work, both formally and informally, women are considered one of the largest investment sources for developing countries. The participation of Iranian women in the labour market has been widespread only 100 years after the presence of their counterparts in industrial societies, and this participation has fluctuated sharply over the last three decades. According to the statistics, the participation rate of women in the labour market is about 50% in the developed countries of North America, while this figure is between 11% and 13% in the Middle East.

According to the statistics of the Management and Planning Organisation, the employment rate of women in Iran is about 11%; however, according to some unofficial statistics, it is over 13%. In the international domain, women's welfare index can be determined by their level of education, fertility and average life expectancy. Statistics in this area have shown significant progress in the Middle East and North Africa (Salamzadeh et al., 2014). However, regarding women's participation in the economy and the promotion of their capabilities in the political arena, we have witnessed these countries' insignificant presence in this field. In the 1980s, with the onset of the recession and increasing economic pressures on households, women's employment outside the home became necessary. In recent years, with an increase in women's level of education in society, their attitudes have also changed. Besides, they have become aware of the importance of missed opportunities. This, in turn, has led to a reasonable reduction in fertility and to the control of population growth as well as an increase in women's demand to enter the labour market and gain financial independence.

Although the rate of women's economic participation is doubled in Iran compared to about 70 years ago, women still have a minimal share of the Iranian economy and labour market. According to economic studies, the rate of women's economic participation in Iran is about 16%. It is noteworthy that women's economic participation in Iran has increased in recent decades. Official reports show that women's economic participation has increased from 9.2% in 1956 to more than 16% in 2019. But

Exhibit 4.8 Bazaar; photo © 2021 by Aidin Salamzadeh

women, who make up half of the population, still have a small share of the Iranian economy. On average, women should contribute to about 47% of the economy. According to the World Bank report, the rate of women's economic participation in Qatar was the highest among OECD countries with 58% in 2017. The rate of women's economic participation in Iraq was 19%. Kuwait, Bahrain and the UAE reported the highest participation in the region following Qatar, with participation rates of 47%, 44% and 41%, respectively. Meanwhile, the economic participation of Iranian women has yet to reach 20%. In this regard, there is a need for a big leap so that women can reach a suitable position in the Iranian economy.

Iran's economic policies since 1979 and the isolation from international economic relations have had a fundamentally deteriorating impact on Iran's economic development and Iranians' welfare. In addition, GDP per capita has never reached its previous status before the Revolution. Reviewing the history of the Islamic Republic regime, it can be seen that, immediately after the revolution, pro-Iranian students seized the US embassy in Tehran. Since then, Iran's relationship with the US government has deteriorated, and it has imposed sanctions on Iran (Farzanegan and Hayo, 2019). The Islamic Republic's relationships with the European Union have also been strained over the past 40 years due to allegations of terrorism, human rights and the lack of transparency in Iran's nuclear activities. The international sanctions against the Islamic Republic of Iran discouraged multinational enterprises (MNEs) from investing in Iran and in general doing business with Iran. Since the Islamic Revolution, Iran's net inflows of foreign direct investment (FDI) have been very low compared to that of many other countries in the region.

In 2002, incentives for FDI were introduced by the Foreign Investment Promotion and Protection Act (FIPPA), which was passed by the Iranian parliament with the reformist perspective.

Economic sanctions will always have positive and negative effects on any country. Different phenomena such as self-sufficiency, independence, economy and self-confidence can be mentioned as the positive effects of sanctions. However, many effects such as higher imports, reduced exports, smuggling and quasi-smuggling, lack of currency and corruption as well as seeking rent are among the negative effects that cause the most damage to the country in the face of sanctions. The degree of dependence of each economic sector on other countries is the most important component in determining that sector's vulnerability in the face of sanctions. In the industrial sector, there are certainly parent industries and industries that mainly supply their technology and production factors, including raw materials and intermediates, from other countries. It also includes industries that are considered as export markets by other countries and are considered export-oriented; they will suffer the most from international sanctions accordingly.

In 2019, GDP shrank by 7.6% amid declining consumption, oil exports and construction activity. The IMF predicts that Iran's economy will slowly rebound from a recession. Meanwhile, GDP will still be negative in 2020, at –6% because of the outbreak of the COVID-19 pandemic, and it is expected to grow to 3.1% in 2021, mainly due to its diversification and the post-pandemic global economic recovery (April 2020 World Economic Outlook IMF). The non-oil sectors generate most of Iran's economic output and jobs; these sectors have been proven more resilient under US sanctions than the energy sector.

Furthermore, Iran has been on the path of reform and reinforcement with the pressures of sanctions, willingly or unwillingly (forced success). We will examine the effects and consequences of sanctions on Iran's foreign investment and Iran's plans for foreign investors in the following section.

The long-term and continuous economic growth in any country is achieved by optimally equipping investment resources in that country's economy. Using foreign investment is a means to equip resources through proper and principled planning that leads to economic growth and development.

Given the importance of investing in the world economy, economists and governments all agree on the vital importance of foreign investment; they consider investment an important factor in creating broad economic changes for all the countries, especially developing countries. Foreign investors can act as a factor and tool for growth and development and most countries, especially developing countries with lower liquidity, seek to attract foreign capital to implement their economic and industrial projects. And for this reason, foreign investment has a wide range of political and economic dimensions. However, the sanctions are imposed to deprive the country of access to the global market for goods and services as well as capital and to isolate the country that prevents access to foreign capital. Iran's plan in this regard is the solution based on the resilience economy; Resilience economics is about reducing dependencies, highlighting the benefits of domestic production and striving for self-reliance. In FDI literature, three economic incentives are of particular importance. Attracting this investment in developing countries is aimed at resource search, market search and efficiency. The expansion of foreign investment inflows to these countries is mainly in response to the provision of productive and financial resources for investment and an increase in productive capital. Also, the goals of foreign investment and host companies are to expand export markets through the development of productive capacities, which is pursued within the framework of a national economy and a regional or transnational economy.

Accordingly, these issues and problems have prevented the effective and serious presence of Iran in the dynamic flow of FDI in recent years. Apart from political issues, this has increased the risk of investing in Iran, and foreign investors have not yet shown any desire to operate in Iran in the usual way. Therefore, there is a need for foreign investors in Iran, where the economic structure requires foreign financial resources and advanced technologies.

The most important condition for attracting foreign investment is the public belief in the efficiency and usefulness of these resources in the process of economic development of the country. The general belief of the political elites in Iran, based on their understanding of the current realities of the world and the country, concluded that attracting foreign investment for the development of the country and its life in the global economy is necessary. It does not mean that others' domination should be accepted in the name of foreign investment, but like other countries, a framework should be designed to attract foreign capital.

Beneficial and constructive interventions of the government in providing the grounds and infrastructure for attracting foreign investment are as follows:

- Creating the necessary economic security.
- Strengthening the private sector by respecting and guaranteeing individual and private property.
- Ensuring contracts and economic activities through the adoption of transparent and efficient laws.

Removing barriers to foreign investment will be discussed in the next section.

Reducing political risk: The reduction of political risk has been as crucial to the Iranian government as reducing economic risk in attracting FDI. Therefore, the country's diplomatic apparatus has played an important role in this regard by reliably regulating bilateral relations and raising the country's political position.

Specific planning for the proper use of foreign investment: Prior to accepting foreign investments, a specific plan is presented to decide how to use these resources. This programme is based on prioritising the use of foreign investment, that is, compensation of financial resources, absorption of modern technologies or efficient management systems, or all these three procedures at the same time. Economic sectors or industries that are more profitable for the country in terms of generating more foreign exchange earnings, increasing employment and helping to successfully enter global markets have been given priority in attracting foreign investment.

Linking foreign investments with the private sector: Foreign investment is attracted when it is linked to the private sector of the host country to perform a joint activity. Therefore, a strong private sector is a prerequisite for foreign investment.

Towards the Future

Due to the particular climatic and geographical conditions in their country and the existence of vast and rich underground resources, especially in the field of oil, gas and petrochemicals, Iranians provide a very suitable platform to attract foreign capital and its achievements; however, it seems that not much success has been achieved due to some shortcomings because of the lack of an efficient legal system concerning the issue, primarily until the adoption of the Law on Encouragement and Support of Foreign Investment at the macro level of the country's management.

The government welcomes foreign investment in Iran and also urges foreign investors to peruse the Foreign Investment Promotion and Support Law and its bylaws, to be acquainted with their rights, facilities and protections resulting from investment and to be informed of their legal obligations and requirements within the framework of this Law (Adesnik and Ghasseminejad, 2018). The use of external financial resources and credits for the implementation of projects and the purchase of equipment and capital goods for production projects as well as technical and engineering services of projects are sought following financial contracts that are concluded with foreign creditors.

The implementation process of this method is based on the latest approval of the esteemed Council of Ministers of the Government of Iran and the criteria of the Fifth Development Plan, which is as follows:

- Acceptable activities
- Required guarantee
- Interest rates and costs
- Payment ceiling
- Duration of using the facility
- Repayment period
- Government and non-government sector

The Guide to Providing Foreign Resources refers to the process of reviewing the application of foreign investors in the investment organisation up to the stage of issuing a foreign investment license:

- The process of reviewing the application of foreign investors in the investment organisation up to the stage of issuing the investment license
- Guaranteed and supportive coverage by the Iranian government
- Law, facilities and support of foreign investors by the Iranian government
- Obligations and legal requirements of foreign investors
- Total benefits and guaranteed facilities to the foreign investor

Large financial companies are exploring strategies to enter Iran's financial markets and use domestic potential to achieve this goal. According to foreign experts, the fields of "Information Technology and Online Commerce", "Petroleum and Petrochemical", "Medicine", "Banking", "Insurance" and "Transportation" are the leading investment destinations in Iran (Garousi Mokhtarzadeh et al., 2020; Rahimdel et al., 2020).

According to the World Bank, the country has one of the most lenient rules and regulations on foreign investment among developing countries. At the moment, foreign investors can easily invest in almost all sectors of the Iranian economy. If their investments are in agriculture, mining and industry, they can withdraw their income entirely from Iran.

Foreign investment is increasing rapidly in Iran, and the government is removing other barriers to investment in the country (Habibi and Sharif Karimi, 2017). The approval of the "Law on Encouragement and Protection of Foreign Investment" and the acceptance of its executive regulations in the cabinet is an essential part of the set of reforms in the structure of macroeconomics. The trend in demand for foreign investment in Iran following the enacting of the new law indicates that the new economic environment, as well as the legal and regulatory regime, have created enormous potential for foreign investment. Besides, by focusing efforts on the transparent transfer of the latest developments in economic dynamics and foreign investment frameworks, the country will be implemented more quickly.

The expansion of the scope of activities of foreign investors, conceivable investment in infrastructure, recognition of new investment methods other than FDI such as project financing, the establishment of a unit called the Foreign Investment Services Centre in the Investment Organisation are considered as the developments of the new law in the area of foreign investment. Moreover, this new law has resulted in economic and technical assistance to provide centralised and practical support for foreign investors' activities in Iran and the liberalisation of more foreign exchange mechanisms for the optimal use of foreign investors.

Direct investment and interest using foreign capital are considered as two portions of foreign investment in Iran. While controlling the capital in indirect investment, the investor also participates in its management, makes decisions regarding capital management, buys the production agents, hires unskilled workers as well as specialised personnel and deals with the type of goods, marketing and pricing. This method of investment establishes a "multinational company" in a foreign branch, lends to its foreign components or reinvests the profits from the company's activities abroad. Transnational corporations transfer technology, create jobs and pay taxes to the investable government and provide an environment of competition, stability and economic prosperity. In foreign indirect investment, the investor does not seek to control or manage the company or interfere in the decisions and management of a group, and generally refers to the purchase of securities including stocks and bonds. In this regard, it is evident that the investor intends to buy shares at a lower price and sell them at a higher price, which does not lead to real development, prosperity and job creation and income; and it is only functioning in the direction of making more profit. In recent years, significant investments have been made in the field of oil in Iran that has also been successful in using financial resources, BOT or other forms of foreign resources. In some cases, foreign companies have invested in the country either directly or with the participation of Iranian parties (Yusof and Salami, 2013).

According to the latest statistics of the Foreign Investment Organisation, the foreign investment volume reached more than 24 billion and 381 million dollars in Iran from 1993 to the end of April 2020. In this regard, the share of Asia was $10.2 billion, the share of Europe was $9.7 billion, the share of Africa was $1.6 billion, and the share of the United States was $1.4 billion. Between 1993 and 2007, the majority of the investment volume in Iran belonged to 2005 and 2006; and after that, we have observed the highest volume of investment in Iran only in the first month of this year (Leila, 2020).

Foreign investment may have different effects depending on the circumstances and the type of approach. In the past, many developing countries were reluctant to welcome FDI, mostly by multinational corporations. It was believed that these companies were merely thinking of plundering the country's resources, endangering national sovereignty and independence as well as intensifying economic dependence. In recent years, the attitude of developing countries has changed with the clarification of the influential role that FDI can play in the process of economic growth and development of a country; there is no doubt that foreign investment seeks to make a profit, but this does not necessarily lead to the detriment of the host countries. Instead, with proper policy and planning, the presence of a foreign investor can be beneficial. However, in this case, the investors of developed countries can result in more profit compared to the investing and developing country. According to the standards of economics, the efficiency of any rare factors is higher than other factors. For this reason, interest rates in these countries are at a lower level due to the existence of capital in developed countries. Consequently, the quality of return on capital in these countries is lower than that of the developing countries.

The Law on Encouraging and Protecting Foreign Investment allows for investment in all the areas of economic activity in Iran; however, army, ammunition and national security sites are forbidden for foreign investment. The Foreign Investment Encouragement and Protection Law has also provided comprehensive security against the risks that are commonly referred to as non-commercial risks. In terms of the issues related to the transfer of profits and the return on capital, this law respects investors' rights by facilitating the transfer and providing the currency required for the transfer. There are no restrictions on the amount of transfer interest as well as the amount of capital or return on capital gains. It also recognises foreign investors' rights in cases where the implementation of a project is stopped or interrupted as a result of a law or a governmental decision. The law has also introduced new legal options in government–investor relations, which indicates the Iranian government's receptive and constructive approach to protect the interests of foreign investors.

According to the global indicators that are published every year by relevant institutions in various fields, Iran's position in the region and the world indicates that, in recent years, Iran has had an upward trend in most indicators, which has improved its economic situation. Some of these economic indicators such as business ease, credit-business risk, entrepreneurship, global development and competitiveness can directly affect the business environment (Dana et al., 2013). As many developed countries have experienced, economic growth can be achieved through effort, transparency, clear rules, anti-corruption strategies, resolution of other barriers, facilitating business and improving entrepreneurial trends (Dana, 2007; 2011; Salamzadeh and Kawamorita, 2017; Jafari Sadeghi et al., 2019).

To clarify the issue, it is necessary to observe which practical strategies have been implemented by more prosperous countries in terms of economic indicators. Of course, there is no single pattern for all the economies, but it is essential to include each country's cultural, political, social, national and resource factors in development programmes. When there is an improvement in indicators such as business ease, credit risk and economic freedom, one can hope to attract foreign investment, which can be the right stimulus for economic development and improvement of the business environment (Singh and Gal, 2020). The Business Space Index consists of 10 sub-indices. From one perspective, this index is the most critical global index whose degree of difficulty and convenience directly impact the creation of a business for the entrepreneurs (Salamzadeh, 2018). Iran's position in 2017 indicates that although the internal situation has improved in recent years, more business reforms are needed to strengthen its function. For example, according to the latest statistics, countries like Indonesia and the UAE have made significant progress in the region. Proceedings include eliminating the minimum capital for establishing SMEs, creating a single form for submitting a group application for company registration and business licenses.

Iran outperforms its neighbour countries such as Turkey, the UAE and Saudi Arabia to ease doing business in the region. One of the most important reasons for the superiority of these countries is the availability of adequate infrastructure as well as appropriate laws and regulations (Doshmanli et al., 2018). Iran has taken some steps to improve its environmental conditions, including creating a single national window, facilitating cross-border trade, simplifying the registration process for companies, reducing access to electricity, and improving access to credit information. Nonetheless, costly procedures for setting up an economic unit in Iran are still regarded as obstacles to starting a business in Iran (Zarghamee et al., 2020).

Iran is one of the developing countries that need foreign financial resources and investment for development; however, they have either prevented the inflow of foreign capital or have restricted them with the introduction of sanctions during recent decades. These sanctions are imposed in order to deprive the country of access to the global market for goods, services and capital as well as to isolate the country; in addition, because investors are looking for more profit and a safer place to invest, they are more willing to enter the markets where these opportunities are available. Given that investment in advanced industrialised countries is saturated, the markets of developing countries are considered as the best markets in the current situation. It is important to note that in recent years, in the field of the business environment, we have witnessed the establishment of appropriate laws and regulations in different parts of Iran such as the provisions of the Fifth Development Plan law and finally the law of continuous improvement of the business environment (Khaledi and Shirazi, 2013). To gain a higher share in attracting foreign investment worldwide and move towards progress and development, Iran needs to continuously amend and implement the rules of development plans in the country's business environment to provide an appropriate platform for trust and entry of foreign investors into the country.

References

Adesnik, David, and Saeed Ghasseminejad (2018), "Foreign Investment in Iran: Multinational Firms' Compliance with US Sanctions," (Retrieved from SSRN 3257581)

Ahmadi, Ali, Farzad Esmaeilion, Ali Esmaeilion, Mohammad Ali Ehyaei, and John L. Silveira (2020), "Benefits and Limitations of Waste-to-Energy Conversion in Iran," *Renewable Energy Research and Application* 1 (1), pp. 27–45.

Biancone, Paolo Pietro, Silvana Secinaro, and Vahid Jafari-Sadeghi (2016), "Risk Management in Export Compliance: Concepts, Procedures, and Solutions," in Valter Cantino, Paola De Vincentiis, Maria Gabriella Racca, eds., *Risk Management: Perspectives and Open Issues,* London: McGraw-Hill, pp. 64–78.

Boudlaie, Hasan, Hanan Amoozad Mahdiraji, Sabihe Shamsi, Vahid Jafari-Sadeghi, and Alexis Garcia-Perez (2020), "Designing a Human Resource Scorecard: An Empirical Stakeholder-Based Study with a Company Culture Perspective," *Journal of Entrepreneurship, Management, and Innovation* 16 (4), pp. 113–147.

Dana, Léo-Paul (2000a), "Change and Circumstance in Kyrgyz Markets," *Qualitative Market Research: An International Journal* 3 (2), pp. 62–73.

Dana, Léo-Paul (2000b), "Economic Sectors in Egypt and Their Managerial Implications," *Journal of African Business* 1 (1), pp. 65–81.

Dana, Léo-Paul (2007), *Asian Models of Entrepreneurship from the Indian Union and the Kingdom of Nepal to the Japanese Archipelago: Context, Policy and Practice,* London, Singapore & Hong Kong: World Scientific.

Dana, Léo-Paul (2011), "Entrepreneurship in Bolivia: An Ethnographic Enquiry," *International Journal of Business and Emerging Markets* 3 (1), pp. 75–88.

Dana, Léo-Paul, Hamid Etemad, and Richard W. Wright (1999a), "Theoretical Foundations of International Entrepreneurship," in Richard W. Wright, ed., *International Entrepreneurship: Globalisation of Emerging Businesses,* Stamford: JAI Press, pp. 3–22.

Dana, Léo-Paul, Hamid Etemad, and Richard W. Wright (1999b), "The Impact of Globalisation on SMEs," *Global Focus* 11 (4), pp. 93–105.

Dana, Léo-Paul, Hamid Etemad, and Richard W. Wright (2013), "Toward a Paradigm of Symbiotic Entrepreneurship," *International Journal of Entrepreneurship and Small Business* 5 (2), pp. 109–126.

Dana, Léo-Paul, and Richard W. Wright (2015), "Bazaar Economies, Modern Networks and Entrepreneurship," in Cary L. Cooper, Michael H. Morris, and Donald F. Kuratko, eds., *Wiley Encyclopedia of Management,* United Kingdom, Wiley, pp. 13–18.

Doshmanli, Mansoureh, Yashar Salamzadeh, and Aidin Salamzadeh (2018), "Development of SMEs in an Emerging Economy: Does Corporate Social Responsibility Matter?" *International Journal of Management and Enterprise Development* 17 (2), pp. 168–191.

Farzanegan, Mohammad Reza, and Bernd Hayo (2019), "Sanctions and the shadow economy: Empirical evidence from Iranian provinces," *Applied Economics Letters* 26(6), pp. 501–505.

Garousi Mokhtarzadeh, Nima, Hannan Amoozad Mahdiraji, Vahid Jafari-Sadeghi, Arash Soltani, and Ali Asghar Abbassi Kamardi (2020), "A Product-Technology Portfolio Alignment Approach for Food Industry: A Multi-Criteria Decision Making with Z-Numbers," *British Food Journal* 122 (12), pp. 3947–3967.

Ghodsi, Mahdi, Vasily Astrov, Richard Grieveson, and Robert Stehrer (2018). The Iranian Economy: Challenges and Opportunities (No. 429). wiiw Research Report.

Habibi, Fateh, and Mohammad Sharif Karimi (2017), "Foreign Direct Investment and Economic Growth: Evidence from Iran and GCC," *Iranian Economic Review* 21 (3), pp. 601–620.

Jafari-Sadeghi, Vahid (2020), "The Motivational Factors of Business Venturing: Opportunity Versus Necessity? A Gendered Perspective on European Countries," *Journal of Business Research* 113, pp. 279–289.

Jafari-Sadeghi, Vahid, Dev Dutta, Alberto Ferraris, and Manlio Del Giudice (2020), "Internationalisation Business Processes in an Under-Supported Policy Contexts: Evidence from Italian SMEs," *Business Process Management Journal* 26 (5), pp. 1055–1074.

Jafari-Sadeghi, Vahid, Paolo Pietro Biancone, Robert B. Anderson, and Jean-Marie Nkongolo-Bakenda (2019), "International Entrepreneurship by Particular People 'on their Own Terms': A Study on the Universal Characteristics of Entrepreneurs in Evolving Economies," *International Journal of Entrepreneurship and Small Business* 37 (2), pp. 288–308.

Khaledi, Koohsar, and Andisheh Haghighatnezhad Shirazi (2013), "Estimates of Factors Affecting Economic Growth in the Agricultural Sector in the Fifth Development Plan of Iran (Emphasis on Investment)," *World Applied Sciences Journal* 22 (10), pp. 1492–1499.

Leila, A. S. (2020), The Revival of the Iranian Revolutionary Economy: Studying the Structural Causes of Its Failure, International Institute for Iranian Studies, https://rasanah-iiis.org/english/wp-content/up loads/sites/2/2020/09/The-Revival-of-the-Iranian-Revolutionary-Economy-Studying-the-Structural-Causes-of-Its-Failure-1.pdf

Light, Ivan, Shahamak Rezaei, and Léo-Paul Dana (2013), "Ethnic Minority Entrepreneurs in the international Carpet Trade-An Empirical Study," *International Journal of Entrepreneurship and Small Business* 18 (2), pp. 125–153.

Moghadam, Saeed Jafari, and Aidin Salamzadeh (2018), "Do Senior Bankers Care about Entrepreneurial Behaviour?: Case of Senior Managers of Iranian Vanguard Banks," *World Review of Entrepreneurship, Management and Sustainable Development* 14 (1–2), pp. 271–287.

Rahimdel, Mohammad Javad, and Hossein Noferesti (2020), "Investment Preferences of Iran's Mineral Extraction Sector with a Focus on the Productivity of the Energy Consumption, Water and Labor Force," *Resources Policy* 67, p. 101695.

Rezaei, Shahamak (2011), "Trust as a Coopetititive Strategy in a Global Co-Ethnic Market: Towards an Empirically Supported Theory," *International Journal of Business and Globalisation* 7 (3), pp. 265–302.

Rezaei, Shahamak, Birte Hansen, Veland Ramadani, and Léo-Paul Dana (2019), "The Resurgence of Bazaar Entrepreneurship: 'Ravabet-Networking' and the Case of the Persian Carpet Trade," in Veland Ramadani, Léo-Paul Dana, Vanessa Ratten, and Abdylmenaf Bexheti, eds., *Informal Ethnic Entrepreneurship: Future Research Paradigms for Creating Innovative Business Activity,* Switzerland AG: Springer, pp. 63–82.

Rezaei, Shahamak, Léo-Paul Dana, and Veland Ramadani (2017), *Iranian Entrepreneurship: Deciphering the Entrepreneurial Ecosystem in Iran and in the Iranian Diaspora,* Switzerland AG: Springer.

Rezaei, Shahamak, Marco Goli, and Léo-Paul Dana (2013), "Informal Opportunity among SMEs: An Empirical Study of Denmark's Underground Economy," *International Journal of Entrepreneurship and Small Business* 19 (1), pp. 64–76.

Sadeghi, Vahid Jafari, Jean-Marie Nkongolo-Bakenda, Robert B. Anderson, and Léo-Paul Dana (2019), "An Institution-Based View of International Entrepreneurship: A Comparison of Context-Based and Universal Determinants in Developing and Economically Advanced Countries," *International Business Review* 28 (6), p. 101588.

Sadeghi, Vahid Jafari, and Paolo Pietro Biancone (2017), "Exploring the Drivers of Gender Entrepreneurship: Focus on the Motivational Perspectives in USA, Italy, and France," in Vanessa Ratten, Veland Ramadani, Léo-Paul Dana, Robert D. Hisrich, and Joao Ferreira, eds., *Gender and Family Entrepreneurship,* United Kingdom: Routledge, pp. 124–141.

Sadeghi, Vahid Jafari, Paolo Pietro Biancone, Charles Giacoma, and Silvana Secinaro (2017), "Export Compliance: A Missing Component of International Entrepreneurship," *International Journal of Business and Management* 12 (11), pp. 103–110.

Sadeghi, Vahid Jafari, Paolo Pietro Biancone, Charles Giacoma, and Silvana Secinaro (2018), "How does Export Compliance Influence the Internationalisation of Firms: Is it a Thread or an Opportunity?" *Journal of Global Entrepreneurship Research* 8 (3), pp. 1–15.

Salamzadeh, Aidin (2018), "Start-Up Boom in an Emerging Market: A Niche Market Approach," in Datis Khajeheian, Mike Friedrichsen, and Wilfried Mödinger, eds., *Competitiveness in Emerging Markets,* Cham: Springer, pp. 233–243.

Salamzadeh, Aidin, and Hiroko Kawamorita (2017), "The Enterprising Communities and Startup Ecosystem in Iran," *Journal of Enterprising Communities* 11 (4), pp. 456–479.

Salamzadeh, Aidin, and Léo-Paul Dana (2021), "The Coronavirus (COVID-19) Pandemic: Challenges among Iranian Startups," *Journal of Small Business & Entrepreneurship* 33 (5), pp. 489–512. https://doi.org/10.1080/08276331.2020.1821158

Salamzadeh, Aidin, and Veland Ramadani (2021), "Entrepreneurial Ecosystem and Female Digital Entrepreneurship – Lessons to learn from an Iranian Case Study," in Shahamak Rezaei et al. eds., *The Emerald Handbook of Women and Entrepreneurship in Developing Economies,* Bingley, UK: Emerald.

Salamzadeh, Aidin, Zahra Arasti, and Ghanbar Mohammadi Elyasi (2017), "Creation of ICT-Based Social Start-Ups in Iran: A Multiple Case Study," *Journal of Enterprising Culture* 25 (1), pp. 97–122.

Salamzadeh, Yashar, Mehran Nejati, and Aidin Salamzadeh (2014), "Agility Path through Work Values in Knowledge-Based Organizations: A Study of Virtual Universities," *Innovar* 24 (53), pp. 177–186.

Singh, Devesh, and Zoltán Gal (2020), "Economic Freedom and its Impact on Foreign Direct Investment: Global Overview," *Review of Economic Perspectives* 20 (1), pp. 73–90.

Tajpour, Mehdi, and Aidin Salamzadeh (2019), "The Effect of Spiritual Intelligence on Organisational Entrepreneurship: Case Study of Educational Departments in University of Tehran," *International Journal of Management and Enterprise Development* 18 (3), pp. 205–218.

Tajpour, Mehdi, Elahe Hosseini, and Aidin Salamzadeh (2020), "The Effect of Innovation Components on Organisational Performance: Case of the Governorate of Golestan Province," *International Journal of Public Sector Performance Management* 6(6), pp. 817–830.

World Bank (2018), *Doing Business 2018. Reforming to Create Jobs. Economy Profile of Iran,* Washington: World Bank, (Retrieved from http://www.doingbusiness.org/~/media/WBG/DoingBusiness/Documents/Profiles/Country/IRN.pdf, accessed 21 November 2020)

Yusof, Aminah Binti, and Bahman Salami (2013), "Success Factors for Build Operate Transfer (BOT) Power Plant Projects in Iran," *International Journal of Modern Engineering Research* 3 (1), pp. 324–330.

Zarghamee, Mehdi S., Yahya Tabesh, and Dariush Zahedi (2020), *Building an Innovation Economy in Iran,* Berkeley, California: Berkeley University of California.

Successors to the Russian Empire

Chapter 5

The Context for Business in Armenia

Shqipe Gërguri-Rashiti, Veland Ramadani, Maia Chiabrishvili &
Vladimir Dzenopoljac

Abstract: This chapter focuses on the important aspects of the business environment of Armenia. In the beginning an overview of historical, political and economic development of Armenia, since its inception, is provided. The work addresses the characteristics of the Armenian business framework conditions, with details describing the ecosystem dimensions. The chapter concludes with providing a brief outlook for the future and provides insights and few recommendations.

Keywords: Business context, entrepreneurship, bazaar, ecosystem, Armenia

Introduction

Armenia is a landlocked, mountainous country in Western Asia, on the crossroads between Europe and Asia. It is located in Southern Caucasus, the Eurasian Region. Armenia borders Georgia on the north, Azerbaijan on the east and south, Iran on the south and Turkey on the west (Exhibit 5.1). Armenia became a United Nations member on 2 March 1992 (Mokyr, 2003). It covers an area of 29,743 km².

Yerevan (Exhibit 5.2) is the country's capital and the largest city representing its administrative, industrial and cultural centre. Yerevan is located along the Hrazdan River. Mount Ararat, Turkish Ağrı Dağı overlooks the point where borders of Turkey, Iran, and Armenia meet (Britannica, 2020a). Mount Ararat is thought to be the holy land where Noah landed

Exhibit 5.1   Map of Armenia; courtesy of Nations Online Project

his ark. Armenians consider Ararat the symbol of their state, It is visible from many places in Yerevan, It is central to Armenian identity. The city was designed so that Ararat could be the centre of views all around the city.

Around 3 million people are living in Armenia, with a population density of 103 people per square kilometre. Regarding the population ethnicity, 98.1% are ethnic Armenians, 1.2% Yazidis, 0.4% Russians and 0.3% other minorities (Assyrians, Georgians, Ukrainians, Belarusians, Greeks, Kurds and Jews). Armenia has a relatively large diaspora, estimated at about 10 million people (Bolsajian, 2018), which is spread all around the world. Armenian communities can be found in Russia, Ukraine, Iran, Georgia, Syria, Israel, Lebanon, the United States, Canada, Argentina, Brazil, France, Australia, Poland, Greece and Cyprus (Cohen, 2010). According to some estimations, around 40,000–70,000 Armenians still live in Turkey (Turay, 2008). Based on a Gallup research from 2017, Armenia is characterised by the highest migrant acceptance rates in eastern Europe (Esipova et al., 2017).

The official language of the country is Armenian, while Russian and English are the most used foreign languages. According to research that

Exhibit 5.2 Mount Ararat and the Yerevan skyline; photo courtesy of Serouj Ourishian

was conducted in 2013, it was confirmed that 95% of Armenians speak Russian, where 24% in the advanced level, 59% in the intermediate level and 11% beginners; around 40% speak English, where 4% advanced, 16% intermediate and 20% beginner level (Caucasus Research Resource Centers, 2013).

Considering the ethnic homogeneity of the Armenian population, Christianity is the religion of the most Armenian people, respectively, 92.5% are members of Armenian Apostolic Church, while 2.3% are other Christians, 0.8% belongs to Yazidism, 0.4% other religions and 4.0% do not practise any religion. A very few practice Islam and Judaism as religions. The Armenian Apostolic Church was founded in the 1st century A.D., and in 301 A.D., it became the first branch of Christianity to turn into a state religion (Scott, 2016). The spiritual centre of the Church is at the Etchmiadzin Cathedral (Exhibit 5.3). Some monuments and sculptures are presented in Exhibits 5.4–5.6.

Armenian national flag and emblem are presented in Exhibit 5.7. The Armenian national flag consists of three equal-width horizontal bands with red colour on the top, followed by blue in the middle and orange on the bottom. Based on the Constitution of the Republic of Armenia,

Exhibit 5.3   Etchmiadzin Cathedral Entrance; photo courtesy of Pixabay (https://pixabay.com/photos/etchmiadzin-cathedral-gate-entrance-1781463/)

Exhibit 5.4   Zvartnots Cathedral; photo courtesy of Pixabay (https://pixabay.com/photos/cathedral-column-arch-ruin-1781012/)

Exhibit 5.5 Fountain Flower; photo courtesy of Pixabay (https://pixabay.com/photos/fountain-flower-art-sculpture-1762755/)

Exhibit 5.6 Lion Sculpture and Cascade in Yerevan, Armenia; photo courtesy of Pixabay (https://pixabay.com/photos/lion-head-sculpture-art-statue-1761473/)

Exhibit 5.7   Flag and emblem of the Republic of Armenia; courtesy of The Government of the Republic of Armenia

these colours mean: "The *red* emblematises the Armenian Highland, the Armenian people's continued struggle for survival, maintenance of the Christian faith, Armenia's independence and freedom. The *blue* emblematises the will of the people of Armenia to live beneath peaceful skies. The *orange* emblematises the creative talent and hard-working nature of the people of Armenia". The Armenian Supreme Soviet adopted this flag on 24 August 1990, while the National Assembly of Armenia has governed its usage on 15 June 2006 based on the Law on the National Flag of Armenia. The Coat of Arms is a national emblem of Armenia, adopted on 19 April 1992 by the Supreme Soviet of the Republic of Armenia (The Government of the Republic of Armenia, 2020).

The remaining parts of this chapter provide a picture of Armenia's historical aspects and its impact on doing business in this country, Armenian general business context and useful suggestions for the further development of the business ecosystem in Armenia.

Historical Context

Armenia is a mountainous country (about 80% is mountainous) with a variety of scenery and geologic instability and situated along the Great Silk Road. The country is landlocked with limited natural resources. It is a 'land of rugged mountains and extinct volcanoes, its highest peak is Mount Aragats, 4095 m (FAO, 2021). The country is located in the southern Caucasus, between the Black Sea and the Caspian Sea. From the 3rd to 19th century, Armenia was experiencing continuous attacks and invasions from neighbouring empires – Persians, Romans, Arabs and Turks. In 17–18th centuries, Armenia was divided between Persia and Turkey because of destructive wars. In 1828, west of Armenia became a part of the Russian empire. During World War I, in 1915–16, Ottoman authorities deported hundreds of thousands of Armenians from their homeland in the eastern Ottoman Empire. After World War I, many Armenians were massacred by the Ottomans. Others formed the Armenian diaspora. The Guardian refers to the source (see under Exhibit 5.8) to provide the number of Armenians in diasporas of different countries in the world.

The Armenian provinces declared their first independence from the Russian Empire in May 1918. Shortly after, in 1920, the country was invaded by the Soviet Red Army. Armenia was formed as the Soviet Republic on 29 November 1920. In 1922, Soviet Union made Armenia as part of the Transcaucasian Soviet Federated Socialist Republic, which

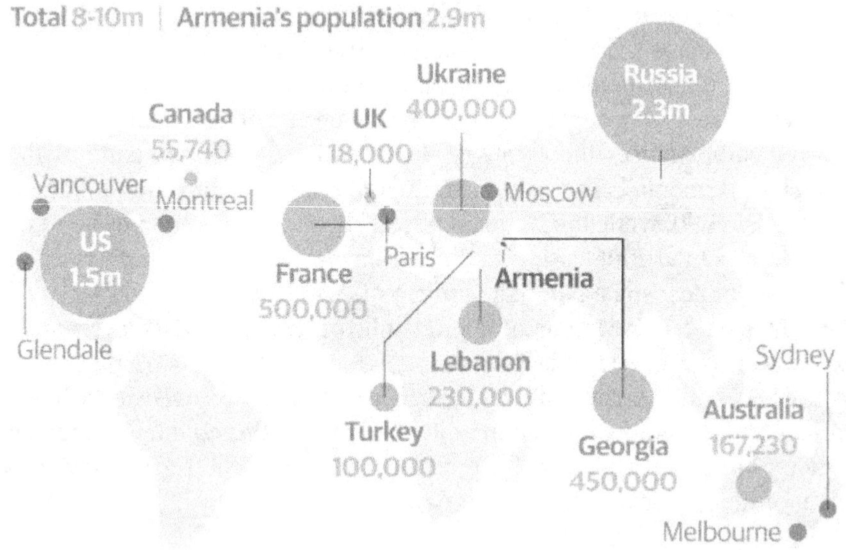

Exhibit 5.8   Number of Armenians living outside Armenia

Source: Ministry of Diaspora of the Republic of Armenia, FCO, Statistics Canada, Australian Bureau of Statistics

was dissolved in 1936, and Armenia became a constituent republic of the Soviet Union. On 23 August 1990 Armenia declared sovereignty and after the breakdown of the Soviet Union, the country declared its independence (on 21 September 1991). The Nagorno-Karabakh (Artsakh), an enclave of 4400 km^2 in southwestern Azerbaijan, persisted to be the zone of frozen conflict between Armenia and Azerbaijan since 1988. It is populated primarily by ethnic Armenians. By the mid-1990s, Karabakh Armenian forces had occupied much of southwestern Azerbaijan.

Soon after Pashinyan took office, clashes between Armenian and Azeri troops erupted on Armenia's border with Azerbaijan's exclave of Nakhichevan. The clashes were short-lived, Pashinyan was criticised for not responding aggressively. Peaceful resolution appeared impossible and after a devastating war in 2020, Armenia's troops "compelled to withdraw from most of that area" (Mints, 2021). Armenia appeared "in a deep socio-political crisis coupled with economic hardships connected to the war, refugees, ruined infrastructure and housing in Artsakh, not to mention the aggravated COVID-19 situation". Russian influence on the country has increased and apparently will be increasing further. The government has already asked Russians to provide patrol services in some parts of the southeast border with Azerbaijan. Most probably, national security issues are connected to and often provided by Russia (Kanadyan, 2021). The tragedy is that "For Armenians, it is families uprooted, a homeland lost, thousands of soldiers killed while defending against a fearsome 21ˢᵗ-century war machine. For Azerbaijanis, it is the legacy of a quarter-century of expulsion from their Soviet-era houses, from the territory that is now recaptured but that may not become habitable for years" (The New York Times, 2021).

Even before the war in Nagorno Karabakh, most Armenian strategic infrastructures, especially in the energy sector, were owned/managed by Russia. Armenia heavily depends on Russian economic and governmental support. Armenia's economy and business are vulnerable to instability in the global commodity markets and Russia's economic challenges due to its geographic and political isolation from Azerbaijan and Turkey, a limited market for export and monopolies in important business sectors. The amount of government debt is reaching the threshold of debt to gross domestic product (GDP) ratio, which is set by the country's legislation. This leads Yerevan to tighten its fiscal policies (CIA, 2020).

Bazaar represents an essential part of the trade activities in Armenia. In the past and today, the bazaar in Armenia (Exhibits 5.9 and 5.10) remains

Exhibit 5.9 Outdoor stall; photo courtesy of VdmBrmyn, used under the Wikimedia Creative Commons License

Exhibit 5.10   Agricultural bazaar in Armenia; photo courtesy of Narek75, used under the Wikimedia Creative Commons License

a place where smaller businesses provide their products (Dana, 2011). A bazaar is a "social and cultural system, a way of life and a general mode of commercial activity, which has been in existence for millennia. In the bazaar, economic transactions are not the focus of activities. Instead, the focus is on relationships and alliances. In this scenario, consumers do not necessarily seek the lowest price or the best quality. A person buys from a friend, sometimes to help the friend and sometimes to ensure that the friend will reciprocate" (Dana et al., 2008, p. 113). This aspect of doing business is important because of the fact that this is informal employment in Armenia and it accounts for around 52.1% of all jobs in the country, according to the data in 2010 (National Statistical Service of the Republic of Armenia, 2011). Additionally, the officially registered unemployed population in Armenia per 1000 persons in 2020 was 60.9%, according to the latest available data of Statistical Committee of the Republic of Armenia (2021). In this regard, it is unclear to what extent there is an overlap between informal employment and officially published data on unemployment. But this is certainly an area where small and medium enterprises arise and develop.

Context for Enterprise and Implications for Doing Business

From 1920 to 1991 under the Soviet Union, the Armenian economy was transformed from primarily agricultural to industrial. However, agriculture (together with manufacturing and services) remains an important sector contributing significantly to GDP and employment (accounting for about one-fifth of GDP and employing one-fifth of the labour force. The privatisation of industry and agriculture, structural reforms in tax and financial systems, and price liberalisation created an institutional and legal basis for a market economy after regaining the independence (Savenjuk, 2020).

U.S. Department of State in its report – 2020 Investment Climate Statements: Armenia – discusses "Policies Towards Foreign Direct Investment" as "relatively open", stating that the law entitles foreign companies the same treatment as Armenian companies. It characterises Armenia's human capital as strong, especially in science, technology, engineering and mathematics. This leads to considerable investment in the IT and high-tech sectors. The qualified specialists encourage international companies to establish branches and subsidiary companies. Although, small market, geographic isolation, low per capita GNI and insufficient rule of law create unfavourable business and investment climate, change of government in April/May 2018 has been opened new paths to competition. The hope to eliminate systemic corruption has arrived. "The Armenian National Interests Fund and Investment Support Center are responsible for attracting and facilitating inward foreign direct investment" (U.S. Department of State, 2020).

The economy relies on remittances from migrants that work in Russia. These remittances comprise about 12%–14% of GDP. The country heavily depends on imports of energy and raw materials and government continuously counts on loans from Russia and global financial institutions. In 2015, Armenia joined Russia's Eurasian Economic Union. Export of goods and services is limited primarily to the Russian market. Since 2017, Armenia is the part of Comprehensive and Enhanced Partnership Agreement with the European Union. Small and medium enterprises mostly represent the business in Armenia. They provide nearly 80% of all jobs, although they make up only 27% of Armenia's GDP (Akulic, 2019). The European Union's EU4Business Initiative assists SMEs in accessing EU funds. This initiative is the part of EU's broader efforts towards fostering small business development and is aiming at improving their access to finance, promoting quality business regulations, upgrading services to existing and potential businesses, and benefiting from trade opportunities. Armenia is one of the six countries where EU4Business programme helps small and medium enterprises to develop a favourable business and investment environment and effectively use their full capacity by "improving access to finance and new markets, target women entrepreneurs and SMEs working in green energy and also encourage social entrepreneurship". (EU4Business, 2020). In 2019, Armenia received 76.33 million Euros through this initiative.

The reform agenda of the new government that has been formed in Armenia after 2018 and political changes includes SME development among other priorities. The OECD's assessment of the implementation of the Small Business Act (SBA) for Europe states, that Armenia's progress on the SBA is not impressive due to the lack of medium-term SME strategy. Although, there were some improvements such as institutional and regulatory framework for SME policy; extended scope of support provided to SMEs by the special agency; upgraded electronic procurement system; and policy focus on the importance of entrepreneurial human capital. Finalisation, adoption and implementation of the SME Development Strategy for 2020–24, its monitoring and evaluation system; improvement of e-governance services; supporting export operations and competitive business environment are policy objectives for the coming period (OECD, 2020c).

The World Bank in Armenia indicates that the economy has experienced a profound transformation since independence. Maintaining sustainable growth, determined reforms together with inflows of capital and remittances largely supported to development of a market-oriented environment. Unfortunately, the global financial crisis has impacted the economy significantly (The World Bank, 2020). In its report on Armenia, the United Nations Conference on Trade and Development (UNCTAD) provides information on FDI and external financial resources (Table 5.1).

FDI inflows as well as outflows are not characterised with stability. Personal remittances represent an impressive percentage of GDP.

Despite challenges, Armenia provides a considerably safe environment for international businesses to operate. The country's economic freedom score is 70.6, making its economy the 34th most free in the 2020 index. Armenia is ranked 18th among 45 countries in the Europe region (Economic Freedom, 2020). According to the Ministry of Economy of Armenia, country has improved its position in the Index of Economic

Table 5.1. Financial Flows (Millions of US$)

	2005	**2010**	**2015**	**2019**
FDI Inflows	292	529	184	254
FDI Outflows	5	27	28	−142
Personal remittances, % of GDP	17	16	14	11

Source: UNCTAD (2020)

Freedom, released by the Heritage Foundation (2020), promoting to the 34th place compared to the 47th place in 2019. The country is included in the list of Mostly Free countries with 70.6 score, whereas last year it was in the group of Moderately Free countries with 67.7 points (Armenpress, 2020).

During the last 20 years, Armenia has demonstrated stability. The country's overall score is above the regional average and well above the world average. Armenia's 2019 value of Human Development Index (HDI) was 0.776 (higher than the average of 0.753 for countries in the high human development group and lower than the average of 0.791 for countries in Europe and Central Asia). In Table 5.2, among European and Central Asian countries, Armenia is compared with countries in the region (Azerbaijan and Georgia), with HDIs ranked 88 and 61, respectively (UNDP, 2020). Armenia is at 77th place according to the 2019 Corruption Perceptions Index (CPI) reported by Transparency International.

In the global rankings, Armenia follows neighbouring Georgia but is ahead of its three other neighbours, Azerbaijan, Iran and Turkey. Armenia has set developments in education, taxes, service delivery in the police and health sector, as a priority, it conducted accurate risk assessments and elaborated action plans for these sectors (OECD, 2020b). The government has made some tax and customs administration improvements in recent years. In 2013, Transparency International in its Overview of Corruption and Anti-Corruption in Armenia was stating that "Corruption in Armenia is endemic and widespread, permeating all levels of society. The public administration, particularly the judiciary, the police and the health sector, are especially vulnerable to corruption" (Transparency International, 2013). Unfortunately, anti-corruption measures appeared mostly ineffective. In its Armenia Corruption Report, GAN Integrity provides a snapshot: although progress has been made on the fight against persistent corruption, still "businesses operating or planning to invest in Armenia face high corruption" (GAN, 2020). Due to its economic isolation from Azerbaijan and Turkey, Armenia will need to plan for and implement the additional economic reforms under strengthened rule of law to pursue sustainable economic growth and enhance economic competitiveness and employment opportunities. (CIA, 2020). According to a report by the Istanbul Anti-Corruption Action Plan (IAP) "Armenia should step up its fight against corruption by ensuring an effective enforcement of laws and giving institutions the resources they need to tackle it" (OECD, 2020a).

Ranking countries against each other under the Ease of Doing Business Index aims at providing information on how the regulatory environment is conducive to business operations and property rights protection. Economies with a high rank (1–20) have more straightforward and friendly regulations for businesses. According to the latest World Bank annual ratings, Armenia is ranked 47 among 190 economies in the ease of doing business. The rank of Armenia deteriorated to 47 in 2019 from 41 in 2018 (Table 5.3).

In the Global Competitiveness Report (World Economic Forum, 2019), Armenia has improved its competitiveness index by 1.4 points. It is ranked 69th (70th in 2018) in the list of 141 countries. The country scored 61.28 points (out of 100) in the 2018 report.

In January 2003, Armenia joined the World Trade Organisation. This was the fact of great importance because the country has only two open trade borders – Iran and Georgia (due to Armenia's conflict with Azerbaijan over the separatist Nagorno-Karabakh region, its border with Azerbaijan is closed since 1991, and with Turkey since 1993). International merchandise trade is characterised by a negative balance, though international trade in services showed a positive balance in 2019. Transport and travel are the main categories in the services (Table 5.5).

Export of merchandise mostly is represented by food, ores and metal, and manufactured goods. Russian Federation, China, Switzerland, Lichtenstein, Iraq and Georgia are Armenia's top six trade partners and the Russian Federation has the biggest share.

Data for Armenia for the trade openness (exports plus imports as percent of GDP) from 1990 to 2019 show that the average value during that period was 77.94% with a minimum of 54.54% in 2008 and a maximum of

Table 5.2. Armenia's HDI and Component Indicators for 2019 Relative to Selected Countries and Groups

	HDI Value	HDI Rank	Life Expectancy at Birth	Expected Years of Schooling	Mean Years of Schooling	GNI per Capita (2017 PPP US$)
Armenia	0.776	81	75.1	13.1	11.3	13,894
Azerbaijan	0.756	88	73.0	12.9	10.6	13,784
Georgia	0.812	61	73.8	15.3	13.1	14,429
Europe and Central Asia	0.791	-	74.4	14.7	10.4	17,939
High HDI	0.753	-	75.3	14.0	8.4	14,255

Source: UNDP (2020)

Table 5.3. Ranking of Armenia and its Neighbour Countries in Ease of Doing Business

Economy	2010	2011	2012	2013	2014	2015	2016	2017	2018	2019
Armenia	61	55	40	49	38	43	38	47	41	47
Georgia	17	16	9	8	24	23	16	9	6	7
Azerbaijan	69	66	71	70	63	61	65	57	25	34
Russia	124	120	111	92	54	36	40	35	31	28
Iran	140	144	152	152	119	117	120	124	128	127
Turkey	73	71	72	69	51	63	69	60	43	33

Source: Trading Economics (2020a)

Table 5.4. Scores of Armenia and its Neighbour Countries in Global Competitiveness

Economy	2010	2011	2012	2013	2014	2015	2016	2017	2018	2019
Armenia	3.71	3.75	3.88	4.02	4.1	4	4.01	58.85	59.86	61.28
Georgia	3.8	3.86	3.95	4.07	4.15	4.21	4.22	59.85	60/88	60.61
Azerbaijan	4.3	4.28	4.31	4.41	4.51	4.53	4.5	60.28	60.04	62.72
Russia	4.15	4.23	4.21	4.19	4.24	4.37	4.44	62.97	65.62	66.74
Iran	-	4.14	4.25	4.21	4.07	4.02	4.09	54.41	54.85	52.97
Turkey	4.16	4.24	4.28	4.45	4.45	4.46	4.37	61.42	61.6	62.14

Source: World Economic Forum (2020)

Table 5.5. International Merchandise Trade and Total Trade in Services
(Millions of US$)

	2005	2010	2015	2019
Merchandise exports	974	1011	1485	2640
Merchandise imports	1802	3783	3239	5514
Merchandise trade balance	−828	−2771	−1754	−2874
Services exports	430	1013	1512	2402
Services imports	578	1274	1608	2322
Services trade balance	−148	−261	−95	80

Source: UNCTAD (2020)

112.43% in 1994. The latest value from 2019 is 91.43% (the world average in 2019 based on 143 countries is 94.26%).

Armenia was affected by the spread of COVID-19 in March 2020. It has introduced tight restrictions and imposed a full lockdown in April. The early removal of restrictions led to a wider spread of the virus and a number of reported cases and fatality rates appeared. As a result, growth has turned negative since March after among the highest in the Europe and Central Asia region. According to the World Bank, following an impressive growth in the past three years, which also continued in the first two months of 2020 (of more than 9% year-on-year [y-o-y]), and registered a 5.7% y-o-y reduction for the first half of the year. Inflation remains low, averaging 0.91% for the year, due to the deflation in food and world oil prices and low aggregate demand. (The World Bank, 2020)

Roughly, 2.3% of GDP was allocated for 25 economic and social measures to mitigate the pandemic. According to the assumptions, lower revenue collection and the increased current spending will increase the state budget deficit from an originally planned 2.3% of GDP to 5.4%, elevating public debt to above 60% of GDP (The World Bank, 2020). United Nations Economic Commission for Europe (UNECE, 2020) reported that majority of the MSMEs appeared in debt despite the government's comprehensive financial support measures, they were, "postponed business expenditures and loan repayments to survive falling revenues". Around 79% pointed out the decisive meaning of receiving government support for their survival. They expected deferrals of tax payment and subsidising of loans. Approximately 62% of those surveyed covered their wage bill and maintained operations using their personal savings. "This came at the expense of their families' welfare, as they had to cut back on food expenditure and postpone household payments, including personal loans, rent, and utility bills." "Trade reforms are urgently needed to cushion blow" (UNECE, 2020).

Academic works provide more specifics on SMEs. Results show that being employed by an SME doubles the likelihood of layoff and pay reduction. Findings call for more targeted government assistance to SMEs and low-skilled workers (Beglaryan and Shakhmuradyan, 2020).

Towards the Future

Armenia has seen a turbulent past and usually was a subject of occupation mainly due to its geographical location and relatively small size. The country gained independence twice. The first time Armenian provinces declared their independence from the Russian Empire in 1918. The second one occurred after the break of the Soviet Union, in 1991. Armenia experienced and still undergoes geopolitical unrests, especially around the Nagorno-Karabakh region, located in southwestern Azerbaijan and continued to be the zone of frozen conflict between Armenia and Azerbaijan since 1988, which escalated in armed conflict in 2020. As it is mentioned before, all these unrests have led to having one of the world's biggest diasporas (relatively speaking). Most Armenians live outside Armenia.

In economic terms, the country sees certain positive outlooks. When looking at the GDP (current prices, U.S. dollars), the country will experience a growth rate around 5% in the period 2020–25. At the same time, inflation in terms of average consumer prices (per cent change) of Armenia had increased from −1.41% change in 2016 to 0.91% change in 2020, growing at an average annual rate of 24.40%. Towards the year 2025, the inflation rate will grow from 2.03% in 2021 to 3.78% in 2025, according to the most recent data obtained from the International Monetary Fund (IMF). The projected increase of GDP will be followed by a relatively constant unemployment rate, which will revolve around 21% between 2021 and 2025. This is an improvement compared to the year 2020, when 22.27% of the total labour force was unemployed.

The industrial production in Armenia is expected to be 2.50% at the end of the last quarter of 2020. In the next 12 months, it is forecasted that this indicator will grow to 5%, while in the long term the percentage should rise to 8% by the end of 2022, according to the econometric models used by Trading Economics (2020b). On the other hand, the manufacturing production in Armenia increased by 9.2% in October 2020, when compared to the same month in the previous year. By the end of the last quarter of 2020, the manufacturing in Armenia was around 6.5%. By the end of 2021, manufacturing is estimated to rise to 9.5%. Additionally, it is expected that this economic activity keeps the trend at 8.5% in 2022 (Trading Economics, 2020b).

The significant political changes happened in Armenia in 2018: Nikol Pashinyan, a former journalist and legislator, created and developed his image as a politician close to the people. Prime Minister Sargsyan has resigned as a result of protests that were turned to so-called Armenia's Velvet Revolution. The ruling party resisted but opposition parties united around Pashinyan and voted him as prime minister. Pashinyan pledged to lead reforms to root out corruption. The new parliament was established. It set the development of small and medium-sized enterprises in Armenia as one of the priorities for future economic growth and development. Many institutional mechanisms were put in place to support SME development (e.g., e-procurement system). However, the country needs to finalise and implement the SME Development Strategy 2020–2024 to enhance e-government services, improve bankruptcy procedures, offer better services to exporters and create a competition-friendly business environment (OECD, 2020b). The government showed significant support to small businesses in the private sector during the COVID-19 pandemic and provided direct aid to companies by allowing them to take interest-free loans to pay salaries, purchase raw materials and export products. Besides this, assistance was provided to entrepreneurs who did not reduce the number of employees during the epidemic and continue to pay them wages (Khachatryan, 2020).

The history of private business and entrepreneurship in Armenia is relatively young and dates back to late 1986 when the law on individual labour activity was introduced. Afterwards, in 1987, the law on cooperatives was adopted, which allowed a certain level of private economic activity. This law was further enhanced in 1988, making it possible for this new form of enterprise to earn income legally. In a certain way, we can say that doing business in Armenia still suffers from certain forms of "child diseases", which imply the slow development of organisational structure, lack of clear strategy, proper planning and control mechanisms, as well as financial discipline. In contrast, according to the study implemented in

2017, small business owners still prefer simple-rent extraction in the country, they have distrust towards the market economy, and significant discrepancies in regard to the approach to doing business exist between large, medium and small businesses. Firstly, entrepreneurs, as representatives of micro and small business are usually mainly concerned about bare survival and lack ambition and long-term orientation in their business (Mikaelian, 2017). On the other hand, if any small business develops its operations outside the bare survival scope, the organisation tends to become more formal. In terms of types of industry and share of employment, small enterprises have a high share in overall employment in industries, like manufacturing, construction, wholesale and retail trade, accommodation, real estate, professional services, administrative services and repair of computers. On the other hand, large enterprises are big employers in mining, energy, water supply, transportation and ICT (OECD, 2018).

It is interesting to note that the individuals engaged in agriculture do not consider their activity as a business but rather consider themselves unemployed, which skews the economy image slightly. In Armenia, the regulatory environment in which small and micro enterprises operate is considered to have a relatively low level of corruption. However, mainly due to historical prejudices, the perceived level of corruption of people is very high. This is the main reason why small business owners tend to avoid contact with state institutions and often operate in the economy's grey area. This trend is partly caused by the Soviet experience and partly is considered an attempt to avoid paying taxes. However, these trends tend to die down due to globalisation and lowered trade barriers (Mikaelian, 2017).

References

Akulic, Oksana (2019), "Сравнительный анализ состояния малого и среднего бизнеса и форм государственной поддержки в России и в Армении," *Russian Colloquium – Journal* 6 (39), pp. 1–10.

Armenpress (2020), Armenia's economy becoming more and more free – PM. Available at: https://armenpress.am/eng/news/1020073.html (Accessed 10 June 2021)

Beglaryan, Mane, and Gayane Shakhmuradyan (2020), "The Impact of COVID-19 on Small and Medium-sized Enterprises in Armenia:

Evidence from a Labor Force Survey," (Retrieved from https://sbir. upct.es/index.php/sbir/article/view/298, accessed 28 February 2021)

Bolsajian, Monique (2018), "The Armenian Diaspora: Migration and its Influence on Identity and Politics," *Global Societies Journal* 6 (1), pp. 29–40.

Britannica (2020a), "Mount Ararat, Mountain, Turkey, The Editors of Encyclopaedia Britannica," (Retrieved from https://www.britannica. com/place/Mount-Ararat, accessed 1 March 2021)

Caucasus Research Resource Centers (2013), *The South Caucasus between the EU and the Eurasian Union,* Bremen: CRRC.

Central Intelligence Agency (2020), "Armenia, The World Factbook," (Retrieved from https://www.cia.gov/the-world-factbook/countries/ armenia/, accessed 25 December 2020)

Cohen, Robin (2010), *Global Diasporas: An Introduction,* London: Routledge.

Dana, Léo-Paul (2011), "Entrepreneurship in Bolivia: An Ethnographic Enquiry," *International Journal of Business and Emerging Markets* 3 (1), pp. 75–88.

Dana, Léo-Paul, Etemad Hamid, and Richard W. Wright (2008), "Toward a Paradigm of Symbiotic Entrepreneurship," *International Journal of Entrepreneurship and Small Business* 5 (2), pp. 109–126.

Economic Freedom (2020), "Armenia Records Progress in Heritage Foundation's Economic Freedom Index 2020," (Retrieved from www. armenpress.am/eng/news/1009102, accessed 18 December 2020)

Esipova, Neli, John Fleming, and Julie Ray (2017), *New Index Shows Least, Most-Accepting Countries for Migrants,* Washington: Gallup.

EU4Business (2020). Country Report 2020: Armenia. Available at: https:// eu4business.eu/reports/eu4business-country-report-2020-armenia/ (Accessed 10 June 2021)

Food and Agriculture Organization in Armenia (2021), "Armenia at a Glance," (Retrieved from http://www.fao.org/armenia/fao-in-armenia/ armenia-at-a-glance/en/, accessed 5 March 2021)

Gall, Carlotta, and Anton Troianovski (2021), "After Nagorno-Karabakh War, Trauma, Tragedy and Devastation, by Carlotta Gall and Anton Troianovski," (Retrieved from https://www.nytimes.com/2020/12/11/ world/europe/nagorno-karabakh-armenia-azerbaijan.html, accessed 1 March 2021)

GAN Risk and Compliance Portal (2020), "Armenia Corruption Report," (Retrieved from https://www.ganintegrity.com/portal/country-profiles/armenia/, accessed 28 February 2021)

The Government of the Republic of Armenia (2020), "General Information," (Retrieved from https://www.gov.am/en/official/, accessed 21 December 2020)

Heritage Foundation (2020), "Index of Economic Freedom," (Retrieved from https://www.heritage.org/index/country/armenia, accessed 18 December 2020)

International Monetary Fund (2020), "World Economic Outlook Database, October 2020," (Retrieved from https://knoema.com/IMFWEO20 20Oct/imf-world-economic-outlook-weo-database-october-2020? country=1000060-armenia, accessed 10 January 2021)

Kanadyan, Hovsep (2021), "Implications of the 2020 Artsakh War on Regional Countries, EVN Report," (Retrieved from https://www. evnreport.com/politics/implications-of-the-2020-artsakh-war-on-regional-countries, accessed 2 March 2021)

Khachatryan, Arthur (2020), "Armenia: Forecasts for Business and the Economy Amid the State of Emergency," JAM News, (Retrieved from https://jam-news.net/armenia-economy-coronavirus-emergency/, accessed 20 January 2021)

Mikaelian, Hrant (2017), "Self-employment, Micro and Small Business in Armenia – Emerging Culture of Entrepreneurship, Caucasus Institute, Gebert Ruf Foundation, Yerevan," (Retrieved from https://c-i.am/wp-content/uploads/Entrepreneurship-Armenia.pdf, accessed 25 January 2021)

Mints, Aleksey (2021), "Armenia," Encyclopaedia Britannica, (Retrieved from https://www.britannica.com/place/Armenia, accessed 20 January 2021)

Mokyr, Joel (2003), *The Oxford Encyclopedia of Economic History,* Oxford: Oxford University Press.

National Statistical Service of the Republic of Armenia (2011), "The Informal Sector and Informal Employment in Armenia, Country Report 2010," (Retrieved from https://www.adb.org/sites/default/files/ publication/28437/informal-sector-armenia.pdf, accessed 7 March 2021)

Organisation for Economic Co-operation and Development (2018), "Compendium of Enterprise Statistics in Armenia," (Retrieved from https://www.oecd.org/eurasia/competitiveness-programme/eastern-partners/Compendium-Entreprise-Statistics-Armenia-2018-EN.pdf, accessed 7 March 2021)

Organisation for Economic Co-operation and Development (2020a), "Anti-Corruption Progress Report on Eastern Europe and Central Asia,"

(Retrieved from https://www.oecd.org/corruption/acn/publications documents/, accessed 25 January 2021)

Organisation for Economic Co-operation and Development (2020b), "Armenia: Small Business Act Country Profile," (Retrieved from https://www.oecd-ilibrary.org/sites/95f303db-en/index.html? itemId=/content/component/95f303db-en, accessed 25 January 2021)

Organisation for Economic Co-operation and Development (2020c), *SME Policy Index: Eastern Partner Countries 2020, Assessing the Implementation of the Small Business Act for Europe,* Armenia: Small Business Act Country Profile, (Retrieved from https://www.oecd-ilibrary.org/development/sme-policy-index-eastern-partner-countries-2020_95f303db-en, accessed 28 February 2021)

Savenjuk, Galina (2020), "Бизнес и жизнь в Армении – чем привлекает страна нерезидентов?," International Wealth, (Retrieved from https://internationalwealth.info/best-offshore-services/business-and-life-in-armenia-attractiveness-to-non-residents/, accessed 18 December 2020)

Scott, Michael (2016), *Ancient Worlds: A Global History of Antiquity,* New York: Basic Books.

Statistical Committee of the Republic of Armenia (2021), "Statistical Committee of the Republic of Armenia," (Retrieved from https://www.armstat.am/en/?nid=12&id=08009, accessed 7 March 2021)

Trading Economics (2020a), "Armenia – Ease of Doing Business Index, Trading Economics," (Retrieved from https://tradingeconomics.com/armenia/ease-of-doing-business-index-1-most-business-friendly-regulations-wb-data.html, accessed 12 December 2020)

Trading Economics (2020b), "Armenia Industrial Production," (Retrieved from https://tradingeconomics.com/armenia/industrial-production, accessed 12 January 2021)

Transparency International (2013), Global corruption barometer. Available at: https://transparency.am/en/gcb (Accessed 10 June 2021)

Turay, Anna (2008), *Tarihte Ermeniler,* Istanbul: Bolsohays.

United Nations Conference on Trade and Development (2020), *Investment Promotion Strategy in times of the Global Crisis and Beyond,* Joint Report by the Office to the President of the Republic of Armenia and United Nations Conference on Trade and Development.

United Nations Economic Commission for Europe (2020), "Armenia Addresses COVID-19 Impact on Businesses through Streamlined Trade Procedures and Upgraded Quality Infrastructure: United Nations Economic Commission for Europe Study Proposes Measures for Supporting Further Efforts," (Retrieved from https://unece.org/general-unece/press/armenia-addresses-covid-19-impact-businesses-through-streamlined-trade, accessed 28 February 2021)

United Nations Development Programme (2020), "Human Development Report," Armenia, (Retrieved from http://hdr.undp.org/en/countries/profiles/ARM/, accessed 12 January 2021)

U.S. Department of State (2020), "Investment Climate Statements: Armenia, Report Overview," (Retrieved from https://www.state.gov/reports/2020-investment-climate-statements/armenia/, accessed 28 February 2021)

World Bank (2020). The World Bank in Armenia. Available at: https://www.worldbank.org/en/country/armenia (Accessed 10 June 2021)

World Economic Forum (2020), "Armenia Improves Position in Global Competitiveness Report," (Retrieved from https://armenpress.am/eng/news/991024.html, accessed 18 December 2020)

Chapter 6

The Context for Business in Azerbaijan

Aidin Salamzadeh & Yashar Salamzadeh

Abstract: Azerbaijan is an oil and gas–producing country with both traditional and modern aspects. The country is a fascinating place to run a business as it was ranked 34th globally in terms of the Doing Business index in 2020. Azerbaijan is a land of old bazaars for traditional sellers and modern markets for innovative firms. Besides oil and gas products, agriculture, tourism, construction and transportation are among the country's major sectors. With a whale of touristic destinations in which there are different bazaars, Azerbaijan's economy has kept these historical mechanisms to meet its people's current demands and attract more tourists. After its independence, the country has profoundly developed in terms of socio-economic factors and entered into several innovative and emerging markets. Thus, there are plenty of business opportunities to be explored, evaluated and exploited by potential individuals or companies in this country.

Keywords: Business, bazaar, entrepreneurship, economic development, Azerbaijan

Introduction

Azerbaijan is the largest country in the Caucasus region of Euroasia, which connects Eastern Europe to Western Asia. The country is bounded by Iran (south), Turkey and Armenia (west), Georgia (northwest), the Russian republic of Daghestan (north), and the Caspian Sea (east). Besides, through the Caspian Sea, Azerbaijan is connected to Turkmenistan and

Kazakhstan (Exhibit 6.1). The official language is Azerbaijani (a Turkic language) used by the majority of people (Mokari and Werner, 2017), yet, in some small regions, people speak in Russian and Armenian. As a Muslim-majority country, it stands in second place for Shia Muslims in the world (Balci, 2004). Nevertheless, the minorities of Christians live in peace with Muslims in this secular country (Ergun and Çitak, 2020), despite several disputes among Azerbaijan and Armenia, especially in the last few decades.

Azerbaijan has considerable oil and natural gas resources (Zulfigarov and Neuenkirch, 2019). One could easily see several pumping units for extracting oil near Baku (Exhibit 6.2). Besides, several oil and gas pipelines date back to the late 19th century. Azerbaijan has considerable gold, silver and mineral resources. Agriculture, tourism, transportation, construction, and science and new technologies are among the other major economic sectors (Nasirov, 2013). Due to its geographic location, the country is

Exhibit 6.1 Map 3761 of Azerbaijan; courtesy of the United Nations

considered a critical crossroad for several countries to transport various goods, such as raw materials (Swietochowski, 1999). The country plays a significant role, as south–north corridor, which was connected historically to the silk road through Iran (Ghorbanpoor, 2010). Also, Azerbaijan is a part of the connection between the Asian and the Eastern European countries.

Based on its economic and geographic situation and its old history, Azerbaijan is a country with a remarkable history of bazaars and marketplaces (Exhibit 6.3), in which different agricultural and cultural goods are sold (Asadov, 2019). Bazaars are places to sell and buy routine products for Azerbaijanis and also a place to sell or buy souvenirs. There are several bazaars in different cities, such as *Taza Bazaar* (New Bazaar), *Yashil Bazaar* (Green Bazaar), *Nasimi Bazaar*, and the like – each of which is a place to sell or buy various products. On the one hand, the bazaar economy is well developed for centuries (Baratin et al., 2012). On the other hand, like several emerging economies (Dana, 2005), science and technology markets are also emerging following the market economy's logic (Hasanov and Akbulaev, 2020).

Exhibit 6.2 The City of Baku; photo © 2021 by Aidin Salamzadeh

Exhibit 6.3   Bazaar in Baku; photo © 2021 by Kitti Gould

Exhibit 6.4   Flag of the Republic of Azerbaijan

Azerbaijan's flag, which is shown in Exhibit 6.4, contains bright blue, red and green. There are a white crescent and an eight-pointed star in the centre of its flag. The earlier flag of the Azerbaijan Soviet Socialist Republic (SSR) has replaced by this flag in 1991. Each colour has a specific meaning. The bright blue colour stands for Azerbaijan's Turkic origins, the red colour symbolises progress and the green colour represents Islam, the main religion of Azerbaijanis.

Historical Context

Azerbaijan is among the old places in the world, where early civilisations used to reside. There is evidence of human settlement in this region during the Stone Age (Farajova, 2010; Liberman, 2003). The country went through several historical changes. First, Scythians were the early inhabitants of the region during the 9th century BC (Kashkay, 1997). Then, Medes dominated the area (Genito, 1986), and this region became a part of their broad empire for around two centuries until the Achaemenids became the rulers of the Persian Empire around 550 BC and ruled over this region after Medes (Gagoshidze et al., 2007). During this era, they initiated and spread Zoroastrianism in their empire (Chen, 2003). In the 4th century, Christianity spread in this region after the Sasanian Empire turned them into a vassal state in 252 (Mousavi and Daryaee, 2012), named Caucasian Albania (Vacca, 2015). After the emergence of Islam in the 7th century, the state became a Muslim state (Lemercier-Quelquejay, 1984). In the 11th century, one of the first Turkic dynasties was established, that is, the Seljuk Empire (Peacock, 2015). They entered the region now known as Azerbaijan by 1067. After centuries, the Safavid dynasty became the rulers and converted Sunni Muslims to Shia in 1501 (Zarinebaf, 2019). In the Ottoman-Safavid war (1578–1590), the Ottomans occupied parts of current Azerbaijan (Scherberger, 2011). After more than a century, as a result of the Russo-Persian war (1722–1723), parts of northern Azerbaijan were occupied by Russians. After the Safavids, the Afsharid dynasty ruled over Azerbaijan. Several self-ruling *Khanates* ruled over different parts of this region as the Iranian King's vassals and subjects during this time (Bournoutian, 2016). Iran mainly ruled the area to the north of the Aras Revier until the 19th century, when Russia occupied it and forced Iran to leave the region based on the Gulistan and Turkmenchay treaties. Afterwards, the Aras River became the border of Iran and the Soviet Union (Farrokh, 2003).

During World War I and after the Russian Empire's collapse, the Transcaucasian Democratic Federative Republic was formed (Mamoulia, 2020). This country included the present-day republics of Azerbaijan, Georgia and Armenia. Nevertheless, this did not last long (22 April to 28 May 1918). In May 1918, the republic was dissolved, and the Azerbaijan Democratic Republic (ADR) declared its independence (Yusifova, 2014). After 23 months, the Soviet Union invaded ADR and established the Azerbaijan SSR (28 April 1920) (Huseynov and Mokhtar, 2019). In 1920, Armenia declared its independence. In 1921, Azerbaijan, Georgia, the Soviet republics of Russia and Armenia signed the Treaty of Kars (Uslu and Ok, 2013; Vagnini, 2012). The Nakhichevan Autonomous SSR was included in the Azerbaijan SSR by this treaty in 1924. According to its strategic importance during World War II, Azerbaijan fought against invaders and around 250,000 people – of about 3.4 million population – were killed. In this war, more than 130 Azerbaijanis were titled as the Heroes of the Soviet Union. In 1990, Black January (*Qara Yanvar*) was happened according to a state emergency due to the dissolution of the Soviet Union. Sadly, 147 civilians of Baku were killed on this day. People in Azerbaijan remember this day as the Day of Nationwide Sorrow (January 20). Azerbaijan declared its independence on 18 October 1991 (Khan, 2014).

After its independence, the First Nagorno-Karabakh War affected Azerbaijan and Armenia's relationship, which was historically controversial (Mkrtchyan, 2007). Armenia supported the Armenian population of Karabakh and occupied some parts of Azerbaijan. Afterwards, in 1993, the United Nations Security Council Resolutions obliged Armenians to withdraw all Armenian forces from the occupied territories immediately (Zourabian, 2006). Nevertheless, still, Karabakh remained a source of dispute between these two countries. On 27 September 2020, new issues were raised, according to which the Azerbaijani and Armenian forces entered into a new war (Burke, 2020). This war took around six weeks. Based on Azerbaijan's victory, this region turned entirely back to them, and Azerbaijanis celebrated this day (Carey, 2020).

In addition to its remarkable history, Azerbaijan is a country with several cultural characteristics. Azerbaijan's culture includes, and is not limited to, its historical places, poets, artists and modern artefacts. The Maiden Tower, Shirvanshah Palace, Ateshgah, Gobustan, Gamigaya Drawings, Chiraggalaand and Azkyh Cave are among Azerbaijan's main historical places (Broers, 2020). Besides, there are two main Azerbaijani literature traditions, that is, folk literature, and written literature (e.g., Uceinov et al., 1963). The first tradition includes the epic tradition and folk poetry, which deal with the most profound traditions and customs of the Azerbaijani people and is commonly used in daily conversations. The second tradition includes Safavid literature and the classical era. This tradition is closely connected to Persian history. In addition to these two traditions, from the 19th century, the literature was mainly known by Soviet Azerbaijani and Persian Azerbaijani traditions (e.g., Avetikyan, 2009; Salamzadeh et al., 2013; Swietochowski, 1999). Nevertheless, modern literature has borrowed from all the mentioned traditions and combined them with mainstream global literature. This led to post-modern literature in Azerbaijan. Besides, artists like Gamar Salamzade, the first Azerbaijani female film director, or Muslim Magomayev, the King of Song, the Azerbaijani opera singer, are among the leading artists in this region.

As mentioned earlier, besides the oil and gas industries, Azerbaijanis are proactively engaged in agriculture, tourism, transportation, construction, manufacturing, and science and technology-based sectors (Aras et al., 2016) (Exhibit 6.5 & Exhibit 6.6). Besides, throughout several centuries, Azerbaijanis saved their remarkable history of bazaars (Dana, 2007; Hoffman, 1999). In the earliest historical civilisations, they were engaged in the agriculture industry. Several pieces of evidence exist regarding their agricultural techniques and technologies during those years (Aliyev and Gasimov, 2018). They were expert farmers who used to work on the fertile soils of Azerbaijan. Besides, Azerbaijan was always a corridor for transporting products, based on its geographic location. Then, there were several bazaars for selling agricultural and exported or imported goods. Taza Bazaar, Yashil Bazaar and Nasimi Bazaar are among the remained bazaars (Exhibit 6.7) that have borrowed a lot from their historical versions. *Taza* means new. Then, Taza Bazaar means new bazaar, where one could find fresh fruits, vegetables, berries, nuts as well as dried fruits. The goods sold in this market are not limited to these things, and one might buy several delicious products in this bazaar. *Yashil* means green. Then,

Exhibit 6.5 Heydar Aliyev Centre; photo © 2021 by Aidin Salamzadeh

Exhibit 6.6 Flame Towers in Baku; photo © 2021 by Aidin Salamzadeh

Exhibit 6.7 Bazaar in Baku; photo © 2021 by Kitti Gould

Yashil Bazaar means green bazaar. This bazaar is considered the most diversified bazaar in Baku. In this bazaar, one could barely find anything one needs, mostly what belongs to Azerbaijan. People even could taste some products before they buy them (Exhibit 6.8). Nasimi Bazaar was named based on the name of a well-known poet, that is, Imamaddin Nasimi. It is primarily a place for plant lovers. One could buy several delicious products here in this bazaar. As mentioned, most of the bazaars are dedicated to agricultural products, but there are also bazaars for selling other products (Exhibit 6.9).

In addition to its remarkable history of bazaars, Azerbaijan is experiencing new technological trends based on new firms' innovative development in various economic sectors, primarily through its technology parks (Hasanov and Akbulaev, 2020). Like several emerging economies, innovations have influenced Azerbaijan's economic development, as several other countries are also investing in these markets (Barrichello et al., 2020; Dana, 2000; Salamzadeh et al., 2017). The establishment of the *BARAMA Innovation and Entrepreneurship Centre* in 2009, opening coworking spaces in technoparks in 2012, and the foundation of *High Technology Park* in 2013 paved the way for startups and innovative teams to realise their innovative dreams. Besides, Baku Business Factory, Next Step Innovation

Exhibit 6.8 Handicrafts in Baku; photo © 2021 by Kitti Gould

Centre and Sup.az Accelerator in 2015 started to act, and in 2016, Colab Co-Working space started to act in this market (Exhibit 6.10) (Huseynova and Zeynalova, 2015; İbrahimova, 2019; Salamzadeh, 2018; Salamzadeh and Markovic, 2018). Such issues have considerably changed the competition scene in Azerbaijan, and thus new niche and technology-based markets have emerged accordingly. Besides, significant improvements in the e-government sector have paved the way for Azerbaijan's further

Exhibit 6.9 Vendor in Baku bazaar;
photo © 2021 by Kitti Gould

Exhibit 6.10   Coworking space in Baku; photo © 2021 by Aidin Salamzadeh

economic development (Babayev, 2018). Besides its historical connection with countries like Iran and Georgia (Doshmanli et al., 2018; Tajpour et al., 2020), Azerbaijan's economy has dramatically changed through the last two decades by expanding economic relationships with various countries, including Italy, Turkey, Israel, Czech Republic, Germany, India and China as its main export partners, and Russia, Turkey, United Kingdom, China, Germany and Georgia as the major import partners (Exhibit 6.11). It is noteworthy that Azerbaijan's international relationships are not limited to these countries (Ahmadova, 2019).

Context for Enterprise and Implications for Doing Business

Azerbaijan is an oil and natural gas-rich country with a strategic position as a hub in the Caucasus region (Feizullaev et al., 2020). In 2018, the real GDP of Azerbaijan had expanded by 1.4% based on higher exports of gas, stable oil production and other economic facts. Besides, after 2018, the government of Azerbaijan has experienced significant changes, including

Exhibit 6.11   Port of Baku; photo © 2021 by Aidin Salamzadeh

critical changes of the ministers and the Karabakh war in late 2020 (Tugrul and Karimli, 2020). Significant economic reforms in the key sectors have planned to recover the economic growth rate, which was affected by the coronavirus pandemic in 2020, like several other neighbouring countries in this region (Expert Group, 2020). Nevertheless, this economic reform highly relies on rising gas exports, which might lead to medium-term accelerated growth. Supporting the private sector by improving investments or collaborating on various projects, reducing governmental projects, facilitating competition and considering human development plans would improve the economic growth rate (Allahverdiyev, 2020; Ganbarov et al., 2020). Hopefully, the budget for education and healthcare raised significantly in 2019, respectively, by 13% and 44.5%, which might improve Azerbaijani human capital and pave the way for long-term economic growth (Zeynalli, 2020). Nevertheless, other issues need more attention from policymakers of Azerbaijan.

Table 6.1 shows the significant specifications of the country. According to Table 6.1, the general state of Azerbaijan has improved significantly in terms of essential indexes such as life expectancy and education. Besides, the time required to start a business has decreased dramatically to four days. The mobile penetration rate and Internet users have also increased, which is a positive indication for improving e-commerce.

Table 6.1. Statistics of Azerbaijan

	1990	2000	2010	2018
Population, total (millions)	7.16	8.05	9.05	9.94
Population growth (annual %)	0.4	0.8	1.2	0.9
Surface area (sq. km) (thousands)	86.6	86.6	86.6	86.6
GNI, Atlas method (current US$) (billions)	4.42	4.87	48.63	40.40
GNI per capita, Atlas method (current US$)	590	610	5,370	4,060
GNI, PPP (current international $) (billions)	24.55	25.95	126.29	137.13
GNI per capita, PPP (current international $)	3,280	3,220	13,950	13,800
People				
Income share held by lowest 20%	..	7.4	..	..
Life expectancy at birth, total (years)	65	67	71	73
Mortality rate, under-5 (per 1,000 live births)	95	75	37	22
Primary completion rate, total (% of relevant age group)	99	90	90	100
School enrollment, primary (% gross)	114.6	97.2	93.8	99.7
School enrollment, secondary (% gross)	92	74	..	94

(continued)

Table 6.1. Major Specifications of Azerbaijan (*continued*)

	1990	2000	2010	2018
Economy				
GDP (current US$) (billions)	8.86	5.27	52.90	47.11
GDP growth (annual %)	–0.7	11.1	4.8	1.5
Inflation, GDP deflator (annual %)	83.5	12.5	13.8	12.2
Agriculture, forestry, and fishing, value added (% of GDP)	27	16	6	5
Industry (including construction), value added (% of GDP)	30	43	60	52
Exports of goods and services (% of GDP)	44	40	54	54
Imports of goods and services (% of GDP)	39	38	21	38
Gross capital formation (% of GDP)	27	21	18	20
Revenue, excluding grants (% of GDP)	..	..	44.0	36.4
Net lending (+) / net borrowing (–) (% of GDP)	..	..	15.5	9.5
States and markets				
Time required to start a business (days)	..	105	8	4
Domestic credit provided by financial sector (% of GDP)	..	..	..	13.1
Tax revenue (% of GDP)	..	..	12.2	13.0
Military expenditure (% of GDP)	2.4	2.3	2.8	3.6
Mobile cellular subscriptions (per 100 people)	0.0	5.2	100.7	103.9
Individuals using the Internet (% of population)	0.0	0.1	46.0	79.8
High-technology exports (% of manufactured exports)	..	..	1	4
Statistical capacity score (overall average)	..	..	79	78

Source: The World Bank – World Development Indicators database

According to the IMF, in 2019, GDP of Azerbaijan increased by 2.3%. Nevertheless, due to the coronavirus pandemic, a decrease of GDP to 2.2% is expected in 2020. Hopefully, an increase to 0.7% is expected as the coronavirus pandemic would be controlled, and the understanding of policymakers about facing this global challenge would be improved. Like the World Bank, IMF believes that the threats of the country's reliance on hydrocarbons and the declining oil production are significant (Davudova, 2020; Mukhtarov et al., 2019; Orujov et al., 2019). According to the Corruption Perceptions Index 2019, Azerbaijan has improved from 152 to 126 among 180 countries (Suleymanli, 2020). This shows a substantial improvement, but yet it is not satisfactory. According to the World Bank reports in 2019, employment rates in agriculture, industry and services sectors are 35.5%, 15% and 49.5%. It reveals that most of the population is in the services and agriculture sectors.

Doing Business in Azerbaijan

Azerbaijan is an upper-middle-income country with a doing business score of 76.7, which is ranked 34th in terms of Ease of Doing Business in 2020 (do Carmo Silva et al., 2020). Azerbaijan is ranked first in terms of getting credit. It reveals that getting credit for doing a business is easy, and intended individuals could easily access credit. Besides, in terms of starting a business, Azerbaijan is ranked ninth, as the process has only three phases and takes less than four days. In terms of enforcing contracts, the country stands in 28th place. Besides, the most straightforward processes of registering a company for foreigners made Azerbaijan a fascinating destination for them. In addition, regarding dealing with construction permits, Azerbaijan is ranked 59th. It shows that it is relatively easy to build a warehouse, obtain required permits, receive necessary inspections and get utility connections. In terms of getting electricity for a newly constructed warehouse, Azerbaijan is modestly ranked 80th globally. The steps, time and cost of registering property are other pillars of doing business. Azerbaijan is ranked 40th in these pillars. It reveals that registering properties such as land and buildings is almost easy. In terms of protecting minority investors, the country is ranked 105th. It shows that minority shareholders could hardly secure themselves against the misuse of corporate assets by managers, secure their rights, and lower the risk of abuse. Paying taxes is another index in which Azerbaijan is ranked 40th. It shows that tax payment is reasonable in this country, and medium-sized companies typically pay their taxes. In terms of trading across borders, the country is ranked 83rd globally. It shows that still the time and cost of the logistical processes for exports and imports are moderately high. Nevertheless, one should take into account that Azerbaijan has paved the way for foreign investment, and this pillar has improved throughout time. Resolving insolvency is the last pillar in which the country is ranked 47th. It reveals that there are several options for those who become insolvent, and therefore, it is not so much time-consuming and does not impose so much cost.

Similar to any country, the context of doing business has some specifications in Azerbaijan. For instance, its conflicts with Armenia have led to setting some unwritten rules. According to such unwritten rules, one might not speak Armenian or about Armenia in Azerbaijan. Besides, one must not travel to the country after travelling to Armenia. These are mostly due to the historical issues mentioned in the previous sections. Moreover, if people feel that one respects their Azeri roots and history, they will become more friendly. It is noteworthy that due to their geopolitical location as well as their remarkable history, the Azerbaijani people are so friendly to their guests. This is a fact that one could easily see in their routine lives and bazaars. People could negotiate the prices and decide which products to buy (Dana and Wright, 2015). If the sellers feel that one person is a tourist, they might even ask him/her to pay lower prices in Azerbaijani manat instead of USD or Euros.

Overall, Azerbaijan has become an exciting country for doing business, and this made several investors interested in investing in this country. That has changed Azerbaijan's state in the region and made it both a touristic destination and an investment choice for foreigners. According to their friendly and hospitable business environment, Azerbaijan has experienced remarkable economic growth, especially after its independence and transition as a post-communist economy (Dana and Dana, 2003). Besides, after emphasising on sectors other than the oil and gas sector, business opportunities have been diversified.

As a foreign businessperson, one might choose from different company types, including limited liability, joint-stock or closed-stock companies, as well as general or limited partnerships, for which varied rules and regulations are applicable. Limited liability companies are among the most suitable forms of a company for foreigners. Despite many countries, the rules and regulations do not require any specific amount for company capital and allow foreign ownership in local companies. Besides, no requirements regarding the manager's nationality or hiring local employees for specific positions are applicable. Additionally, laws provide flexible rules for forming joint ventures. These rules do not restrict foreign shareholders' rights, intervene in their financing issues and oblige them to transfer funds to and from the country. All the issues mentioned earlier make Azerbaijan an exciting destination for foreign investors.

On the one hand, these positive elements have promoted the business environment. On the other hand, the high corruption rate and the gap between poor and rich people push the economy back. Hopefully, the current trend shows that positive forces have been more powerful and effective than negative ones. Therefore, one could witness a growing economy in this country. Despite the challenges, and according to the abundance of opportunities, Azerbaijan has become a desirable destination for international businesspersons.

Towards the Future

Azerbaijan's economy relies mainly on gas and oil, chemical and petrochemical products, steel, iron and textiles. Besides, in addition to these resources, agriculture, construction, transportation and emerging technology sectors are among the country's main economic sectors. Also, according to its historical and geotouristic attractions, Azerbaijan is a fantastic destination for tourists. Based on these potentials, the country is going towards becoming a highly competitive economy. The government has planned to form a new economic model that pays attention to (i) revising the existing rules and regulations in order to let the market economy play its role, (ii) developing the non-oil sector, (iii) improving the economic structure, (iv) supporting innovative activities, (v) improving the transportation infrastructure, (vi) developing ICT sector and realising the information society concept and (vii) developing human capital. These are among the essential aspects of the new economy in Azerbaijan. Besides, the government continuously improves the business rules and regulations, which is evident in its Doing Business index. As a touristic destination, the country pays specific attention to its cultural heritage, as well as its ecological and environmental issues.

Azerbaijan revived after its independence, and the economy has substantially improved under the leadership of Heydar Aliyev. Today, the country stands among the leading countries in its region and has gained foreign investors' attention who could easily enter into its market and invest in various projects. By paving the way for foreign direct investment (FDI) and highlighting new opportunities for potential investors, it is projected that

Azerbaijan will become more prosperous and wealthy. Besides its emerging economy, the old history of bazaars helps Azerbaijanis stand among the most potential candidates for doing business in traditional bazaars and modern markets. Nevertheless, the country faces some challenges, such as (i) coping with the innovative waves of the new technologies compared to other countries, (ii) decreasing its reliance on the oil and gas economy, (iii) coping with the Globalisation risks and threats as the competition has become tense and (iv) paying attention to both industrialisation wave and environmental issues.

References

Ahmadova, Akima (2019), "The Analysis of the Current State of Foreign Trade Relations of Azerbaijan Republic," *Massachusetts Review of Science and Technologies* 1 (13), pp. 167–174.

Aliyev, Khatai, and Ilkin Gasimov (2018), "Retrospective of Economic and Trade Policies Focused on Agricultural Development: Case of Azerbaijan," in Vasily Erokhin, ed., *Establishing Food Security and Alternatives to International Trade in Emerging Economies,* IGI Global, pp. 177–195.

Allahverdiyev, Madat (2020), "World Economy and Sustainable Political-Economic Welfare of Azerbaijan," *Randwick International of Social Science Journal* 1 (2), pp. 337–344.

Aras, Osman Nuri, Elchin Suleymanov, and Karim Mammadov (2016). *Economy of Azerbaijan,* Baku: Sharg-Garb Publishing House.

Asadov, Farda (2019), "Trade Routes, Trading Centers and the Emergence of the Domestic Market in Azerbaijan in the Period of Arab-Khazar Domination on the Silk Road," *Acta Via Serica* 4 (1), pp. 1–2.

Avetikyan, Gevorg G. (2009), *Ethnicity in Contemporary Islamic Republic of Iran,* Doctoral dissertation, Central European University.

Babayev, Emin (2018), *Electronic Government as an Element of the Digital Economy: Experience of the Republic of Azerbaijan.* St. Petersburg Russian Presidential Academy of National Economy and Public Administration.

Balci, Bayram (2004), "Between Sunnism and Shiism: Islam in Post-Soviet Azerbaijan," *Central Asian Survey* 23 (2), pp. 205–217.

Baratin, Lara, Sara Bertozzi, Elvio Moretti, and Michele Spinella (2012), "Gis and 3D Models as Support to Documentation and Planning of the Baku Historical Centre (Republic of Azerbaijan)," *International Journal of Heritage in the Digital Era* 1, pp. 71–76.

Barrichello, Alcides, Emerson Gomes dos Santos, and Morano Rogerio (2020), "Determinant and Priority Factors of Innovation for the Development of Nations," *Innovation & Management Review* 17 (3), pp. 307–320.

Bournoutian, George (2016), "Arthur Tsutsiev: Atlas of the Ethno-Political History of the Caucasus, Translated from Russian by Nora Seligman Favorov, New Haven: Yale University Press, 2014, xv+ 221," *Iran and the Caucasus* 20 (2), pp. 253–258.

Broers, Laurence (2020), "Cartographies of Consensus and Grievance: Visualising the Territory of Azerbaijan," *Europe-Asia Studies,* 72 (9), pp. 1–30.

Burke, Róisín (2020), "International Law in the Buffer: Nagorno-Karabakh and Intractable Territorial Disputes," *Journal of International Peacekeeping* 23 (3–4), pp. 249–302.

Carey, Seamus (2020), The NATO of the Indo-Pacific. *Guardian (Sydney),* 1941 (Retrieved from https://search.informit.com.au/documentSum mary;dn=549654037772094;res=IELAPA)

Chen, Sanping (2003), "From Azerbaijan to Dunhuang–A Zoroastrianism Note," *Central Asiatic Journal* 47 (2), pp. 183–197.

Dana, Léo-Paul (2000), "Change and Circumstance in Kyrgyz Markets," *Qualitative Market Research: An International Journal* 3 (2), pp. 62–73.

Dana, Léo-Paul (2005), *When Economies Change Hands: A Survey of Entrepreneurship in the Emerging Markets of Europe from the Balkans to the Baltic States,* New York: Routledge.

Dana, Léo-Paul (2007), *Asian Models of Entrepreneurship from the Indian Union and the Kingdom of Nepal to the Japanese Archipelago: Context, Policy, and Practice,* London, Singapore & Hong Kong: World Scientific.

Dana, Léo-Paul, and Teresa Dana (2003), "Management and Enterprise Development in Post-Communist Economies," *International Journal of Management and Enterprise Development* 1 (1), pp. 45–54.

Dana, Léo-Paul, and Richard W. Wright (2015), "Bazaar Economies, Modern Networks and Entrepreneurship," in Cary L. Cooper, ed., *Wiley Encyclopedia of Management,* New Jersey: John Wiley & Sons, pp. 1–7.

Davudova, Revana I. (2020), "A VECM Analysis of the Relations the CPI, PPI, GDP Per Capita, Exchange Rate in the Republic of Azerbaijan,"

Asian Journal of Economics, Business and Accounting 19 (3), pp. 22–46.

do Carmo Silva, Marcela, Helder Gomes Costa, and Gomes Carlos Francisco Simões (2020), "Multicriteria Decision Choices for Investment in Innovative Upper-Middle Income Countries," *Innovation & Management Review* 17 (3), pp. 321–347.

Doshmanli, Masoumeh, Yashar Salamzadeh, and Aidin Salamzadeh (2018), "Development of SMEs in an Emerging Economy: Does Corporate Social Responsibility Matter?," *International Journal of Management and Enterprise Development* 17 (2), pp. 168–191.

Ergun, Ayça, and Zana Çitak (2020), "Secularism and National Identity in Post-Soviet Azerbaijan," *Journal of Church and State* 62 (3), pp. 464–485.

Expert Group (2020), A Preliminary Assessment of the Impact of the COVID-19 Pandemic on Azerbaijani Economy, Center for Economic and Social Development, (Retrieved from https://ssrn.com/abstract=3676919, accessed 19 August 2020 or http://dx.doi.org/10.2139/ssrn.3676919)

Farajova, Malahat (2010, September), "Pleistocene Art in Azerbaijan," in Jean Clottes, ed., *L'art Pléistocene Dans Le Monde/Pleistocene Art of the World/Arte Pleistoceno En El Mundo,* Tarascon-Sur-Ariege: Actes Du Congres IFRAO, pp. 929e942.

Farrokh, Kaveh (2003), "A Case of Historical Misconceptions? — Congressman Rohrabacher's Letter to Hillary Clinton Regarding Azerbaijan," *Forum of EthnoGeoPolitics* 1 (1), pp. 9–30.

Feizullaev, Ahmet, Shaker Kocharli, and Abbasova, Samat (2020), "Oil and Gas Potential of Superimopsed Depressions in Azerbaijan," *Mining Science and Technology* 5 (2), pp. 72–81.

Gagoshidze, Iulon Knauß, and Florian Ilyas Babaev (2007), "An Achaemenid «Palace» At Qarajamirli (Azerbaijan) Preliminary Report On The Excavations In 2006," *Ancient Civilisations from Scythia to Siberia* 13 (1–2), pp. 31–45.

Ganbarov, Fuad, Gunay Alieva, and Babazade Isgender (2020), "The Role of Exchange Rates in Non-Oil Export Activity: Evidence from Azerbaijan," *Journal of Eastern European and Central Asian Research* 7 (3), pp. 340–350.

Genito, Bruno (1986), "The Medes A Reassessment of the Archaeological Evidence," *East and West* 36 (1–3), pp. 11–81.

Ghorbanpoor, Mahmood (2010), "Regional Position of Iran in Foreign Trade with Republic of Azerbaijan," *World Applied Sciences Journal* 9 (1), pp. 69–75.

Hasanov, Niyazi, and Nurkhodzha Akbulaev (2020), "Innovative Development of Key Sectors of Economy Based on the Creation of Technological Parks in the Republic of Azerbaijan," *New Trends and Issues Proceedings on Advances in Pure and Applied Sciences* 12, pp. 44–56.

Hoffman, David I. (1999), "Oil and Development in Post-Soviet Azerbaijan," *NBR ANALYSIS* 10, pp. 5–28.

Huseynov, Elchin Shahinovich, and Tunku Mohar Mokhtar (2019), "A Critique of Tadeusz Swietochowski's Works on the Azerbaijan Democratic Republic (1918–1920) Under the Prism of Edward Said's Orientalism," *IIUM Journal of Religion and Civilisational Studies* 2 (1), pp. 24–38.

Huseynova, Khatira, and Elmira Zeynalova (2015), "The Role Business Incubators in the Building Regional Innovation System," *The Business & Management Review* 6 (3), p. 190.

İbrahimova, Khayala (2019), "Influence of Innovations on Economic Development in Azerbaijan," *Academic Journal of Economic Studies* 5 (3), pp. 58–63.

Kashkay, Solmaz (1997), "The Material Culture in Azerbaijan During the Scythian Campaigns – A New Interpretation of Herodotus," *Altorientalische Forschungen* 24 (2), pp. 251–258.

Khan, Shazia Mehmood-Ul-Hassan (2014), "Black January: Day of Martyrs," *Defence Journal* 17 (7), pp. 1–26.

Lemercier-Quelquejay, Chantal (1984), "Islam and Identity in Azerbaijan," *Central Asian Survey* 3 (2), pp. 29–55.

Liberman, Sherri (2003), *A Historical Atlas of Azerbaijan,* New York, USA: The Rosen Publishing Group.

Mamoulia, Georges (2020), "Azerbaijan and the Transcaucasian Democratic Federative Republic: Historical Reality and Possibility," *Caucasus Survey* 8 (1), pp. 21–30.

Mkrtchyan, Tigran (2007), "Democratisation and the Conflict of Nagorno-Karabakh," *Turkish Policy Quarterly* 6 (3), pp. 79–92.

Mokari, Payam Ghaffarvand, and Stefan Werner (2017), "Azerbaijani," *Journal of the International Phonetic Association* 47 (2), pp. 207–212.

Mousavi, Ali, and Touraj Daryaee (2012), "The Sasanian Empire: An Archaeological Survey, c. 220–AD 640," *A Companion to the Archaeology of the Ancient Near East* 2, pp. 1076–1094.

Mukhtarov, Shahriyar, Jeyhun Mammadov, and Ahmadov Fariz (2019), "The Impact of Oil Prices on Inflation: The Case of Azerbaijan," *International Journal of Energy Economics and Policy* 9 (4), p. 97.

Nasirov, Gani (2013), "The City Built on Gold," *New Eastern Europe* 2 (7), pp. 131–135.

Orujov, Samir, Elnur Alakbarov, and Javid Maharramov (2019), "Econometric Assessment of the Effect of Small and Medium Enterprises on Economic Development (The ASE of Azerbaijan)," *Информация и инновации* 14 (2), pp. 35–42.

Peacock, Andrew C. S. (2015), *Great Seljuk Empire,* Edinburgh, United Kingdom: Edinburgh University Press.

Salamzadeh, Aidin (2018), "Start-Up Boom in an Emerging Market: A Niche Market Approach," in Datis Khajeheian, Mike Friedrichsen, and Wilfried Mödinger, eds., *Competitiveness in Emerging Markets,* Cham: Springer, pp. 233–243.

Salamzadeh, Aidin, Mohammad Ali Azimi, and David A. Kirby (2013), "Social Entrepreneurship Education in Higher Education: Insights from a Developing Country," *International Journal of Entrepreneurship and Small Business* 20 (1), pp. 17–34.

Salamzadeh, Aidin, Zahra Arasti, and Ghanbar Mohammadi Elyasi (2017), "Creation of ICT-Based Social Start-Ups in Iran: A Multiple Case Study," *Journal of Enterprising Culture* 25 (1), pp. 97–122.

Salamzadeh, Aidin, and Mirjana Radovic Markovic (2018), "Shortening the Learning Curve of Media Start-Ups in Accelerators: Case of a Developing Country," in Albert Gyamfi, and Idongesit Williams, eds., *Evaluating Media Richness in Organisational Learning*, IGI Global, pp. 36–48.

Scherberger, Max (2011). "The Confrontation between Sunni and Shi'i Empires: Ottoman-Safavid Relations between the Fourteenth and the Seventeenth Century," in Ofra Bengio, and Meir Litvak, eds., *The Sunna and Shi'a in History,* New York: Palgrave Macmillan, pp. 51–67.

Suleymanli, Kamran (2020), *The Azerbaijani Economy and the Development of Non-Oil Sector*, Master's Thesis, Politecnico Di Torino: Italy.

Swietochowski, Tadeusz (1999), "Azerbaijan: Perspectives from the Crossroads," *Central Asian Survey* 18 (4), pp. 419–434.

Tajpour, Mehdi, Elahe Hosseini, and Aidin Salamzadeh (2020), "The Effect of Innovation Components on Organisational Performance: Case of the Governorate of Golestan Province," *International Journal of Public Sector Performance Management* 6 (6), pp. 817–830.

Tugrul, Tugba Orten, and Kanan Karimli (2020), "The Evalution of Sustainable Development Policies of Azerbaijan Since Independence: A Four-Capital Model Approach," *Present Environment and Sustainable Development* 1, pp. 44–254.

Uceinov, Mehmet, Aziz Bretanitski, and Abdul Vahab Rahim oglu Salamzadeh (1963), *History of Azerbaijan Architecture*, Moscow.

Uslu, Ramazan, and Nuri Ok (2013), "Common Cultural and Spiritual Values, and the Role of Historical Factors in the Development of Azerbaijan–Turkey Economic Relations," *West East Journal of Social Sciences* 2 (2), pp. 109–116.

Vacca, Alison (2015), "Nisbas of the North: Muslims from Armenia, Caucasian Albania, and Azerbaijan in Arabic Biographical Dictionaries (4th-7th centuries AH)," *Arabica* 62 (4), pp. 521–550.

Vagnini, Alessandro (2012), "Great War in Transcaucasia: From Ottoman Occupation to the Treaty of Kars," *Mediterranean Journal of Social Sciences* 3, pp. 93–112.

Yusifova, Shabnam (2014), "The Recognition of the Independence of Azerbaijan Democratic Republic in Paris Peace Conference and the Attitude of Iran," *Mediterranean Journal of Social Sciences* 5 (19), pp. 355–355.

Zarinebaf, Fariba (2019), "Azerbaijan between Two Empires: A Contested Borderland in the Early Modern Period (Sixteenth–Eighteenth Centuries)," *Iranian Studies* 52 (3–4), pp. 299–337.

Zeynalli, Latif (2020), "The Impact of Stimulating the Development of Human Capital on Economic Development," *European Journal of Social Impact and Circular Economy* 1 (1b), pp. 38–52.

Zourabian, Levon (2006), "The Nagorno-Karabakh Settlement Revisited: Is Peace Achievable?," *Demokratizatsiya* 14 (2), pp. 1–11.

Zulfigarov, Farid, and Matthias Neuenkirch (2019), "Azerbaijan and Its Oil Resources: Curse or Blessing?" *Universitat Trier, Research Papers in Economics* No. 11/19. (Retrieved from https://ssrn.com/abstract=3391732, accessed 21 May 2019 or http://dx.doi.org/10.2139/ssrn.3391732)

Chapter 7

The Context for Business in Georgia

Irine Guruli & Giorgi Ormotsadze

Abstract: The single best condition defining Georgia's past, present and future is its location. From being the trade route to being the battleground, or being the land for mediation, Georgian soil has seen it all. Multiculturalism has been one of the key characteristics of Georgia's existence. Trade and exchange of goods have been an integral part of building the Georgina identity since the late bronze age. Bazaars have played a major role in developing the nation. Modern Georgia readopted liberal policies and once again recommitted itself towards international trade and partnerships. The future of Georgia rests in the Georgians' ability to reside and blend into the multicultural environment, encourage economic adaptation and modernise the existing markets to better meet global tendencies.

Keywords: Orthodox Christianity, transition economy

Introduction

Georgia (in Georgian *Sakartvelo*) is a Transcaucasian country located on the Black Sea's eastern bank and the southern flanks of the Great Caucasian Mountains. Alongside the Black Sea, four countries border: Russia from the north and northeast, Azerbaijan from the east and southeast, and Armenia and Turkey from the south. The capital of Georgia is Tbilisi (Map of Georgia can be seen on Exhibit 7.1).

The area of Georgia is 69,700 km^2 (Government of Georgia, 2020a). More than 81.3% of the territory of Georgia is located above 400 m, and 55% above 1000 m (Bondyrev et al., 2015). The general extent of the borders of Georgia is about 1916 km. Georgia is subdivided into nine regions

Exhibit 7.1   Map 3780 of Georgia; courtesy of the United Nations

(Samegrelo-Zemo Svaneti, Guria, Imereti, Racha-Lechkhumi and Kvemo Svaneti, Samtskhe-Javakheti, Shida Kartli, Mtskheta-Mtianeti, Kvemo Kartli and Kakheti) and two autonomous republics (Abkhazia and Adjara); See Exhibit: 7.2. After the Soviet Union's dissolution, conflicts erupted in the autonomous republics of Georgia, namely the Republic of Abkhazia and Tskhinvali region (South Ossetia). After Russian invasion on Georgia's territory in 2008, the Russian Federation recognised the self-declared independence of Abkhazia and the Tskhinvali regions. According to the Georgian law, these territories and territorial waters are titled "the occupied territories". None of them is recognised by the international community and practice the de-facto state status (Government of Georgia, 2020b).

A major part of the territory of Georgia has a subtropical climate. Due to the uneven nature of the Georgian landscape, the average temperature varies significantly. In January temperature fluctuates from +3°C to −2°C, and in July it varies from +26°C to 27°C in the flat parts of Georgia. In the mountains, the temperature sharply falls to −18°C in January and rises to +12°C in July. Similarly the average precipitation varies from 300 mm in the east to 2800 mm in the west. The western part of the country and

Exhibit 7.2 View of Batumi, Georgia; photo courtesy of Grisha Bruev used under Shutterstock license

the high mountains seem to have a tendency towards warming, but it is overshadowed by the influence of the Black Sea (Bondyrev et al., 2015).

According to the National Statistics Office of Georgia (Geostat) Georgian population by 1 January 2020 equals 3.7 million people. Since 1994, Georgia's population has been declining steadily (from 4.9 million); however, the recent years demonstrate that the slope of decline was plateaued and the population of Georgia remains stagnant (National Statistics Office of Georgia, 2020d). Furthermore, Georgia has recorded a negative index of migration for several years. On average, 2.2 people per thousand migrated from Georgia from 2013 to 2019 (National Statistics Office of Georgia, 2020d). According to the 2014 census, 86.8% of the Georgian population is ethnically Georgian. The largest ethnic minority groups are Azeris – 6.3%, followed by Armenians – 4.5%; Russians – 0.7%; Ossetians – 0.4%; Yazidis – 0.3%; Ukrainians – 0.2%; Kists – 0.2%; Greeks – 0.1%; and Assyrians – 0.1% (National Statistics Office of Georgia, 2016).

Historically, Georgia was located on the intersection of the trade routes between Europe and Asia – East and West. Furthermore, Georgia was placed on the borderline of two great civilisations – Christianity and Islam and for centuries attracted the interest of the major empires. Hence the Georgian culture carries both Asian and European characteristics. Georgia does not have an official religion. However, most of the population is Orthodox Christian (83.4%). The largest religious minorities are Muslims – 10.7%, followed by Armenian Apostolic – 2.9%; Catholics – 0.5%; Jehovah's Witnesses – 0.3%; Yazidis - 0.2%; and Protestants – 0.1% (National Statistics Office of Georgia, 2016).

According to Article 8 of the Constitution, Georgia's official language is Georgian (Constitution of Georgia, 2010). The Georgian literary tradition, in the form of inscriptions, dates back to the 5th century. The New Georgian literary language originated in the secular literature of the 12th century; it became fully established in the middle of the 19th century. Until the beginning of the 19th century, Old Georgian was used for religious purposes (Tikkanen, Amy and Team of Editors of Encyclopedia, 2016).

During the Soviet rule, Georgian heraldry was largely suppressed; however, with the regained independence, it was revived. The modern history of Georgia records two flags. The first was used during 1918–1921 and 1990–2004 and the second one from 2004 till today. The first flag was cherry red with a canton of black and white stripes. Cherry red was (and still is) considered the national colour; black stood for the tragedies of the past, white for hopes for the future. The 1918–1921 flag was readopted on 14 November 1990, and independence was again proclaimed on 9 April 1991 (Smith, 2011). The modern flag consists of five red crosses (the Cross of St. George and four smaller ones). The design of the flag came from medieval Georgia and was reintroduced in 2004 after the change of the government. Another important piece of Georgian heraldry is the coat of arms of Georgia. It is partly based on the medieval arms of the Georgian royal house. It portrays Saint George on the silver horse with the silver spear on the red shield. The shield is crowned with the Iberian (Georgian) crown and is supported by two golden lions. Below the shield is the silver field with the writing "Strength is in Unity" ("ძალა ერთობაშია") (Parliament of Georgia, 2004).

Georgia is the parliamentary representative democratic republic with a multi-party system. The President of Georgia is the ceremonial head of state while the Prime Minister of Georgia is the head of the government (Constitution of Georgia, 2010). The executive powers are practised by the Government and the President of Georgia. Legislative power is vested in both the Government and the unicameral Parliament of Georgia (Nakashidze, 2016). The National Currency of Georgia is Georgian Lari, which replaced the coupon currency on 2 October 1995. "Lari", the name chosen for the basic monetary unit of the Georgian national currency, is an old Georgian word denoting a hoard or property (National Bank of Georgia, 2020).

Though the modern history of Georgia few names defined the political development of the country. Initially, it was Zviad Gamsakhurdia, the first president of the Republic of Georgia. He was in charge of the freedom movement from The Soviet Union. Even though his presidency was cut short and lasted less than a year, his legacy had a major effect on Georgian politics

(Nodia, 1996). The second president of Georgia was Eduard Shevardnadze, who became the head of state from 1995. Politics of Shevardnadze was controversial. He was in charge of the state through the harshest years of Georgia's modern history. In 2003 as the result of the Rose revolution, Shevardnadze left the position and politics (Geyer, 2010). In the aftermath of Rose Revolution, Mikheil Saakashvili became the third president of Georgia. His domestic and international policies were bold and pro-Western (Dana et al., 1999). Saakashvili had strong support from the Western partners who assisted Georgia's liberal reforms. However, Saakashvili's popularity started to quickly shrink after the 2008 war and human rights violations. In 2012, united opposition under the aegis of "Georgian Dream" came to power. The opposition was led by the Georgian billionaire Bidzina Ivanishvili, who since then left official positions but still remains as the key figure on the Georgian political landscape and the leader of the governing party. Meanwhile, Georgian Dream is still the majority political party forming the governance (Oravec and Holland, 2019). After 2020 parliamentary elections, the country entered into a political crisis, with the opposition parties boycotting to enter the parliament. On December 11 the first plenary session was held with the representation of only the ruling party members. As a result, for the first time in the history of independent Georgia, the country functions with one-party parliament as of now.

Historical Context

The geographical location of Georgia has played a major role in forging the Georgian identity and culture. Located on the verge of East and West, Georgian culture has been developed as the counter-response of the influences from the Eastern and Western superpowers. Tracing back to BC, the history of the Georgian people starts with the Colchis and Iberian tribes. Centuries of war and peace have transformed small state under the Caucasus mountains into the home for various ethnic, linguistic and confessional groups. The modern history of Georgia starts on 26 May 1918, when the Democratic Republic of Georgia was founded (Janelidze, 2018; Jones, 2014). On 26 May 1918, the National Council was elected by the Georgian National Congress, and the Act of Independence was adopted. The newly founded nation remained independent for a brief period of time. On 25 February 1921, Tbilisi, was occupied by the Red Army (Natmelidze et al., 2012). The occupation lasted for 99 years, and Georgia regained its independence only on 9 April 1991 (Supreme Council of the Republic of Georgia, 1991). Since regaining independence, two separate wars have been fought on the Georgian soil, both of them causing the loss of territories and creation of the de-facto states – Abkhazia and South Ossetia. Moreover, the collapse of the Soviet Union and regained independence were not enough to fully escape the Russian influence. In both wars, in Abkhazia and Samachablo, Russia was involved openly. In both cases, it was supporting the separatists' movements and justifying them. The war in Abkhazia started on 14 August 1992, and ended on 27 September 1993. Georgia lost *de jure* control over Abkhazia. However, till today, Georgia claims that Abkhazia is an area occupied by Russia. Abkhazia's self-proclaimed independence is recognised only by Russia, Syria, Venezuela, Nicaragua and Nauru. The rest of the international community supports the Georgian position (Bursulaia, 2020; Hewitt, 2014). Similarly, on 7 August 2020, Georgian troops entered South Ossetia's breakaway region as the response to the violence and unauthorised military actions. Georgian military forces managed to fight their way through the Ossetian forces till the capital Tskinvali, although Georgian forces were stunned finding themselves to fight against Russian Army troops (which had been quietly moving into the region for several days). After five days, when the war was over, Russia ejected Georgian military forces from South Ossetia (Cheterian, 2009; Hamilton, 2018; Lanskoy and Areshidze, 2008).

The geopolitical order of the region disabled Georgia to achieve the Western aspirations its counterpart from the Baltic state managed to attain in 2004 in the form of EU and NATO memberships. However, since 1991 Georgia has been expressing its commitment towards the Western values, and today it remains the close partner and ally for both the European Union and NATO.

One of the major milestones on Georgia's path towards NATO membership was the Bucharest Summit held on 3 April 2020. On the summit, NATO member states agreed and issued the statement that Georgia and Ukraine would become members of the organisation.

> "NATO welcomes Ukraine's and Georgia's Euro-Atlantic aspirations for membership in NATO. We agreed today that these countries will become members of NATO ... MAP is the next step for Ukraine and Georgia on their direct way to membership" (Bucharest Summit Declaration, 2008)

Currently, Georgia is the NATO aspirant country. It is actively involved in NATO initiatives and contributes to the NATO missions all around the globe. Georgia is one of the largest non-member state contributors to the NATO mission in Afghanistan (North Atlantic Treaty Organization, 2014).

The cornerstone for Georgia–EU relations was the Association Agreement signed on 27 June 2014. The agreement entered into force on 1 July 2016. Agreement introduced a preferential trade regime for Georgia. The Deep and Comprehensive Free Trade Area (DCFTA) is the regime that enables Georgia to access the EU market with zero import tariff (Association Agreement, 2014).

Due to the location and multicultural nature, Georgia has been an active participant of the economic and trade relations within the region and beyond. Since the late Bronze Age, Georgians have been present on the great silk road (Hauptmann and Klein, 2009). Historical traces demonstrate that trade centres and bazaars started to appear on Georgian land from the Medieval Times (Javakhishvili, 1930). Throughout medieval times, crossroads of the trade routes and meeting places of the different ethnic groups became the locations where major Georgian cities started to flourish (Khutsishvili, 2018). International trade was essential for peace and prosperity. Hence, Georgian kings were eager to support it. Bazaars and markets allowed multicultural populations to reside peacefully. Georgian markets were attracting traders from the whole Caucasus. Even during the difficult periods, bazaars on the Georgian soil remained as the peaceful places for meeting and trade. Sadakhlo bazaar on the border of Georgia, Armenia and Azerbaijan did not stop functioning even during the war between Armenia and Azerbaijan (Dabaghyan and Gabrielyan, 2011). Similarly, Ergneti market in Tskhinvali remained an active trade hub even after Georgian relations with South Ossetia became complicated (Closson, 2010; Freese, 2005).

Trade markets and bazaars were highly favoured in medieval Georgia; however, conditions started to change with the Soviet rule. Soviet elite intended to abolish the private economical entities and build the socialist economy. However, compared to the rest of the Soviet Union, the Caucasian traders were in a favourable position and to some extent remained exemption to the rule (Khutsishvili, 2018). During the Soviet times privately organised economic activities were forbidden, although such activates were never fully abolished in the Caucasus. Traders from Georgia and neighbouring countries were known as merchants and vendors trading in Moscow and other cities of USSR, through both formal and informal means. Flowers, fruits and vegetables were the most common products sold by the Georgian vendors in Soviet cities (Sik and Wallace, 1999). The trade chains remained rather durable after the collapse of the

Soviet Union. Till today Russia remains a significant trade destination for the Georgian exporters of the agricultural products. According to the gross output 2019, 11.6% of the Georgian economy is made up of wholesale and retail trade, and repair of motor vehicles and motorcycles. Trade and repair sector employs 15% of formally employed in Georgia (Geostat); the number is a lot higher if self-employed are taken into account.

There are some notable active bazaars in Georgia, one of which is Deserter Market (Exhibit 7.3). It is currently the central market in Tbilisi. The name came from the 1920s when the soldiers were buying their harnesses, weapons and other items in the market area. The old Deserter Market building, built in the 1960s, was demolished in 2007, but it still functions in its original form today. Deserter markets niche is the agricultural product. Although it is not limited only with agricultural products and anything can be found if such need arises. Meanwhile, one of the most artsy and interesting markets in Tbilisi is the Dry Bridge Market (Exhibit 7.4), which is located in the centre of Tbilisi. The mixture of a flea market with the arts defines the characteristic of the Dry Bridge Bazaar. It attracts tourists as the goods sold on the market are the reflection of the Georgian history. Artefacts from soviet times alongside with the replicas of Georgia's medieval art create the eclectic nature of the market and make

Exhibit 7.3 Deserter Market in Tbilisi, Georgia; photo courtesy of Grisha Bruev used under Shutterstock license

Exhibit 7.4 Dry Bridge Market in Tbilisi, Georgia; photo courtesy of Magdalena Paluchowska used under Shutterstock license

it one of the must-see sights for international visitors. Dry Bridge market's one of the names is *the market of memories*, which perfectly describes the emotional nature of the place. Another touristic destination bazaar is Maidani, which is located in the city centre on the most touristy location of the capital (Exhibit 7.5 and 7.6). Unlike the Dry Bridge, Maidani does not offer customers second-hand goods but rather specialises on the souvenirs and authentic Georgian goods.

Open markets and bazaar still remain an integral part of Georgians' everyday economy. According to the National Statistics Office of Georgia in 2019, there were up to 208 markets in Georgia. Most of them are located in Tbilisi (30.8%). Furthermore, daily trade is carried out in 163 markets, while 19 of them are organised on Sundays. Length of the stands reach 53.1 thousand metres. Georgian markets offer costumers a wide variety of products; in 2019, 32.2% of the economic actors engaged in trading on the Georgian bazaars were selling only non-food goods (Awang et al., 2016). Currently, in Georgia, there is only one market that trades only with food goods, three markets trading with cars and five markets trading livestock.

Exhibit 7.5 Old Town Tbilisi, Georgia; photo courtesy of Iryna Hromotska used under Shutterstock license

Exhibit 7.6 Old Town Tbilisi, Georgia; photo courtesy of Monticello used under Shutterstock license

All the other markets have mixed products. There are 55.7 thousand daily trade places and on average 45.1 thousand sellers on the Georgian markets. Economic agents engaged in the organisation of bazaars amounted $50 million in income in 2019 (National Statistics Office of Georgia, 2019).

Context for Enterprise and Implications for Doing Business

According to the World Bank classification, Georgia is an upper-middle-income country in Eastern Europe. The country embarked on a road to transition to democratisation and market liberalisation after regaining independence in 1991. Larger-scale reforms and transformations started after the rose revolution in 2003, resulting in the World Bank's Top Reformer in the Region title.

By looking at the GDP composition, one can assume that Georgia lacks activities in high value-added sectors that translate into a narrow export base. As of 2019, the largest shares in the GDP were made up of manufacturing and trade sectors.

Conventional sectors of agriculture and businesses such as metal are not sufficient to back Georgia's integration within the exceedingly competitive worldwide economy. New sectors such as tourism and transportation started to emerge in recent years, but the global pandemic in 2020 already had a harsh effect on both, and it is unlikely that those sectors will recover swiftly.

The country mainly struggles to mobilise both domestic and foreign investments for supporting growth. Various studies concluded that job market also represents a challenge with high levels of unemployment and underemployment. Almost half of the country's labour force is engaged in the agricultural sector, which produces only 7.7% of GDP (National Statistics Office of Georgia, 2020a). Exhibit 7.7 gives a snapshot of key economic indicators for Georgia.

The World Bank acknowledges Georgia as one of the easiest countries to do business (World Bank Group, 2020). Steady reforms of the economic liberalisation from 2003 enabled Georgia to have liberal laws, procedures and taxes for the entrepreneurs (Dana, 2011; Dana and Ramadani, 2015). Due to the small size, the Georgian economy is highly dependent on international trade. Deepening trade relations, boosting and diversifying the Georgian export base has been the priority of the Government of Georgia (GoG) for the past decade, evidence of this is the successfully completed FTAs with EU (in 2014), EFTA countries (in 2016), China (in 2018), with ongoing negotiations with the United States, Israel and India. With the negative trade balance of US$5.7 billion (as of 2019) export remains the priority for the Georgian government. State policies are adopted to encourage the entrepreneurs to produce in Georgia and then export to the international markets. Furthermore, Georgian export has been supported not only by the local actors but also by the international community. Although,

Key Economic Indicators for Georgia	
Population in thousands (2019)	3718.2 (Urban 59%; Rural 41%)
Gross Domestic Product (GDP) at current prices, mil. USD (2018)	16,207.1
GDP per capita (at current prices) USD (2018)	4345.5
Share of the population under the absolute Poverty line (2019)	19.5%
Unemployment rate (2019)	17.6%
Self-employed as percentage of employed (2019)	30.7%
FDI inflows as percent of GDP (2016)	9%
Remittance inflow as percent of GDP (2019)	12.9%

Exhibit 7.7 Key Indicators of Georgia. Data were extracted from the web pages of the National Office of Statistics of Georgia and the World Bank

recent years have demonstrated the growth for both import and export in Georgia, while the trade balance remained more stagnant, over US$5 billion. Furthermore, the share of the import in turnover has been reduced from 77.5% in 2016 to 70.6% in 2019, while the value of export rose from 22.5% (2016) to 29.4% (2019) (National Statistic Office of Georgia, 2020) (Exhibit 7.8).

Strong historical ties alongside with the logistical conveniences define the list of destinations for the Georgian export. Russia, Azerbaijan, Armenia and Turkey still remain as one of the leading destinations for Georgian goods (Batrancea et al., 2019). While export to the CIS (The Commonwealth of Independent States) countries (including Ukraine) equals 54% of total export. European Union is also one of the major partners for Georgia, and the annual export in 2019 topped over US$800 million (22% of Georgia's export). Largest exporting destinations for Georgian exporters in 2019 were Azerbaijan (13%), Russia (13%), Armenia (11%), Ukraine (7%), Bulgaria (7%), China (6%) and Turkey (5%).

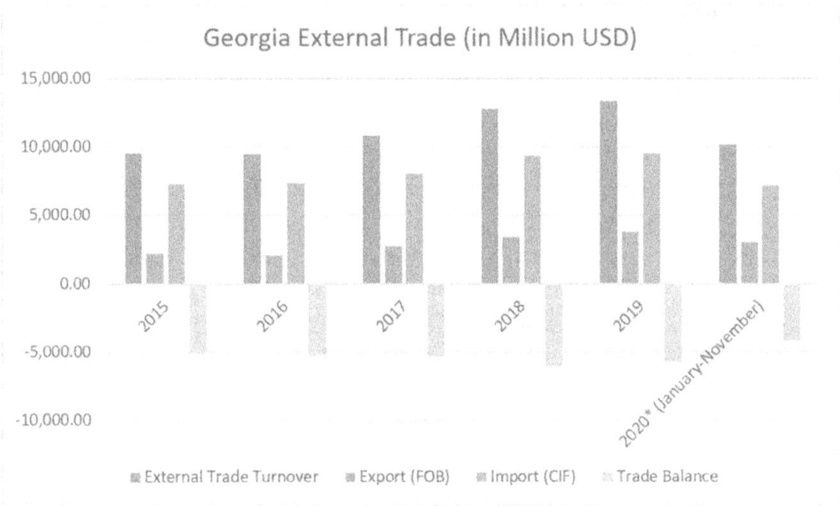

Exhibit 7.8 External Trade. Data were extracted from the National Office of Statistics of Georgia (National Bank of Georgia, 2020)

Equaling US$686.7 million or 18.2% of total exports motor vehicles were the most exported product from Georgia in 2019. A large majority of exported motor vehicles are re-exported from Georgia into landlocked neighbouring countries such as Armenia and Azerbaijan. The exports of copper ores and concentrates totalled US$651.6 million, and their share in the total exports amounted to 17.3%. Third on the list of the top exported products was Ferro-alloys with the value US$303.0 million, constituting 8.0% of the total exports, while wine and fresh grapes were the fourth most exported product from Georgia with a value of US$222.9 million (4.6%)

Leading importers in Georgia are Turkey (18%), Russia (11%), China (10%), Azerbaijan (6%), Germany (5%), Ukraine (5%) and the United States (4%). Two major groups of countries contributing to the Georgian import are CIS and EU. However, the disparity among the two is smaller compared to the export. In 2019, Georgian imports from CIS countries totalled US$2.4 billion (26.9%) while the value of imported goods from EU equalled US$2.2 billion (25.6%).

The large share of Georgian imports is petroleum and petroleum oils. Georgia has limited oil resources. Hence it is imported from abroad. In 2019, the value of imported petroleum was US$756.9 million (8.4%). Followed by motor vehicles US$653 million (7.2%) most of which are re-exported to the neighbouring countries. Copper ores and concentrates were the third most imported product with a value of US$603.7 million (6.7%). The fourth was pharmaceuticals with a value of US$355.4 million (3.9%).

An important aspect for ensuring economic growth and development is related to the inflow of Foreign Direct Investments (FDI). Georgia is highly dependent on the inflows of foreign capital. After regaining independence, the inflow of foreign investments played an important role in Georgia's Transition into the market-based economy (Silagadze and Zubiashvili, 2016; Charaia et al., 2020). In 2019 FDI in Georgia amounted to US$1.3 billion 0.3% more than in 2018. However, it falls short compared to the numbers recorded in 2017 (National Statistics Office of Georgia, 2020b) (Exhibit 7.9).

Major investors in Georgia in 2019 were the United Kingdom (18%), Turkey (13.4%); Ireland (10.2%), the United States (8.5%), Netherlands (7.7%), Panama (5.9%), Luxembourg (5.3%); China (3.3%) and Japan (3%). The share of the three largest investors in total FDI reached 41.6%. Notably, the United Kingdom and Netherland have been among the largest investors in Georgia for the last three years.

Meanwhile the economic sectors attracting the most foreign investments were the Financial Sector (20.8%); Energy Sector (20%); Transports and Communication (9.7%); Hotels and Restaurants (9.2%),

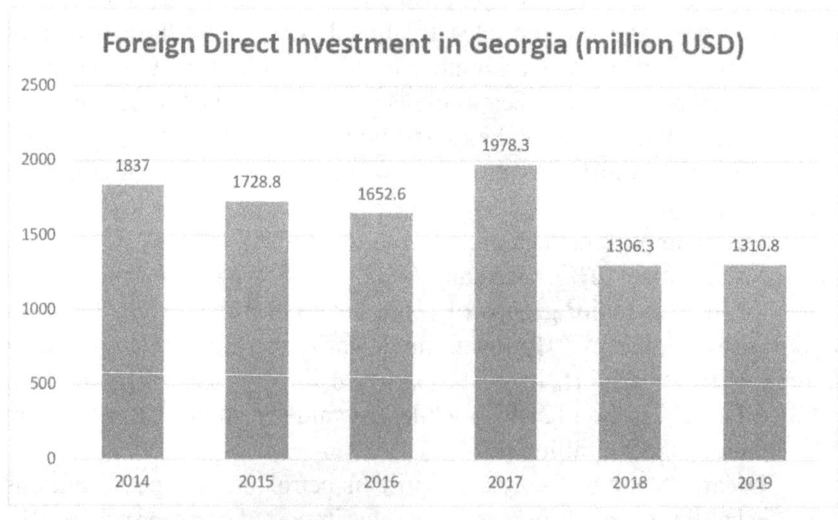

Exhibit 7.9 FDI Tendencies. Data were extracted from the web page of National Statistics Office of Georgia (National Statistics Office of Georgia, 2020c)

Manufacturing (8.8%); Mining (4%); Construction (2.7%); Health and Social Work (1%); Real Estate (0.7%). The energy sector has been one of the most attractive sectors for international investors in Georgia since 2013. On the other hand, Construction, and Transport and Communication have recorded reduced interest among the investors and the inflow of the foreign recourses has decreased in recent years compared to the numbers from 2015 to 2017.

Towards the Future

Even the most brilliant past is not a guarantee of a successful future. Georgian's historical memory keeps the record of glory and prosperity, as well as decades of oppression, war and hardship. It is hard to foresee what the future holds for Georgia; however, the readiness of Georgian society and economy for the future transformations and challenges can be assessed and explained.

Reforms undertaken during the course of the past years and steps taken towards EU integration involved significant changes for the Georgian economy as a whole. These changes brought simplification and improvement of the business environment and presented opportunities by the opening of new markets and new possibilities. However, like other similar countries (Anggadwita and Palalić, 2020; Dana, 2005; Palalić et al., 2018; Ramadani et al., 2018; Salamzadeh and Dana, 2020), further reforms and steps need to be taken towards achieving an increased capacity of Georgian entrepreneurs to become sources of innovation, job creation and sustainable economic development. Some of the key challenges Georgian economy faces are the following: further development of the business and investment environment, labour market and renovation of the infrastructure. Without, solving or at least improving the mentioned conditions, Georgia would fail to compete with more developed economies.

Covid-19 pandemic resulted in heavy economic and social implications (Kawamorita et al., 2020). Projections of international organisations are quite pessimistic, projecting shrinkage of Georgian economy by at least 5%. Given the structure of the Georgian economy, the dominance of the informal sector, lack of diversification and low innovation levels made the impact even harsher. The largest negative impact is projected for commodity exporters and those engaged in the tourism sector. Lockdown measures implemented by the government as a response to minimise the Covid-19 spread strongly affected the normal functioning of enterprises and bazaars. Economic turnaround will be a hard path to walk, especially due to the need for a substantial technological shift (Doshmanli et al., 2018; Salamzadeh, 2018). Many economic activities were not just paused; it will be challenging to get back to normal. Given the fact that the country is dominated by small enterprises, and the role of informal employment is significant, dependence on cash is heavy and the level of technological development is low, the movement of cash flow (including international receipts) is of crucial importance for all economic sectors in order to prevent them from suffering permanent long-term damage.

Opportunities ahead are related to the utilisation of international partnership agreements and making use of the unique nature of being located on the verge of East and West, and are related with both Christian and Muslim cultures, which enables Georgians to adapt to the multicultural nature of the future. This will be fostered through heavy investment in infrastructural projects and promoting international joint ventures, knowledge and information transfers. Lastly, the historical memory of being the trade route is the cultural advantage Georgian's should encourage, however, the low added value created on the domestic bazaars is not enough for the future development; hence economic adaptation and modernisation of the existing markets are required for better future.

References

Anggadwita, G., and R. Palalić (2020). "Entrepreneurship in Indonesia: some contextual aspects," in Paresha Sinha, Jenny Gibb, Michèle Akoorie, and Jonathan M. Scott, eds., *Research Handbook on Entrepreneurship in Emerging Economies.* Cheltenham, UK: Edward Elgar Publishing. doi: https://doi.org/10.4337/9781788973717.00018

Association Agreement (2014), Brussels: EUR-Lex, (Retrieved from https://eur-lex.europa.eu/legal-content/EN/TXT/?uri=CELEX: 02014A0830(02)-20180601)

Awang, Amran, Shazwani Amran, Mohamad Niza Md Nor, Ilyani Ibrahim, and Mohd Fazly Mohd Razali (2016), "Individual Entrepreneurial Orientation Impact on Entrepreneurial Intention: Intervening Effect of PBC and Subjective Norm," *Journal of Entrepreneurship, Business and Economics* 4 (2), pp. 94–129.

Batrancea, Larissa, Anca Nichita, Jerome Olsen, Christoph Kogler, Erich Kirchler, Erik Hoelzl, Avi Weiss, et al. (2019), "Trust and Power as

Determinants of Tax Compliance Across 44 Nations," *Journal of Economic Psychology* 74, p. 102191.

Bondyrev, Igor, Zurab Davitashvili, and Vijay Singh (2015), *The Georgrapy of Georgia Problems and Perspectives,* London: Springer.

Bucharest Summit Declaration (2008), Heads of State and Government Participating in the Meeting of the North Atlantic Council in Bucharest, (Retrieved from https://www.nato.int/cps/en/natolive/official_texts_8443.htm)

Bursulaia, Guranda (2020), The Voices of Silence: The Case of Georgian History Textbooks. *Caucasus Survey* 8, pp. 1–16.

Charaia, Vakhtang, Archil Chochia, and Mariam Lashkhi (2020), "The Impact of FDI on Economic Development: The Case of Georgia," *TalTech Journal of European Studies* 10 (2), pp. 96–116.

Cheterian, V. (2009), "The August 2008 War in Georgia: From Ethnic Conflict to Border Wars," *Central Asian Survey* 28 (2), pp. 155–170.

Closson, Stacy (2010), "Networks of Profit in Georgia's," *Journal of Intervention and Statebuilding* 4 (2), pp. 179–204.

Constitution of Georgia (2010, October 15), Parliament of Georgia, (Retrieved from: https://matsne.gov.ge/en/document/download/30346/35/en/pdf)

Dabaghyan, Artak, and Mkhitar Gabrielyan (2011), "Rural Transcaucasian Trade before and after National Borders," *Acta Ethnographica Hungarica* 56 (2), pp. 333–357.

Dana, Léo-Paul (2005), *When Economies Change Hands: A Survey of Entrepreneurship in the Emerging Markets of Europe from the Balkans to the Baltic States*, New York, Routledge.

Dana, Léo-Paul, ed. (2011), *World Encyclopedia of Entrepreneurship*, Cheltenham, UK, Edward Elgar.

Dana, Léo-Paul, Hamid Etemad, and Richard W. Wright (1999), "The Impact of Globalisation on SMEs," *Global Focus* 11 (4), pp. 93–106.

Dana, Léo-Paul, and Veland Ramadani (2015), "Context and Uniqueness of Transition Economies," in Léo-Paul Dana, and Veland Ramadani, eds., *Family Businesses in Transition Economies,* Cham: Springer, pp. 39–69.

Doshmanli, Mansoureh, Yashar Salamzadeh, and Aidin Salamzadeh (2018), "Development of SMEs in an Emerging Economy: Does Corporate Social Responsibility Matter?" *International Journal of Management and Enterprise Development* 17 (2), pp. 168–191.

Freese, Theresa (2005), "A Report from the Field: Georgia's War against Contraband and the Struggle for Territorial Integrity," *SAIS Review of International Affairs* 25 (1), pp. 107–121.

Geyer, Georgie Anne (2010), "Conversations with Eduard Shevardnadze," *The Washington Quarterly* 23 (2), pp. 55–66.

Government of Georgia (2020a), Regions of Georgia, web page of the Government of Georgia (Retrieved from: http://gov.ge/index.php?lang_id=geo&sec_id=419)

Government of Georgia (2020b), About Georgia, web page of Government of Georgia, (Retrieved from http://gov.ge/index. php?lang_id=ENG&sec_id=193)

Hamilton, Robert E. (2018), *August 2008 and Everything After,* Philadelphia: The Foreign Policy Research Institute.

Hauptmann, Andreas, and Sabine Klein (2009), "Bronze Age Gold in Southern Georgia. Archeo Sciences," *Revue d'archéométrie* 33, pp. 75–82.

Hewitt, George (2014), "History of the Context of the Georgian-Abkhazian Conflict," *Iran and the Cuacasus* 18 (3), pp. 289–314.

Janelidze, Otar (2018), "The Democratic Republic of Georgia (1918–1921)," *Remembrance and Justice (pamięć i sprawiedliwość)* 31 (1), pp. 168–189.

Javakhishvili, Ivane (1930), *Georgia's Economic History,* Tbilisi: Georgian Book (ქართული წიგნი).

Jones, Stephen F. (2014), *The Making of Modern Georgia, 1918-2012,* New York: Routledge.

Kawamorita, Hiroko, Aidin Salamzadeh, Kursat Demiryurek, and Mahyar Ghajarzadeh (2020), "Entrepreneurial Universities in Times of Crisis: Case of COVID-19 Pandemic," *Journal of Entrepreneurship, Business and Economics* 8 (1), pp. 77–88.

Khutsishvili, Ketevan (2018), *Marketplaces: Meeting Places in Border Zones of Georgia,* Tbilisi: VolkswagenStiftung.

Lanskoy, Miriam, and Giorgi Areshidze (2008), "Georgia's Year of Turmoil," *Journal of Democracy* 19 (4), pp. 154–168.

Nakashidze, Malkhaz (2016), "Semi-presidentalism in Georgia," in Robert Elgie and Sophia Moestrup, eds., *Semi-Presidentialism in the Caucasus and Central Asia* (pp. 119–142), London: Springer Nature.

National Bank of Georgia (2020), nbg.gov.ge, (Retrieved from https://nbg.gov.ge/en)

National Statistics Office of Georgia (2016), *2014 General Population Census Main Results,* Tbilisi: National Statistics Office of Georgia (GEOSTAT).

National Statistics Office of Georgia (2019), *Activities of Economic Agents Engaged in Organization of Markets in 2019,* (Retrieved from https://www.geostat.ge/en/single-news/1899/information-on-activities-of-economic-agents-engaged-in-organization-of-markets-2019

National Statistic Office of Georgia (2020a), *External Merchandised Trade in Georgia 2019,* Tbilis: National Statistic Office of Georgia, (Retrieved from https://www.geostat.ge/media/28996/saqonlit-sagareo-vachroba-saqartveloshi-20.01.2020-%28eng%29.pdf)

National Statistic Office of Georgia (2020b), Geostat.ge, (Retrieved from https://www.geostat.ge/en/modules/categories/41/population)

National Statistics Office of Georgia (2020c), *Foreign Direct Investment in Georgia 2019,* Tbilisi: National Statistics Office of Georgia, (Retrieved from https://www.geostat.ge/media/32981/FDI-in-2019_17.08.2020.pdf)

National Statistics Office of Georgia (2020d), Number of Population, Tbilisi, National Statistics Office of Georgia (Retrieved from https://www.geostat.ge/media/30991/Number-of-Population-2020.01.01.pdf)

Natmelidze, Memet, Akin Bendiani Svili, and Alishka Daushvili (2012), *Georgia in XIX–XX Centuries,* Tbilisi: Palitra.

Nodia, Ghia (1996), Political Turmoil in Georgia and the Ethnic Policies of Zviad Gamsakhurdia. *Contested Borders in the Caucasus,* pp. 73–89, (Retrieved from https://www.vub.be/sites/vub/files/nieuws/users/bcoppiet/129nodia.pdf)

North Atlantic Treaty Organization (2014), NATO-Georgia Relations, (Retrieved from https://www.nato.int/nato_static_fl2014/assets/pdf/pdf_2014_04/20140331_140401-media-backgrounder-georg.pdf)

Oravec, Phillip, and Edward C. Holland (2019), "The Georgian Dream? Outcomes from the Summer of Protest," *Demokratizatsiya: The Journal of Post-Soviet Democratisation* 27 (2), pp. 249–256.

Palalic, Ramo, Léo-Paul Dana, and Veland Ramadani, eds. (2018), *Entrepreneurship in Former Yugoslavia: Diversity, Institutional Constraints and Prospects,* Cham: Springer.

Parliament of Georgia (2004), Legislative Herald of Georgia, (Retrieved from Matsne.ge: https://matsne.gov.ge/en/document/view/32764?publication=12)

Ramadani, Veland, Vanessa Ratten, and Ramo Palalić (2018), "Special Issue on Family Entrepreneurship in Transition and Emerging Economies," *International Journal of Transitions and Innovation Systems* 6 (2), pp. 103–107.

Salamzadeh, Aidin (2018), "Start-up Boom in an Emerging Market: A Niche Market Approach," in Datis Khajeheian, Mike Friedrichsen, and Wilfried Mödinger, eds., *Competitiveness in Emerging Markets*, Cham: Springer, pp. 233–243.

Salamzadeh, Aidin, and Léo-Paul Dana (2021), "The Coronavirus (COVID-19) Pandemic: Challenges among Iranian Startups," *Journal of Small Business & Entrepreneurship* 33 (5), pp. 489–512.

Sik, Endre, and Claire Denise Wallace (1999), "The Development of Open-air Markets in East-Central Europe," *International Jurnal of Urban and Regional Research* 23 (4), pp. 697–714.

Silagadze, Avtandil, and Tamaz Zubiashvili (2016), "Foreign Direct Investment in Georgia," *International Journal of Arts & Sciences* 9 (2), pp. 63–72.

Smith, William (2011), Encyclopædia Britannica, Flag of Georgia, Encyclopædia Britannica, Inc. (Retrieved from https://www.britannica.com/topic/flag-of-Georgia national-flag)

Tikkanen, Amy and Team of Editors of Encyclopedia (2016). "Georgian Language." Encyclopedia Britannica, (Retrieved from https://www.britannica.com/topic/Georgian-language)

The State Council of Heraldy (n.d.). The State Flag of Georgia, National Symbols. Retrieve from: http://heraldika.ge/index.php?m=26

Supreme Council of the Republic of Georgia (1991), Legislative Herald of Georgia, (Retrieved from matsne.gov.ge: https://matsne.gov.ge/en/document/view/32362?publication=0)

World Bank Group (2020), *Doing Business 2020,* Washington: World Bank Publications.

Successors to the Ottoman Province of Cyprus, an Early British Protectorate

Chapter 8

The Context for Business in Cyprus

Kanellos-Panagiotis Nikolopoulos, Léo-Paul Dana & Hans-Ruediger Kaufmann

Abstract: The island of Cyprus was annexed by the Ottoman Empire in 1571 and in 1573 the Venetians left the island. Cyprus gained independence from 1861 to 1868 and again from 1870 until 1878 when the British and the Ottoman sultan signed the Convention of Constantinople, putting Cyprus under British control. In 1914, the island was annexed by the United Kingdom. Cyprus was granted independence in 1960 but divided by Turkish occupation in 1974. This chapter is about the section of Cyprus that was not occupied in 1974.

Keywords: Cyprus, business

Introduction[1]

Cyprus is the third largest island in the Mediterranean Sea, with 648 km of shoreline (Exhibit 8.1). The name Cyprus is believed to be derived from the Latin term for copper – *Cyprium aes* – the principal economic resource on the island. This is reflected in the national flag of the Republic of Cyprus, which is white, with a copper-coloured silhouette of the entire island. Below the silhouette are two olive branches symbolising the hope for peace between the Greeks and the Turks who comprise the island's two ethnic communities. Cypriot is a dialect of the Greek language; Greek and Turkish are official languages here, while English is also widely spoken (Exhibit 8.2). Seventy percent of the island's population is Greek Orthodox; most (99.5%) of these people reside in the

---

[1] This section is based on Dana and Dana (2000).

Exhibit 8.1   Cyprus shoreline; photo © 2021 by Léo-Paul Dana

Exhibit 8.2 Trilingual signage; photo © 2021 by Léo-Paul Dana

Republic of Cyprus, where churches are many (Exhibits 8.3 and 8.4). The majority of the Muslims on the island (98.7%) reside in northern Cyprus, the topic of Chapter 9. The two entities are divided by the Green Line (Exhibit 8.5).

The Cyprus pound (C£), linked to the European Currency Unit (ECU) in 1992 at the rate of 1.7086 ECU per pound plus or minus 2.25%, was replaced by the euro on 1 January 2008. Becoming a member of the European Union (EU) in 2004 and the subsequent introduction of the euro in Cyprus was expected to result in greater political stability (Orphanides, 2014). An EU car plate is featured in Exhibit 8.6. Today, the Republic of Cyprus is an export-oriented country, with a thriving service sector as well as thriving family businesses including family farms (Exhibit 8.7), often with elaborate terrace farming (Exhibit 8.8). Some families own sheep (Exhibit 8.9).

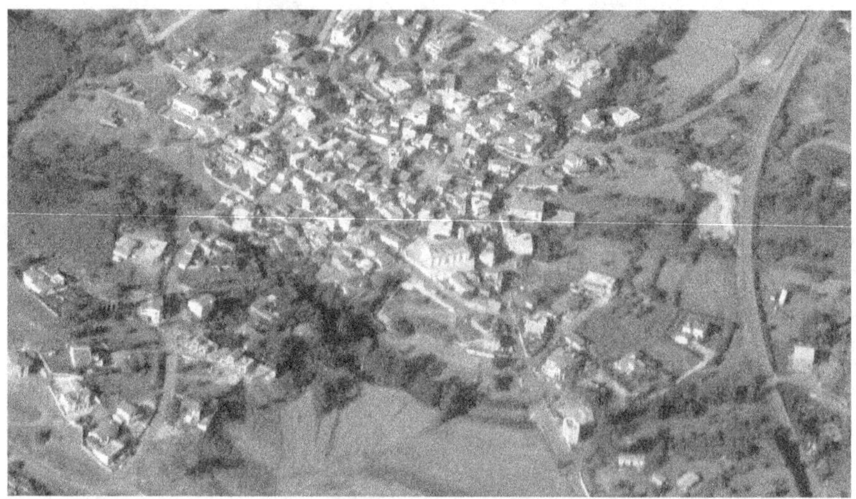

Exhibit 8.3   Church is central to typical community; photo © 2021 by Léo-Paul Dana

Exhibit 8.4   Inside a village church; photo © 2021 by Léo-Paul Dana

Exhibit 8.5 Green Line; photo © 2021 by Léo-Paul Dana

Exhibit 8.6 EU car plate; photo © 2021 by Léo-Paul Dana

Exhibit 8.7 Artisanal production of exquisite halloumi cheese in Frenaros; photo © 2021 by Léo-Paul Dana

Exhibit 8.8 Terrace farms; photo © 2021 by Léo-Paul Dana

Exhibit 8.9   Chios sheep; photo © 2021 by Léo-Paul Dana

Historical Context[2]

Due to its geostrategic bridgehead position to three continents in the most southeastern part of Europe, Cyprus became a commercial hub for early traders, and, over the years, various powers have wanted to rule it. Fortified walls still remain, as evidence of Venetian rule that lasted until 1571. Then, the Turks conquered the island, and it remained Ottoman until 1878, at which time the British took over its administration. For a detailed discussion, see Cassia (1986). In 1925, Cyprus became a British colony, with King George V as head of state. Despite British occupation, the island kept alive Greek folklore, music and dance (Exhibit 8.10).

During World War II, Cyprus became a haven for Greek refugees escaping the Nazis on the Aegean Islands. Between 1942 and 1945, about 12,000 Greek refugees were settled in camps provided by the state and

---

2 This section is based on Dana (2000) and Dana and Dana (2000). For detailed historical accounts, see: Hatzivassiliou (2005); Heraclidou (2014); Nevzat and Hatay (2009); and Yiangou and Heraclidou (2017).

Exhibit 8.10   Greek folklore in Cyprus; photo © 2021 by Léo-Paul Dana

the Cyprus Mines Corporation. Most of these refugees settled in Cyprus permanently. During the 1950s, agriculture accounted for 40% of gainful employment in Cyprus. This contributed greatly to exports.

After conducting one of the most successful anti-colonial struggles in the 1950s, and with competition about control over the island between Greece and Turkey having begun well before its independence, based on the Agreements of Zurich and London, Cyprus became an independent state in 1960.

On August 16, 1960, the Republic of Cyprus was formally declared independence from the United Kingdom, and for the first time established its own ruling body. The national constitution was drafted by the United Kingdom and endorsed by both Greece and Turkey. Article 185 stipulated that "the territory of the Republic of Cyprus is one and indivisible." The new republic maintained close trading links with the United Kingdom and with other members of the British Commonwealth. However, the constitution according to which the two major ethnic communities of the island, Greek and Turkish Cypriot were supposed to coexist presented them with formidable challenges due to its provisions for representation in the administration and legislature and extended veto rights to decision-making. Soon, clashes between the two dominant communities in the island erupted and wider military confrontation with the participation of Greece and Turkey was just a matter of time.

In 1974, the military junta in Athens organised a coup that succeeded in overthrowing the President of the Republic of Cyprus, Archbishop Makarios

III. Immediately, Turkey, in its capacity as guarantor power, invaded the northern part of the island, where the Turkish forces are still stationed, and in 1983 proclaimed its independence under the official name of Turkish Republic of Northern Cyprus. Until today only Turkey recognises the existence of the northern part of the island as a state entity separated from the Republic of Cyprus by the Green Line. Beginning in April 2003, movement was allowed across the Green Line. (There are now nine crossing points across Cyprus.) As tourism grew, a new airport terminal was built at Larnaca and the old one was closed (Exhibit 8.11).

The discovery of natural gas in Cyprus in 2011 and the already initiated gas explorations motivated Homayoon (2019) to develop an innovative conceptual framework for preventing Cyprus from experiencing a possible "Natural Curse" possibly occurring on potential revenues. The researcher discussed whether natural gas revenues could contribute to relief Cyprus from its current political, social and economic pressures as anticipated by Cyprus governmental officials and how to sustainably manage the income to gain the highest possible return on investments, and inter-generational equity.

Exhibit 8.11 Old LCA terminal served from 1975 to 2009; photo © 2021 by Léo-Paul Dana

In June 2020, the Cyprus Minister of Finance, Petrides, stressing the crucial role of tourism for the country (12%–15% of GDP), called the EU to avoid that the "symmetric shock" related to the pandemic consequences become an "asymmetric recovery" and, hence, called the EU to employ more instruments to ensure the economic recovery. For the first time, Petrides foresaw upward estimates due to Cyprus' success to contain the pandemic (Petrides, 2020). This optimism was partially shared by Mihai-Yiannaki and Mullen (2020) who noted that the COVID-19 pandemic in Cyprus led to a sharp fall in output but a smaller decline in employment, thanks to a range of government support schemes. The crisis resulted in the acceleration of digitisation.

Context for Enterprise and Implications for Doing Business

The Republic of Cyprus joined the United Nations in 1960. Since 1961, it has been a member of the British Commonwealth, of the Council of Europe, and of the Non-Aligned Movement. The Association Agreement between Cyprus and the European Economic Community (the predecessor to the EU) came into effect in 1973. The Republic of Cyprus is a member of the International Monetary Fund and of the World Bank, both of which classify it as a developed nation. It is a full member of the International Standards Organisation (ISO), and its activities include preparation and publication of standards, inspection, conformity assessment and certification.

According to a consulting view, Cyprus is a favourable environment for businesses. Key factors for this are low taxation and the rapid process of starting a company (Dionysiou and Partners, n.d.); however, in the wave of a global and euro zone crisis, for the first time since 1978, Cyprus experienced from 2010 to 2015 a dramatic economic downturn (see Exhibits 8.12 and 8.13).

The Republic of Cyprus has long had a developed infrastructure, including access to excellent drinking water (see Exhibit 8.14). Telecommunications and transportation networks are well developed. There has long been an excellent inter-city public transportation system (Exhibit 8.15). For international travel, there are regular ferry services to and from Greece, Egypt and Israel. There are two international airports, one near Larnaca and the other near Paphos.

Thanks to its favourable location, Cyprus managed to be attractively positioned in a number of business domains, including tourism, real

Exhibit 8.12 Closed while business was slow; photo © 2021 by Léo-Paul Dana

Exhibit 8.13 Little shopping; photo © 2021 by Léo-Paul Dana

Exhibit 8.14　Larnaca water administration; photo © 2021 by Léo-Paul Dana

Exhibit 8.15　Vintage inter-city bus; photo © 2021 by Léo-Paul Dana

estate, holding location and most of all as a financial centre. In addition, a longstanding maritime tradition boasting over 250 shipping companies makes Cyprus a world-class maritime hub as the largest third-party ship management centre, the largest crew management centre in the world and the third-largest international ship register in Europe (Maritimecyprus, 2019).

Larnaca (Exhibit 8.16) and Limassol are ports for merchant marine and passenger traffic (see Exhibit 8.17). Limassol is the home of important shipping fleets. It is the home of family-owned Jasmine Maritime Ltd and EDT Shipmanagement, respectively owner and operator of support vessels including suction dredger EDT Yam (Exhibit 8.18); the family owns cargo ships and specialises in the management and operation of towage and salvage vessels.

The Cypriot law system is based on a mixture between the Anglo-Saxon system and the Continental one. The principal sources of law in Cyprus are the EU directives, the constitution, the statutory laws and the judicial laws. The Cypriot commercial or company law falls under the Companies' Law Chapter 113 (Lawyers-Cyprus, 2015).

Exhibit 8.16 Old Larnaca; photo © 2021 by Léo-Paul Dana

Exhibit 8.17   Lighthouse west of Larnaca; photo © 2021 by Léo-Paul Dana

Exhibit 8.18   Family-owned suction dredger built in 1983; photo © 2021 by
Léo-Paul Dana

The entry of Cyprus into the EU entailed a re-organisation of the tax system to comply with European Community legislation. There are now some 32,000 offshore companies in Cyprus and the Central Bank registers approximately 350 new ones every month (CompanyRegister.Net, n.d.).

The often-stated view that the tax regime combined with the Doble Test Assistant (DTA) web might be regarded as Cyprus' main competitive advantage is a reason of concern for the European Commission (2020) and might be subject to changes: The absence of withholding taxes, the design of the Cypriot corporate tax residence rules and the residence and citizenship by investment schemes (abolished in late 2020) became a cause for concern. In addition to the implementation of European and internationally agreed initiatives, Cyprus announced some unilateral measures. These include the introduction of withholding taxes on dividend, interest and royalty payments to countries on the EU list of non-cooperative jurisdictions on tax matters, the introduction of a tax residency test based on incorporation and the reviewing of the transfer pricing framework to take into account the transfer pricing recommendations from the OECD base erosion and profit shifting project (European Commission, 2020).

A major business player in the Cypriot economy has been the Orthodox Church of Cyprus. Roudometov (2019) in his seminal work on the topic explains that secularism stemming from British colonial rule economic involvement favoured the model of the businessman bishop, especially in the banking and tourism sector.

Through various ecclesiastical institutions the Holy Archbishopric of Cyprus has been for many years the main shareholder in the Hellenic Bank (currently holdings of 7.15%), the second-largest bank in Cyprus and used to have considerable stock holdings in the Bank of Cyprus and a smaller number of stock holdings in Marfin Popular Bank (Roudometov, 2019). The Church is a major property owner, the Kykkos monastery constituting a prime example, offering immovable property for long-term rentals, while other bishoprics also own hotels or tourist resorts (Roudometov, 2019).

In industry, the Church has been a major stockholder in some of the island's largest businesses, the KEO beverages industry, Vassilikos Cement Works Ltd. and the Greek Mining Group (Roudometov, 2019). Finally they retain an important presence in mass media, founding and owning a private broadcasting station in 1991, O Logos (The Word), and being a major shareholder in the Cyprus branch of the Greek TV Channel Mega (Roudometov, 2019).

The prospect of Cyprus becoming an energy hub for the wider region is more than just a possibility, also considered in the light of the cooperation with Israel that has improved dramatically over the recent years. Despite its marked anti-Western rhetoric and maintaining close ties with the Arab countries, early on as an independent state Cyprus also cultivated its economic and commercial relations with Israel (Stergiou, 2016). The successive natural gas and oil reserves discovered in the offshore Tamar field in 2009 and Leviathan in 2010 in Israel and the offshore Aphrodite field discovered in 2011 in Cyprus, in a region covered by Cyprus and Israel's EEZs acted as a catalyst in bilateral relations. This is also reflected in the remarkably increased bilateral trade volume. Cyprus exports to Israel increased from €16.7 million in 2009 to €77.3 million in 2014 and its imports from Israel from €389.1 in 2009 to €487.4 million in 2014 (Stergiou, 2016). More importantly, this translated to increased military cooperation to safeguard Cypriot offshore natural gas fields, the first relevant agreement signed in February 2012 (Stergiou, 2016).

The best is yet to come. In 2020, Greece, Cyprus and Israel signed a deal to build a 1,900 km (1,180 mile) underwater pipeline, the EastMed project to carry natural gas from the eastern Mediterranean's rapidly developing gas fields to Europe. The project is estimated to cost $6 to $7 billion and the initial quantities of gas from Israel and Cyprus to the Greek island of Crete and from there to Italy and Europe through mainland Greece. This is only part of a much bigger pipeline to convey gas to Europe via Greece and Italy (Reuters, 2020).

The EastMed Gas Forum (EMGF) resulting from the deal includes Cyprus, Greece, Italy and the Palestinian Authority as members, as well as Israel, Egypt and the United Arab Emirates (UAE) with associated status Globes (2021). In addition to the above, Israel and the UAE signed a binding memorandum of understanding in Abu Dhabi in October 2020 to use the existing overland Israeli pipeline, the Europe-Asia Pipeline the Eilat-Ashkelon Pipeline Co (EAPC) that will save the expense and time of shipping oil from the Persian Gulf through the Suez Canal by using the Red Sea route instead and continuing through Israel (Globe, 2020).

Presenting the Cyprus business environment one cannot omit the economic relations between Russia and Cyprus, which have proven extremely solid and durable despite the various crises. The largest provider of foreign direct investment (FDI) to Russia by far is Cyprus. Some 32% of total inward FDI stock ($499.7 billion) flowed into Russia from Cyprus at the end of September 2017 (Korhonen et al., 2018). Following the economic crisis and after a dramatic decline in the years 2013–2015, the FDIs of the Russians to and from Cyprus in 2016 returned to pre-crisis levels of 2013. Cyprus ranks first in inward FDI and outward FDI with almost 35% of total flows from Russia (Repousis et al., 2019). Liuhto (2018) explains that among Russian businesses the main incentive to move to Cyprus by almost 60% is the favourable tax regime. Almost 70% of Russian companies are situated in Limassol (Liuhto, 2018) or *Limassolgrad* because of the presence of the large Russian community there.

According to the census, the total population of Russian citizens that numbered 8,663 in 2001 increased by 93% in 2011 and today it is estimated that approximately 40,000 Russians live in Cyprus, mainly in Limassol (Revita Turnarounds, 2020). Due to the business incentives offered, the Russians take advantage of them to the benefit of the country's economy. They still consider Limassol attractive due to its infrastructure, the relative low corporate tax, modern telecommunications and professional services, as well as its healthy climate and the interest in acquiring real estate in Limassol is still high among Russians (Revita Turnarounds 2020). It remains to be seen how the whole image will be affected by the recent changes such as the golden visa abolition.

Towards the Future

Peace and unification talks have been continuing up until now and communication and cooperation between the Republic of Cyprus and the northern part of the island have improved over the years. However, the reunification of the island is still not yet in sight. The accession of Cyprus as a member state in the EU in 2004 raised new hopes for progress in the reunification talks but this has failed to materialise up until now. In 2011, the discovery of what seems like vast resources of oil and natural gas worth exploiting was heralded as a turning point in the development of the island's economy. However, this discovery has triggered another round of dispute among Greece, Turkey and the Republic of Cyprus over exploitation rights including Turkish Cypriots in the northern part of the island.

Regarding financial support, Mihai-Yiannaki and Mullen (2020) refer to the EU's Recovery and Resilience Facility (RRF) being conditional for the government's recovery plan with its seven policy axes (public health; labour market and social and educational/training policy; new growth model and economic diversification; investment-friendly business environment, supporting small- and medium-sized enterprises [SMEs] and promoting public sector and judicial efficiency; digital efficiency and productivity; transition to a green economy; fiscal/financial): Under the EU's €750 billion RRF agreed by EU leaders in July 2020, Cyprus was entitled to €978 m in (conditional) direct grants and, according to the Employers and Industrialists Federation (OEB), a total of €1.09 billion to address the COVID-19 pandemic, undertake green and digital transition and becoming more sustainable and resilient by 2026. Mihai-Yiannaki and Mullen (2020) evaluated the achievement of the short-term goals by October 2020 as broadly successful specifically in terms of supporting employment growth due to previously achieved fiscal consolidation; a better capitalised banking sector; revised down forecasts for real GDP contraction; the acceleration of digitisation of government services mainly due to a new ministry for research, innovation and digital policy; the engagement of the government for STEM and digital education; ecological transformation due to the EU's RRF. Possible concerns, on the other hand, relate to an expected increase of non-performing loans; a sharp increase of young women leaving the labour force; a reduced state contribution to GDP due to increasingly necessary means to support incomes; underachieving the intended Horizon 2020 objective of spending 3% of GDP for research and development (R&D). The authors recommend future labour force surveys to differentiate inactives additional by age and to more frequently update the data on those parts of the population being at risk of poverty.

The Cyprus Recovery Plan addressed a number of gaps highlighted by the Cyprus Country Report for 2020 by the European Commission (2020). In the following, a few of the future priorities are exemplified. The previous emphasis on mass tourism and services based on "sun and sea" (Kaufmann et al., 2011) resulted in a lack of environmental sustainability and diversification of tourism being mainly dependent on British and Russian tourists (European Commission, 2020). Policy Axis 3, for example, referring to green tourism addresses this gap. Further suggestions to upgrade the tourism offers might relate to better align tourism products and services to the values of the diverse tourism segments (Gronau and Kaufmann, 2009) and to develop new markets to overcome over-dependency on individual markets. Furthermore, agro-tourism is suggested to be both an excellent avenue to revitalise villages in Cypriot rural areas and letting authenticity seekers actively experience the identity of Cyprus people and products (Gronau and Kaufmann, 2009). The village of Lefkara, for example, is well known for its lace and silverware. Not far, the monastery of Ayios Minas is famous for the production of honey and painting of icons. The monks of the Chrysoroyiatissa Monastery are said to produce some of the island's best vintage wines. However, the agricultural sector is continuously on the decline as initially funds were diverted to other industry branches (Dana, 2000).

An income tax reform, in 1990, favoured entrepreneurs in tertiary industries as opposed to those in agriculture. To stimulate growth in agriculture, the European Commission (2020) suggests to register more quality schemes, following the example of EU protected designation of origin (PDO) and protected geographical indication (PGI). Furthermore, quality assurance schemes addressing current consumer preferences, such as low carbon footprint, no use of pesticides, organic farming, high landscape diversity features, high standards of animal welfare, mountain products, could generate more added value. In 2020, 1.98% of the Cyprus labour force (down from 3.8% in 2010) was employed in agriculture, compared to 81.74% in services (increase from 75.8% in 2010) and 16.28% in industry (decrease from 20.4% in 2010) (Statista, 2021a).

The European Commission's statement that growth relies heavily on specific sectors, such as tourism, foreign-funded residential construction and services linked to foreign companies, which are vulnerable to potential negative external developments, is accommodated, especially by aim 2 of the national recovery plan to "strengthen the resilience of the economy and society, promote diversification and upgrade the economy's efficiency and productivity" (Mihai-Yiannaki and Mullen, 2020), and in terms of new positionings, by Policy Axis 1 to develop Cyprus to a new public health hub and by Policy Axis 2 suggesting to expand on the existing strength regarding the tertiary educational sector to be stronger internationalised.

The European Commission (2020) holds that investment lags behind future growth areas such as digital transformation, R&D, renewable sources of energy (potential in renewable sources of energy, notably solar energy), sustainable transport and the circular economy – among the member states with the highest green-house gas emissions per person. According to the European Commission (2020), in Cyprus, no progress can be recognised regarding privatisation. The national recovery plan considers these points by a suggested growth model stated in Policy Axis 3: Redesign and diversify the economy; bring more technology to agriculture; promote the efficiency and branding of Cyprus products; enhance the use of biotech; promote the greening of tourism; develop tertiary education and attract more international students; establish key performance indicators (KPIs) for the use of government funds; fast-track innovative businesses and facilitate the commercialisation of ideas; connect with the Cypriot diaspora for synergies and create centres of excellence. In this context, Cyprus recovery plan aim 3 is to foster the green and digital transition, in line with the EU's strategic goals. Also, the measures of Policy Axis 6 aim to accelerate the transition to a green economy.

The call for a new economic model is supported by Price Waterhouse Coopers (2020); the consultants provide suggestions and reforms for the recovery and transformation of the county's economy targeting reforms in the realms of the state, businesses as well as society as a whole towards sustainable growth for the 21st century. In particular, the report refers to measures as to how achieving economic competitiveness, economic and social resilience, increasing productivity levels and creating jobs aligned with the EU priorities with regards to digital and green economy. As additional pillars for an innovative business model for Cyprus, Price Waterhouse Coopers (PWC) suggests research and innovation, education, transportation as well as other sectors, such as alternative investments, that is aggrotech) and sustainable tourism. Interestingly, the PWC study points to the importance of culture in this context. The study also highlights the impact of culture in the development and success of countries' economic initiatives. According to PWC, now is the right time for Cyprus to study thoroughly and utilise the cultural characteristics of our country following the example of other countries and similar proposals by the EU. In cultural terms, Cyprus belongs to the same culture group as Greece. The reason is the geographical proximity, common traditions, language, national origin and religion. In the cultural setting, Kaufmann et al. (2013) investigated the degree of correlation between intercultural competence, emotional intelligence, communication styles and character traits. Further competences, specifically in an intercultural context, relate to knowledge creation, sharing and transferring knowledge across cultures (Sánchez Bengoa et al., 2012).

In addition, the European Commission (2020) suggests to ensure that growth benefits all groups of the population, more investment is needed in vocational education and training, adult learning, early childhood education and care and health. The measures of Policy Axis 2 addressing the labour market, social policy, education and human capital (in co-operation with the Human Resources Development Authority aim to improve this perceived gap. Furthermore, the European Commission (2020) perceives a lack of effectiveness of the justice system and payment discipline in setting up a reliable system to issue and transfer immovable property rights and in accelerating anti-corruption reforms and safeguarding the independence of the prosecution. This point is addressed by Policy Axis 4 of the Cyprus recovery plan aiming to promote public sector and judicial efficiency. A final suggestion refers to fine-tune the Cyprus recovery plan in terms of providing a time stage plan for achieving the priorities added by concrete KPIs to measure the respective level of progress towards achieving the aims.

After riding on the rollercoaster through Cyprus' breathtaking history and economic changes, the impression emerges that the island gained resilience to master its future. This optimism is based on the improving economic figures pointing to the dawn of a better future, a serious reflection process, learning from, albeit, painful experiences in the recent economic crisis leading to new structures, which is mirrored by the content of the Cyprus recovery plan, and a high motivation to embark for new shores. The journey should succeed embedded in supportive European partnerships. Yet, the desired new economic model will still be a challenging task, which is best to be achieved by concerted multidisciplinary think tanks.

The growing need for energy as well as new and safer trade routes for its transportation points towards the direction that initiatives like the EastMEd pipeline, which, once materialised successfully, will benefit countries like Cyprus by turning them into hubs that respond thus to global demands in this sector.

References

Cassia, Paul Sant (1986), "Religion, Politics and Ethnicity in Cyprus during the Turkocratia (1571–1878)," *European Journal of Sociology* 27 (1), pp. 3–28.

CompanyRegister.Net (n.d.), (Retrieved from http://companyregister.net/about/, accessed 19 March 2021)

Dana, Léo-Paul (2000), *Economies of the Eastern Mediterranean Region: Economic Miracles in the Making,* Singapore, London & Hong Kong: World Scientific.

Dana, Léo-Paul, and Teresa E. Dana (2000), "Taking Sides on the Island of Cyprus," *Journal of Small Business Management* 38 (2), pp. 80–87.

Dionysiou & Partners (n.d.), (Retrieved from https://dplawcyprus.com/2020/01/29/more-than-12-000-new-companies-registered-in-cyprus-in-2019/, accessed 19 February 2021)

European Commission (2020), "Cyprus Country Report for 2020," (Retrieved from https://ec.europa.eu/info/sites/info/files/2020-european_semester_country-report-cyprus_en.pdf, accessed 20 March 2021)

Globes (2020), "Agreement Signed to Operate Israel Pipeline for UAE oil," (Retrieved from https://en.globes.co.il/en/article-agreement-signed-to-operate-israel-uae-oil-pipeline-1001346340)

Globes (2021), "Israel and Egypt to Lay Underwater Pipeline" (Retrieved from https://en.globes.co.il/en/article-israel-and-egypt-to-lay-underwater-gas-pipeline-1001361489)

Gronau, Werner, and Hans-Ruediger Kaufmann (2009), "Tourism as a Stimulus for Sustainable Development in Rural Areas: A Cypriot Perspective," *TOURISMOS: An International Multidisciplinary Journal of Tourism* 4 (1), pp. 83–95.

Hatzivassiliou, Evanthis (2005), "Cyprus at the Crossroads, 1959–63," *European History Quarterly* 35 (4), pp. 523–540.

Heraclidou, Antigone (2014), "Politics of Education and Language in Cyprus and Malta during the Inter-war Years," *Journal of Mediterranean Studies* 23(1), pp. 75–88.

Homayoon, Morvarid (2019), Cyprus' Gas: "National Wealth" or "Natural Curse"? Will Cyprus as a Newly Acquired Natural Resource Country Benefit from this Windfall? PhD Thesis, University of Nicosia.

Kaufmann, Hans-Ruediger, Maria Englezou, and Ana Garcia-Gallego (2013), "Tailoring Cross-Cultural Competence Training," *Thunderbird International Business Review* 56 (1), pp. 27–42.

Kaufmann, Hans-Ruediger, Werner Gronau, and Savvas Sakkadas (2011), "Nicosia-Concerted Retailing and Tourism Strategies to Awaken a Neglected and Sleeping Beauty," *TOURISMOS: An International Multidisciplinary Journal of Tourism* 6 (1), pp. 15–29.

Korhonen, Iikka, Heli Simola, and Laura Solanko. "Sanctions, Counter-Sanctions and Russia: Effects on Economy, Trade and Finance," (2018). BOFIT Policy Brief 2018 No. 4

Koutantou, Angeliki (2020), "Greece, Israel, Cyprus Sign EastMed Gas Pipeline Deal," (Retrieved from https://www.reuters.com/article/us-greece-cyprus-israel-pipeline-idUSKBN1Z10R5)

Lawyers-Cyprus (2015), "Company Law in Cyprus," (Retrieved from https://www.lawyers-cyprus.com/commercial-law-in-cyprus, 23 March 2021)

Liuhto, Kari (2018), The Economic Relations between Cyprus and Russia, Presentation https://www.researchgate.net/publication/323143804

Maritimecyprus (2019), "Cyprus Ship Registry and World Class Maritime Hub," (Retrieved from https://www.maritimecyprus.com/2019/03/18/

cyprus-international-ship-registry-world-class-maritime-hub/, accessed 23 March 2021)

Mihai-Yiannaki, Simona, and Fiona Mullen (2020), *The Recovery Plan in Cyprus: Setting the Course for a Climate-Neutral and Digital Future?* Nicosia: Friedrich-Ebert-Stiftung, (Retrieved from http://library.fes.de/pdf-files/bueros/zypern/17208.pdf, accessed 18 March 2021)

Nevzat, Altay, and Mete Hatay (2009), "Politics, Society and the Decline of Islam in Cyprus: From the Ottoman Era to the Twenty-First Century," *Middle Eastern Studies* 45 (6), pp. 911–933.

Orphanides, Athanasios (2014), "What Happened in Cyprus? The Economic Consequences of theLast Communist Government in EuropeInstitute for Monetary and Financial Stability Goethe University Frankfurt am Main," Working Paper Series, N. 79, (Retrieved from https://ideas.repec.org/p/zbw/imfswp/79.html, accessed 19 March 2021)

Petrides, Constaninos (2020), "EU Must Deploy More Instruments to Ensure Economic Recovery: Cyprus Finance Minister Interview," (Retrieved from https://www.cnbc.com/video/2020/06/03/eu-must-use-more-stimulus-to-ensure-recovery-cyprus-finance-minister.html, accessed 20 March 2021)

Price Waterhouse Coopers (2020), "New PWC Cyprus Study to Transform the Economy," (Retrieved from https://www.pwc.com.cy/en/press-releases/press-releases-2020/restart-cyprus-now.html)

Repousis, Spyridon, Petros Lois, and Pavlos Kougioumtsidis (2019), "Foreign Direct Investments and Round Tripping between Cyprus and Russia." *Journal of Money Laundering Control*, 22 (3), pp. 442–450.

Revita Turnarounds (2020), "The Effect of the Russian Community on the Economy of Cyprus," (Retrieved from https://www.revita.com.cy/the-effect-of-the-russian-community-on-the-economy-of-cyprus/)

Roudometov, Victor (2019), "The Economic Activities of the Orthodox Church of Cyprus," *Archives de Sciences Sociales des Religions* 1, pp. 107–124.

Sánchez Bengoa, Dolores, Hans-Ruediger Kaufmann, and Demetris Vrontis (2012), "A New Organisational Memory for Cross-Cultural Knowledge Management," *Cross Cultural Management: An International Journal* 19 (3), pp. 336–351.

Statista (2021), "Cyprus: Distribution of Employment by Economic Sector from 2010 to 2020," (Retrieved from https://www.statista.com/statistics/382141/employment-by-economic-sector-in-cyprus/, accessed 23 March 2021)

Stergiou, Andreas (2016), "Turkey–Cyprus–Israel Relations and the Cyprus Conflict," *Journal of Balkan and Near Eastern Studies* 18 (4), pp. 375–392.
Yiangou, Anastasia, and Antigone Heraclidou, eds. (2017), *Cyprus from Colonialism to the Present: Visions and Realities: Essays in Honor of Robert Holland,* Oxon: Routledge.

Chapter 9

The Context for Business in Northern Cyprus

Gözde İnal-Cavlan & Léo-Paul Dana

Abstract: In 1974, the northeastern portion of the island of Cyprus was occupied by Turkey. It has since been recognised as an independent country only by Turkey, upon whom it is highly dependent. This chapter is about this de facto entity.

Keywords: Northern Cyprus, Turkish Republic of Northern Cyprus

Introduction

Since the division of the island of Cyprus, only Turkey recognises the northern part as a political entity. Although northern Cyprus has long been the object of an international economic boycott, Turkey facilitates northern Cypriot enterprise – allowing goods to be labelled as Turkish. Since 2004, it is possible for northern Cypriots to move goods through the south, as long as it is shown that no formerly Greek Cypriot property was used in production. Many Turkish Cypriots whose families lived on the island pre-1974 have claimed their rights to a Republic of Cyprus passport; these people can freely cross to the south. Some Turkish Cypriots work in the south and occasionally get contracts as Turkish-owned firms.

While the official language is Turkish, English is widely spoken and understood in official and commercial circles. The religion is Islam, with Muslims making up 99% of the population (State Planning Organisation, 2020). The country is rich with mosques (see Exhibit 9.1). Many of the Turkish settlers who have arrived after 1974 were pious Muslims from rural areas. Turkish Cypriots have close cultural and

Exhibit 9.1   This mosque was formerly a church; photo © 2021 by Léo-Paul Dana

economic ties to Turkey (see Exhibit 9.2), with societal and organisational culture being a blend of Western and Eastern values (Dexter et al., 2007; Tanova, 2003).

Historical Context[1]

Cyprus is a Mediterranean island with an area of 3,572 square miles (Parker, 1969, p. LXXIII). It was first colonised by the ancient Greeks and successively conquered by every ruling empire in the region, including the Phoenician, Assyrian, Egyptian and Persian (Manisali, 2000, pp. 5–6).

---

[1] Much of this section is based on Dana (2000) and Inal (2008). See also Mallinson (2005; 2016).

Exhibit 9.2 Flags of Turkey and northern Cyprus side by side, with the image of Kamal Ataturk in the background; photo © 2021 by Léo-Paul Dana

Within a Greek sphere of influence, the Ptolemaic Empire, and later the Romans, Byzantines, Richard Coeur de Lion of England, Lusignans (French crusaders), Venetians and Ottomans ruled the island (Gunnis, 1936). The Turkish population came after the conquest of Cyprus by the Ottomans (Özkul, 2005). During the Ottoman period (1571–1878), a population of predominantly Greek Cypriots grew to include almost 20% Turkish Cypriots, descendants of soldiers, settlers and others of Islamic, Turkish origin (Fisher, 2001, p. 309). Turks in Cyprus were mainly involved in agricultural activities, including growing fruit (see Exhibit 9.3) and raising livestock (see Exhibit 9.4), similar to most other Muslims under the Ottoman administration. Tax regulations during the Ottoman administration were designed to encourage non-Muslims to trade and Muslims to engage in agriculture. This structure continued under British rule after 1878. (Until 1914, Cyprus was technically still an Ottoman territory, administered by Britain.)

Cyprus was under the British between 1878 and 1960 (Necatigil, 1998) and declared a British Colony in 1925 (Persianis, 2003). For detailed discussions of the British rule of Cyprus, see Faustmann and Peristianis (2006), Hatzivassiliou (1991), Hill (1952), Holland (1993; 1999), Rappas (2008; 2014) and Yiangou (2012). Remnants of British rule are still visible (Exhibits 9.5 and 9.6).

Exhibit 9.3　Oranges; photo © 2021 by Gözde İnal-Cavlan

Exhibit 9.4　Sheep grazing in an olive orchard; photo © 2021 by Léo-Paul Dana

Exhibit 9.5 The GR of King George V still visible; photo © 2021 by Léo-Paul Dana

While the fight for the liberation of Cyprus was mainly the work of the Greek–Cypriot organisation EOKA, undeniably there were Turkish Cypriots who were inspired by the cause and participated actively in the fight of EOKA. They also formed paramilitary organisations who assisted the British with dealing with the guerrillas in accordance with Turkey's directions.

In August 1960, with the agreement of Turkey, Greece, the United Kingdom and Turkish and Greek Cypriot communities, Cyprus became an independent country, a functional federation with Greek and Turkish Cypriots as founding partners (Hannay, 2005; Müftüler-Bac, 1999; Theophanous, 2000). Union with Greece (enosis) or with Turkey was expressly forbidden, as was the partition of the island and the union of either part with Greece or Turkey. Taksim (partitioning) was the Turkish Cypriot position. The independence of the Republic of Cyprus was guaranteed by Turkey, Greece and the British (Ertekün, 1984; Hannay, 2005).

During armed clashes in December 1963, a result of the disagreements in changing the constitution in Cyprus, Greek Cypriots, seized total control of the island, including the airport and the harbours (see Exhibit 9.7).

Government institutions became exclusively Greek Cypriot. Turkish Cypriot members of Parliament were barred from the House of Representatives, located in south Nicosia, in a Greek area. Turkish Cypriots gathered together for mutual protection in enclaves where they had local majorities; a few villages remained mixed. Turkish Cypriots workers continued to work in Limassol port, and in the courts and justice system. The Greek Cypriot rump of the government was recognised by the

Exhibit 9.6   Royal Mailbox with GVR for King George V embossed and yellow painted over the original red; photo © 2021 by Léo-Paul Dana

United Nations (UN) as the Government of Cyprus. The UN operated convoys between Nicosia and Kyrenia, to protect Greek Cypriots travelling through the Turkish enclave in Gonyeli and northern Nicosia.

Between 1963 and 1974, many Turkish Cypriot businesses shut down or were negatively affected by the restrictions imposed on their trading and other business activities. Many Cypriots subsequently left the island and

Exhibit 9.7 Old Kyrenia Harbour; photo © 2021 by Gözde İnal-Cavlan

migrated mainly to the United Kingdom as well as Australia, Canada and Turkey in pursuit of better economic and social conditions (Alicik, 1997; Issa, 2005; Manisali, 2000).

In July, 1974, Greek troops carried out a *coup d'état* in Cyprus with the intention of uniting the island with Greece (Hannay, 2005). This happened under the guidance and planning of the junta that had seized power in Athens in 1967. The fighting started between rival Greek factions and then between Greeks and Turks (Issa, 2004). Turkey then sent her troops to the island in order to re-establish the constitutional order established in 1960; this was regarded by the Turks as compliant with the tripartite agreement between Greece, Turkey and the United Kingdom, made during the creation of the Republic of Cyprus in 1960 (Issa, 2004, p. 72). The Greeks considered this as an unjustified act of aggression (Issa, 2004). After the division, 37% of the island came under the control of Turkey. During the military operations, around 160,000 Greek Cypriots who had been residing in what became the Turkish-controlled area were forced to migrate to the south (Davies, 2006).

By an agreement between the two communities on the population exchange, around 40,000 Turkish Cypriots living in the south were relocated to the north (Fisher, 2001). Problems in housing and employment occurred as a result of the mass population exchange and forced migration between the two communities in Cyprus. Because of the extent of demographic issues, this was the first time in modern history that an Orthodox church – the Church of Cyprus – permitted legal abortions. During this period, both the Turkish and the Greek administrations allocated houses, land, property and offices that were vacated by the other community members to their own people. Greek Cypriots were short of accommodation, and refugee housing estates were built. There was little attempt to keep people from the same village together. The Turkish Cypriots who escaped/ migrated to the north had a larger housing stock to use, and villages often settled together in formerly Greek Cypriot villages in the north. The migration of Turkish Cypriots to the north of the island changed demographics and the economy. Beginning in 1974, the inflow of Turkish migrants from Turkey also contributed to the increase of the population and the growth of the economy in the north.

Separating the two entities of Cyprus is the Green Line – a UN buffer zone – 180-km long and covering 4% of the island's land surface. The Green Line first appeared in December 1963 to divide the communities in Nicosia – it then extended across the whole island (except north of the British Eastern Sovereign Base Area) as a buffer zone. Common institutions were very limited after 1963.

Until the creation of this boundary, both sides of Cyprus had shared a common history, one government, a unified infrastructure and equal access to foreign markets. Then, significant changes were introduced. Whereas English, Greek and Turkish had been common prior to the split, the Turkish authorities in Cyprus opted for one official national language – Turkish. Monolingual Turkish signs replaced bilingual and trilingual signs.

On 15 November 1983, the Turkish Cypriots declared the independence of northern Cyprus, only recognised by Turkey (Dana, 2000; Giritli et al., 2014; Østergaard-Nielsen, 2003). Because of international trade embargoes, northern Cyprus has remained heavily dependent on Turkey for financial support (Østergaard-Nielsen, 2003, Turkish Cypriot Chamber of Commerce, 2002) and adopted the use of Turkish lira, the currency of Turkey. In the southern part of the island, the administration continued to exist as an internationally recognised state, the Republic of Cyprus.

Prior to the crossing point openings between the north and south sides of Cyprus, a person wishing to travel from Nicosia in the Republic of Cyprus, to the northern section of the same city – a stone's throw as the crow flies – travelled first to Turkey (via Greece, as there was no direct connection between south Cyprus and Turkey) and then to northern Cyprus. A Greek Cypriot needed a visa for Turkey. A few people could get permission to live in the north and travel in and out via the south (the minister at St Andrew's Kyrenia, and diplomats, for example) and British service personnel. Also, non-Greeks on holiday in the south could get a pass to travel to the north.

Since 1 May 2004, the unilateral European Union (EU) membership bid of the Republic of Cyprus was accepted and for the time being the EU acquis is only applicable in the Republic of Cyprus. After the failure of the UN initiative and the entry of the island of Cyprus into the EU, the problem was considered by the EU and vigorous efforts are continuing to find a mutually acceptable solution for the island to be reunified as a federal state. In addition, Green Line Regulation started on 1 May 2004 and the execution of Green Line Trade from northern Cyprus to the Republic of Cyprus began on 20 August 2004 (Adaoğlu, 2005) and trade of goods between the two entities began in May 2005 (Hatay et al., 2008). After the access of the Republic of Cyprus to EU, Turkish Cypriots were provided funding for economic development. Buildings in the Arabahmet Area in Nicosia were renovated with these funds (see Exhibit 9.8).

The failure of peace talks in 2017 was a big setback. In 2020, Turkish Cypriots elected a hard-line leader, committed to a two-state

Exhibit 9.8 Arabahmet area of Nicosia; photo © 2021 by Gözde İnal-Cavlan

solution, with recognition of northern Cyprus as a separate country. This, of course, is anathema to the Republic of Cyprus. Nevertheless, there is a hope among people to be unified again and live a prosperous life again (see Exhibit 9.9).

Exhibit 9.9 Looking forward to better times; photo © 2021 by Gözde İnal-Cavlan

Context for Enterprise and Implications for Doing Business

In contrast to the outward-looking economy of the Republic of Cyprus, that of northern Cyprus is limited by the fact that the latter is not recognised by any international organisation. As a result of the non-recognition and the economic embargo placed by the international community in northern Cyprus, the latter has no official economic ties with any country outside Turkey (Dana, 2000) and the growth rates of northern Cypriot firms and also of the northern Cypriot economy have been slow compared to that of the south (Giritli and Kalmaz, 2020; Howells and Krivokapic-Skoko, 2010; Özkul, 2010; Tanova, 2003) – especially before the opening of crossing points in 2003 with the partial easing of embargoes.

Officially, no country other than Turkey has trade links or transportation links with northern Cyprus. Thus, in contrast to the Republic of Cyprus, which is industrialised and export-oriented, northern Cyprus is largely shut off from the global economy (Dana, 2000). Furthermore, production costs negatively affects economic growth in northern Cyprus due to the political situation, limitations on trade and commerce, and dependence on the Turkish economy (Giritli and Kalmaz, 2020).

Furthermore, non-recognition created multiple issues for northern Cypriots ranging from the symbolic (e.g., having no direct international telephone dialling code) to the material (all flights to and from the island operate via Turkey) (Mertkan-Özünlü and Thomson, 2009, p. 100). Employment in northern Cyprus depends heavily on the public sector, some 26.8% of the total in 2018 (State Planning Organization, 2018).

In addition, research reveals that business people often face bureaucratic problems when trying to expand/start up businesses (Howells and Krivokapic-Skoko, 2010). People rely on their own/family resources or get loans from families (Howells and Krivokapic-Skoko, 2010). In addition, the lack of knowledge in business idea development as well as in business start-up have been widely brought forward, and hence the training and development in entrepreneurship and financial support such as grants were highly required (Şeşen and İnal Cavlan, 2017).

Since April 2003, movement was allowed across the Green Line. Measures have been introduced to assist the Turkish Cypriots. From this date onwards and further with the accession of Cyprus into the EU, Turkish Cypriots have obtained Republic of Cyprus birth certificates, and following this, Republic of Cyprus ID cards and Republic of Cyprus Passports. Overall, the opening of crossing points in 2003 and crossings to the south and north was a positive move and development (Yorucu et al., 2010). Turkish Cypriot officials have to comply with the EU standards and completed the necessary work to bring their laws more in line with the *acquis communautaire*.

Currently, there are nine crossing points across Cyprus. The country's capital, Nicosia, has three crossing points: Agios Dhometios (*Metehan* in Turkish), opened in 2003, which serves both pedestrians and cars, and Ledra Palace (also opened in 2003) and Ledra Street (opened in 2008), both of which can only be used by pedestrians (Europa, 2018).

Agriculture had been the backbone of the northern Cypriot economy and provided employment for many Turkish Cypriots (Dana, 2000; Dana and Dana, 2000; Tanova, 2003). However, the agriculture industry lost its importance after 1994 as a result of the decision taken by the European courts, which abandoned agricultural imports from northern Cyprus (Ünlücan, 2010). The economy in northern Cyprus has limited resources and carries the characteristics of an island economy. Consumer goods are mainly imported and generally the volume of imports exceeds exports.

Today, the economy of the country is dominated by the services sector, which includes the public sector, trade, tourism and higher education (Giritli et al., 2014; SABER Report, 2016). Particularly the service sector holds an important position in the northern Cypriot economy and has gained importance starting since the 1980s (Ekemen and İnal-Cavlan, 2016; Ünlücan, 2010). During the 1990s the demand for the higher education sector has increased (Katırcıoğlu, 2010). There are 20 universities in northern Cyprus (YODAK, 2019). Some excellent Turkish academic institutions – both private and public – operate campuses in northern Cyprus; these include Bahcesehir and the Middle East Technical University. Higher education institutions have a 35% share of GDP (State Planning Organization, 2018). Data showed that the number of students reached 102,944 in the academic year 2018–2019 (Giritli and Kalmaz, 2020).

The private sector in northern Cyprus is relatively small and focused on low value-added production, mostly in the service sector, and composed of family-run micro and small enterprises. There are different working conditions in the private and public sectors; mainly in the private sector, there is a lack of labour regulations and contacts. Turkish people from Turkey mainly work in low-skilled jobs, according to Labour Force Survey data, one-third of the Turkish Cypriot labour force is composed of Turkish people (SABER Report, 2016). According to the same source, the contraposition of the large, well-paying "public" administration with the low-productivity, small and medium-sized enterprises (SMEs) in the private sector contributes to an image of the labour market in northern Cyprus as a dual one in which human capital is not allocated in the most efficient way (SABER Report, 2016, p. 11). Ninety-five percent of privately set-up businesses are SMEs, and they provide employment to 88% of the private sector (Tanova, 2003).

According to the State Planning Organization (2018) Household Workforce Survey, the total size of the workforce in northern Cyprus is 132,411. Out of this number, 1,145 employees, that is, 0.9% are working in Republic of Cyprus. The same research reveals that 81.1% of working people are employed in the service sector, 9.1% in industry, 2.7% in agriculture and 7% in construction.

It is also important to mention that as of April 2003, arrangements are such that SMEs in northern Cyprus are harmonised with EU standards. A centre for SMEs, KOBI Centre, has been established, which gives professional support to individuals who would like to start businesses. The EU has been continuing to providing support such as training young people, women and other groups and providing grants to set up and develop small businesses.

Since the 2004 opening of the boundary between the Republic of Cyprus and northern Cyprus, the Republic of Cyprus has become the third trade partner of northern Cyprus after Turkey and the United Kingdom (Senhaz et al., 2016). Trade then increased at an average annual rate of 35.9% (Gökcekus et al., 2012; Senhaz et al. 2016). In the first year of the crossing point opening, the total value of goods traded exceeded €1 million. By 2018, it increased to about €5 million. Different types of goods are being traded such as vegetables, stone products, paper goods, furniture and fish (Europa, 2018). As the Ledra Street Lokmaci Gate in Nicosia was opened on 3 April 2008, the growth and expansion of firms in the area have been significant. According to official statistics, both Greek and Turkish Cypriots have benefited from such a win-win condition (Jacobson et al., 2009). This shows that mutual agreements and collaborative efforts are worthwhile and should be cherished.

Despite the bankruptcies of several banks, there is a developed banking system in northern Cyprus, but banks here can only have limited access to the international financial system through Turkish institutions (SABER Report, 2016). In addition to the Central Bank and the Development Bank, there are 21 onshore commercial banks and seven International Banking Units (State Planning Organization, 2020). Complementing Western-style banks (Exhibit 9.10), Islamic banks (Exhibit 9.11) and investment companies (Exhibit 9.12) have been providing Islamic banking services.

Among the primary objectives of northern Cyprus is the encouragement of foreign investment. As a result, potential investors are aware of the positive attitude of the government towards themselves. Export-oriented industries are more preferable due to the development policy in the country. Co-operation between local and foreign firms in the form of joint ventures is promoted, and northern Cyprus offers numerous advantages and incentives to foreign investors (State Planning Organization, 2020).

Another form of investment is in housing – particularly holiday homes. The Karmi scheme is an example of the surplus housing stock inherited in 1974 being put to use.

The Cyprus Turkish Investment Development Agency (YAGA) is meant to assist investors in order to promote economic development of the country. It provides necessary information and consultancy services to investors, before, during and after investment in cooperation with the relevant institutions. (State Planning Organization, 2020).

Exhibit 9.10 Western-style bank; photo © 2021 by Léo-Paul Dana

Exhibit 9.11 Faisal Islamic Bank; photo © 2021 by Léo-Paul Dana

Towards the Future

Northern Cyprus is only recognised by Turkey, and the contemporary expansion of Turkey into Cyprus remains a problem yet to be resolved by the involved actors, with the support of the international community and

Exhibit 9.12   Faisal Islamic Investment Co; photo © 2021 by Léo-Paul Dana

in respect to international law. The future is still unclear; see Ker-Lindsay (2011).

Another challenge is that COVID-19 greatly affected fragile economies, including the Turkish Cypriot economic structure that was greatly damaged; many businesses in the private sector were shut down, student flow stopped and unemployment increased. These negative impacts will take a long period to be overcome. A small economy will always have less resilience than a larger one.

Meanwhile, overcoming internal issues is an important goal. Northern Cyprus has the potential to become an attractive destination for international business as well as tourists and there is some "hope value" in investing (that the Cyprus problem will be solved); developing businesses that benefit from "illegality" is more difficult. Tourism benefitted from being able to fly to Larnaca and then cross to the north; low-cost higher education draws in students, including many from Africa in recent years. Medical, tourism and other niche markets might have possibilities.

References

Adaoğlu, Hacer S. (2005), "AB ve KKTC Hukuku Açısından Yeşil Hat Tüzüğü," *Ankara Avrupa Çalışmaları Dergisi* 5 (1), pp. 15–28.

Alicik, Hasan (1997), *Kimlik, Yabancılaşma, Asimilasyon, Lefkoşa:* Galeri Kültür Yayınları.

Dana, Léo-Paul (2000), *Economies of the Eastern Mediterranean Region: Economic Miracles in the Making,* Singapore, London and Hong Kong: World Scientific.

Dana, Léo-Paul, and Teresa E. Dana (2000), "Taking Sides on the Island of Cyprus," *Journal of Small Business Management* 38 (2), pp. 80–87.

Davies, Elizabeth (2006), "Land Dispute Casts New Shadow over Cyprus," *Independent*, p. 20.

Dexter, Barbara, Cynthia Forson, Gözde İnal, Mine Karataş-Özkan, Fatma Küskü, Mustafa F. Özbilgin, Cem Tanova, and Jeongkoo Yoon (2007), "Convergence and Divergence of Influences on Career Choice: A Comparative Analysis of Influences China, Ghana, Greece, Israel, Korea, North Cyprus, Turkey and the UK," in Mustafa Özbilginand Ayala Malach-Pines, ed., *Career Choice in Management and Entrepreneurship,* Cheltenham: Edward Elgar, pp. 23–51.

Ekemen, Mehmet A., and Gözde İnal-Cavlan (2016), "Antecedents of Growth in Higher Education Institutions of North Cyprus: Resource-Based Approach," *Business Management and Strategy* 7 (1), pp. 1–28.

Ertekün, Necati (1984), *The Cyprus Dispute and the Birth of the Turkish Republic of Northern Cyprus,* Oxford: K. Rüstem and Bro.

Europa (2018), Bringing Cypriot Communities Closer Together EU Promotes Free Movement Across Cyprus, Nicosia, TCC Aid Programme- European -(Funded), (Retrieved from https://ec.europa.eu/info/sites/info/files/tcc_aid_programme_green_line_regulation_booklet_en_0.pdf)

Faustmann, Hubert, and Nicos Peristianis, eds. (2006), *Britain in Cyprus: Colonialism and Post-colonialism 1878–1960 (Peleus)*, Mannheim, Germany: Bibliopolis.

Fisher, Ronald J. (2001), "Cyprus: The Failure of Mediation and the Escalation of an Identity-Based Conflict to an Adversarial Impasse," *Peace Research* 3 (3), pp. 307–326.

Giritli, Nuru, Glenn P. Jenkins, and Sevin Ugural (2014), "Economic Repercussions of Opening the Border to Labour Movements Between North and South Cyprus," *Economic Research* 27 (1), pp. 729–739.

Giritli, Nuru, and Demet B. Kalmaz (2020), "Re-Examining the Impact of Financial Development on the Economic Growth of North Cyprus Through the Moderating Role of the Education Sector," *Journal of Public Affairs* p. e2517, (Retrieved from wileyonlinelibrary.com/journal/pa)

Gökcekus, Ömer, Jessica Henson, Dennis Nottebaum, and Anthony Wanis-St John (2012), "Impediments to Trade Across the Green Line in Cyprus: Classic Barriers and Mistrust," *Journal of Peace Research* 49 (6), pp. 863–872.

Gunnis, Rupert (1936), *Historic Cyprus,* London: Methuen and Co.

Hannay, David (2005), *Cyprus: The Search for a Solution,* London: I.B. Tauris & Co.

Hatay, Mete, Julia Kalimeri, and Fiona Mullen (2008), *Intra-island Trade in Cyprus: Obstacles, Oppositions and Psychological Barriers*, PRIO Cyprus Centre Paper.

Hatzivassiliou, Evanthis (1991), "Blocking Enosis: Britain and the Cyprus question, March-December 1956," *The Journal of Imperial and Commonwealth History* 19 (2), pp. 247–263.

Hill, Sir George (1952), *A History of Cyprus, Vol. IV: The Ottoman Province, The British Colony 1571–1948,* Cambridge: Cambridge University Press.

Holland, Robert (1993), "Never, Never Land: British Colonial Policy and the Roots of Violence in Cyprus, 1950–54," *The Journal of Imperial and Commonwealth History* 21 (3), pp. 148–176.

Holland, Robert (1999), *Britain and the Revolt in Cyprus, 1954–1959,* Oxford: Clarendon Press.

Howells, Karen, and Branka Krivokapic-Skoko (2010), "The Dilemma of the Turkish Cypriot Entrepreneur: The View From the 'Green Line'," *International Journal of Business and Globalisation* 4 (1), pp. 4–17.

Inal, Gozde (2008), *A Comparative Study of the Reasons for and Means of Setting-Up A Small Business: The Case of Turkish Cypriot Restaurateurs and Lawyers in North Cyprus and Britain,* PhD thesis, Queen Mary University of London, London.

Issa, Tözün (2004), "Turkish-Speaking Communities in Britain: Migration for Education," *The Welsh Journal of Education* 13 (1), pp. 69–94.

Issa, Tozun (2005), *Talking Turkey: The Language, Culture and Identity of Turkish Speaking Children in Britain,* Oakhill: Trentham Books.

Jacobson, David, Bernard Musyck, Stelios Orphanides, and Craig Webster (2009), *The Opening of Ledra Street/Lockmaci Crossing in April 2008: Reactions from Citizens and Shopkeepers,* PRIO Cyprus Centre Paper. Nicosia: PRIO Cyprus Centre.

Katırcıoğlu, Salih T. (2010), "International Tourism, Higher Education and Economic Growth: In the Case of North Cyprus," *The World Economy* 33, pp. 1955–1972.

Ker-Lindsay, James (2011), *The Cyprus Problem: What Everyone Needs to Know,* Oxford: Oxford University Press.

Mallinson, William (2005), *Cyprus: A Modern History,* London: I.B. Tauris & Co.

Mallinson, William (2016), *Kissinger and the Invasion of Cyprus: Diplomacy in the Eastern Mediterranean*, Newcastle upon Tyne: Cambridge Scholars.

Manisali, Erol (2000), *Cyprus: Yesterday and Today,* Istanbul: Der Publications.

Mertkan-Özünlü, Sefika, and Pat Thomson (2009), "Educational Reform in North Cyprus: Towards the Making of a Nation/State?" *International Journal of Educational Development* 29 (1), pp. 99–106.

Müftüler-Bac, Meltem (1999), "The Cyprus Debacle: What the Future Holds," *Futures* 31, pp. 559–575.

Necatigil, Zade Mehmet (1998), "The Legal System of the Turkish Republic of Northern Cyprus," *Journal of Cyprus Studies* 4 (2), pp. 213–255.

Østergaard-Nielsen, Eva (2003), "The Democratic Deficit of Diaspora Politics: Turkish Cypriots in Britain and the Cyprus Issue," *Journal of Ethnic and Migration Studies* 29 (4), pp. 683–700.

Özkul, Ali Efdal (2005), *Kıbrıs'ın Sosyo-Ekonomik Tarihi (1726–1750),* Istanbul: Iletişim Yayınları.

Özkul, Zeki Kaan (2010), "Entrepreneurship and Women's Empowerment in North Cyprus," *The Cambridge Undergraduate Journal of Development Economics* 3 (1), pp. 4–17.

Parker, Robin (1969), *Aphrodite's Realm: An Illustrated Guide and Handbook to Cyprus,* Nicosia: Zavallis Press.

Persianis, Panayiotis (2003), "British Colonial Higher Education Policy-Making in the 1930s: The Case of a Plan to Establish a University in Cyprus," *Compare* 33 (3), pp. 351–368.

Rappas, Alexis (2008), "The Elusive Polity: Imagining and Contesting Colonial Authority in Cyprus During the 1930s," *Journal of Modern Greek Studies* 26 (2), pp. 363–397.

Rappas, Alexis (2014), *Cyprus in the 1930s: British Colonial Rule and the Roots of the Cyprus Conflict,* London: I.B. Tauris & Co.

Senhaz, Zehra, Eminer Fehiman, and Okan V. Şafaklı (2016), "The Comparative Advantage of North Cyprus in the Green Line Trade: Emrical Analysis During Periods of 2005–2013," *International Journal of Research in Commerce & Management* 6 (11), pp. 23–30.

Şeşen, Harun, and Gözde İnal Cavlan (2017), "Girişimcilik ve KKTC Örneği," in Okan V. Şafaklı and H. Sesen, eds., *Kıbrıs Türk Ekonomisinin Dünü ve Bugünü,* Ankara: Detay Yayıncılık, pp. 43–77.

State Planning Organization (2018), *Household Workforce Research 2018*, Nicosia: SPO.

State Planning Organization (2020), *Economic & Social Indicators-TRNC,* Nicosia: TRNC Government Pub.

Tanova, Cem (2003), "Firm Size and Recruitment: Staffing Practices in Small and Large Organisations in North Cyprus," *Career Development International* 8 (2), pp. 107–114.

Theophanous, Andreas (2000), "Cyprus, the European Union and the Search for a New Constitution," *Journal of Southern Europe and the Balkans* 2, pp. 212–233.

Turkish Cypriot Chamber of Commerce (2002), *Embargoes and Isolation of North Cyprus*, Nicosia: TRNC Deputy Prime Ministry and Ministry of Foreign Affairs, Public Relations Department, (Retrieved from http://www.trncinfo.com/TANITMADAIRESI/2002/ENGLISH/EMBARGOES/040302.htm, accessed 3 September 2020)

Ünlücan, Dogan (2010), "Characteristics of SMEs in North Cyprus: A Small Island," *Problems of Perspective in Management* 8 (3), pp. 139–146.

World Bank (2016), Turkish Cypriot Community Workforce Development, *World Bank,* (Retrieved from https://openknowledge.worldbank.org/handle/10986/26513)

Yiangou, Anastasia (2012), *Cyprus in World War II: Politics and Conflict in the Eastern Mediterranean,* London: I.B. Tauris & Co.

YODAK (2019), Higher Education Planning, Supervision, Accreditation and Coordination Board, North Cyprus, (Retrieved from http://yodak.gov.ct.tr/)

Yorucu, Vedat, Özay Mehmet, Resmiye Alpar, and Pinar Ulucay (2010), "Cross-Border Trade Liberalization: The Case of Lokmaci/Ledra Gate in Divided Nicosia, Cyprus," *European Planning Studies* 18 (10), pp. 1749–1764.

Successors to Other Early British Protectorates

Chapter 10

The Context for Business in Yemen

Mugaahed Abdu Kaid Saleh & K. Rajappa Manjunath

Abstract: Yemen is one of the least developed countries in Western Asia, and the most impoverished economy in the region, especially with the current instability in the country. The condition of Yemen acts as a prohibitive factor for the business sector to grow and contribute to the country's gross domestic product (GDP), which is difficult to overcome without enforcing the laws, developing and reforming the education system and infrastructure and providing incentives to the business sector to encourage competition and establish a conducive business environment. This chapter is an attempt to present an overview of the business context in Yemen as an underdeveloped economy being different from neighbouring economies in the Gulf region and Western Asia in general.

Keywords: Bazaars, business context, development, doing business, Yemen

Introduction

The Republic of Yemen was born in 1990, upon the unification of two existing republics, North Yemen and South Yemen. Industry and business have been in basic forms during the two previous republics, essential products were made locally such as cotton fabrics, pottery industry, jewellery, boats, rugs and swords. These crafts were used to cover the needs of the locals and used to be exported to neighbouring areas too. Power and technology were the main obstacles to develop industrial establishments. However, leather processing units, domestic utensils units, cement factory and textile industry existed in North Yemen during the 1960s, this industrial sector contributed around 1.2% to the gross domestic product

(GDP), whereas in South Yemen, better establishments existed during the 1960s due to the British existence in the country, therefore, the industrial sector was more expansive than in North Yemen, it consisted of cigarette, paints, bags, fragrance, furniture and construction sectors and so on (Alawadhi, 2003).

The urbanisation process after the revolution in the 1960s began to achieve remarkable growth during the 1970s due to factors such as remittances of workers abroad and urban migration (World Bank, 1981), along with such urban growth and with oil discovery, the industrial sector witnessed significant development during the late 1980s and early 1990s. After the unification of Yemen and establishing the new republic in 1990, the government paid attention towards developing the business sector, industrial sector and business environment, as a new constitution was promulgated based on which the government issued the commercial law in 1991. Further, with the existence of power supply, there was an increase in the number of establishments and their employment as well as their contribution to the country's GDP.

After the unification of the country and the merger of two different administrative systems in both countries, efforts were made to organise the business sector and legalise its functions. The government initiated reform programmes with the support of the World Bank in 1994, majorly the civil service sector. The International Labour Organisation (ILO) surveyed the Yemen labour force in 2014 and reported that 13.4 million of the population (total population was estimated to be 28.4 million) are working-age population, out of them only 4.8 million are considered labour force in the country with a labour force participation rate of 36.3% (International Labour Organization, 2015).

When considering education, only 23% are possessing secondary education and 8% having higher education qualifications. The service sector accommodates more than half of the labour force in Yemen (55.6%), particularly the trade sector (22.7%) and public administration (12.7%). The agricultural sector absorbs 29.2% of the labour force, whereas 14.5% of the labour force is in the industry sector. It is also worth noting that almost half of the labour force (42.4%) work for their account or working for family business. Further, the majority of the labour force (73.2%) are employed in the informal sector and 8% have informal jobs in the formal sector enterprises (International Labour Organization, 2015). This can lead to assuming the high tendency of the Yemeni society towards undertaking entrepreneurial activities and business establishments. It also explains the nature of the Yemeni bazaar being different from neighbouring countries of the Gulf region.

This chapter aims to shed some light on the business context in Yemen as an underdeveloped economy in West Asia; it presents a historical overview of the business context and practices in Yemen, then it gives an overview about the context of doing business in the country compared to other countries in Asia, America and Europe. Then an overview of the potential future of doing business in Yemen is presented, including success stories of countries that managed to transform from underdeveloped economies to become fast-developing economies.

Historical Context

Yemen has a long history. Jewish people were here for about 3,000 years. The Ottomans ruled twice (1539–1636) and (1872–1911), and then was the Mutawakkilite Kingdom of Yemen (1918–1948), while in the south, the British occupied it (1839–1962), then two republics were announced in North and South Yemen until they became one country "The Republic of Yemen" in 1990 (Rabi, 2014).

Within the plural society of former British Aden and its environments (in South Yemen), since Aden has been a province of the British Raj (1839–1937), and then a British protectorate, the Jewish population created a mercantile community integrated within the new opportunities in trade since 1869 following the opening of the Suez Canal, when the port city became a centre of distribution (*éntrepôt*) of coal. Considered a loyal group to the British authorities in contrast to their potential competitors, members of the ethno-national groups of both Indian and Somali migrants, these Jews served as middlemen. They mainly engaged in small-scale trade in commodities as well as in money exchange. Following the 1947 massacre of Jewish people in Yemen, most survivors migrated to Israel (Ariel, 2013). Later, following the exit of the British, others left for Israel and Britain (Meron, 2011). With the slogan "Convert or die", in March 2021, Houthi Islamists expelled 12 remaining Jews along with Yemen's Rabbi Yahya Youssef who had long identified more as an Arab than as a Jew.

Until 1970, the only two countries where oil has not been found yet in the Arabian Peninsula were North Yemen and South Yemen. Discovery of crude oil in neighbouring countries led to foreign commercial banks announcing their investments in these countries. During these times, and due to the lack of necessary infrastructure, the business sector was mainly centred on local handcrafts in basic and traditional bazaars.

Bazaar economies have been investigated in the literature (Dana, 2000a; 2000b; 2011; 2014; Dana et al., 2013; Dana and Wright, 2015; Edo, 1975; Fanselow, 1990; Geertz, 1978); authors such as Professor Léo-Paul Dana have distinguished the bazaar economy from the firm-based and state-controlled economies. The bazaar sector is more common in low-income countries. Yemen, as an underdeveloped economy, is an example of witnessing the practices of bazaar sectors among individuals and business units. Before becoming a republic, that is, before the 1960s, development in business or infrastructure was not occurring in reality. Therefore, the business transactions were conducted through traditional bazaars as traditional bazaars have been a primary source for doing business (Exhibits 10.1, 10.2 and 10.3). Traditional bazaars are of two types in Yemen, regular bazaars, which function on a daily basis, and weekly bazaars, which operate only one day per week, which is more common in rural areas in the country. It is also worth mentioning that urbanisation began to develop in Yemen during the 1970s, which implies that rural area bazaars were very common all over the country.

Léo-Paul Dana argued that sticking to traditions contributed to the continuous adoption of traditional bazaars in Egypt where personal relationship plays a significant role in conducting business transactions among small businesses (Dana, 2000b). Similarly, the society of Yemen is known as tribal, traditional and often described as a primitive society as it has not evolved or become modern yet (Caton, 2013), which somehow contributes to the spread of traditional bazaars whether in the cities or rural areas of the country.

Before the unification of Yemen, and more particularly in 1972, the industrial sectors in the country consisted of eight manufacturing plants, 8 workshops for metal and furniture fitting, seven workshops for machinery and automobile repair, 13 workshops for manufacturing construction materials, four plants for soft-drinks bottling and packaging and 11 plants for manufacturing miscellaneous goods and commodities (World Bank, 1973; 1979). After the crude oil discovery and its production in the country, and particularly after the unification of Yemen, the enterprises and small companies started to spread all over the country, as the existence of crude oil facilitated the power and electricity sources, and factories and business units were more comfortable to seek for than before.

There is economic growth and development that has been achieved since the unification of Yemen in terms of policies, practices, laws and amendments, and support to the business sector. Yet, Yemen is still famous

Exhibit 10.1 Traditional market (bazaar) as the main venue for doing business; photo © 2021 by Björn Wenngren, used with permission

Exhibit 10.2 Weekly bazaar as an essential source of doing business in rural areas; photo © 2021 by Björn Wenngren, used with permission

for being primarily dominated by an informal economic sector as more than 95% of business units fall into the category of small and medium enterprises. This somehow limited technological development in the country. Yet, traditional markets or bazaars are still the main sources for doing business in cities and rural areas. The weekly bazaars are more common as a source for doing business in rural areas of Yemen.

The structural developments that took place during the last two decades in terms of managerial economics, particularly after the reform programmes initiated by the government, led to the expansion of the activities of the private sector. This played a crucial role in the economic development due to the limited role of the public sector while applying the reform programmes, as well as the globalisation and global changes that triggered the need for the private sector to absorb the workforce and increase investments towards developing the economy. Yet its contribution is limited due to the unorganised labour market, which renders the outcome of structural efforts to be less contributing to economic development (Alhawery, 2004; Saeed, 2005). However, traditional bazaars, whether weekly bazaars or regular traditional bazaars, are still widespread and expanding all over the

Exhibit 10.3 Weekly bazaar to buy and sell animals; photo © 2021 by Björn Wenngren, used with permission

Exhibit 10.4 Daily (regular) bazaar - Taiz; photo © 2021 by Albaraa Mansoor, used with permission

Exhibit 10.5 Daily bazaar; photo © 2021 by Albaraa Mansoor, used with permission

Exhibit 10.6　Weekly bazaar; photo © 2021 by Albaraa Mansoor, used with permission

country in terms of the process of doing business while being more common in rural areas (see Exhibits 10.4, 10.5, and 10.6).

Context for Enterprise and Implications for Doing Business

Among Arab oil-exporting countries, Yemen as well as Syria are the minor oil exporters. In contrast, major exporters are Kuwait, Saudi Arabia and Iraq, and importers are the countries, such as Jordan (United Nations, 1991). Economic sectors have witnessed significant development in the Yemeni economy during the last two decades, as the manufacturing sector used to contribute around 5.17% to the country's GDP in 2000 has contributed with 11.14% to GDP in 2017. At the same time, the sectors of agriculture, forestry and fishing have grown from 12.04% of GDP in 2000 to 18.86% in 2017. Another primary contributing sector is wholesale and retail trade, which has been moderately contributing towards the country's GDP (i.e., 12.10% in 2000 and 16.62% in 2017).

The sector of transport and storage is another major contributor towards GDP in Yemen, as it contributed around 10.03% during 2000 and 12.39% during 2017. The other sectors are minor contributors towards

GDP such as electricity and water (1.01% in 2017), maintenance (1.40% in 2017), construction (4.53% in 2017), communications (2.80% in 2017) and restaurants and hotels (2% in 2017) (Central Statistical Organization, 2017). This implies that more business opportunities can be sought and found along with preparing a conducive business environment for entrepreneurs to invest and expand their functions and contribution towards GDP growth and development.

According to the statistical yearbook of 2017, there were 608,450 registered full-time employees in various sectors in the country. The education sector employs the majority of employees (302,264), followed by the public administration sector (63,588); the health sector (61,168); electricity and gas supply (29,139); construction (25,325); transport, storage and communications (23,629); stockbroker (23,176) and the manufacturing sector (18,540) (Central Statistical Organization, 2017). According to the labour survey of the ILO in Yemen, the most common occupations among labour force in Yemen are field crops and vegetable growers (785,700), shop salespersons (762,100), dairy and livestock producers (207,200), construction labourers (117,400), office clerks (109,300) and car, taxi and van drivers (109,200). Out of the surveyed labour force, 6.90% are employers, 50.30% are employees, whereas 31.00% are own-account workers and 11.40% are contributing family workers (International Labour Organization, 2015).

It is worth noting that the current conflict and political instability in the country have affected the business environment during the last five years. The same can be reflected on the outcome of the business sectors in the country, more particularly the mining and quarrying sectors, which dropped down drastically from 42.05% of total industry outcome in 2014 to 8.77% in 2017, as extracting crude oil is significantly more vulnerable to the political condition than other sectors. This led to the increase of the contribution of manufacturing industries as it has effectively grown from 43.91% in 2004 to 83.35% in 2017.

In the manufacturing sector, the major contributing industries are food processing and non-alcoholic beverages with a contributing percentage of 10.89% in 2004, 21.83% in 2014 and 42.02% in 2017; refined petroleum products with a contribution of 21.34% in 2004, 15.53% in 2014 and 10.20% in 2017 (Table 10.2). Other industries, such as textiles, dressmaking and fur dyeing, furniture, recycling products, paper products, printing, publishing and photocopying, plastic products, are minor contributors to with less than 5% of total industry, let alone technological and electronic manufacturing (Central Statistical Organization, 2004; 2010; 2014; 2017). This implies the possibility and availability of a rich business environment to indulge in doing business and manufacturing, which in turn reduces the imports into the country through increasing locally manufactured goods and commodities by investing in the manufacturing sector, which may also increase the export activities, as well. The statistics show a decline in exports during the last 20 years (Table 10.1).

Small and medium enterprises are the most common business in the world, almost all economies consist of small and medium enterprises as a major component among others. They create the bulk of job opportunities in low- and middle-income countries (LMICs). The economy of Yemen is the most impoverished economy among the Middle East economies, attempting

Table 10.1. Export and Imports 2003–2017 (Percentage of GDP)

Year	Imports	Exports
2003	30.96	31.45
2004	28.86	29.53
2005	28.24	29.48
2006	26.63	29.28
2007	33.22	24.65
2008	34.39	25.02
2009	32.25	22.00
2010	30.87	21.48
2011	30.65	22.93
2012	35.22	22.03
2013	38.67	20.96
2014	44.46	19.88
2015	26.65	3.88
2016	34.32	1.85
2017	19.00	0.53

Source: Central Statistical Organization

Table 10.2. Percentage of Various Industries to Total Industry

	2004	2010	2014	2017
Mining and quarrying	52.85%	40.29%	42.05%	8.77%
Oil and gas	52.66%	39.88%	41.62%	7.92%
Other mines and quarrying sites	0.19%	0.41%	0.44%	0.85%
Manufacturing	43.91%	56.26%	53.26%	83.35%
Foodstuffs and non-alcoholic beverages	10.89%	19.72%	21.83%	42.02%
Tobacco products	1.78%	2.04%	2.14%	4.79%
Textiles making	0.27%	0.32%	0.37%	0.68%
Dressmaking and fur dyeing	0.74%	1.49%	1.58%	2.88%
Bags, shoes and hides tanning	0.28%	0.18%	0.22%	0.40%
Wood products excluding furniture	0.63%	0.71%	0.88%	1.61%
Paper and paper products	0.73%	0.13%	0.22%	0.40%
Printing, publishing and photocopying	0.43%	0.36%	0.37%	0.75%
Refined petroleum products	21.34%	22.66%	15.53%	10.20%
Chemicals and chemical by-products	0.53%	0.46%	0.55%	1.16%
Plastic products	1.38%	1.58%	2.03%	3.79%
Constructional non-metallic products	2.80%	2.56%	2.84%	5.84%
Manufacture of alkaline metals	0.00%	0.01%	0.02%	0.02%
Worked metal products	1.52%	3.30%	3.73%	7.04%
Machinery and equipment	0.02%	0.04%	0.04%	0.08%
Electric equipment and appliances	0.01%	0.07%	0.05%	0.09%

(*continued*)

Table 10.2. Percentage of Various Industries to Total Industry (*continued*)

	2004	2010	2014	2017
Medical equipment and instruments	0.00%	0.00%	0.00%	0.00%
Manufacture of engine vehicles	0.00%	0.00%	0.00%	0.01%
Other transport equipment	0.01%	0.04%	0.03%	0.04%
Furniture	0.56%	0.59%	0.83%	1.55%
Recycling manufacture	0.00%	0.00%	0.00%	0.01%
Electricity and Water	3.24%	3.45%	4.69%	7.88%
Electricity supplies	2.61%	2.61%	3.61%	5.92%
Accumulation, purification and distribution of water	0.64%	0.84%	1.08%	1.95%
Total	100.0%	100.0%	100.0%	100.0%

Source: Central Statistical Organization

to build new resources for income for replacing the declining oil production. However, the private sector is still at its basic stage of development. Micro, small and medium enterprises in Yemen are the major component of the Yemeni economy, they are considered the principal employer in the country through generating job opportunities for people entering the labour market each year (Aliriani, 2013; Donor Committee for Enterprise Development, 2017; Reeg, 2015). Small- and medium-sized enterprises (SMEs) comprise around 97% of the recorded firm in the country; this makes the economy of Yemen based primarily on small and medium enterprises. Medium and large enterprises are few, with a presence of state-owned enterprises (Aliriani, 2013; World Bank, 2008), these enterprises have grown since the unification of Yemen in 1990, playing a significant role in the economy and job creation after the agricultural sector (Cetin et al., 2007). Regardless of this, there is no universal definition of micro-, small- and medium-sized enterprises (MSMEs) adopted in Yemen, even though there have been many attempts to define them by sponsors and authors. However, according to Social Fund for Development, which is a major tool of the government of Yemen supported by international organisations (the World Bank, International Monetary Funds) to alleviate poverty and encourage development, as well as the report of these international organisations, enterprises are classified into:

- Micro enterprises: any firm operating with a capital less than one million Yemeni rial and up to five employees.
- Small enterprises (SEs): any firm operating with a capital of more than 1 million and less than 20 million Yemeni rial with employees not exceeding 10 employees.
- Medium-sized enterprises (MEs): any firm operating with a capital more than 20 million Yemeni rial and up to 50 employees (Alsabai, 2016; Cetin et al., 2007).

MSMEs in Yemen are characterised by being an important segment of the economy, employment generation, their contribution to the national productivity, being more flexible than large firms as they adapt quickly to the economic and social changes, requiring less capital, and their existence in almost all activities. At the same time, they face obstacles and constraints such as the lack of access to advanced technologies, managerial skills, international markets, access to finance, the challenge of political insta-bility, and weak legislative system (Cetin et al., 2007; World Bank, 2013).

Around 70% of owners launch their enterprises using their funds, as the formal financial sector in Yemen is highly underdeveloped. Around 8% of entrepreneurs are illiterate, 37% completed primary and secondary education, 27% of entrepreneurs only completed primary education and 21% have a university education (Cetin et al., 2007). Around 46.4% of micro, small and medium enterprises do not have a bookkeeping system of any kind, most enterprises do not use banking services, and 57.7% of enterprises have informal loans (Cetin et al., 2007).

Most of the SEs have no structured management or official structures, job description by the owners who are the managers in 44.5% of enter-prises makes the business lack the clarity in respect to decision-making and having no management cycle. Around 10% of enterprises have access to advanced technology in production. "Low skills" is a major staffing problem according to 42% of the enterprises in Yemen. Further, the lack of commitment from the part of the staff and the high turnover of staff are also significant issues to enterprises, which make the enterprises reluctant to invest in training programmes for employees due to the high turnover (Al-Maqaleh, 2012).

Multinational companies can play a significant role in the development of life standards of the poorest people in underdeveloped economies by serving and making profits to improve the local economic conditions by investing in such economies. The role of multinationals such as Digicel in Haiti, and Telenor in Pakistan and Bangladesh has been an example of the development that can be realised among the poor people in underdeveloped economies where people live on less than two dollars a day (Warnholz, 2008). However, regulatory environment, difficult business environments and the perceived high risk act as prohibitive factors for the flow of capitals to the underdeveloped economies (Warnholz, 2008). This forces developing countries to prepare a conducive business environment that induces entrepreneurs to undertake entrepreneurial activities.

Yemen, like any other developing country, aims for developing the process of doing business due to the role played by the business sectors in underdeveloped economies and their contribution to the growth of GDP. Even though more than 95% of the business sector in Yemen falls in the category of SMEs, yet the legislative perspective in Yemen did not give due attention towards small and medium enterprises as they are essential to economic development, GDP growth, employment creation and income generation. The laws and regulations are dedicated to organising the existence and activities of large companies in the economy, while there is no official definition and classification of small and medium enterprises adopted in the concerned rules and regulations.

The Yemeni commercial law was promulgated in 1991, regardless of being a comprehensive law towards large companies, it, and its amendments, did not give due attention to the sector of small and medium enterprises as a critical component of the business sector in the economy. Moreover, a special law for the companies was issued in 1997, which organises establishing, running and closing companies does not give any characterisation or classification for small and medium enterprises. Further, incentives and initiatives from the government to the small and medium enterprises sector are almost absent in all regulations (Raymanpress, 2013).

SMEs, as a significant component in the economy, face the challenge of lacking the government's protection and support. This can be solved by establishing a supervising unit as an authority for small and medium enterprises, as the official support for small and medium enterprises can be grouped into three aspects, the first aspect is the legal aspect, which involves the rules and regulation including initiatives to support and encourage SMEs, the second aspect is related to financing enterprises and facilitating their access to the required loans, whereas the third aspect is related to providing the needed training and consultation (Raymanpress, 2013). The lack of these three aspects leaves the enterprises being a target to many challenges that hamper their functions.

Countries such as Saudi Arabia and India have a specific ministry for micro, small and medium enterprises. Further, initiatives and incentives are identified to encourage growth and investments in the SMEs sector. Financing enterprises and providing the needed training and consultation are also organised through specific official organisations that are directed to provide such support to entrepreneurs and their enterprises (Al-Dhafiri, 2020; Kannan and Sudalaimuthu, 2014).

Governance experts state that governance deficiencies are related to the political condition when the political environment is not conducive; it yields more chaotic and not promising results in terms of governance. Concentrating locally in regards to governance is a useful tool to improve the supply of governance. Furthermore, the supply of these governance practices cannot take place without agencies and states that rethink their internal governance (Carothers and Diane de Gramont, 2011).

Table 10.3 shows statistics related to the change in the rank between 2010 and 2020 of the ease of doing business and the other parameters for measuring doing business in Yemen compared with other countries in Asia as well as Europe and America. As it can be observed in the table, the rank of 2010 is deducted from the rank of 2020, therefore, the negative values in the table mean an improvement in the rank of the country, whereas the positive value means a decline in the rank of a country. For instance, the rank of Yemen in 2010 was 99 and 187 in 2020, so 88 is the result of deducting 99 from 187 to explore the amount of improvement/deterioration that happened between the ranks of 2010 and 2020 of each country included in the table.

As for the ease of doing business, Jordan and the United Arab Emirates (UAE) (see relevant chapters in this book) have developed their rank during the last 10 years, whereas the rest of the Asian countries below achieved a negative development to their ranks, Yemen has the most deteriorated rank during the same period.

Challenges and difficulties face businesses and hamper their chances for growth and development. In a previous study, we empirically examined the obstacles, barriers and challenges faced by Yemeni SMEs and the effect on their performance during the current instability in the country. The temporary challenges that are related to the economic and political

Table 10.3.   Change in Ranks of Countries in Doing Business Between 2010 and 2020

Parameter	Yemen	Oman	Saudi Arabia	UAE	Syria	Jordan	Germany	France	Sweden	Brazil	Canada	USA
Ease of doing business	88	3	49	−17	33	−25	−3	1	−8	−5	15	2
Starting a business	103	−30	25	−27	10	−5	41	15	−4	12	1	47
Procedures (number)	0	−1	−1	−6	0	−1	0	0	1	−5	1	0
Time (days)	28	−8	5	−11.5	−2	−1	−10	−3	−7.5	−107	−3.5	−2
Cost (% of income per capita)	−42.8	0.9	−2.3	11	−19.7	−26.2	1.8	−0.2	−0.1	−3.3	−0.1	0.5
Dealing with construction permits	136	−83	−5	−24	54	46	12	35	12	57	35	−1
Registering property	36	32	18	3	80	−28	19	−60	−11	13	1	27
Getting credit	36	17	19	−23	−5	−123	33	61	9	17	−15	0
Protecting investors	30	−5	−13	−106	−22	−14	−32	−28	−29	−12	2	31
Paying taxes	−59	3	50	26	−14	36	−25	2	−11	34	−9	−36
Trading across borders	68	−59	63	87	60	4	28	−24	11	8	13	21
Enforcing contracts	108	−37	−89	−125	−16	−14	6	10	−12	−42	42	9
Closing a business	70	31	108	−63	71	16	−31	−16	−1	−54	9	−13

Source: World Bank data

instability in the country were found to be the most influential challenges on the performance of small and medium enterprises, whereas the legal challenges were found to be the second most influential challenges to their performance. Furthermore, we asked the respondents to identify one obstacle that they considered to be the most challenging. Infrastructural factors, theft and disorder, instability and the absence of a supervising authority for SMEs have been identified as major obstacles by 21.8%, 16.8%, 11.2% and 10.2% of enterprises, respectively, more details of the most challenging obstacles are presented in Exhibit 10.7.

In another study, we investigated the barriers that hamper the ability and tendency of entrepreneurs and business owners to adopt digitalisation in their business processes. The results revealed a considerable effect of the environmental barriers, which include lacking government support, regulatory system and appropriate networks; technical and economic barriers were influential but not as much as environmental barriers. Interestingly, individual barriers were not found significantly influential, which implies the high tendency of entrepreneurs to expand their entrepreneurial activities in terms of digitalising their business process. Similarly, respondents were asked to identify the most challenging barrier to their tendency and ability to digitalise their business process. The inadequate infrastructure and the absence of government support were identified as the most challenging barriers to 54.8% and 34.8% of enterprises, respectively. This implies that creating and preparing a conducive business environment is

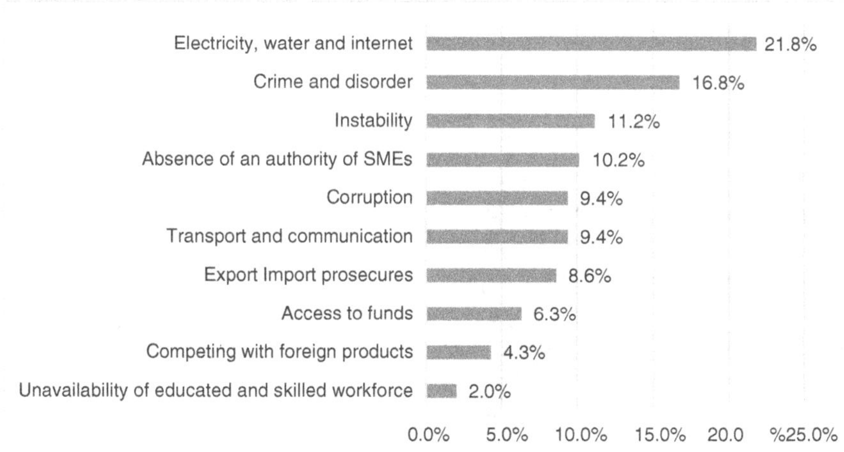

Exhibit 10.7 The most challenging obstacles for SMEs in Yemen

an earnest need for small and medium enterprises to realise their objective business goals and in turn contribute to the development and economic welfare.

Governments, usually, support the business sector to overcome such challenges and obstacles by attempting the needed reforms which enable the business sector to function innovatively towards achieving objective business goals and development. In a comparative study, Yemen was compared to other four underdeveloped economies, namely Afghanistan, Bangladesh, Rwanda and Sudan, in terms of reforms attempted to ease the process of doing business, which can attract entrepreneurs in terms of investments and undertaking entrepreneurial activities. The results indicated that Yemen was the least to attempt any reforms related to facilitating the business process, and the best reforms attempted took place in Rwanda, which made a massive transition in the process of doing business during the last 10 years, which we will refer to later in this chapter.

According to the Doing Business reports issued by the World Bank, the United Arab Emirates and Saudi Arabia are the two countries that have the highest number of reforms attempted for the purpose of facilitating doing business during the last 10 years (World Bank, 2009; 2018). Similarly, when considering the ranks of European and American countries, some developed countries such as France and Sweden have attempted more reforms than Yemen did, considering the fact which goes without saying that the developed countries with conducive business environments may rarely attempt reforms due to the good governance applied in developed countries as such countries maintained high ranks of good governance during the last 10 years as reflected in their ranks in the Good Governance Indicators issued by the World Bank, while Yemen along with Syria have witnessed a drastic fall in their ranks of the parameters of good governance (World Bank, 2019c). This implies the lack of attention drawn towards the business sectors and the procedures that could contribute to facilitating the process of doing business in the country.

The world development report (World Bank, 2017b) emphasised the importance of governance to developing countries in overcoming the challenges related to growth, equity and security, as the policies' effectiveness in such countries is highly affected and interfered by the unequal distribution of power in a society, which also hampers the chances of curbing corruption, improving municipal services and generating long-term savings. The importance of good governance increases with the increase in demand for good infrastructure in an economy, effective service delivery and fair institutions, which is very common in the least developed countries; therefore, adopting good governance leads to achieving development goals by working with civil society, harnessing the private sectors and maximising the efforts to curb corruption.

The investment sector is crucial for developing countries, especially if they aim and plan to increase the extent of development and graduate into middle-income countries. However, the investment sector is subject to changes and development based on the investment environment and investment atmosphere in a country. Therefore, focusing on developing the investment environment and atmosphere is one of the basic requirements for achieving economic growth and development (Al-Afandi, 2010). The legislative aspects towards encouraging investment in Yemen have been taken into consideration in the amendment to the investment law in 2002, which emphasised on the freedom to invest in projects and enterprises; equality among Yemeni, Arabic and foreign capitals investing in the country; rights to obtain lands and buildings; rights to maintain being private investments; rights for foreign investors to transfer their benefits abroad, granting enterprises customs and tax exemption, protecting local manufacturing by increasing customs on importing competitive foreign products, exempting manufacturers for export from partial and full fees related to exporting and many other aspects that act as key factor enticing investors to invest in Yemen (Amendment to investment law (No. 22) 2002, Yemen).

Yet, governance remains a chronic problem in the republic of Yemen. According to Transparency International (2019), Yemen is listed, along with other four countries that are Venezuela, Syria, South Sudan and Somalia, in the category of bottom countries in the corruption perceptions index (CPI). The governance in Yemen transmitted from extreme centralisation during the previous regime into a status of fragmentation during the current instability (Rogers, 2019), such fragmentation was increased due to the failure to decentralise during the last 10 years coupled with the active unrest (Al-Rawhani, 2019).

Towards the Future

The continuous existence of the challenges facing businesses in Yemen triggers an earnest need for official efforts by the government and its international development partners to work towards creating a conducive and competitive business environment that could induce investments by entrepreneurs to thrive and make added values to the development process and economic welfare.

A major issue witnessed in lower-income economies is prohibitive, inefficient or costly regulations that hamper the chances for business to grow and expand as well as resultantly impairing the business environment for potential entrepreneurship activities ("Environment for Business", 2013). For such condition, instead of relying on international aid provided to Yemen by development partners, efforts could be geared towards establishing a regulatory environment that would facilitate establishing a conducive business environment that could attract investments and entrepreneurial activities, in other words, adopting entrepreneurial change is the way out from prohibitive environment towards conducive business environment and achieving entrepreneurial development.

This is not new in the business world, many developing countries that are currently classified as middle-income countries have been underdeveloped two decades ago, and they created a success story by adopting such changes and reforms to become a reference point for other countries; here in this section, we will mention few of such experiences.

First, the Singaporean experience (see also Dana, 1999, 2014): For the success of its industrialisation process, Singapore had to create a safe and corruption-free environment with low taxes. For that, penalties were set for any illegal trade, illegal activities or corruption, which led to the need for developing human resources and infrastructure in the country through establishing technical schools and educational institutions; this helped Singapore to reach full employment during the 1970s (Zhou, 2019; Huff, 1994; World Bank, 2019d).

Such development was mainly based on reforms. During the 1960s, the reform efforts were focused on economic survival and building the state, whereas during the 1970s, reforms were focused on improving the efficiency and effectiveness of the public sector, improving the ability of Singapore to attract foreign investments and establishing statutory boards to foster these efforts towards fulfilling the claimed development goals. In the 1980s, the reform process was dedicated to human resources through driving for more productivity, talent as well as achieving higher value-added investments in the country. During the 1990s, the reform was geared towards the change that Singapore plan for to transition into a high-income country, and one of the remarkable changes adopted during the 1990s was launching Public Service for the 21st century (PS21) in 1995

(Lim, 1997), which addressed the internal and external issues of the public administration (Becerra, 2013; Lim, 1997; Quah, 2010) such as staff well-being, work improvement team and Staff Suggestion Scheme, quality service and finally the organisational review (Jones, 1997), by adopting initiatives for quality service that are courtesy, accessibility, responsiveness and effectiveness, which have the acronym as CARE (Ma, 2000; Quah, 2010).

The outcome of the long series of reforms resulted in the real transition of the Singaporean economy into one of the first world economies today. Such transition is reflected on the rank of Singapore in the international indexes such as Doing Business, Human Development Index (HDI), Global Competitiveness Index, Index of Economic Freedom and the continuous growth of GDP.

The reforms in Malaysia began with establishing Development Administration Unit (DAU) in 1965 to be responsible for planning and guiding the programmes and plans of administrative development (Alfaqi, 2012; Siddiquee, 2007; Taib and Mat, 1992); the Malaysian Administrative Modernisation and Management Planning Unit (MAMPU) that kept the development process going forward by focusing on the facilities that run and manage the public affairs (Ramli, 2012).

The industrial development in Malaysia increased the investments on heavy industries and attracted foreign direct investment (FDI), further, privatisation was practised through a policy called "Malaysia Incorporated" to reduce the burden on the government (Atory, 1995; Rasiah, 1993; Sundaram, 2017). The government also instituted the "Look East policy", which was concerned about two main elements that the methods of work in Japan and South Korea are supposed to be a model for Malaysia and the other element was about exchanging training and education with these two countries (Milne, 1986).

The National Development Policy and the Wawasan 2020 or Vision 2020 was announced, which is a master plan that aims for transforming the economy into market-driven, dynamic and customer-oriented for the purpose of transitioning into the first world economy (Khattab, 2004; Siddiquee, 2002), along with announcing many awards related to quality for the institutions in the public and private sectors to improve competition (Idris et al., 1996; Tuck, 2005).

At time of writing, Malaysia is ranked as a fast developing country; it is the 12th country in the ease of doing business in 2020 (World Bank, 2020), the 23rd country in the global competitiveness index (Schwab,

2018), the 22nd country in the Index of Economic Freedom (Miller et al., 2019), along with remarkable development in human development and GDP growth.

After the effect of World War II on the newly established Turkish republic, reforms were attempted by establishing commissions to tackle problems and challenges in the administrative system through the help of foreign experts (Altunok 2018; Gezici et al., 2016; Kapucu and Palabıyık, 2008; Sözen, 2005; Younis et al., 1992).

Along with the five-year plans aiming for development and addressing the issues in public administration (Coşkun, 2005; Younis, et al., 1992), administrative reforms became of more priority to the new government in 2003, such reforms focused on the development of the economy, improving efficiency and effectiveness of the public sector, whereas governance reforms aimed at improving accountability, transparency, responsiveness and participation in public administration. The reforms were geared towards privatisation, decentralisation, outsourcing, performance-oriented budgeting, organisation of public institutions and public employment (Berkman and Heper, 2001; Çelenk, 2009; Sezen, 2011; Sozen and Shaw, 2003).

The World Bank described the Turkish performance, economic and social development as "impressive" as it led to increasing the employment and rendering Turkey to an upper-middle-income country (World Bank, 2019a). Today, Turkey is the 43rd country worldwide in terms of the ease of doing business after it was the 93rd country in 2006 (World Bank, 2006; 2019b). The HDI score of Turkey grew from 0.576 in 1990 to 0.791 in 2018 to be ranked the 64th country out of 188 countries, putting Turkey in the category of high human development countries (United Nations Development Programme, 2018). See Chapter 15 of this book.

Last, the Rwandan experience: Where the genocide that took place in 1994 impoverished the population, the economy and the ability to attract investments. But the efforts continued to reduce inflation to single digits, and reduce poverty as well, by focusing on investments, infrastructure and education (BBC, n.d.; Central Intelligence Agency, 2018).

Major policies were issued and adopted to pursue the economic growth in Rwanda such as Rwanda Vision 2020, which focused mainly on building a knowledge-based and private sector-led economy along with developed human capital (Government of Rwanda, 2000); Poverty Reduction Strategy Paper as a reaffirmation of the government's commitment towards sustainable poverty reduction (Government of Rwanda, 2002); Economic Development and Poverty Reduction Strategy,

2008–2012, as a medium-term strategy to achieve the long-term development goals (Government of Rwanda, 2007); Economic Development and Poverty Reduction Strategy II, 2013–2018, which focused on major five priority areas: increasing the domestic interconnectivity of the economy, boosting the exports of the economy and increasing its connectivity with other economies, transitioning and developing the private sector through investments, increasing urban development as a new sector to transform the economic geography, transforming through pursuing a green economy (Government of Rwanda, 2013).

The results of such efforts can be seen in the ranks of the Rwandan economy among other economies in terms of doing business, as Rwanda was ranked the 139th country in the ease of doing business in 2006, while it is the 21st country during 2019 (World Bank, 2005; 2019b), along with significant improvement in human development, economic growth and GDP improvement.

The United Nations Secretary-General Kofi Annan (1998) stated that governance is of crucial importance for countries over the world to eradicate poverty and promote development (Annan, 1998). Therefore, taking this into consideration while checking the success stories of the countries mentioned earlier, it can be concluded that good governance, when applied, contributes towards promoting the development chances whether in an undeveloped economy such as in Rwanda or developing economy such as the Turkish economy. Further, it is worth mentioning that countries such as Rwanda and Singapore began the struggle towards development regardless of the required recourses, as they began developing the regulatory environment to encourage the business activities, and the human capital to take part in the development process, which is now reflected in the ranks of these countries in the HDI.

A major potential that can make doing business in Yemen an efficient opportunity is that the human capital is available in Yemen, as Yemeni workforce exists in the Gulf countries, more particularly, Saudi Arabia due to the common relationship and characteristics the two countries share. The remittance for such a workforce abroad acts as an essential role player in income generating in the economy (Wadhah Ahmed et al., 2019). Another potential could be the availability of opportunities in the manufacturing sector as the imports of Yemen are much higher than its exports (Central Statistical Organization, 2017), investing in the manufacturing sector can get the benefit of the availability of workforce, less domestic competition (than other West Asia countries), the encouragement of the regulatory aspect to investing in the country. However, it is worth mentioning that the current instability witnessed in the country acts as a major reason preventing investment initiatives from growing in the country plus being a cause for investors to consider other business environments to invest their capitals. Therefore, the following points can be suggested based on the abovementioned discussion for the purpose of improving the business environment in Yemen and prepare a competitive and conducive environment for investment and doing business:

Reforming the education system; to be directed towards developing skilled and qualified human capital. Currently, employers in Yemen consider the lack of skilled workforce as a major challenge hampering their ability to develop and expand their business activities, further, there is a mismatch between the educational institutions' outcome and the private sectors' employability needs (International Labour Organization, 2015). This creates an earnest need to re-engineer the education system to facilitate the chances of developing a better outcome that is needed by the private sector employers, which helps in achieving sustainable development through education. The World Development Report (Filmer, et al., 2018) quoted Kuan Chung's saying, which is "If your plan is for one year, plant rice. If your plan is for ten years, plant trees. If your plan is for one hundred years, educate children", this implies the importance of the role that education can facilitate if set properly and developed regularly.

Enforcing the laws; the world development report in 2017 (Lopez-Calva et al., 2017) was mainly focused on governance and the importance of improving governance to meet today's challenges. Singapore has been a perfect example of enforcing the laws for the purpose of development. The first Prime Minister Lee Kuan Yew set the strict laws and regulations to be followed in order to aim for development, which include specific bans and laws against litter, spitting, chewing gum, jaywalking, graffiti and so on. Plate (2010) wrote that chewing gum and sticking the remaining of it in every which place is thought of by authorities as a palpable attack on Singapore's ambition to be perfect. Therefore, Lee Kuan Yew succeeded in transforming Singapore from a small port into a global trading hub (Metz, 2015). The same can be aimed in Yemen if there is due attention towards enforcing the law, which could provide protection to businesses, investors and capitals in the country, which in turn acts as an attraction to FDIs.

Developing the infrastructure; infrastructural factors are majorly affecting the performance of small and medium enterprises in Yemen, be it factors related to roads, water and electricity or technological infrastructure such as the internet and telecommunication networks. A developing country could witness development in its infrastructure if it succeeded in overcoming the challenges of developing infrastructure such as dearth of visionary leaders, demand and supply, which can occur through techniques such as PESTLES analysis, which means the infrastructural development challenges could be political, economic, social, technology, legal, environmental and safety; PARETO analysis, which is a statistical method in decision-making to identify a specific number of tasks that produce major impact, it uses the 80/20 rule, which means that by doing specific 20% of the work, you can generate 80% of the benefits of doing the whole job; development matrix, which means that the four requirements of any physical infrastructure projects are design, finance, technology and management (Oyedele, 2016).

Providing motivations to businesses to grow and expand; nowadays, governments whether national, state or local governments vie for attracting and retaining investments to increase the chances for development, this happens through increasing values and ranges of incentives granted to businesses to invest, operate and expand (Rondinelli and Burpitt, 2000). Incentives to business act as a key factor leading to sustainability, further, incentives are not exclusively financial, for other incentives can bring financial effects to businesses and enterprises. Holt et al. (2010) divided incentives into economic incentives, regulatory incentives, social incentives, technical incentives and other incentives, which include incentives that are not part of the previous incentives such as free advertising or the opportunity to participate in advisory groups.

It can be then concluded that harvesting good outcomes in the business sector is based on preparing a conducive business environment with the regulatory framework, providing incentives to business and enforcing the laws and regulations. Future research might investigate the role of Yemenite women (Exhibit 10.8).

Exhibit 10.8 Dressed up in traditional looking dress; photo courtesy of
Tima Miroshnichenko

References

Al-Afandi, Mohammed Ahmed (2010), Investment Atmosphere in Yemen, Evaluation a Fifteen Year Experience (1990–2005), Proceedings of the Conference "Yemen – Economy – Future" Organised by Yemeni Center for Strategic Studies, Sanaa, Yemen, October 25–27.

Alawadhi, Hamid M. (2003), *The Yemeni Encyclopedia* (Vol. 3), Sanaa, Yemen: Alafif Cultural Foundation, pp. 1870–1880.

Al-Dhafiri, Faisal Mudhi (2020), The Role of Small and Medium Sized Enterprises in Achieving Kingdom of Saudi Arabia Vision 2030 and Supporting the Economic Security. Doctoral dissertation, Naif Arab University for Security Sciences, Riyadh, Saudi Arabia.

Alfaqi, Abeer (2012), "Administrative Reform Experiences: The Malaysian Public Administration Reform ... Four Decades of Development," *African Journal of Political Sciences* 1 (1), pp. 78–93.

Alhawery, Mohammed Ahmed (2004), "The Requirements to Promote the Role of the Private Sector in Economic Development," *Shoon Alasr Journal,* 8 (17), pp. 85–109.

Aliriani, Kais (2013), Role of SMEs in the Economy: The Case of Yemen. Proceeding of Yemen: Challenges for the Future, International Conference, January 11–12, London.

Al-Maqaleh, Ali (2012), Small Enterprises in Yemen, Master dissertation, Queen Arwa University, Yemen. Proceedings of Yemen: Challenges for the Future, International Conference, January 11–12, London.

Al-Rawhani, Osama (2019), A Strong Central State: A Prerequisite for Effective Local Governance in Yemen, Arab Reform Initiative, (Retrieved from https://www.arab-reform.net/publication/a-strong-central-state-a-prerequisite-for-effective-local-governance-in-yemen/)

AlSabai, Sadiq Ahmed Abdullah (2016), "The Role of Microfinance Institutions and Programs in Developing and Funding SMEs in Yemen 2009–2014," *SUST Journal of Economic Sciences* 17 (2), pp. 104–123. (Retrieved from http://repository.sustech.edu/handle/123456789/17903)

Altunok, Mustafa (2018), "Development of Turkish Public Administration," in Ali Farazmand, ed., *Global Encyclopedia of Public Administration, Public Policy, and Governance,* Cham: Springer.

Annan, Kofi A. (1998), *Partnerships for Global Community: Annual Report on the Work of the Organization, 1998,* New York: United Nations, Department of Public Information.

Ariel, Ari (2013), *Jewish-Muslim Relations and Migration from Yemen to Palestine in the Late Nineteenth and Twentieth Centuries,* Leiden: Brill.

Atory, Hussain Ahmad (1995), "Administrative Reforms in Malaysia Strategies for Promoting Efficiency and Productivity in the Public

Service, 1981–91," *Indian Journal of Public Administration* 41 (1), pp. 78–91.

BBC (n.d.), Rwanda Country Profile, (Retrieved from https://www.bbc.com/news/world-africa-14093238)

Becerra, Pedro A. Villezca (2013), "Public Sector Management in Singapore: Examining the Public Service for the 21st Century Reform," *Explanans* 2 (2), pp. 33–45.

Berkman, A. Umit, and Metin Heper (2001), "Political dynamics and administrative reform in Turkey," in Ali Farazmand, ed., *Administrative Reform in Developing Nations,* Westpost, Connecticut: Praeger, pp. 151–162.

Carothers, Thomas, and Diane de Gramont (2011), *Aiding Governance in Developing Countries: Progress Amid Uncertainties* (Vol. 1), Washington, DC: Carnegie Endowment for International Peace.

Caton, Steven C. (2013), *Yemen, Middle East in Focus*, Santa Barbara, California: ABC-CLIO.

Çelenk, Ayse Aslihan (2009), "Europeanization and Administrative Reform: The Case of Turkey," *Mediterranean Politics* 14(1), pp. 41–60.

Cetin, Özlem, Sylvie Hoster, and Jürgen Kathmann (2007), Assessment of MSE Financial Needs in Yemen (No. 44471), Washington, DC: World Bank.

Central Intelligence Agency (2018), *The World Factbook 2018,* Washington, DC: Central Intelligence Agency, Government Printing Office.

Central Statistical Organization (2004), *Statistical Year Book for 2004,* Sanaa: Central Statistical Organization.

Central Statistical Organization (2010), *Statistical Year Book for 2010,* Sanaa: Central Statistical Organization.

Central Statistical Organization (2014), *Statistical Year Book for 2014,* Sanaa: Central Statistical Organization.

Central Statistical Organization (2017), *Statistical Year Book for 2017,* Sanaa: Central Statistical Organization.

Coşkun, Betül (2005), "Türkiye'de Kamu Yönetiminde Yeniden Yapılanma Tarihsel Geçmiş Ve Genel Bir Değerlendirme," *Türk İdare Dergisi* 448, pp. 13–47.

Dana, Léo-Paul (1999), *Entrepreneurship in Pacific Asia,* Singapore, London and Hong Kong: World Scientific.

Dana, Léo-Paul (2000a), "Change and Circumstance in Kyrgyz Markets," *Qualitative Market Research: An International Journal* 3 (2), pp. 62–73.

Dana, Léo-Paul (2000b), "Economic Sectors in Egypt and Their Managerial Implications," *Journal of African Business* 1 (1), pp. 65–81.

Dana, Léo-Paul (2011), "Entrepreneurship in Bolivia: An Ethnographic Enquiry," *International Journal of Business and Emerging Markets* 3 (1), pp. 75–88.

Dana, Léo-Paul (2014), *Asian Models of Entrepreneurship from the Indian Union and Nepal to the Japanese Archipelago: Context, Policy and Practice,* Singapore, London and Hong Kong: World Scientific.

Dana, Léo-Paul, Hamid Etemad, and Richard W. Wright (2013), "Toward a Paradigm of Symbiotic Entrepreneurship," *International Journal of Entrepreneurship and Small Business* 5 (2), pp. 109–126.

Dana, Léo-Paul, and Richard W. Wright (2015), "Bazaar Economies, Modern Networks and Entrepreneurship," in Sir Cary L. Cooper, ed., Wiley Encyclopedia of Management, 3rd edition, John Wiley & Sons, Volume 3, Michael Morris and Don Kuratko, volume editors, pp. 13–18.

Donor Committee for Enterprise Development (2017), *Technical Report: Policies That Promote SME Participation in Public Procurement,* Washington, DC: Donor Committee for Enterprise Development.

Edo, Michael. E. (1975), "Currency Arrangements and Banking Legislation in the Arabian Peninsula," *Staff Papers* 22 (2), pp. 510–538.

Environment for Business in Low-Income Countries (2013), openphilanthropy. (Retrieved from https://www.openphilanthropy.org/research/cause-reports/business-environment)

Fanselow, Frank S. (1990), "The Bazaar Economy or How Bizarre is the Bazaar Really?" *Man* 25 (2), pp. 250–265.

Filmer, Deon, Margarita Langthaler, Robert Stehrer, and Thomas Vogel (2018), *Learning to Realize Education's Promise*, Washington, The World Bank.

Geertz, Clifford (1978), "The Bazaar Economy: Information and Search in Peasant Marketing," *The American Economic Review* 68 (2), pp. 28–32.

General Investment Authority (2002), Law Investment Amendment No. 22, 2002, Sanaa, Yemen: National Information Center.

Gezici, Hikmet Salahaddin, Yasin Taşpınar, and Selcuk Aslan (2016), "Attempts for Reform in Turkish Public Administration After 1950," in *Second International Congress on Economics and Business (ICEB 2016),* Sarajevo, pp. 1418–1429.

Goetz, Kimberly S. (2010), "Encouraging Sustainable Business Practices Using Incentives: A Practitioner's View," *Management Research Review* 33 (11), pp. 1042–1053.

Government of Rwanda (2000), Rwanda Vision 2020, Kigali: Ministry of Finance and Economic Planning.

Government of Rwanda (2002), Poverty Reduction Strategy Paper 2002, Kigali: Ministry of Finance and Economic Planning.

Government of Rwanda (2007), *Economic Development and Poverty Reduction Strategy, 2008–2012,* Kigali: Ministry of Finance and Economic Planning.

Government of Rwanda (2013), *Economic Development and Poverty Reduction Strategy II, 2013–2018,* Kigali: Rwanda Standards Board.

Huff, W. Greg (1994), *The Economic Growth of Singapore: Trade and Development in the Twentieth Century,* New York: Cambridge University Press.

Idris, Mohd. Ashari, William McEwan, and Nicolo Belavendram (1996), "The Adoption of ISO 9000 and Total Quality Management in Malaysia," *The TQM Magazine* 8 (5), pp. 65–68.

International Labour Organization (2015), *Yemen Labour Force Survey 2013–14,* Beirut, Lebanon: International Labour Organization.

Jones, Lawrence R. (1997), "Public Service for the 21st Century – PS21," in Jon S. T. Quah, ed., *Public Administration Singapore-Style,* Bingley: Emerald.

Kannan, A. S., and S. Sudalaimuthu (2014), "Indian MSMEs: Initiatives and Financing Trends," *International Journal of Management* 5 (10), pp. 58–70.

Kapucu, Naim, and Hamit Palabıyık (2008), *Turkish Public Administration: From Tradition to the Modern Age* (Vol. 17), Ankara, Turkey: USAK Books.

Khattab, Umi (2004), "Wawasan 2020: Engineering a Modern Malay (sia) State Campaigns and Minority Stakes," *Media Asia* 31 (3), pp. 170–177.

Lim, Siong Guan (1997), "Sustaining Excellence in Government: The Singapore Experience," *Public Administration and Development: The International Journal of Management Research and Practice* 17 (1), pp. 167–174.

Lopez-Calva, Luis-Felipe, Yongmei Zhou, Edouard Al-Dahdah, David J. Bulman, D. H. Isser, Marco Larizza, Ezequiel Molina, Abla Safir, and Siddharth Sharma (2017), *World Development Report 2017: Governance and the Law* (No. 112303). Washington, DC: World Bank.

Ma, David K. L. (2000), "Delivering Results on the Ground: Improving Service to Citizens in Singapore," *Asian Journal of Political Science* 8 (2), pp. 137–144.

Meron, Orly C. (2011), "Port Jews: Aden (1839–1947) as a Test Case," *Tema: Journal of Judeo-Yemenite Studies* 11, pp. 99–122.

Metz, Elle (2015), Why Singapore Banned Chewing Gum, *BBC News Magazine,* (Retrieved from https://www.bbc.com/news/magazine-32 090420)

Miller, Terry, Anthony B. Kim, and James M. Roberts (2019), *Index of Economic Freedom,* Washington, DC: The Heritage Foundation.

Milne, Robert S. (1986), "Malaysia – Beyond the New Economic Policy," *Asian Survey* 26 (12), pp. 1364–1382.

Oyedele, Olufemi Adedamola (2016), Infrastructure Problems of Developing Nations and Sustainable Development. International Public Procurement Conference, IPPC7, Bali, Indonesia.

Plate, Tom (2010), *Conversations with Lee Kuan Yew: Citizen Singapore: How to Build a Nation,* Singapore: Marshall Cavendish Editions.

Quah, Jon S. T., ed. (2010), *Public Administration Singapore-Style,* Bingley: Emerald.

Rabi, Uzi (2014), *Yemen: Revolution, Civil War and Unification,* Bloomsbury Publishing.

Ramli, Razlini Mohd (2012), "Malaysian E-government: Issues and Challenges in Public Administration," *International Proceedings of Economic Development and Research* 48 (2), pp. 19–23.

Rasiah, Rajah (1993), "Free Trade Zones and Industrial Development in Malaysia," in Kwame Sundaran Jomo, ed., *Industrializing Malaysia: Policy, Performance, Prospects,* Abingdon, Oxfordshire: Routledge.

Raymanpress (2013), The First Small Enterprises Conference Calls for Change, (Retrieved from http://www.raymanpress.com/print.php?id =33470)

Reeg, Caroline (2015), *Micro and Small Enterprises as Drivers for Job Creation and Decent Work,* Bonn, Germany: Deutsches Institut für Entwicklungspolitik.

Rogers, Joshua (2019), *Local Governance in Yemen: Theory, Practice, and Future Options,* Berlin: Berghof Foundation.

Rondinelli, Dennis A., and William J. Burpitt (2000), "Do Government Incentives Attract and Retain International Investment? A Study of Foreign-Owned Firms in North Carolina," *Policy Sciences* 33 (2), pp. 181–205.

Saeed, Shawqi Hail (2005). Workforce and the Private Sector in Yemen. Presented to: Round-Table Conference in Yemen for Growth, and Social Development, April 9–10, Sanaa, Yemen.

Schwab, Klaus (2018), *The Global Competitiveness Report 2018,* World Economic Forum, pp. 9–14.

Sezen, Seriye (2011), "International Versus Domestic Explanations of Administrative Reforms: The Case of Turkey," *International Review of Administrative Sciences* 77 (2), pp. 322–346.

Siddiquee, Noore Alam (2002), "Administrative Reform in Malaysia: Recent Trends and Developments," *Asian Journal of Political Science* 10 (1), pp. 105–130.

Siddiquee, Noore Alam (2007), "Public Service Innovations Policy Transfer and Governance in the Asia-Pacific Region: The Malaysian Experience," *JOAAG* 2 (1), pp. 81–91.

Sözen, Süleyman (2005), "Administrative Reforms in Turkey: Impretives Efforts and Constraints," *Ankara Üniversitesi SBF Dergisi* 60 (3), pp. 195–214.

Sözen, Süleyman, and Ian Shaw (2003), "Turkey and the European Union: Modernizing a Traditional State?" *Social Policy & Administration* 37 (2), pp. 108–120.

Sundaram, Jomo Kwame (2017), "'Malaysia Incorporated': Corporatism a la Mahathir," *Institutions and Economies* 6, pp. 73–94.

Taib, Tan Sri Data Mahmood Bin, and Johari Mat (1992), "Administrative Reforms in Malaysia Toward Enhancing Public Service Performance," *Governance* 5 (4), pp. 423–437.

Transparency International (2019), *Corruption Perceptions Index 2019,* Berlin, Germany: Transparency International.

Tuck, Cheah Eng (2005), "A Quality Award and Stock Market Reaction: Evidence from Malaysia," *Total Quality Management & Business Excellence* 16 (6), pp. 681–691.

United Nations (1991), *Trade and Development Report, 1991,* New York: United Nations.

United Nations Development Programme (2018), *Human Development Indices and Indicators 2018 Statistical Update,* New York: United Nations.

Wadhah Ahmed, Saleh Zaid, and Yousef Mohsen (2019), *The Essential Role of Remittances in Mitigating Economic Collapse,* Sanaa, Yemen: Sanaa Center for Strategic Studies.

Warnholz, Jean-Louis (2008), "Even the Poorest Can Be a Thriving Market," *Harvard Business Review,* 86 (5), p. 26.

World Bank (1973), Economic Development in the Yemen Arab Republic, Report No. 98a-YAR, Washington, DC: World Bank.

World Bank (1979), *Yemen Arab Republic, Development of a Traditional Economy,* Washington, DC: World Bank Country Study.

World Bank (1981), *Yemen Arab Republic – Urban Sector Report,* Washington, DC: World Bank.

World Bank (2005), *Doing Business Economy Rankings: Removing Obstacles for Growth,* Washington, DC: World Bank and the International Finance Corporation.

World Bank (2006), *Doing Business 2006: Creating Jobs.* Washington, DC: World Bank.

World Bank (2008), *Telling Our Story: Improving Lives – Success Stories* (English, edition no. 4), Washington, DC: World Bank.

World Bank (2009), *Doing Business 2010: Reforming Through Difficult Times,* Washington, DC: World Bank.

World Bank (2013), Enterprise Survey 2013, (Retrieved from https://www. enterprisesurveys.org/en/data/exploreeconomies/2013/yemen)

World Bank (2017a), Doing Business 2018. Reforming to Create Jobs, (Retrieved from http://russian.doingbusiness.org/content/dam/doing Business/media/Annual-Reports/English/DB2018-Full-Report.pdf)

World Bank (2017b), *World Development Report: Governance and Law. 2017,* Washington, DC: World Bank.

World Bank (2018), *Doing Business 2019: Training for Reform,* Washington, DC: World Bank.

World Bank (2019a), Country Snapshot, Turkey, (Retrieved from http:// pubdocs.worldbank.org/en/188761555342422504/Turkey-Snapshot-Spring-2019.pdf, accessed 23 October 2019)

World Bank (2019b), *Doing Business 2019: Training for Reform,* Washington, DC: World Bank.

World Bank (2019c), Good Governance Indicators, (Retrieved from https:// info.worldbank.org/governance/wgi/)

World Bank (2019d), The World Bank in Singapore, (Retrieved from https://www.worldbank.org/en/country/singapore/overview, accessed 15 October 2019)

World Bank (2020), *Doing Business: Comparing Business Regulation in 190 Economies,* Washington, DC: World Bank.

Younis, Talib, S. A. M. Ibrahim, and M. A. McLean (1992), "Administrative Development and Reform in Turkey: A Historical Overview (Part II)," *International Journal of Public Sector Management* 5 (2), pp. 21–31.

Zhou, Ping (2019), The History of Singapore's Economic Development, (Retrieved from https://www.thoughtco.com/singapores-economic-development-1434565, accessed 15 October 2019)

Chapter 11

The Context for Business in Bahrain

Veland Ramadani, Ramo Palalić, Aidin Salamzadeh & Léo-Paul Dana

Abstract: This chapter focuses on several important aspects of the business context of the Kingdom of Bahrain, a tiny desert kingdom linked to Saudi Arabia by the 25-km long King Fahd Causeway. The chapter provides an overview of the historical, political and economic development of Bahrain since its inception, followed by a discussion of characteristics of Bahraini business framework conditions, wherein details of the ecosystem dimensions are described. The chapter concludes with providing a brief outlook for the future and provides a few insights and recommendations.

Keywords: Business context, bazaar, ecosystem, Bahrain

Introduction

The Kingdom of Bahrain is located in the Persian Gulf, between the Qatari Peninsula and the northeastern coast of Saudi Arabia. It consists of a small archipelago with 51 natural islands and 33 artificial islands, which are centred around Bahrain Island (Exhibit 11.1). Bahrain became a member of the United Nations (UN) on 21 September 1971. With an area of 780 km^2, Bahrain is the third-smallest country in Asia after Singapore and the Maldives (Crystal, 2021). With a population of 157,000, Manama (Exhibit 11.2) is its largest city and the national capital. The capital's name comes from the Arabic word, *al-Manãma*, which means "the place of rest" or "the place of dreams" (Room, 1997).

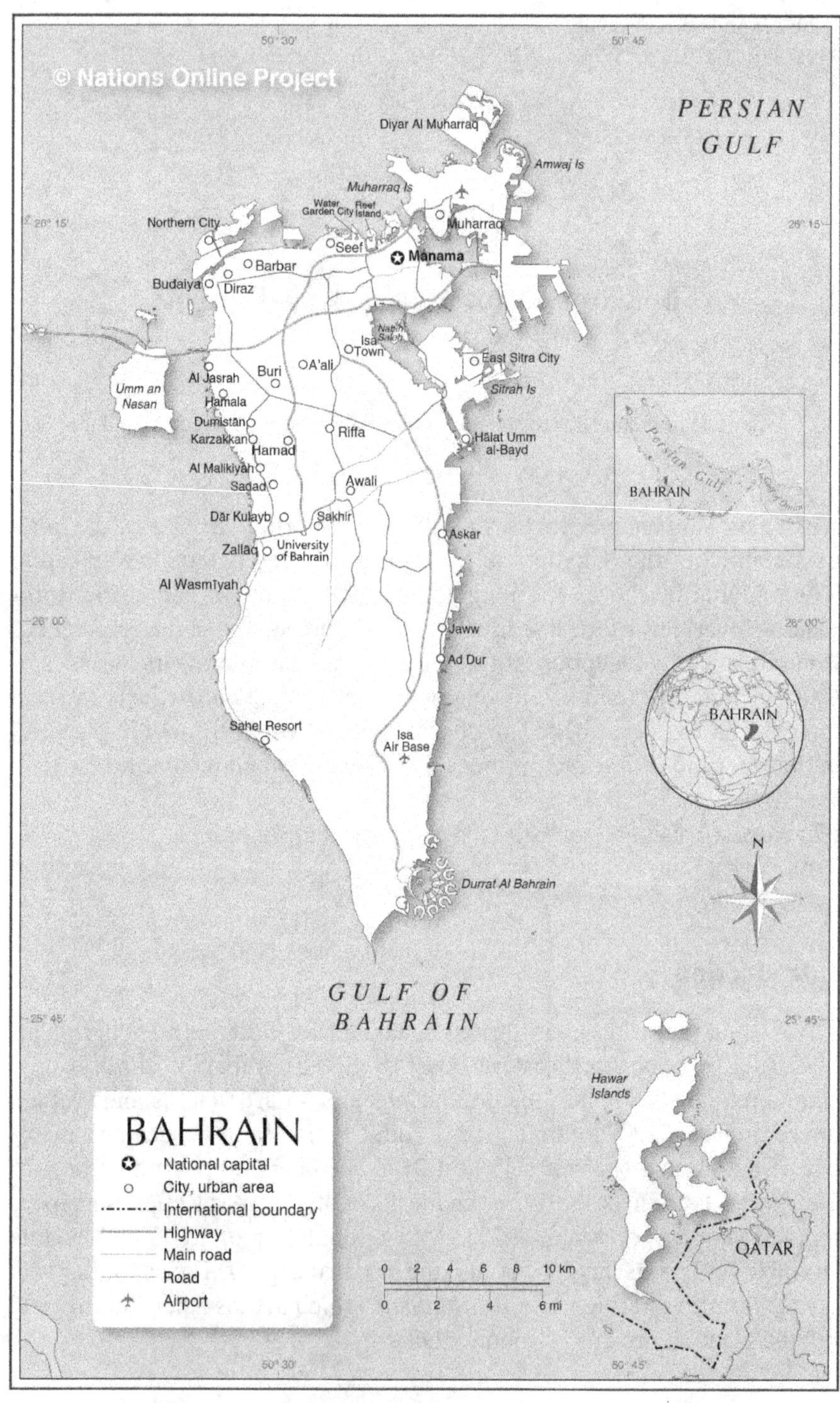

Exhibit 11.1   Map of Bahrain; courtesy of Nations Online Project

Exhibit 11.2 Manama, the capital of Bahrain; photo courtesy of Pixabay

Around 1.6 million people live in Bahrain. Regarding the population ethnicity, 50.7% are Arab (46% Bahraini, 3% Somalis, 1.7% others), 45.5% other Asian, 1% European and 1.2% others (Central Intelligence Agency, 2011). Islam is the state religion with 69.7% of the Bahraini population being Muslim. Shi'a Muslims are the majority (62% of the Muslim people) and are divided into two main groups, Baharna (Arab) and Ajam (Persian) Shi'a. Most of them live in Manama and Muharraq. Even though Sunni Muslims are a minority, they are the most influential people in the country, where they hold the most positions in the government; the royal family is Sunni. Sunni Muslims are divided into Arabs and Huwala, and most of them live in Muharraq, Riffa, Zallaq and Hawar islands (Rentz, 2008). Exhibit 11.3 shows the Al-Fatih Grand Mosque in Bahrain. With regards to the other religions, Christians make up about 14.1% of the population, Hindu 10.2%, Buddhist 3.1%, Jews 0.3%, other religions 1% and less than 2% unaffiliated (Pew Research Center, 2020).

Bahrain's official language is Arabic, while English is the most used foreign language and an obligatory language at all schools. Most of the Bahraini people also speak Persian but mostly in the home. Other languages are Hindi, Urdu and Tagalog, usually used among expatriates (Smith, 2021).

Exhibit 11.3 Al-Fatih Grand Mosque; photo courtesy of Pixabay

Bahrain has developed infrastructures, especially since the development of the petroleum industry. In addition to its robust banking and financial industry (Boadi et al., 2017), the country has invested in telecommunications, as well as science-and-technology-based industries, such as startups (Salamzadeh, 2018; Salamzadeh et al., 2017). Several multinational corporations are operating in this country and selling their goods and services to other countries. Access to biocapacity in this country is lesser than the world's average (Lane, 2009). Then, Bahrain relies heavily on imports of food, meat and fruits from other countries and exports of crude oil to other countries. However, substantial investments in technological advancements have changed the current export ratios that still highly rely on crude oil (Khayati, 2019). Moreover, Bahrain has a long history of bazaars (Exhibit 11.4). For instance, Manama Souq is the oldest bazaar of its capital. This bazaar was shaped to sell various products and underwent a series of incidents, like staying at the centre of a general strike in 1922 (Al-Mdaires, 2002).

Exhibit 11.4 Fruit seller; photo courtesy of Pixabay

The remaining of this chapter provides a picture of Bahrain's historical aspects and its impact on doing business in this country, general business context and ends with useful suggestions for further development of the business ecosystem in Bahrain.

Historical Context

Bahrain was historically civilised by Dilmun and turned into a trade centre in the Bronze Age. Assyrians and Babylonians also ruled over this region thousands of years ago (Larsen, 1983). The Achaemenids ruled over this region for almost three centuries, until Parthias further expanded Persia and ruled over Oman as well. Then, Bahrain became a critical trade zone for them (André-Salvini, 2005). This region exports pearls, cotton and other valuable products to various destinations like the Arab countries and India. This country was home to Arameans, Christians, Persians and Zoroastrians. After the Muslim conquest, Bahrainis mostly converted to Islam (Potts, 2006). Muslims have been dominant in Bahrain ever since. Jews arrived here from Basra (Iraq) during the 1880s and they have had good relations with other Bahrainis ever since.

The Portuguese Empire ruled over Bahrain for around eight decades, beginning in 1521. However, the Safavid Empire expelled the Portuguese from the island in 1602 and expanded Shi'a Islam (Stewart, 1996). Persian rulers governed Bahrain for the next two centuries; however, the country was invaded by Oman in 1717 and 1738. In 1783, Qatar's Bani Utbath tribe defeated Al-Madhkur, and their Khalifa moved to Bahrain in 1799 due to Ottomans' pressures (Zahlan, 2016). Omanis and Al Sauds invaded Bahrain in the early 19th century.

In 1820, the Al Khalifa was supported and recognised as the ruler of Bahrain by the United Kingdom. Agreements were signed between Bahrain and the United Kingdom to protect and empower Bahrain during those years (Fuccaro, 2009), but this led to unrest among Bahrainis in the following years, as the United Kingdom dominated the country. The country was ranked first in the world in pearl fisheries, until the development of petroleum.

During the late 1880s, Jewish traders established a Jewish community in Bahrain. Jews here were largely self-employed. In 1911, some merchants asked for restricting the authority of Britain over Bahrain. Subsequently, they were exiled to India (Kaiksow, 2009). Shortly before British Foreign Secretary Arthur Balfour gave his support for re-establishing a "national home for the Jewish people" in Palestine, there was a discussion about creating a "Jewish State of Eastern Arabia" in the desert near Manama. In 1927, Reza Shah, the Shah of Iran, requested sovereignty over this country, due to the conflicts created between Shi'a and Sunni citizens of Bahrain, as well as some other pressures put by the United Kingdom to Bahrainis.

When oil was discovered in 1932, Bahrain entered its modernisation era. This tightened their relationship with the United Kingdom. Bahrain joined the Allied side in World War II, and this led to being bombarded by Italians (Macris, 2010). After World War II, anti-British movements were initiated among Arabs.

Many Jews moved away from Bahrain left during the late 1940s and immigrated to India and then to Israel. Others left during the late 1960s. Among the Jews who stayed in Bahrain is the prominent Nonoo family, originally from Iraq.

In 1971, the Shah of Iran accepted holding a referendum by the UN, and the country declared its independence and joined the UN (Goudarzi and Nazarpour, 2019). As of 1973, Bahrain's economy was both positively and negatively affected by the oil boom. The country has since diversified its economy. During the Lebanese Civil War, Bahrain replaced Beirut as the Middle East's financial hub (Batrancea et al., 2019; Nuruzzaman,

2013). Afterwards, the country expanded its relationships with its allies and tried to be more open in economic and political negotiations.

In 2001, Ebrahim Dahood Nonoo was appointed as the first-ever member of Bahrain's parliamentary Shura Council. His successor was his cousin, Houda Nonoo, the first Jewish woman on the Shura Council. In 2008, Hooda Nonoo was selected to serve as an ambassador of Bahrain to the United States, making her the first Jewish ambassador to represent an Arab country. Another cousin, Bahrain-born Misha Nonoo was raised in London and is a fashion designer rumoured to have introduced Meghan Markle to Prince Harry.

In 2002, the country's formal name was changed from the State of Bahrain to the Kingdom of Bahrain (Matthiesen, 2013). The Bahraini national flag consists of white and red stripes, separated by five triangles that serve as a serrated line and symbolise the five pillars of Islam. This flag was adopted on 14 February 2002 by the Emir of Bahrain, Hamad ibn Isa Al Khalifa who declared the country to be a kingdom with himself as king. The coat of arms is a national emblem of Bahrain and is based on Charles Belgrave's design of 1932 (De Vries, 2011).

In 2010, Jewish author Nancy Khedouri was appointed to the Bahraini parliament. In 2011, after the Arab Spring, Bahrain's Shi'a majority protested against their Sunni rulers. This led to the death of about 100 Bahrainis but was not covered thoroughly by Arab media (Al-Rawi, 2015; Karolak, 2017).

As of 2015, His Majesty the King, Hamad bin Isa al-Khalifa, officially marked the Jewish holiday of Hanukkah, with Muslim and Jewish Bahrainis celebrating together. In June 2019, the United States sponsored an economic workshop in Bahrain. Among participants was well-known Palestinian businessman Ashraf Jabari, co-founder of the Judaea and Samaria Chamber of Commerce. Jabari expressed support for President Trump's peace plan; Bahrain and Israel signed the 2020 *Abraham Accords: Declaration of Peace, Cooperation, and Constructive Diplomatic and Friendly Relations*. Bahrain has signed agreements with 190 countries and is among the fastest-growing economies in the Arab world.

Context for Enterprise and Implications for Doing Business

Bahrain provides a fertile ground for doing business. As discussed recently by Dana et al. (2021), Palalić, Kahwaji, et al. (2021) and Palalić, Dana, et al. (2021), Bahrain is in a crucial geostrategic position that provides an excellent opportunity for the country to be exposed, open and close to global business activities. Thus, it becomes a vital hub for investors and business people, giving the kingdom sufficient basis for various business activities. In the past few decades such activities were reflected in various international and bilateral agreements, among which are of great importance like General Agreement on Tariffs and Trade (GATT) agreement signed in 1993 and a 1994 agreement signed with the World Trade Organisation.

One of the interesting moments, not for Bahrain only, but for the entire Gulf Cooperation Council (GCC) is that each GCC member sets up a vision for a few decades in the future, which marks such a country being serious in its socio-economic development (Barrichello et al., 2020). Bahrain's vision is set up in 2008 with the name: *The Economic Vision 2030*, which was launched by His Majesty King Hamad bin Isa Al Khalifa. This shows the visionary path for the King for Bahrainis to be recognised globally as the ones who initiate good things. In this line, the slogan has been set up "From Regional Pioneer to Global Contender." This vision is supposed to nurture country's sustainability, competitiveness at a global scale and fairness. These strategic steps are crucial in restructuring the whole country, including the government, society and business environment (Palalić, Dana, et al., 2021). It is hoped that such a momentous strategic vision will positively impact the country in the long term, which will be bounced to domestic human capital as the major force in the country's socio-economic development. It should also be noted that Bahrain's government allocated considerable resources via various funds and organisations to complement its vision in reality.

Palalić, Dana, et al. (2021) noted that Bahrain's government aimed to reduce national poverty and decrease the unemployment rate, especially among youth. In doing this, the government made initiatives in developing other businesses rather than oil and gas production. The friendly legislation made the country in doing business easy, enabling possibilities of getting various business licenses and a huge pool of skilled and trained labour force for entrepreneurial activities (Dana et al., 2009). Considering that Bahrain was formerly a land of nomads, it can be said that this country has transformed itself from an itinerant society into an ultra-modern country.

The kingdom truly invests a lot of resources in building a strong and developed society through different social and economic activities. One of the pillars in a modern economy is innovation, where Bahrain, in the recent past, was not fortunate to improve, but the index has been decreased by 24 points (Table 11.1). It shows that innovation slowed down in Bahrain.

Justification can be found in the recent pandemic (COVID-19), because the primary goal of every government around the globe was to protect society from it, where lots of resources had to be allocated to fight back the pandemic.

According to the same source, Bahrain has been ranked 79th out of 131 global economies for Global Innovation Index (GII) in 2020. Table 11.2 indicates that in recent years there was a decrease in the GII index (World Intellectual Property Organisation, 2021).

In 2020, Bahrain performed less in innovation outputs than innovation inputs. Respectively, it can be observed that innovation inputs are higher compared to 2019 and 2018, while the performance of outputs is lower compared to 2019 and 2018.

Due to lower foreign oil prices and the spread of COVID-19, like other countries in this region (Kawamorita et al., 2020; Salamzadeh and Dana, 2021), Bahrain's economy was projected to contract. In view of

Table 11.1. Innovation Ranking for GCC Countries

No	GCC Member	2019	2020
1	Bahrain	55	79
2	Kuwait	60	78
3	Oman	109	84
4	Qatar	72	70
5	Saudi Arabia	77	66
6	United Arab Emirates	55	34

Source: World Intellectual Property Organisation (2021)

Table 11.2. Bahrain's Ranking for GII

No	Year	GII	Innovation inputs	Innovation outputs
1	2020	79	63	89
2	2019	78	69	87
3	2018	72	70	74

Source: World Intellectual Property Organisation (2021)

lower oil receipts and high off-budget expenditures, the total budget deficit was predicted to only steadily narrow over 2021–2022. Downside risks are triggered by the duration and depth of the two very important factors that could worsen the situation in the future, the weak oil price and the pandemic COVID-19 (World Bank, 2021).

In the face of more pandemic disturbances, combined with a moderate rebound in oil prices over the rest of the year, real GDP is projected to decline by 5% by the end of 2020. Growth could bounce back to an average of 2% over 2021–2022, backed by infrastructure projects and non-oil activity pick-ups. The overall fiscal deficit is expected to expand to over 13% of GDP by 2020 due to lower oil prices and high budgetary expenses, along with limited oil production potential. The continuation of high fiscal deficits would lead to a rapid increase in government debt, which is expected to hit 130% of GDP in 2020 (World Bank, 2021).

As the whole world will depend on global happenings, Bahrain's business landscape will also be dependent. Nonetheless, the kingdom will find other ways to suppress the global impact on doing business in this country.

Towards the Future

Something special in Bahrain is the churches of different denominations, Hindu and Sikh temples, maatams, Shiite mosques, Sunni mosques and the synagogue dating from the 1930s are close together, but more importantly, their members befriend one another. Citizens respect the culture and religions of others and even join each other in religious celebrations. This creates a positive environment for business as well as for social ties. A resident of Bahrain, whose family business is a leading importer of tablecloths and linens, Khedouri (2008) observed that Bahrain has long practised religious tolerance; she explained that Bahraini Jews are proud to be Arab – and they have contributed significantly to the nation. The old market Al Mutanabi Road was formerly known as *Suq al-yahoud* – the Jewish Market. In the old market several shops display Jewish family names across their storefronts. In 2008, King Hamad bin Isa Al Khalifa went to the United Kingdom and to the United States where he invited Jews of Bahraini origin to move back to Bahrain, which he described as their home. He told 50 Bahraini Jews in New York: "It's your country." In September 2020, Bahraini Foreign Minister Abdullatif Al Zayani signed a declaration of peace, cooperation and constructive diplomatic and friendly relations (see Exhibit 11.5) with Israel.

ABRAHAM ACCORDS: DECLARATION OF PEACE, CO-OPERATION, AND CONSTRUCTIVE DIPLOMATIC AND FRIENDLY RELATIONS

Announced by the State of Israel and Kingdom of Bahrain on 15 September 2020

His Majesty King Hamad bin Isa bin Salman al-Khalifa and Prime Minister Benjamin Netanyahu have agreed to open era of friendship and cooperation in a pursuit of a Middle East region that is stable, secure and prosperous for the benefit of all States and peoples in the region. In this spirit Prime Minister Netanyahu of Israel and Foreign Minister Mr. Abdullatif Al Zayani met in Washington today, at the invitation of President Donald J. Trump of the United States of America, to endorse the principles of the Abraham Accords and to commence a new chapter of peace. This diplomatic breakthrough was facilitated by the Abraham Accords initiative of President Donald J. Trump. It reflects the successful perseverance of the United States' efforts to promote peace and stability in the Middle East. The Kingdom of Bahrain and the State of Israel trust that this development will help lead to a future in which all peoples and all faiths can live together in the spirit of cooperation and enjoy peace and prosperity where states focus on shared interests and building a better future.

The parties discussed their shared commitment to advancing peace and security in the Middle East stressing the importance of embracing the vision of the Abraham Accords, widening the circle of peace; recognizing each State's right to sovereignty and to live in peace and security, and continuing the efforts to achieve a just, comprehensive, and enduring resolution of the Israeli-Palestinian conflict.

In their meeting, Prime Minister Benjamin Netanyahu and Foreign Minister Abdullatif Al Zayani agreed to establish full diplomatic relations, to promote lasting security, to eschew threats and the use of force, as well as advance coexistence and a culture of peace. In this spirit, they have today approved a series of steps initiating this new chapter in their relations. The Kingdom of Bahrain and the state of Israel have agreed to seek agreements in the coming weeks regarding investment, tourism, direct flights, security, telecommunications, technology, energy, healthcare, culture, the environment, and the other areas of mutual benefit, as well as reaching agreement on the reciprocal opening of embassies.

The Kingdom of Bahrain and the State of Israel view this moment as a historic opportunity and recognize their responsibility to pursue a more secure and prosperous future for generations to come in their respective countries and in the region.

The two countries jointly express their profound thanks and appreciation to President Donald J. Trump for his untiring efforts and unique and pragmatic approach to further the cause of peace, justice and prosperity for all the peoples of the region. In recognition of this appreciation, the two countries have asked President Donald J. Trump to sign this document as a witness to their shared resolve and as the host of their historic meeting.

Prime Minister Benjamin Netanyahu   Foreign Minister Abdullatif Al Zayani

Witnessed by
President Donald J. Trump

Exhibit 11.5 Signed by Israel, Bahrain and the United States

It appears Bahrain is on the right course for a very bright economic future. Perhaps its success will encourage others to follow suit. Alon and Chase (2005) found that it is in a nation's long-run economic interest to expand not only economic freedom but also religious freedom. Yong (2019) found cultural diversity to be the causal variable of richer ideas, heuristics, perspectives and skills, suggesting the potential sustainability of economic prosperity with creativity-oriented policies. Lu (2021) identified diversity as a causal variable promoting economic expansion. Likewise one might conclude that increasing diversity in Bahrain will also increase prosperity.

References

Al-Mdaires, Falah (2002), "Shicism and Political Protest in Bahrain," *Digest of Middle East Studies* 11 (1), pp. 20–44.

Al-Rawi, Ahmed K. (2015), "Sectarianism and the Arab Spring: Framing the Popular Protests in Bahrain," *Global Media and Communication* 11 (1), pp. 25–42.

Alon, Ilan, and Gregory Chase (2005), "Religious Freedom and Economic Prosperity," *Cato Journal* 25 (2), pp. 399–406.

André-Salvini, Béatrice (2005), *Forgotten Empire: The World of Ancient Persia,* Berkeley, CA: University of California Press.

Barrichello, Alcides, Emerson Gomes dos Santos, and Rogerio Scabim Morano (2020), "Determinant and Priority Factors of Innovation for the Development of Nations," *Innovation & Management Review* 17 (3), pp. 307–320.

Batrancea, Larissa, Anca Nichita, Jerome Olsen, Christoph Kogler, Erich Kirchler, Erik Hoelzl, Avi Weiss, et al. (2019), "Trust and Power as Determinants of Tax Compliance Across 44 Nations," *Journal of Economic Psychology* 74, p. 102191.

Boadi, Isaac, Léo-Paul Dana, Gerard Mertens, and Lord Mensah (2017), "SMEs' Financing and Banks' Profitability: A 'Good Date' for Banks in Ghana?" *Journal of African Business* 18 (2), pp. 257–277.

Central Intelligence Agency (2011), "World Fact Book: Bahrain," (Retrieved from https://www.cia.gov/the-world-factbook/countries/bahrain/, accessed January 31, 2021)

Crystal, Jill A. (2021), "Bahrain," (Retrieved from https://www.britannica.com/place/Bahrain, accessed 31 January 2021),

Dana, Léo-Paul, Mary Han, Vanessa Ratten, and Isabelle M. Welpe, eds. (2009), *Handbook of Research on Asian Entrepreneurship,* Cheltenham: Edward Elgar.

Dana, Léo-Paul, Ramadani Veland, and Palalić Ramo (2021), "The Future," in Léo-Paul Dana, Ramo Palalić, and Veland Ramadani, eds., *Entrepreneurship in the Gulf Cooperation Council Region: Evolution and Future Perspectives,* Singapore: World Scientific, pp. 167–174, DOI: 10.1142/9781786348081_0008.

De Vries, Hubert (2011), "Bahrain," (Retrieved from http://hubert-herald.nl/Bahrain.htm, accessed 31 January 2021)

Fuccaro, Nelida (2009), *Histories of City and State in the Persian Gulf: Manama Since 1800* (No. 30), Cambridge, UK: Cambridge University Press.

Goudarzi, Masoumeh Rad, and Sediqeh Nazarpour (2019), "The Separation of Bahrain from Iran," in Mansoureh Ebrahimi, Masoumeh Rad Goudarzi, and Kamaruzaman Yusoff, eds., *The Dynamics of Iranian Borders,* Cham: Springer, pp. 95–114.

Kaiksow, Sarah E. A. (2009), *Threats to British "Protectionism" in Colonial Bahrain: Beyond the Sunni/Shia Divide,* Doctoral dissertation, Georgetown University.

Karolak, Magdalena (2017), "Social Media and the Arab Spring in Bahrain: From Mobilisation to Confrontation," in Cenap Çakmak, ed., *The Arab Spring, Civil Society, and Innovative Activism,* New York: Palgrave Macmillan, pp. 81–119.

Kawamorita, Hiroko, Aidin Salamzadeh, Kursat Demiryurek, and Mahyar Ghajarzadeh (2020), "Entrepreneurial Universities in Times of Crisis: Case of COVID-19 Pandemic," *Journal of Entrepreneurship, Business and Economics* 8 (1), pp. 77–88.

Khayati, Anis (2019), "The Effects of Oil and Non-Oil Exports on Economic Growth in Bahrain," *International Journal of Energy Economics and Policy* 9 (3), pp. 150–160.

Khedouri, Nancy (2008), *From Our Beginning to Present Day,* Bahrain: Al Manar Press.

Lane, Jan-Erik (2009), "The Environmental Predicament in the Asia-Pacific Region Compared With Other Regions," *Asia Pacific Journal of Public Administration* 31 (2), pp. 135–146.

Larsen, Curtis E. (1983), *Life and Land Use on the Bahrain Islands: The Geoarchaeology of an Ancient Society,* Chicago: University of Chicago Press.

Lu, Zeqi (2021), "The Role of Diversity in Economic Prosperity," *International Journal of Social Science and Humanity* 11 (1), pp. 9–12

Macris, Jeffrey R. (2010), "The Persian Gulf Theater in World War II," *Journal of the Middle East and Africa* 1 (1), pp. 97–107.

Matthiesen, Toby (2013), *Sectarian Gulf: Bahrain, Saudi Arabia, and the Arab Spring that Wasn't,* Palo Alto, CA: Stanford University Press.

Nuruzzaman, Mohammed (2013), "Politics, Economics and Saudi Military Intervention in Bahrain," *Journal of Contemporary Asia* 43 (2), pp. 363–378.

Palalić, Ramo, Léo-Paul Dana, and Veland Ramadani (2021),"Introduction," in Léo-Paul Dana, Ramo Palalić, and Veland Ramadani, eds., *Entrepreneurship in The Gulf Cooperation Council Region: Evolution and Future Perspectives*, Singapore: World Scientific, pp. 1–7, DOI: 10.1142/9781786348081_0001

Palalić, Ramo, Ahmad Taha Kahwaji, Hayan Nasser Eddin, and Ognjen Riđić (2021), "Entrepreneurship in Bahrain," in Léo-Paul Dana, Ramo Palalić, and Veland Ramadani, eds., *Entrepreneurship in the Gulf Cooperation Council Region: Evolution and Future Perspectives*, Singapore: World Scientific, pp. 7–24.

Pew Research Center (2020), "Bahrain: Religious Affiliation," (Retrieved from http://www.globalreligiousfutures.org/countries/bahrain/religious_demography#/?affiliations_religion_id=0&affiliations_year=2020, accessed 1 February 2021)

Potts, Dan T. (2006), "Elamites and Kassites in the Persian Gulf," *Journal of Near Eastern Studies* 65 (2), pp. 111–119.

Rentz, George (2008), "Al- Kawāsim," in Peri Bearman, Thierry Bianquis, Clifford Edmund Bosworth, E. J. van Donzel, and Wolfhart Heinrichs, eds., *Encyclopaedia of Islam,* 2nd edition, Leiden, Netherlands: Brill Online.

Room, Adrian (1997), *Placenames of the World: Origins and Meanings of the Names for Over 5000 Natural Features, Countries, Capitals, Territories, Cities and Historic Sights,* Jefferson, North Carolina: McFarland.

Salamzadeh, Aidin (2018), "Start-Up Boom in an Emerging Market: A Niche Market Approach," in Datis Khajeheian, Mike Friedrichsen, and Wilfried Mödinger, eds., *Competitiveness in Emerging Markets,* Cham: Springer, pp. 233–243.

Salamzadeh, Aidin, Zahra Arasti, and Ghanbar Mohammadi Elyasi (2017), "Creation of ICT-Based Social Start-Ups in Iran: A Multiple Case Study," *Journal of Enterprising Culture* 25 (1), pp. 97–122.

Salamzadeh, Aidin, and Léo-Paul Dana (2021), "The Coronavirus (COVID-19) Pandemic: Challenges Among Iranian Startups," *Journal of Small Business & Entrepreneurship* 33 (5), pp. 489–512, https://doi.org/10.1080/08276331.2020.1821158

Smith, Charles G. (2021), "Bahrain: Additional Information," (Retrieved from https://www.britannica.com/place/Bahrain/additional-info# contributors, accessed 31 January 2021)

Stewart, Devin J. (1996), "Notes on the Migration of 'Amili Scholars to Safavid Iran," *Journal of Near Eastern Studies* 55 (2), pp. 81–103.

World Bank (2021), "Bahrain's Economic Update," (Retrieved from https://www.worldbank.org/en/country/gcc/publication/economic-update-october-2020-bahrain, accessed 2 February 2021)

World Intellectual Property Organisation (2021). "Global Innovation Index 2020," (Retrieved from https://www.wipo.int/edocs/pubdocs/en/wipo_pub_gii_2020.pdf, accessed 2 February 2021)

Yong, Enn Lun (2019), "Understanding Cultural Diversity and Economic Prosperity in Europe: A Literature Review and Proposal of a Culture–Economy Framework," *Asian Journal of German and European Studies* 4 (5), pp. 1–34.

Zahlan, Rosemarie Said (2016), *The Making of the Modern Gulf States: Kuwait, Bahrain, Qatar, the United Arab Emirates and Oman,* London: Routledge.

Chapter 12

The Context for Business in Kuwait

Vladimir Dzenopoljac, Shqipe Gërguri-Rashiti,
Veland Ramadani & Léo-Paul Dana

Abstract: This chapter focuses on several important aspects of the business context of Kuwait. First is giving an overview of Kuwait's historical, political and economic development since its inception. Second, the chapter addresses the characteristics of Kuwait's business framework conditions and continues with Kuwait's ranking in terms of ease of doing business, wherein details of the ecosystem dimensions are described. The chapter concludes with providing a brief outlook for the future and provides a few insights and recommendations.

Keywords: Business, bazaar, economic growth, Kuwait

Introduction

Kuwait is an oil-rich country, located in the Arabian Peninsula, at the northwestern corner of the Persian Gulf (Exhibit 12.1). The country is located between Iraq and Saudi Arabia. Kuwait is positioned in one of the driest deserts in the world (Exhibit 12.2). It has a long shoreline compared to its border. Kuwait is bounded east by the Persian Gulf, while on the south and west it is bordered with Saudi Arabia. Iraq borders Kuwait on the northwest and north. In total, Kuwait has a total land boundary length of 462 km (287 miles) and a coastline of 499 km (310 miles).

The country derived its name from the Arabic diminutive of the Hindustani *kūt* ("fort"). In 1756, the ruling Al-Sabah family established the country as sheikhdom, and at the time, the country's main income was

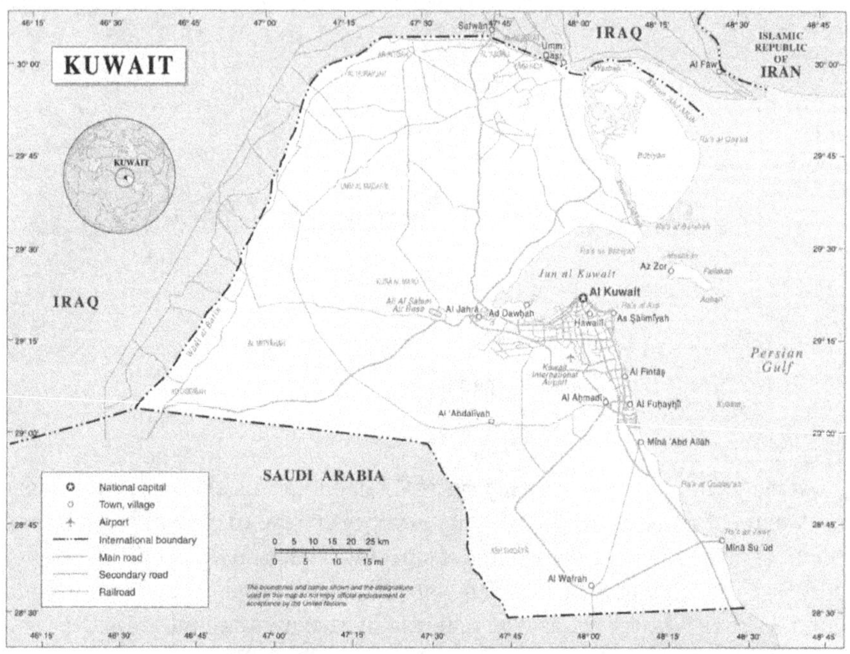

Exhibit 12.1 Map No. 4405 of Kuwait; courtesy of the United Nations

Exhibit 12.2 Skilled for life in the desert; photo courtesy of Pexels

linked to foreign commerce. After a certain time, and with trade growing, this small fort became Kuwait City, which is nowadays a modern metropolis with skyscrapers, apartment buildings and mosques (Exhibit 12.3). Since Kuwait City is the most populated area in Kuwait, the country is considered as one of the world's most-urbanised countries (Anthony, 2021; Dana et al., 2021).

Arabic is the official language, while English is also widely used, primarily in business. Kuwait is divided into several district areas like Farwaniya, Al-Ahmadi, Mubarak Al-Kabir and Jahra, Hawali. Beautiful islands closed by the coast side are Auhha, Bubiyan, Failaka, Kubbar, Miskan, Qaruh, Umm Al-Maradim, Umm Al-Naml and Warba (Khedr, 2019). Kuwait's population is around 4.2 million, where 70% are expats (Abdullah, 2020). The population number is promptly increasing from the 1980s up to the new millennium. Kuwait's flag is similar to several Arab countries, but with the different colour arrangement, containing green, black, red and white where green represents the fertile land of the country, black represents the defeat of the country's enemies, red symbolises the enemies' blood on the Arab warriors' swords and white symbolises noble deeds and purity.

Exhibit 12.3 Kuwait City; photo © 2021 by Shqipe Gërguri-Rashiti

Historical Context

The first recorded inhabitants of one of the islands on Kuwait's coast date back to the 4th century BC. During that time, the ancient Macedonians occupied the Failaka Island near the shore of today's Kuwait. In terms of the existence of the state itself, the earliest recorded history reaches back to 1613 when the central Arabian tribes reached the area of Kuwait. These tribes were moving away from a drought that hit their original habitat. The development of Kuwait's economy started soon when the country became a trade hub for various spices among Europe and India. The focus of the trade business in the 18th century turned to sell pearls. In this period, the people of Kuwait chose their first emir, which was Sabah I bin Jaber. The first emir of Kuwait is the ancestor of the Al-Sabah family that rules Kuwait. Nowadays. This period was the time when Kuwait grew into the trade and commerce centre in the region. This was mainly due to its convenient location that successfully linked India, Africa and Mesopotamia. Additionally, during this historical period, Kuwait developed one of the largest nautical fleets and managed to create a growing industry and trade of pearls. Throughout the 18th century, Kuwait traded mainly pearls, spices, dates, horses and wood (Khedr, 2019). Bazaar played an important role in the trade activities in Kuwait. According to Dana et al. (2008), a bazaar is a "social and cultural system, a way of life and a general mode of commercial activity, which has been in existence for millennia. In the bazaar, economic transactions are not the focus of activities; instead, the focus is on relationships and alliances. In this scenario, consumers do not necessarily seek the lowest price or the best quality. An individual buys from a friend, sometimes to help the friend and sometimes to ensure that the friend will reciprocate" (p.113). The bazaar in Kuwait, called *souq*, in the past and today remains a place where smaller businesses provide their products (Dana, 2011).

The Ottoman Empire grew in power between the 16th and 19th century and Kuwait reached an important agreement with Ottomans in which Kuwait received a special status, *Qada*, which was the first official country jurisdiction over a certain geographical area. The second crucial political agreement for Kuwait happened in 1913, namely the Anglo-Ottoman Convention. Thanks to this agreement, the British and the Ottomans recognised the Emir's status. The Ottomans lost their power during World War I and they were expelled from Kuwait by British and Indian armies. In 1922, Kuwait signed an agreement with Saudi Arabia for having a neutral zone between these two countries. This treaty further strengthened

Kuwait's position in the region. When oil was discovered in Kuwait (during the 1930s), the government decided to take actions in terms of setting country borders that would be accepted internationally, with the aim of protecting the oil wells. After this, Kuwait was officially under British protection. The treaty of British protection of Kuwait lasted until 19 June 1961. Kuwait became a politically and economically independent country on 19 June 1961. At this time, the Kuwaiti dinar was introduced as an official Kuwait currency and replaced the Gulf rupee that was used until that point (Khedr, 2019).

After oil discovery in the 1930s, especially after discovering large oil fields like Burgan oil field, a significant amount of foreign direct investments was directed towards Kuwait. This discovery led to the high growth of Kuwait's petroleum industry and made Kuwait one of the wealthiest countries in the region. This growth continued and by 1952, Kuwait had become the most significant oil producer and exporter in the Gulf. In return, the economy grew rapidly, and this economic development attracted many workers from countries like India and Egypt. At the time, Kuwait was disputing with Saudi Arabia about the border and ownership of certain oil reserves. Ultimately, the two countries agreed to equally share the petroleum reserves that existed in the problematic area. Also, the State of Kuwait experienced a dispute over boundaries with neighbouring country Iraq. However, after a short stand-off, Iraq officially recognised Kuwait as an independent country in October 1963. Soon afterwards, during the 1970s, the government of Kuwait took over the Kuwait Oil Company in an attempt to end the previous partnership with companies British Petroleum and Gulf Oil (Khedr, 2019).

The growth of Kuwait's economy created investment opportunities and raised investor's expectations significantly. In 1982, an unofficial stock market was created. The stock market became known as the Souq al-Manakh. The main objects of trading were stocks of companies outside Kuwait that were unregulated by the Kuwaiti authorities. The biggest interest was trading in stocks of companies from the United Arab Emirates (UAE) and the Kingdom of Bahrain (Colombo, 2006).

Soon after, in 1982, there was a major economic crisis and recession in the state of Kuwait. This crisis was caused by the collapse of Souq Al-Manakh stock market, which was further deepened by the drop in the price of oil on the international market. Luckily, this shock was a short-term one and was overcome by the increase of production of oil by Kuwait's national oil company. Kuwait's increase in oil output managed to reduce the supply shortage caused by the war that was happening between Iraq and Iran at the time. Since Kuwait was supporting Iraq financially during the entire conflict, which lasted for eight years, a number of individual attacks happened during 1983 in Kuwait. Financial support to Iraq amounted to 65 million USD and Iraq asked Kuwait government to write off the debt, which was rejected. This caused increased political tensions between Kuwait and Iraq, and Iraq accused Kuwait that it used their oil fields to drill oil. In the act of retaliation to Kuwait, Iraq attacked Kuwait on 2 August 1990. At that time, the emir was Jaber Al-Sabah who was replaced by Ali Hassan Al-Majid who acted as the governor of Kuwait.

A number of diplomatic meetings occurred with the aim of restoring peace in the region. All of these diplomatic efforts were unsuccessful, which led the United States to initiate a military response against Iraq, together with other 34 nations. This conflict was known as the Gulf War and it lasted until 26 February 1991. The coalition managed to force the Iraqi army to leave Kuwait and the previous emir was returned to power. However, while moving out of Kuwait, the Iraqi military forces set many oil fields in Kuwait on fire, which affected the entire region and damaged Kuwait's economy significantly. The oil production was seriously damaged and the cost of restoring the infrastructure and pre-war oil production was around 50 billion USD and took around two years (Khedr, 2019).

Context for Enterprise and Implications for Doing Business

Kuwait is one of the wealthiest countries in the world. According to the 2019 and 2020 data obtained from International Monetary Fund (IMF), Kuwait is the 59th country in the world in terms of nominal gross domestic product (GDP), with a GDP of 134,761 million USD. Regarding GDP per capita, Kuwait ranks as 40th country in the world with 22,252 USD per capita. The Kuwait economy heavily depends on exporting petroleum products and its main partners in this regard are South Korea, China, Japan, India, Singapore and the United States. On the other hand, the economy of Kuwait is not solely oil dependent. The country has strong production of agricultural fertilisers and other petrochemical products. Additionally, financial services represent an important and growing sector of the economy, while still keeping the tradition of pearl diving. On the import side, the economy of Kuwait is importing a major portion of the food products from around the world, together with clothes and technological equipment.

The economy of Kuwait is considered to be liberal when assessed against the countries in the region. One of the priorities of Kuwait's government is diversifying into sectors like trade and tourism. The current status of Kuwait oil reserves is that the country owns around 102 billion barrels (Szczepanski, 2019).

Since the focus of the chapter is how is doing business in Kuwait different from doing business in other places of Western Asia and different from Europe or America, we will assess mainly the sector of small and medium-sized enterprises (SMEs). In Kuwait, 90% of all registered private entities are SMEs. According to the National Fund for SME Development, SMEs are categorised according to their number of employees, assets and revenues. Companies with less than 50 employees, less than 500,000 KWD in assets, and with achieved revenues below 1,5 million KWD are falling under the category of an SME. Although the SMEs make up 90% of all registered companies, the effective contribution to the GDP is around 3%, with the gross value added by the SMEs of 1216 million KWD in 2019. (Abdullah, 2020; Ramadani et al., 2021). In comparison, the share of SMEs' contribution to GDP is around 40% in emerging economies, 50% in high-income economies and 53% in UAE. In regard to the industry that SMEs in Kuwait belong to, 40% of them are in wholesale/retail trade, together with hotels and restaurants. On the other hand, 33% of SMEs operate in the construction and industry sectors.

Finally, when we talk about employment in Kuwait, the national workforce is made of approximately 390,000 individuals able to work. Out of this number, 81% work in the public and government sector. Private sector employs 19% of working people or around 73,500. However, only 7% of Kuwaiti nationals work in the SME sector. This is mainly due to the imbalance between the levels of salaries in the private and public sectors (Kuwait Financial Centre, 2020). A number of employees are presented in Tables 12.1, 12.2 and 12.3.

The context of an economy can be adequately asserted with the inclusion of criteria for ease of doing business. This means that analysis should include national economic and regulatory factors that significantly affect domestic small and medium-size companies through their life cycle. One such comprehensive analysis is *Doing Business*, provided by the World Bank Group that compares certain economies with other 190 and assesses the ease of doing business on annual basis (World Bank Group, 2020a).

Table 12.1. Number of Employees in the Government Sector

Year	Kuwaiti			Non-Kuwaiti		
	Male	**Female**	**Total**	**Male**	**Female**	**Total**
2015	118,191	148,918	**267,109**	56,923	38,984	**95,907**
2016	120,936	156,999	**277,935**	58,571	41,209	**99,780**
2017	122,919	164,317	**287,236**	59,673	42,761	**102,434**

Source: Central Statistics Bureau of Kuwait (2020)

Table 12.2. Number of Employees in the Private Sector

Year	Kuwaiti			Non-Kuwaiti		
	Male	**Female**	**Total**	**Male**	**Female**	**Total**
2015	36,085	39,223	**75,308**	1,254,153	113,030	**1,367,183**
2016	34,735	36,122	**70,857**	1,369,171	120,500	**1,489,671**
2017	35,180	36,438	**71,618**	1,423,887	123,896	**1,547,783**

Source: Central Statistics Bureau of Kuwait (2020)

Table 12.3. Labour Force Survey 2016/2017

Index	**Kuwaiti**	**Non-Kuwaiti**	**Total**
Labour force participation rate	39.5%	82.2%	73.8%
Unemployment rate	6.4%	1.7%	2.2%
Proportion of workers who work in the government sector and public sector	89.9%	10.6%	18.6%

Source: Central Statistics Bureau of Kuwait (2020)

The report entails the results for two comprehensive measures: (1) the score related to the ease of doing business and (2) the ranking in terms of ease of doing business in the country. The latter measure gives a comparison between economies, while the first measure evaluates different economies with respect to the existing best practices worldwide. *Doing Business* report is implemented annually and points to the extent to which certain regulatory measures for local entrepreneurs have improved over time in absolute terms. On the other hand, the ease of doing business ranking focuses on the relative improvements compared to other economies (World Bank Group, 2020b).

This specific analysis shows important elements within the regulatory environment and shows how these affect local firms. The report gives an overview of different quantitative indicators regarding the issues like starting a business, dealing with construction permits, getting electricity, registering property, getting credit, protecting minority investors, paying taxes, trading across borders, enforcing contracts and resolving insolvency. Additionally, the report also measures features of employing workers (World Bank Group, 2020a). The main indicators when assessing the ease of doing business in a certain economy are presented in Table 12.4.

Table 12.4. Indicators of Ease of Doing a Business in an Economy

No.	Indicator	Definition
1	Starting a business	Procedures, time, cost and paid-in minimum capital to start a limited liability company
2	Dealing with construction permits	Procedures, time and cost to complete all formalities to build a warehouse and the quality control and safety mechanisms in the construction permitting system
3	Getting electricity	Procedures, time and cost to get connected to the electrical grid, and the reliability of the electricity supply and the transparency of tariffs
4	Registering property	Procedures, time and cost to transfer a property and the quality of the land administration system
5	Getting credit	Movable collateral laws and credit information systems
6	Protecting minority investors	Minority shareholders' rights in related party transactions and in corporate governance

(continued)

Table 12.4. Indicators of Ease of Doing a Business in an Economy (*continued*)

No.	Indicator	Definition
7	Paying taxes	Payments, time, total tax and contribution rate for a firm to comply with all tax regulations as well as post-filing processes
8	Trading across borders	Time and cost to export the product of comparative advantage and import auto parts
9	Enforcing contracts	Time and cost to resolve a commercial dispute and the quality of judicial processes
10	Resolving insolvency	Time, cost, outcome and recovery rate for commercial insolvency and the strength of the legal framework for insolvency
11	Employing workers	Flexibility in employment regulation and redundancy cost

Source: World Bank Group, 2020a

Kuwait had a score of 67.4 and ranks 83rd among 190 economies in terms of doing business indicators in 2020. The country was placed in high-income group of economies, with a population of 4,137,309. The report covered the businesses in the most advanced and dynamic business area in Kuwait, known as the Al-Asimah Governorate. This governorate, compared to the other five (Jahra, Farwaniya, Hawalli, Mubarak Al-Kabeer, and Ahmadi) is the smallest in geographical size but has the most convenient position. Some of the other areas are largely in desert (e.g., Jahra), which significantly affects the business operations. Finally, one must note that businesses are mostly registered in the area of Kuwait City but operate throughout the country.

The first indicator shows how an economy is ranked compared to the best practices in the world. For example, in Kuwait an entrepreneur needs 19–20 days to start his/her own business, while the best world practice is recorded in New Zealand, where average time to start a business is 0.5 days. Additionally, starting a business in Kuwait on average costs 1.7% of income per capita. For comparison purposes, in Slovenia these costs are 0. The good side of starting a business in Kuwait is the fact that entrepreneurs do not need minimum paid capital for a limited liability company, which is the most common legal form of starting a new venture. Overall,

Kuwait ranks at 82nd place with a score of 88.4 in starting a business, while the best score in the Middle East is achieved by Oman (93.5), which ranks 32nd in the world.

In terms of dealing with construction permits, Kuwait ranks on average (68th worldwide). On average, procedures in this area take longer than developed economies. For example, in Kuwait an average entrepreneur needs 103 days to obtain all necessary construction permits. At the same time, high-income economies in OECD take 152.3 days on average. On the other hand, costs in this area are higher than in developed economies. Finally, the positive side of this indicator in Kuwait is that building quality control index ranks at 14 out of 15, which is very close to the best practices worldwide (e.g., China; Luxembourg; UAE). Overall score for Kuwait here is 71.9 out of 100, with a rank of 68 worldwide (out of 190 countries).

Getting electricity is the next indicator where Kuwait ranks fairly well among the analysed countries (score 81.9, rank 66th). For instance, the average time needed for entrepreneur to complete this is 49 days, while high-income OECD economies have an average of 74.8 days. The best economies in this regard are the Republic of Korea, St. Kitts and Nevis, and UAE where entrepreneurs need on average only 18 days. In terms of costs of getting electricity, in Kuwait 55.7% of income per capita is needed, while developed OECD economies require 61%. In the majority of other Middle Eastern and Northern African economies, this cost is around 420% of income per capita. In China, Japan and UAE these costs are non-existent.

Registering property for a new venture in Kuwait requires many procedural steps, but it is relatively cheap and takes on average 17 days (in OECD the average is 23.6). This is why Kuwait has a score of 75.1 and the rank of 45 among 190 analysed economies. The countries with the best practices are Georgia, Norway and Portugal where only one procedural step exists (in Kuwait there are seven). On the other hand, in Kuwait the cost of registering property is at 0.5% of income per capita. The lowest cost in this is in Saudi Arabia (0%).

Getting credit for entrepreneurs describes the strength of credit reporting systems and the effectiveness of collateral and bankruptcy laws in facilitating lending. This is a criterion where Kuwait ranks fairly low (score is 45, rank is 119th out of 190 economies). The main reason for this is low ranking in the strength of legal rights (1 out of 12 scores). Countries with the best practices are Brunei Darussalam, Montenegro and New Zealand with the maximum score in this regard.

When discussing protecting minority investors, Kuwait has a score of 66, which places it at 51ˢᵗ position worldwide. This is relatively positive and sends the message to potential investors that their stakes are secure, especially when knowing that Kuwait has the highest index of corporate transparency (7 out of 7) and extent of ownership and control index (6 out of 7). However, the extent of the disclosure the index and the extent of the shareholder rights index are fairly lower.

In the area of paying taxes, Kuwait ranks sixth worldwide with a score of 92.5. This is mainly due to the total tax and contribution rate (% of profit), which is the lowest in the world (13%, compared to OECD high-income economies that have 39.9%). When analysing trading over borders, Kuwait ranks the lowest of all indicators so far (score of 52.6, rank 162ⁿᵈ out of 190). When entrepreneurs in Kuwait think of internationalisation, the obstacles are high, due to complicated export procedures, the time needed to implement export, as well as import or export costs.

In the area of enforcing legal contracts, Kuwait ranks average (score 61.4, rank 74). When monitoring the days needed to enforce the contract, Kuwait judicial system takes on average 566 days (OECD developed economies 589.6, while the best practice is in Singapore, only 120 days). Costs reach 18.6% of the claim value, which is lower than in developed OECD economies (21.5%) but higher than the best example, which is Bhutan with only 0.1% of the claim value. Finally, when discussing resolving insolvency in Kuwait, the country ranks poorly (ranked 115ᵗʰ with a score of 39.2). The main causes for this stand are the low recovery rate (32.2 cents on the dollar) and the time needed to resolve insolvency, which is 4.2 years in Kuwait, while developed economies complete the process in 1.7 years on average.

The indicator of research and development (R&D) transfer explains to what extent national research and development activities in Kuwait will lead to new commercial opportunities and to what level this transfer is available to SMEs. This indicator has a value of 2.09/5. Again, among regional economies, Qatar ranks the highest with the index at 3.48 in 2018, while UAE was ranking at the level of 2.64 in the same period. The lowest ranking country in terms of R&D transfer was Saudi Arabia with an index value of 1.75. For comparison purposes, developed economies range around 3 (e.g., Switzerland 3.26, the Netherlands 3.15, Ireland, Spain and Portugal 2.76, the United States 2.65, and Canada 2.86).

Towards the Future

In light of economic development, The Gulf Cooperation Council (GCC) countries need to prepare for diversification of their economies and leaving oil-dependent practices behind. There are many similarities among GCC countries' attempts to develop their economies as knowledge and innovation based (Zainal, 2020). In Kuwait, the Kuwait National Development Plan (KNDP) was launched in 2017 with the title "New Kuwait" also, referred to as the Kuwait Vision 2035 programme. The main objective of the programme is to transform Kuwait into a financial, cultural and trade leader. One of the main targets to achieve is increasing the GDP share of the private sector that now represents approximately 30% of Kuwait's GDP. The private sector in Kuwait is dynamic and different from Kuwait's regional peers as it focuses more on collaboration than on competition. In this regard, Kuwait developed many quality initiatives to empower youth through entrepreneurship (Pupic, 2018).

Kuwait's economy is rich with human, innovation and financial capital. It is especially interesting to note that around 67% of the country's university graduates are women. However, the issue here is that majority of these graduates do not have the necessary skills to excel when they get hired. For example, within the Zain Group, one of the largest telecommunication services providers in the country, the percentage of females in the company is only 23%. This is low comparing to the global average of around 40%. Hence, the Zain Group initiated its Women Empowerment Initiative with the purpose of motivating women to engage in higher leadership positions. At the moment there is only 14% in these positions and the company aims at increasing this number to 25% by the end of 2020. On the national level, the government of Kuwait invests around 14,300 USD on education per student per year. This is among the biggest investments in students in the world. The downside is that only around 3300 USD is the approximate value of the education received. In other words, the received value accounts only for 23% of the invested amount. For those with innovative business ideas, the country serves as a good steppingstone towards business success. This is mainly due to the inception of the Kuwait National Fund for Small and Medium Enterprise Development in 2013 with invested capital of 6.1 billion USD (Pupic, 2018; Saleh, 2020). Based on *The Global Innovation Index (GII)*, which provides information on the capacity and success of innovations in particular countries, Kuwait is

Table 12.5. Global Innovation Index Rankings in 2019

Country/Index	Global Innovation Index	Innovation Input Index	Innovation Output Index
GCC countries	UAE (36th)	UAE (24th)	**Kuwait (56th)**
	Kuwait (60th)	Saudi Arabia (49th)	UAE (58th)
	Qatar (65th)	Qatar (53rd)	Qatar (70th)
	Saudi Arabia (68th)	Oman (57th)	Saudi Arabia (85th)
	Oman (80th)	Bahrain (69th)	Bahrain (87th)
	Bahrain (78th)	**Kuwait (75th)**	Oman (101st)

Source: Based on Dutta et al., 2020

ranked in 60th place. In Table 12.5 the rankings of Kuwait and other GCC countries are indicated, according to Global Innovation Index, Innovation Input Index and Innovation Output Index.

According to the New Kuwait 2035 national development plan, the country has set seven pillars and five main strategic directions towards changing the economic, demographic and political landscape. The pillars are enhancing Kuwait's global position in diplomacy, trade, culture and philanthropy, reforming the education system, improving the national healthcare system, enhancing the living environment, developing and modernising country's infrastructure, diversifying the economy and averting future growth away from oil and upgrading the public administration to reduce bureaucracy and increase transparency and accountability. The major strategic directions are citizenship participation and respect of law, effective government, prosperous economy, nurturing nation and becoming globally relevant player (Kuwait National Development Plan, 2017).

Entrepreneurship will play a crucial role in this development plan, together with the reformed education system (Ramadani et al., 2021; Tlaiss, 2015). In this regard, one must expect significant improvements in entrepreneurial culture and framework, where the country must increase the ranking in all aspects of ease of doing business. Additionally, it is expected that the country motivates and fosters entrepreneurship education, formal and informal. Creation of entrepreneurship hubs, new venture capitalist companies and reducing the expenditures in subsidising the employment in public and government sectors will all aid to shifting the mindset of latent entrepreneurs and, when graduating from any school, to seriously consider the start of a new venture. Future research might include studies of the entrepreneurial ecosystem as well as the traditional Kuwait bazaar.

References

Abdullah, Mahdi Nour (2020), "Family Entrepreneurship and Banking Support in Kuwait: Conventional vs Islamic Banks," *Journal of Family Business Management* 11 (3), pp. 313–331. https://doi.org/10.1108/JFBM-06-2020-0049

Anthony, John Duke (2021), "Kuwait," (Retrieved from https://www.britannica.com/place/Kuwait, accessed 28 July 2021)

Central Statistics Bureau of Kuwait (2020), "Statistical Bulleting," (Retrieved from https://www.csb.gov.kw/Pages/Statistics_en?ID=69&ParentCatID=3, accessed 13 November 2020)

Colombo, Jesse (2006), "Kuwait's Souk Al-Manakh Stock Bubble, The Bubble Bubble," (Retrieved from http://www.thebubblebubble.com/souk-al-manakh/, accessed 13 October 2020)

Dana, Léo-Paul (2011), "Entrepreneurship in Bolivia: An Ethnographic Enquiry," *International Journal of Business and Emerging Markets* 3 (1), pp. 75–88.

Dana, Léo-Paul, Hamid Etemad, and Richard W. Wright (2008), "Toward a Paradigm of Symbiotic Entrepreneurship," *International Journal of Entrepreneurship and Small Business* 5 (2), pp. 109–126.

Dana, Léo-Paul, Ramo Palalić, and Veland Ramadani, eds. (2021), *Entrepreneurship in the Gulf Cooperation Council Region: Evolution and Future Perspectives,* Singapore: World Scientific.

Dutta, Soumitra, Lanvin Bruno, and Sacha Wunsch-Vincent (2020). *The Global Innovation Index 2019: Creating Healthy Lives — The Future of Medical Innovation,* Geneva and New Delhi: Cornell University, INSEAD, and the World Intellectual Property Organization.

International Monetary Fund World Economic Outlook (2019), Global Manufacturing Downturn, Rising Trade Barriers. Available at: https://www.imf.org/en/Publications/WEO/Issues/2019/10/01/world-economic-outlook-october-2019 (accessed 14 June 2021)

International Monetary Fund World Economic Outlook (2020), A Long and Difficult Ascent. Available at: https://www.imf.org/en/Publications/WEO/Issues/2020/09/30/world-economic-outlook-october-2020 (accessed 14 June 2021)

Khedr, Ahmed A. (2019), *Kuwait Legal System and Research,* New York: Hauser Global Law School Program at NYU School of Law, (Retrieved from https://www.nyulawglobal.org/globalex/Kuwait1.html, accessed on 6 November 2020)

Kuwait Financial Centre (2020), "Kuwait SMEs Post COVID-19 – Current Situation," (Retrieved from https://www.markaz.com/getmedia/653b185f-65b8-4fe7-8e62-3017f3e678c0/Note-on-Kuwait-SMEs-ENG-16-07-2020_1.pdf.aspx, accessed 1 October 2020)

Kuwait National Development Plan (2017), "New Kuwait 2035, Plan Overview," (Retrieved from https://s3.amazonaws.com/assets.new kuwait.gov.kw/wp-content/uploads/2016/09/KNDP_Inforgraphics_ ProjectOverview_ENG.pdf, accessed 2 December 2020)

National Fund for Small and Medium Sized Enterprise Development (2017), "Annual Report 2016-2017," (Retrieved from https:// nationalfund-new.s3.amazonaws.com/media/En-opt.pdf?AWSAcce ssKeyId=AKIAQZTLSBVASLOW2JPX&Signature=TFPzokvEX 9rnMSCuljPmu%2BD5bRw%3D&Expires=1607006452, accessed 1 December 2020)

Pupic, Tamara (2018), "A Cultural Shift: Changes in Kuwait's Entrepreneurship Discourse as Seen at Nuqat's Human Capital Forum, Entrepreneur Middle East," (Retrieved from https://www.entrepreneur.com/article/310279, accessed 1 December 2020)

Ramadani, Veland, Ramo Palalić, Léo-Paul Dana, and Azra Bico (2021), "Entrepreneurship in Kuwait," in Léo-Paul Dana, Ramo Palalić, and Veland Ramadani, eds., *Entrepreneurship in the Gulf Cooperation Council Region: Evolution and Future Perspectives,* Singapore: World Scientific.

Saleh, Yasser (2020), "ICT, Social Media and Covid-19: Evidence from Informal Home-Based Business Community in Kuwait City," *Journal of Enterprising Communities: People and Places in the Global Economy,* 15 (3), pp. 395–413. https://doi.org/10.1108/JEC-07-2020-0131

Szczepanski, Kallie (2019), "Kuwait Fact and History," (Retrieved from https://www.thoughtco.com/kuwait-facts-and-history-195060, accessed 18 November 2020)

Tlaiss, Hayfaa (2015), "How Islamic Business Ethics Impact Women Entrepreneurs: Insights from Four Arab Middle Eastern Countries," *Journal of Business Ethics* 129 (4), pp. 859–877.

World Bank Group (2020a), "Doing Business 2020, Kuwait Economy Profile," (Retrieved from   https://www.doingbusiness.org/content/dam/doingBusiness/country/k/kuwait/KWT.pdf, accessed 29 October 2020)

World Bank Group (2020b), "Explanation of how the Ease of Doing Business Rankings and the Ease of Doing Business Score Measure are Calculated," (Retrieved from https://openknowledge.worldbank.org/bitstream/handle/10986/32436/9781464814402_Ch06.pdf, accessed 30 October 2020)

Zainal, Mohammad (2020), "Innovation Orientation and Performance of Kuwaiti Family Businesses: Evidence from the Initial Period of COVID-19 Pandemic," *Journal of Family Business Management,* https://doi.org/10.1108/JFBM-09-2020-0086

Chapter 13

The Context for Business in Qatar

Ramo Palalić, Léo-Paul Dana, Veland Ramadani & Aidin Salamzadeh

Abstract: One of the countries where tradition and modernity meet is Qatar. From a very poor country in the 20th century to ultra-modern in the 21st century, Qatar became a place in which visitors, workers and business people can find what they look for. The richness of the country's diversified business outlook and culture appeals various stakeholders to stay, visit and do business in this country. In this line, the chapter portrays fundamental information on Qatar, its traditional doing of business through bazaars, the current context of business pursued in this country and the future regarding the country's business stand up.

Keywords: Qatar, Doha, bazaar, business, tradition, culture, *souq*

Introduction

The Persian Gulf and Arabian Peninsula have been very famous since ancient times and they remain attractive regions in today's world. The history goes even far beyond the Islamic era. That time marks this region as the most significant hub for the trade of various spices and goods brought from the Far East and Central Asia, and transmitted to the Western world. As recently narrated by Palalić et al. (2021), this area is known due to several important reasons: "First, it is known for being The Land of the Prophets, the place from which Islamic religion came. Second, throughout history, this place has been the centre for trading (Mecca). Third, today this region is again known for business where several global financial centres are located. Fourth, most oil production is produced in this region, and it is still the land of huge world oil reserves. Fifth, tremendous progress in education is happening in this region, where worldwide, famous, universities have established modern campuses (2021, p. 1)."

In the modern era, the Gulf Cooperation Council (GCC) region is split into several countries. Each of them has its position in the region along with its history and cultural values, which are many of them common. One of these countries is Qatar, which is regarded as the richest GCC member.

Qatar is the second smallest country (11,586 km^2) that is sometimes called the Qatari Peninsula, which is the extension of the Arabian Peninsula, and it continues into the Persian Gulf. It borders Iran (on the east), United Arab Emirates (UAE) on the south, Saudi Arabia (SA) on the west and Bahrain on the northwest (Exhibit 13.1). Further, 564 km of its border is the coastline and maritime with Iran, Bahrain and UAE (Sahli, 2021). The capital city of Qatar is Doha, which is the most populated area in the country, comprising 40% of the total population of Qatar. It has eight municipal regions, namely (1) Madinad Ash-Shamal (North), (2) Al-Khor, (3) Ar-Rayyan (Central and Southwest of Qatar), (4) Al-Daayen (Northeast), (5) Umm-Salal (Central), (6) Ad-Dawhah (today's Doha; Central-East), (7) al-Wakrah (South), and (8) Al-Shahaniya (Central). Among them, Ar-Rayyan and Doha regions are the most populated. Doha, on the other side, represents the most modern city in Qatar.

It should also be mentioned that Doha is one of the important financial centres in the Gulf region. Qatar's GDP per capita is $64,787 (World Bank, 2020), which determines Qatar as the wealthiest country in the GCC region, and places Qatar among the high-income countries (World Bank, 2020). With this, Qatar attracts immigrants, especially from Asian countries, to come and work until they retire. However, such an immigration policy has been halted recently. All GCC countries started with the policy where local nationals will take over most of the managerial positions as well as other key operations in respective countries. In Qatar, for instance, it is called *Qatarisation*. It will bring more involvement of local people in contributing to socio-economic development. Immigrants are still welcomed but not as it is used to be.

Historical Context

The history of this region is very rich, and it goes to ancient times. When writing about Qatar, Sahli (2021) pointed out that the history of the

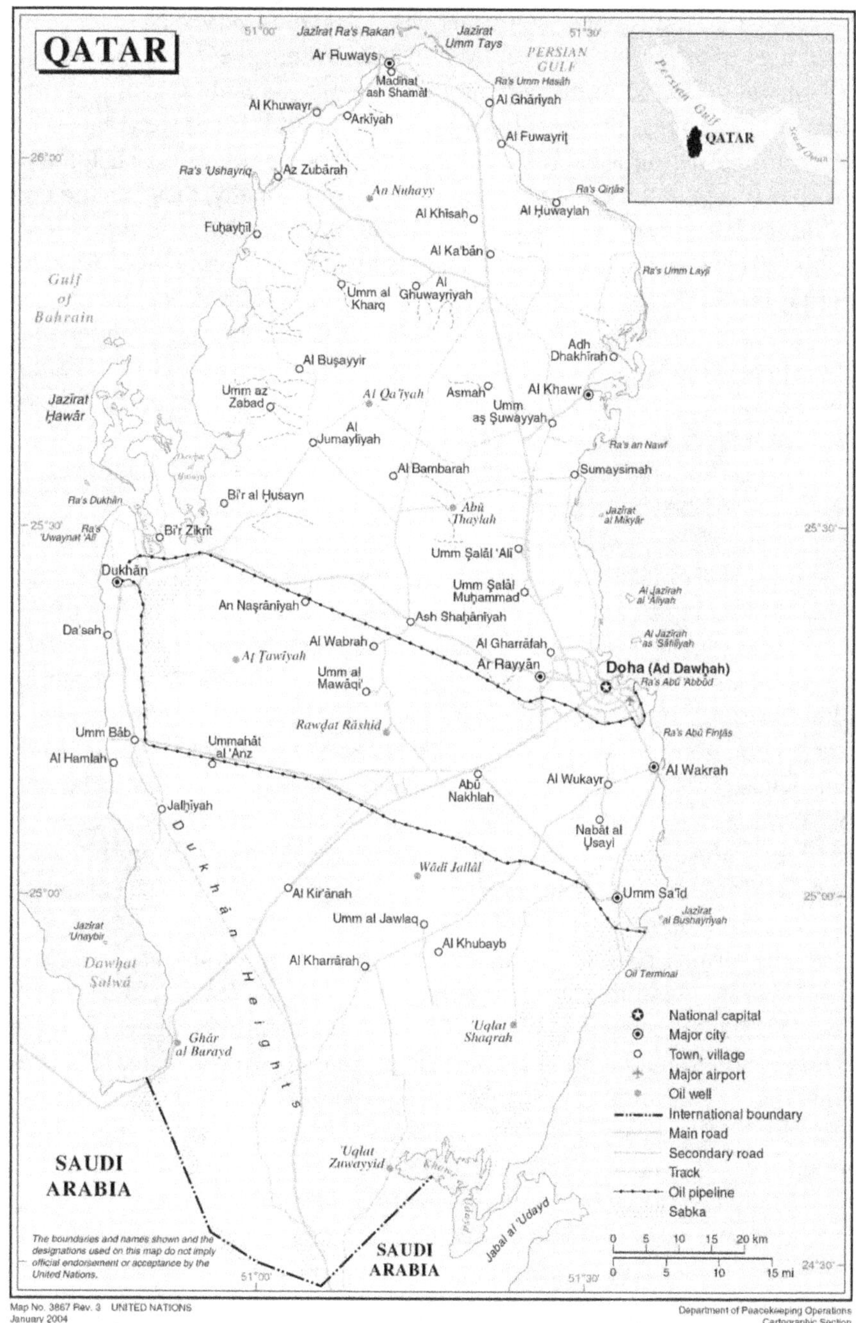

Exhibit 13.1   Map 3867 of Qatar; courtesy of the United Nations

7th century of the Arabian Peninsula was marked as very significant. The teachings of Islam spread very rapidly throughout the whole peninsula, which was reflected in many positive happenings among which is unifying the Arab tribes. The hostilities between the Arab tribes were ended by Islam, declaring all Muslims as one nation. The period of expansion and prosperity began with this new philosophy. Additionally, that was the end of the paganism era, which was the predominant religion in the region. Sahli (2021) also highlighted that Islam spread from today's Spain to India during the Umayyad Reign. In the Arab world, traces of Islamic culture and its influence can be found everywhere, particularly the architectural style that demonstrates the cultural commonalities between the Islamic countries. Many bazaars had been built across the GCC countries under such architectural style, so is in Qatar.

Before the 15th century, Qatar was under Islamic Caliphate for six centuries (632–1258) (Dana et al., 2021, p. 2), and the majority of its population were Muslims and traded according to Islamic (Sharia) Law. Then, an unfortunate time for Qataris was after the Caliphate's ruling, when Mongolians came and destroyed Baghdad as the capital city of the Arabian Empire (Palalić et al., 2021). Before the Ottoman Empire, before the 15th century, this region was conquered by the Portuguese, establishing their position for two decades. Qatar's area was known for trade because it was a good geostrategic position that connects two different worlds. After Portuguese, Qatar became a part of the Ottoman Empire, until the end of World War I. In the late 18th century, the British came to this area and tried to establish a socio-economical system of Qataris, from one perspective, and more importantly, to help them to be independent of the Ottoman Empire, from another side.

The British presence in this region started with the General Treaty in 1820 that aimed to eliminate piracy in this region (Smith, 2004, p. 2). In 1853, the "Perpetual Maritime Truce" Agreement was signed. By this the existing "Shaikhdoms of Abu Dhabi, Sharjah, Dubai, Ajman, Ras al Khaimah, and Umm al Qaiwain became known as the Trucial States" (Smith, 2004, p. 2). Such status remained until 1971, when the British withdrew.

Many disputes were between tribal families of Bahrain and Qatar at that time due to pearl treasures from one perspective, and other things. However, besides those disputes, both countries were looking to be independent.

Notably, Qatar was one of the poor British protectorates in the mid-1800s, but now it has grown into one of the world's largest gas and oil producers. Due to huge reserves of gas and oil, Qatar nowadays is a high-income country with the highest GDP per capita in the world (Qatar Chamber).

The first representative leader of Qatar, Sheikh Mohammed bin Thani, appeared in 1869, formally recognised by the British.[1] Ottomans left Qatar during World War I. Later on, his leadership was replaced by his son's. In the meantime, Qatar tried to join the Shaikhdoms with Emirates; however, there were some disputes, and Qatar obtained its independence on 3 September 1971.

The pearl and the jewellery made of it were at that time very precious and very well known in the rest of the world. This pearl business and trades were the main milestones for Qatar's economy, until the early 1950s, during which time started Qatar's modern era. The discovery of oil in 1935 and its production in the 1950s have changed Qatar into a modern country but with preserved traditional values. These two facts make the country very attractive to visitors and investors.

Nowadays, booms, from one side, and traditional trade and activities, from another, make Qatar popular and very appealing for the rest of the world (Balaguer, 2016). If one travels to Qatar, besides modern style (Exhibit 13.2), travellers, visitors, even investors, can see and enjoy the traditional bazaars in Qatar. One of the local narrators would narrate the stories from the past that impact the traditional way of life and doing business because it is not primarily a goal to achieve transactions but talk, bargain and build a long-term relationship.

> In the 1960s Doha was a cluster of villages. You'd bring your donkey to the souk, to pick up sugar, salt, kerosene. It would be rice for breakfast, lunch and dinner. I worked for Shell at that time, fifteen days straight on an oil rig. Every night there was nothing to do except tell tales. At home my grandfather would build a fire, make milky ginger tea and then tell stories, he recalls. When it came to my turn, I would tell them better!
>
> —(Khalifa Al Sayed).[2]

These traditional bazaars give the soul to the Qataris, especially during the nightlife. Life in GCC countries begins with sunset due to very hot weather in this region. People try to find an oasis to escape from high temperatures, where they will refresh themselves and enjoy half of the day.

---

[1] See https://www.iexplore.com/articles/travel-guides/middle-east/qatar/history-and-culture. Accessed 3 December 2020.

[2] https://www.matthewteller.com/work/qatars-storytelling-tradition/

Exhibit 13.2   Towards Waqif Souq; photo © 2021 by Amila Jamak used with permission

Such places where one can buy traditional things, have a traditional atmosphere, and enjoy traditional food mixed with Indian and Persian cousins are so-called traditional bazaars. Bazaars were discussed by Dana (2007), where he elaborated on the meaning of bazaars. He narrated that "The bazaar is a social and cultural system, a way of life and a general model of commercial activity, which has been in existence for millennia. In the bazaar, economic transactions are not the focus of activities; instead, the focus is on personal relationships. In this scenario, consumers do not necessarily seek the lowest price or the best quality. An individual gives business to another with whom a relationship has been established, to ensure that this person will reciprocate." (p. 19). Doha, the capital city of Qatar, is very rich with traditional bazaars. According to one of the tourist websites,[3] the main bazaars in Qatar are Souq Waqif, Souq Al Wakrah, Falcon Souq, Gold Souq, Souq Al Asery, Souq Al Dira, Al Faleh Souq, Souq Al

---

[3] https://www.iloveqatar.net/guide/places/a-guide-to-the-souqs-and-markets-in-qatar. Accessed 1 December 2020.

Jabor, Souq Haraj, Omani Souq, Thursday and Friday Souq and Souq al Ali. All these are located in the capital city, Doha.

Souq Waqif[4] (Exhibit 13.3) is the old soul of Qatar. It was established more than 100 years ago. The *souq* could be accessed by land and waterway. The body of the *souq* is decorated with various shops containing artisan products and products from different parts of the world while its heart is full of different restaurants, coffee shops and standing food shops (Exhibit 13.4). In these restaurants, every Qatari and visitor relax and having a joyful evening time.

Exhibit 13.3 Falcon Souq; photo © 2021 by Ramo Palalić

---

4 https://www.iloveqatar.net/guide/places/a-guide-to-the-souqs-and-markets-in-qatar. Accessed 1 December 2020.

Exhibit 13.4 Arabian horses galloping in the herd in front of a sand storm; photo © 2021 by Ramo Palalić

Souq Al Wakrah[5] located at Al Wakrah Main Street, Al Wakrah in Doha. Here, people can find different things from other markets. It is designed in a way that a whole family can spend their free time. A walking area is available and so is for children for their playgrounds. At this *souq*, traditional Qatari's heredity and culture are reflected from the indifferent design of mosques, shops, cafes to old exponents of boats. Traditional goods are sold, such as pearls, jewellery, dates, various spices and traditional sweets.

Falcon Souq (Exhibits 13.5, 13.6 and 13.7) is located at the Al Souq Street, close by Al Waqif Souq. It is another Qatari *souq* where people, locals and visitors can spend their time enjoying old but very rich Qatar's heritage. At this *souq*, different preys and different kinds of falconry equipment are showed. Imagine, holding a falcon in your hand! Or, to see Arab horses (Exhibit 13.7) or camels at this bazaar!

It should be noted that falconry is the traditional way of hunting with falcons across many places worldwide. One of those places is on the Arabian Peninsula. As falcons can fly and they have perfect eyesight, they were used for hunting by Bedouins because of the scarce food in deserts.

Gold Souq represents the place where people sell and buy all gold products. Many gold jewellery shops make the place an awesome location where you can find all you need for your lovely soulmate, as well as for friends. The place is so magical; if you walk through the *souq*, such a gorgeous supply of artisan gold products does not leave you uninterested. The *souq* is located in Doha, at Al Ahmed Street, which is between Al Nakheel Hotel and Souq Waqif.

---

[5] Available at https://www.iloveqatar.net/guide/places/a-guide-to-the-souqs-and-markets-in-qatar. Accessed 1 December 2020.

Exhibit 13.5 Inside the Falcon Souq; photo © 2021 by Ramo Palalić

Exhibit 13.6 Skyline; photo © 2021 by Ramo Palalić

Exhibit 13.7 Symbol of tradition in modern Doha, Qatar; photo © 2021 by Ramo Palalić

Souq Al Asery is the oldest and the most famous *souq* in Doha. It is the place where visitors also like to see and enjoy their time. At this *souq*, all products, from modern products to old-time ones, like electronics products, handbags hand-made, perfumes, and so on, can be found. It is located on the same street as Gold Souq, the Al Ahmed Street.

Souq Al Dira is a place where people can buy different kinds of materials and fabrics regardless of their price, such as lace, silk, cotton, crepe, georgette, cashmere pashmina, and so on. It is located at Al Ahmed Street, and very close by the Al Waqif Souq.

Al Faleh Souq is located in the same street as Souq al Dira, Al Ahmed Street. This bazaar is known for cheap products. The interesting thing about this bazaar is bargaining while buying, and yet, it is very challenging because the lower price is very difficult to get since the products shoppers sell are already so cheap.

Souq Al Jabor is located at the same place, Al Ahmad Street. This bazaar is known where people can buy gifts for family and friends. Both buyers and sellers have something to fight for in such transactions. Buyers are offered different products for gifts, family clothes, jewellery and different types of electronic products. Sellers try to sell it at high prices while buyers try to reduce it. In this haggling, there is joy but pride as well.

Souq Haraj a very specific bazaar where second-hand goods can be bought. However, the bazaar provides also new stuff. Either second-hand or new goods are well-matched needs of people. It is one of the busiest bazaars in Doha. It is located at the junction of Al Najma and Al Mansour, Al Najma, Doha.

Omani Souq is located near to Wholesale Market, Al Sailiya, Doha. It is called the Omani bazaar because it aims to sell goods, which are made originally in Oman. One of the famous products globally known and made in Oman is Frankincense. Others, like perfumes and Omani dried fish, are also available in this bazaar. Those who visit this bazaar should bargain while buying because it is a tradition that GCC countries have.

Thursday and Friday Souq is good if someone is looking for traditional clothes, like abayas,[6] where women can find various types, models and with different prices. This place is also known for a good choice of cafeterias and restaurants where people hang out during the day and night. It is located opposite the Old Wholesale Market, Ain Khaled, Doha.

Souq al Ali is similar to the Thursday and Friday Souq. For those who love food, the gourmets and gastro, it is a perfect place where they can find shawarma. Unlike other bazaars, it is located at Doha Expressway, Al Shamal Road, Al Luqta, Doha.

All these bazaars are traditionally good places to buy, sell and enjoy the daily atmosphere. It is possible to meet all types of people – rich, poor, moderate and find all kinds of foods and all types of goods for home and other needs. Simply, all things in one place. Joy and relaxation are available after hard work. Everything for all!

Bazaars are small-scale businesses. Vendors, keep shoppers, food providers, tailors at these places are competing and taking a small piece of the cake from large companies. This market share for large firms is not that attractive, but it is a magically glorious place to do business and grow gradually for small businesses. Qatar is a special place, where traditional and modern styles of living and doing business are possible. More on doing business in Qatar will be elaborated in the next section.

The Context for Enterprise and Implications for Doing Business

Another side of Qatar is how the country is overseen by global reports that make the country attractive for doing business here. Let us go through

---

[6] *Abaya* is a traditional women's clothes in Islamic culture.

some important indicators, which suggest Qatar as one of the best places for investors.

Globally, the GCC region has improved in terms of doing business by 2.9 points among other regions in the world (World Bank, 2020). Such changes were triggered by the necessity of economic diversification as well as foreign investor appeal. As stated by the World Bank on doing business, Qatar has set high goals in 2019 to improve its business environment and attract foreign investors. Indeed, Qatar has improved its ranking on the global scale of doing business. It has moved from 83rd place in 2019 to 77th in 2020, which gives a strong wind to work a lot more on creating Qatar's business environment favourable, appealing and the first one in the region.

One of the essential pillars for each economy is innovation. In this regard, and according to Global Innovation Index (2020), Qatar in the last two years has improved but not as other GCC members like Oman, UAE or SA.

However, if compared with previous years like 2018, Qatar has been much better now. One of the reasons could be the recent disputes between Qatar and SA, Bahrain and UAE, which was reflected in the coming years from 2018. Moreover, the recent global pandemic (COVID-19) worsened the situation around the globe (Salamzadeh and Dana, 2020), and countries that were shakier before were affected compared to others who did not have pre-pandemic issues, either political or economic.

Moreover, according to Trade Economics (2020), Qatar's economy shrank in the second quarter of 2020 by 6.1% from a year earlier. However, it has followed a 0.9% increase in the previous half. Amidst reduced activity due to Covid-19 containment steps accompanied by a decrease in energy prices and plunging tourist arrivals, it was the most acute economic contraction since the first quarter of 2019. In the more detailed view, sectors like transportation and storage (−39.5%); lodging and food services (−38.7%); wholesale and retail trade and repair of vehicles (−30.4%); arts, entertainment and leisure (−11.8%) and manufacturing (−11.8%); (−11.3%) were the most hit ones. Qatar's GDP contracted by 6.4% quarterly, the most in over a year, following a 1.4% fall in the previous period (Trading Economics, 2020).

Towards the Future

Recent conflicts between Qatar, SA and the UAE have hampered Qatar's further development. However, it has also had an impact on the other two countries. Qatar, as well as other GCC members, should have great relations with each other and have common policies that will encourage foreign investors to invest more. Any disputes can provoke an outflow of foreign direct investment (FDI). The bottom line is that GCC members have common cultural and religious values that should be the milestone for mutual prosperity forever. Simply, Qatar and its neighbours should leverage the development of amity in every sphere of their citizens.

As discussed by Sahli (2021), Qatar's business climate is very conducive to local and foreign investors. There are no impassable obstacles that can decisively restrain businessmen/businesswomen from starting their businesses in Qatar. The government is aware of its importance, and it is putting a tremendous effort to eradicate the financial and bureaucratic obstacles that business people face. However, some adjustments could make Qatar rank among the most favourable economies for starting a company. The World Bank proposes offering more protection to investors with strict disclosure laws, as well as improving the legal rights of borrowers and lenders and providing the various parties with in-depth and open credit information.

On the other hand, a wealthy country with strong traditional values is appealing to many people worldwide. The traditional way of doing business is also very much convenient as it is for the modern way. Culturally comfortable place with various traditional habits and customs, including much respected traditional bazaars, attracts many people to visit and spend some time within such cultural environment settings.

As suggested by Palalić et al. (2019), it should not be forgotten that the GCC is a domesticated area for everyone who respects its culture and way of life. Accepting differences is a virtue that may lead to success regardless of the environment one is exposed to. Thus, Qatar has its valuable tradition, culture and hospitality where every person, businessman, businesswomen, tourist or visitor can find something valuable, breathtaking and appealing enough to think or start a business in this country. Considering the World Bank's report (2020) that the business environment is to be improved in Qatar, it becomes an additional reason to see the country as business/investment potential. Additionally, Qatar National Vision 2030 (Planning and Statistics Authority, 2020) articulates more positive content into it.

References

Balaguer, Pedro Antonio (2016), "Linking Education and Business Across Geography of Erasmus+ Improving Relationships between Vocational Training and Job Market," *Journal of Entrepreneurship, Business and Economics* 4 (1), pp. 73–84.

Dana, Léo-Paul (2007), *Asian Models of Entrepreneurship from the Indian Union and Nepal to the Japanese Archipelago: Context, Policy and Practice,* 2nd edition, London, Singapore & Hong Kong: World Scientific.

Dana, Léo-Paul, Ramo Palalić, and Veland Ramadani, eds. (2021), *Entrepreneurship in the Gulf Cooperation Council Region: Evolution and Future Perspectives,* Singapore: World Scientific.

"Doing Business, 2020," (Retrieved from https://www.doingbusiness. org/content/dam/doingBusiness/country/q/qatar/QAT.pdf, accessed 20 December 2020)

Global Innovation Index (2020), (Retrieved from https://www.global innovationindex.org/analysis-indicator, accessed 20 November 2020)

"Global Innovation Index," (https://www.wipo.int/edocs/pubdocs/en/ wipo_pub_gii_2020.pdf, accessed 20 January 2021)

Palalić, Ramo, Léo-Paul Dana, and Veland Ramadani (2019), "Refugee Entrepreneurship: A Case Study from the Sultanate of Oman," in Sibylle Heilbrunn, Jörg Freiling, and Aki Harima, eds., *Refugee Entrepreneurship,* Cham: Palgrave Macmillan, doi: 10.1007/978-3-319-92534-9_14

Palalić, Ramo, Veland Ramadani, and Léo-Paul Dana (2021), "Entrepreneurship in Bahrain," in Léo-Paul Dana, Ramo Palalić, and Veland Ramadani, eds., *Entrepreneurship in the Gulf Cooperation Council Region: Evolution and Future Perspectives,* Singapore: World Scientific, pp. 79–109.

Planning and Statistics Authority (2020), (Retrieved from https://www. psa.gov.qa/en/statistics1/Pages/default.aspx, accessed 20 December 2020)

"Qatar Chamber," (https://www.qatarchamber.com, accessed 3 December 2020)

Sahli, Sadok (2021), "Entrepreneurship in Qatar," in Léo-Paul Dana, Ramo Palalić, and Veland Ramadani, eds., *Entrepreneurship in the Gulf Cooperation Council Region: Evolution and Future Perspectives,* Singapore: World Scientific, Singapore: World Scientific, pp. 79–109.

Salamzadeh, Aidin, and Léo-Paul Dana (2021), "The Coronavirus (COVID-19) Pandemic: Challenges among Iranian Startups," *Journal of Small Business & Entrepreneurship* 33 (5), pp. 489–512. https:// doi.org/10.1080/08276331.2020.1821158

Smith, Simon (2004), *Britain's Revival and Fall in the Gulf: Kuwait, Bahrain, Qatar, and the Trucial States,* London: Taylor & Francis.

Trading Economics (2020), (Retrieved from https://tradingeconomics.com/qatar/indicators, accessed 23 October 2020)

"Trade Economics," (https://tradingeconomics.com/qatar/gdp-growth-annual, accessed 3 December 2020)

World Bank (2020), (Retrieved from http://documents1.worldbank.org/curated/en/688761571934946384/pdf/Doing-Business-2020-Comparing-Business-Regulation-in-190-Economies.pdf, accessed 29 December 2020; https://www.worldbank.org/en/news/press-release/2019/10/24/doing-business-2020-qatars-ambitious-reforms-improve-its-ranking, accessed 20 December 2020)

"World Bank," (http://documents1.worldbank.org/curated/en/688761571934946384/pdf/Doing-Business-2020-Comparing-Business-Regulation-in-190-Economies.pdf, accessed 29 December 2020)

"World Bank-Doing Business," (https://www.worldbank.org/en/news/press-release/2019/10/24/doing-business-2020-qatars-ambitious-reforms-improve-its-ranking, accessed 20 December 2020)

Successor to the Durrani Empire, Buffer between British India and the Russian Empire

Chapter 14

The Context for Business in Afghanistan

Ahsanullah Mohsen, Sayed Fatah Sadat & Mohammad Sediq Nawabzada

Abstract: Afghanistan is considered a rich country from the natural resources' perspective. This country has high investment potential in energy, mining and agriculture. Recently, the government of Afghanistan signed a contract with an Australian investor to generate solar energy up to 20,000 megawatts. Furthermore, Afghanistan has the largest copper mine in Logar province and is contracted with a Chinese firm. Lithium and gas are other elements that are available in several provinces of Afghanistan. Now, the current government is highly committed to economic development and helping foreign investors. Nonetheless, the Afghan economy is free-market economy, and this makes Afghanistan a market of interest for national and international investors. The geographical location of Afghanistan makes it eye-catching country as it can connect the region and regional countries to Europe through its short routes.

Keywords: Bazaar, silk road, Taliban

Introduction

Afghanistan has been a great trade partner to its neighbouring countries. Additionally, Afghanistan was serving as the easy, safe and short path for trade among the countries in the region. These paths were connecting North Asia to South Asia and giving access to South Asian countries to trade their products in Middle Asian countries and Europe. But due to four decades of continuous wars and conflicts, this country suffered a lot in terms of losing its significance of geographic location and business infrastructure within the country (Mohsen, Ramadani, and Dana, 2020).

After the collapse of the Taliban regime, the new government was established in 2001. This government was the political formula suggested by the United States of America, which took place in Bonn, Germany. The Bonn conference in the named year resulted in the establishment of a transitional government led by Hamid Karzai and later he led the country as the president elect for two terms.

With the new government, the hopes for modernisation and accelerating of business activities were raised and Afghanistan got its new and fresh breath for economic growth and development. However, the country didn't experience much improvement in security, transparency and entrepreneurs trust, which could be the main factors for doing business. If the security and infrastructure get better, there are several business sectors, which could have great investment potential. Afghanistan has great business and investment opportunities in various sectors such as mining, livestock and agriculture. There are magnificent reasons for national and international investors to invest in Afghanistan. This country has a free-market economy, which is mainly led by private sector. Additionally, there is 0% tax on the import machinery and only 1% on the import of raw materials. Besides this, there is a possibility of 100% foreign ownership of the business (Consulate General of Afghanistan, 2020).

Bazaar in Afghanistan is hugely based on the social and cultural relationships between entrepreneurs and customers. According to Dana et al. (2008), bazaar is a "social and cultural system, a way of life and a general mode of commercial activity, which has been in existence for millennia" (p.113). Customers with a long-lasting relationship have the privilege of receiving the offer with lower prices and higher quality. As the market is not highly controlled and monitor in certain cases, it makes it difficult to trust the seller and find a product, which is of quality and durable. This is usually true in the case of highly valued products such as refrigerators and air conditioners.

The bazaar in Afghanistan has a common problem with small-scale enterprises and smaller businesses. The social and culture ties between the business and the customers give a chance to the customers to purchase the products by credit (Dana, 2011). Usually, the loan is repaid by the customers but in certain cases the customers fail to pay the amount of loan resulting in the creation of problems between two parties. The product assortment is usually rich and diverse in bazaars (Exhibit 14.1).

Exhibit 14.1   Chicken and turkey meat in an Afghani bazaar; photo © 2021 by
Sayed Fatah Sadat

Historical Context

Afghanistan has remained economically and geopolitically important
throughout its history. As an intersection of trade crossroads, Afghanistan
has played a vital role in connecting Eastern and Southern Asia with
Central and Western Asia and the rest of the world, as well as in supplying goods and natural resources from one part to another, and vice versa.
Afghanistan not only had been home to various civilisations and empires,
but it is also situated as a buffer zone between Russia, Persia and India
(formerly a colony of the British Empire).

Archaeological evidence shows that early people inhabited in caves
and stone shelters in the prehistoric era in the northern part of present-day
Afghanistan. One of such sites documented to date is Qura Kamar situated near the Sarkar Village, eight kilometres north of Aibak City of
Samangan province. The objects and artefacts obtained from the site contain stone tools, animal bones and horns, ceramics and others, commonly
used by the inhabitants of the caves and rock shelters in Afghanistan and

by other ancient people in the region (Yadgari, 2000). The history of life in caves dates back to 8,000 BC. This is the end of the time when early people slowly descended from the caves in the heights of the mountains and started dwelling along the river terraces. Furthermore, archaeologists have obtained stone and bronze products from the country's second most ancient site of Hazar Sum in Samangan province, and from Aq Kupruk in Mazar-e-Sharif. Hazar Sum is situated on a route that is believed to be the connecting link between India and Central Asia (Micheli, 2007).

The Persians and Greeks considered various parts of Afghanistan as separate regions with separate names, namely vast fertile lands in the north (Bactria), mineral-rich mountains in central areas (Parapamisadea), alluvial plains in the western part (Aria) and deserts and river valleys in the eastern part (Arachosia). The Hindu Kush mountains and its hills provided the basic foods for the inhabitants and their livestock, and the valleys acted as routes for migration, trade and business activities (Hiebert, 2012).

Another important hallmark of the lifestyle of the people living in the Avestan Era in present-day Afghanistan was the developments in the industries of carpentry, metallurgy and goldsmith works. Metalworkers melted various metallic minerals and made metal tools out of them for daily uses. Later, they also used animal skins to make clothing and other necessary items from them. Moreover, during the Avestan Era, Aryans (people of Aryana; the ancient name of present-day Afghanistan) formed villages and they were inhabited in the villages and developed towns and cities, which was a result of masonry skills. Aryans also expanded weaponry industries for protecting their habitations and towns from invaders (Yadgari, 2000). Glasswares from the 1st BC and 1st AD centuries have also been obtained from Bagram, which shows the artistic and industrial abilities of the Aryans. These glasswares include bowls, rhyton, pitchers, beakers, jars and fish-shaped jars (Whitehouse, 2012).

The Kushan Empire, established by nomadic tribes from China, today's Bagram (Kapisa), was a dominant power and established civilisation in Central Asia and Northern India, from the 1st century BC to 3rd AD (Ali, 1963). The Kushans produced various types of gold and silver coins in major cities such as in Balk and Peshawar, and they were engaged in trade with China and Eurasia along the prominent Silk Road. They accumulated a great amount of wealth from commercial activities, urbanisation and constructing monasteries (Sánchez, 2012). The Silk Road connected eastern Asia and southern Asia with central Asia, Europe and the Persian Gulf. The Silk Road was used to transport, trade and exchange merchandise silk products and precious stones, Lapis. In the 5th century BC merchants in Bactria transported and traded precious stones along the Indus River. Also, some of the inhabitants of Bactria were traders who travelled hundreds of kilometres to neighbouring countries to exchange goods. This Silk Road model thus represents one of the earliest models of globalisation (probably the first in the world) (Peters, 2019).

During the Middle Ages, various industries had been developed in Khurasan, which covered almost all of the areas, which is nowadays called Afghanistan. These industries included metallurgy, carpentry, stone carving, textile, papermaking and construction works. Even though Afghanistan has mountains rich in minerals and mine, flowing water, arable land, which could serve as a foundation for industrial development, it has not been a developed nation due to unfavourable political, economic and social reasons (Yadgari, 2000). The Jam minarets situated in Ghur from the Ghurid dynasty (1150–1215) demonstrate the artistic and masonry abilities and skills of the people during that era. Before the Genghis Khan invasion of Afghanistan, the country's economy flourished and had played the role of a trade hub from China to Persia and Mediterranean Sea and from India to Central Asia and Eurasia. Being situated in the intersection of civilisations, and as a crossroad for commerce and transportation, Afghanistan had adopted almost all of the inventions and innovations in industries, arts, skills and crafts that would emerge in other parts of the world, especially the neighbouring regions. The internally manufactured goods were not only sufficient for internal consumption, but some of the products were also exported, namely silk, wool and textiles to other countries.

In the contemporary history of Afghanistan, major cities, roads, mosques and madrasas in the country were (re)built during the sultanate of the founder of Afghanistan, The Great Ahmad Shah Baba, and many years later, Emir Habibullah Khan built some new highways and roads namely Kabul-Torkham Highway and Kabul-Kandahar-Chaman Highway (Ataee, 2003). However, the foundations of the first modern industries were laid in 1887 during the rule of Emir Shir Ali Khan and his successor Emir Abdul Rahman Khan, who followed his steps and further modernised the industries inthe late 19th century.

After the last Anglo-Afghan war in 1919, King Amanullah Khan has launched a series of successful reforms in the administrative, political, economic and legal/judiciary arenas. His economic reforms included construction of new highways and renovation of the current highways, the start of transportation businesses, the building of the Salang Tunnel that connects the northern part of the country with the southern, the construction of a 7-kilometre railway route from Kabul to Daraul Aman (Exhibit 14.2), the plan of building a railway between Kabul and Kandahar and its extension to Herat (though this plan was not executed). Telephone network between Kabul and other main cities and Kabul's connection with international hubs through the telegraph system were also established during the Amanullah Khan's reign. In addition, domestic industries were supported with heavy levies on imports, exports were promoted and direct trade links with Germany, United Kingdom and some other European countries were established (Hotak, 2020).

Exhibit 14.2　Steam Locomotive on Kabul-Darul Aman railway line photo courtesy of the National Museum of Afghanistan

Afghanistan's economic development during the rule of King Mohammad Zahir Shah was also notably important, which was mainly undertaken through four development plans, where each was lasting for five years, and implemented from 1956 to 1976. As a result of the implementation of these development plans, industries were modernised and upgraded, energy resources were utilised for the production of energy, textiles industries were modernised and expanded, minerals and mines were excavated and they were either utilised in domestic industries or exported to foreign countries (Yadgari, 2000).

After the fall of the Taliban in 2001, Afghanistan needed to revitalise its hardly struck economy with the help of foreign aids. The country's constitution approved the free-market economy as its legitimate economic system, which induced investors to start privately owned businesses/enterprises. Despite unstable security and the political situation during the past years, Afghanistan's economy experienced considerable development in various sectors and arenas, namely telecommunication, banking, transportation, agriculture, horticulture, livestock, construction and commercial activities. Fearing the return of the Taliban, carpet dealer and jeweller Zabulon Simantov – the last Jewish man in Kabul – announced his departure from Afghanistan in 2021. The Jewish community here dates back to the 7th century. As recently as 1948, the community consisted of 5,000 people.

Context for Enterprise and Implications for Doing Business

According to the National Statistics and Information Authority (NSIA, 2020) report, the population of Afghanistan at the year of 2020 is estimated about 32.8 million (Exhibit 14.3). The annual growth rate of the population between 2018 and 2020 was around 2%. Kabul (the capital of the country) and Herat (a western province), which are the major cities of the country, contain about 22.3% of the population. Nangarhar, Balkh, Helmand, Kandahar, Ghazni, Kunduz, Faryab, Takhar, Badakhshan and Baghlan, other major cities of the country that are similar in terms of population, totally contain about 40% of the population of the country (NSIA, 2020).

The population of the country increased by 31% between 2011 and 2020 with families of having an average of five children. It is estimated that if the population increment remains similar, the population of the country will double by 2050.

Afghanistan established its first university in 1932 – Kabul University. Throughout its long history since 1932, it has provided tertiary education services to a large number of national students. The university has also enjoyed popularity in the region and has attracted many students from the neighbouring countries of Afghanistan. Prior to long war in the country, the university had a rich culture and academic excellence in teaching and

Exhibit 14.3 Students in a university classroom in Afghanistan; photo © 2021 by Sayed Fatah Sadat

research. The decades of war in the country have devastated the entire sectors of Afghanistan and more specifically higher education and Kabul University. Besides being devastated by war, Kabul University is still the first choice for those who want to pursue their higher education. Later on, in the years 1973–1974, the Ministry of Higher Education was established in order to manage, monitor and control the academic affairs of the universities across the country. Before the establishment of the Ministry of Higher Education, it was the Ministry of Education whose primary responsibility was to manage and control primary and secondary schools, it also has been given the responsibility of managing and controlling Kabul University as well. The Ministry of Higher Education after its establishment has developed the National Law of Higher Education and other regulations in order to provide a legal framework for managing and controlling the academic and research affairs in Afghanistan. Political instability and the change of regimes in the history of the country caused the Ministry to revise the National Law of Higher Education by several times since its inception, and most recently the Ministry has revised the Law of Higher Education in 2018, in order to match it with the strategic objectives of the Ministry and the Higher Education System in general (Azimi and Balakarzai, 2020).

The higher education system of Afghanistan mainly consists of the universities and higher education institutes, which are designed mostly for four-year degree programmes in different disciplines. The country has both public and private universities. There are a total of 39 public universities, out of which 4 are central universities located in the capital Kabul, and the remaining 34 universities are located in different provinces across the country. By the formation of the current government, after the collapse of the Taliban regime, and by establishing a new constitution, the country has provided an opportunity for the private sector to emerge. As a result, the private higher education institutes have been established and grown at a very fast rate than expected. Currently, there are 127 registered private universities and higher education institutes in the country, out of which 63 are located in the capital city of Kabul (Ministry of Higher Education, 2020). Exhibit 14.3 shows a university classroom in Afghanistan.

The higher education system of Afghanistan is highly centralised with all decisions regarding academic affairs are taken by the Ministry of Higher Education. The Ministry of Higher Education has four main pillars including academic, students, administrative and financial affairs, and the quality assurance and accreditation. Each pillar of the higher education system has its own responsibilities to effectively govern both public and private universities of the country. The pillars are the central administrative units of the Ministry, which comprise several directorates and other sub-units, including both academic and admin staff for offering services to students and higher education institutions of the country. Though the Ministry of Higher Education governs both public and private universities, and the system of higher education of the country is highly centralised, there is an exception and that is private higher education institutions are enjoying a full autonomy in financial and investment affairs of their own. The Ministry of Higher Education controls and oversees the academic affairs of the private higher education institutions (Azimi and Balakarzai, 2020).

According to World Bank report, the higher education gross enrolment ratio (GER) is about 5%. This percentage of enrolment ration is one of the lowest enrolment ratios throughout the world. The low enrolment rates in Afghanistan can have two reasons. First, the war and conflicts during the 1980s and 1990s period in the country have caused education attainment to decline. The long periods of war affected all levels of education, including primary, secondary and higher education. Second, historically the education attainment is very low among females in Afghanistan and more specifically it has declined during the Taliban regime. The enrolment rates started to rise, in which 5% consists of mainly male students. In the last years since the inception of the current government under the support of international community, female students got the opportunity to go to schools and enroll in universities of their choice (World Bank, 2013).

Though the literacy rate of 43% is too low for the country, if we compare it with the 2011 data there is a dramatic change in the rate, which is a positive point and illustrates how the country has changed over the last one decade.

The main cause of the low literacy rate is the long period of war in the country, which has devastated every corner of the country and destroyed all the infrastructures, more specifically during the Taliban regime in which the doors of schools were closed to girls and Afghanistan was facing an unprecedented economic, social and security problems, in which they didn't have the opportunity to go to schools and universities resulting in the high rate of illiteracy in the country.

The official school ages of the education system of the country start at the age of 7, in which students enroll to the first grade of school and continue up to 12 years. This 12-year system entirely contains the school education. After successful completion of the 12 years of school education, the students will be able to participate in the general examination in order to continue their tertiary education. If succeeded in the exam, they enroll in the universities of their choice. The duration of the university studies is mostly four years, except for medical sciences, which is six years.

The new government in 2001, under the support of international community, and after the collapse of Taliban Afghanistan, inherited a devastated infrastructure, economic institutions, and a collapsed economy, which was addicted to narcotics. Despite the substantial progress made since then, major challenges of the country have remained unsolved, which, in turn, has led to undermining of the efforts for sustained development, and for attracting further foreign investment in the country. The first and foremost challenge, which remained unsolved, is the security of the country. Despite the presence of the US and NATO forces, the country is still unstable and unsecure, which results in the flee of investors from the country. Though the current economy of Afghanistan constitutes of high growth rates, stable currency and expanding private sector, it also faces major challenges such as the illegal drug industry, aid dependency, lack of adequate and sound infrastructure and trade deficit.

According to National Statistics and Information Authority (2020) report, the nominal GDP of Afghanistan in the year 2019 was Afs

1,389.69 billion equivalent to US\$ 18.04 billion with GDP per capita of Afs 43,157.95. equivalent to US\$ 560.49. The real GDP of Afghanistan in the year 2019 was Afs 1,327.92 billion, equivalent to US\$ 17.24 billion, the growth rate of GDP in the year 2019 was 4.03%.

The agriculture sector had a share of 25.52, the share of industry sector was 12.13 and services had a share of 57.38 in total GDP. According to Consumer Price Index (CPI), the inflation rate was 2.3% (3.8% in food items and 0.9% in non-food items) in the country in 2019. The inflation rate has increased compared to the last year, which was 0.6%.

The share of agriculture in total GDP was 25.52%. The growth rate of agriculture sector was 20.79%. The share of services sector in the total GDP was 57.38% in 2019. The main factors contributing to the share were finance and insurance.

The two sectors that are the main contributors of the GDP of country are agriculture and services and we see a fluctuation in the value of agriculture in the years of 2017, 2018 and 2019. The services sector shows a stable increase from 2017 to 2019. The total number of government employees in 2019 was reported as 422,222, of which 76% were males and 24% were females. The data shows a 4.5% increase in government employees compared to the same period of the last year.

Afghanistan's economy grew by 4.03% in 2019 is driven mainly by strong agricultural growth following the country's recovery from drought. The economy is estimated to decline sharply over the first half of 2020, due to the impacts of the COVID-19 crisis (Ministry of Economy, 2020).

Substantial improvements have been made in Afghanistan since 2001, which can be particularly mentioned as the literacy rate is increased to 43%, 127 private universities with different disciplines were established, administrative reforms have been taken place and the three bodies of the government including executive, judiciary and legislative have been established. The door of schools was opened to both male and female students and hundreds of students pursued their higher education in different countries of the world and now are reliable and developed human resources working with different organisations in the country.

Towards the Future

Afghanistan is a landlocked country with no access to the sea, but at the same time it is located in one of the strategic geographic locations of Asia. The country is located within South Asia and Central Asia.

Afghanistan has considerable natural resources including oil, gas, gold, copper, lithium and so on, in which most of them are untouched and are not extracted yet.

The majority of the population are young and the recent developments in the country provided them the opportunity to develop their skills and increase their level of knowledge by utilising different scholarships and going abroad for pursuing higher education. In terms of human capacity development, the country had a significant achievement in the last years.

The future of the country, however, depends on the political situation of the country. The country is getting ready for yet another withdrawal of foreign forces, in 2020 under the Trump's Administration. Though the country has witnessed such withdrawals in the 1980s by the Soviet and 2014 by the United States, while there are striking similarities, there are also differences on the ground, which could help the situation in Afghanistan turn for the better, the difference is the US–Taliban agreement and the initiation of negotiations between the delegation of Islamic Republic of Afghanistan and the Taliban in Doha. As negotiations are in progress between the delegations of the Islamic Republic of Afghanistan and Taliban in order to reach a peace deal and end the long-lasting war in the country. The international community including the United Nations (UN), United States, the European Union, Britain and the region countries are supporting the peace negotiations, there's a strong hope that the outcome of negotiations will be positive and result in a long-lasting peace.

The Afghanistan people are optimistic of the outcome of the peace process and it is believed that the negotiations would have a positive outcome, and it will end to a peace deal between all the stakeholders, which as a result will bring peace and stability to the country. A peaceful and stable Afghanistan means much higher opportunities in all areas of businesses.

Although the country is a landlocked country, it can also be changed to a land-linked country as it is located within South Asia and Central Asia, which represents the intersect of the regional trade. The country can connect the energy-needed countries such as India and Pakistan to the energy-rich countries such as Uzbekistan and Turkmenistan, and major projects in this regard have been initiated such as TAPI, CASA 1000 and more. Through regional connectivity, the country can play an important role in the region and boost its economy.

References

Ali, Mohammed (1963), *Aryana or Ancient Afghanistan,* Kabul: Historical Society of Afghanistan.

Ataee, Mohammad Ibrahim (2003), *A Brief Overview of the Contemporary History of Afghanistan,* Kabul: Maiwand Publishers.

Azimi, Mohammad Naim, and Abdul Tawab Balakarzai (2020), *Nation Building Through Higher Education,* Singapore: Springer.

Consulate General of Afghanistan (2020), Consulate General of the Islamic Republic of Afghanistan, (Retrieved from Doing Business in Afghanistan: https://www.newyork.mfa.af/business-investment/doing-business-in-afghanistan.html)

Dana, Léo-Paul (2011), "Entrepreneurship in Bolivia: An Ethnographic Enquiry," *International Journal of Business and Emerging Markets* 3 (1), pp. 75–88.

Dana, Léo-Paul, Hamid Etemad, and Richard. W. Wright (2008), "Toward a Paradigm of Symbiotic Entrepreneurship," *International Journal of Entrepreneurship and Small Business* 5 (2), pp. 109–126.

Hiebert, Fredrik T. (2012), "The Bronze Age World of Afghanistan," in Joan Aruz and Elisabetta Valtz Fino, eds., *Afghanistan Forging Civilizations along the Silk Road,* New York: The Metropolitan Museum of Art, pp. 16–27.

Hotak, Zalmai (2020), "Political, Economic and Cultural Reforms under Amanullah Khan's Sovereignty," *International Journal of Science and Research* 9 (1), pp. 825–828.

Micheli, R. Roberto (2007), "South Asian Archaeology 2007," in Dennys Frenez and Maurizio Tosi, eds., *Prehistoric Periods,* Oxford: Archaeopress, pp. 191–199.

Ministry of Economy (2020), *A Study on the Effect of COVID-19 on Economy of Afghanistan,* Kabul: Ministry of Economy.

Ministry of Higher Education (2020), *Ministry of Higher Education,* Kabul: Ministry of Higher Education, (Retrieved from https://www.mohe.gov.af/en/government-educational-institutions)

Mohsen, Ahsanullah, Veland Ramadani, and Léo-Paul Dana (2020), "Chapter 2: Green Entrepreneurship Prospects and Challenges: The Context of Afghanistan," in Paresha Sinha, Jenny Gibb, Michele Akoorie, and Jonathan Scott, eds., *Research Handbook on Entrepreneurship in Emerging Economies,* Edward Elgar, pp. 27–43.

National Statistics and Information Authority (2020), *Afghanistan Estimated Population,* Kabul: National Statistics and Information Authority.

Peters, Michael A. (2019), "The Ancient Silk Road and the Birth of Merchant Capitalism," *Educational Philosophy and Theory,* 53 (10), 955–961. https://doi.org/10.1080/00131857.2019.1691481

Sánchez, Fernando López (2012), *The City and the Coin in the Ancient and Early Medieval Worlds,* Oxford: Archaeopress.

United Nations Educational, Scientific and Cultural Organization (2020, November 29), *Afghanistan Education and Literacy,* (Retrieved from http://uis.unesco.org/en/country/af#slideoutmenu)

Whitehouse, David B. (2012), "The Glass from Begram," in Joan Aruz and Elisabetta Valtz Fino, eds., *Afghanistan Forging Civilizations along the Silk Road,* New York: The Metropolitan Museum of Art, pp. 54–63.

World Bank (2013), *Higher Education in Afghanistan: An Emerging Mountainscape,* Washington, DC: The World Bank.

Yadgari, Mustafa A. (2000), "An Overview of the Development of Industries in Afghanistan," *Kabul University Academic Journal* 6, pp. 60–67.

Section VIII

Successor to the Ottoman Empire

Chapter 15

The Context for Business in Turkey

Bella L. Galperin & Çolpan Karan Galperin

Abstract: This chapter presents several important aspects of the business context of Turkey. Initially, an overview of Turkey's historical, political, and economic development is provided. The chapter then addresses the characteristics of Turkey's business framework conditions and continues with the country's ranking in terms of ease of doing business. The chapter concludes with a brief outlook for the future and provides some insights and recommendations for doing business in Turkey.

Keywords: Business, entrepreneurship, bazaar, economic growth, Ottoman Empire, Turkey

Introduction

Turkey is often seen as a bridge from the west to the east. The country is bound by the Black Sea on the north, Georgia and Armenia by the northeast, Azerbaijan and Iran by the east, Iraq and Syria on the southeast, the Mediterranean Sea and the Aegean Sea on the southwest and west, and Greece and Bulgaria on the northwest. The country, officially known as the Republic of Turkey, is a transcontinental country uniquely situated on the Anatolian peninsula in Western Asia and partly on the Balkan peninsula. The country is known to be located at the crossroads of the Balkans, Caucasus, Middle East and eastern Mediterranean (Britannica, 2020).

Due to its unique location, Turkey is a modern country that is rich in heritage, culture, and tradition. Over the centuries, Turkey has been the home of many urban civilisations that have influenced Turkey's cultural fabric. Although its archaeological sites date back to as early as 7,000 BC, with evidence of nomadic tribes during the Palaeolithic and Mesolithic civilisation periods on the Anatolian peninsula (Turkish Cultural Foundation, 2020a), signs of civilisations of Classical Europe and Islamic Middle East can be seen today. Known as Constantinople until 1930, Istanbul was the heart of the Ottoman Empire. Today, it is Turkey's most populous city.

Turkey's blend of Eastern and Western traditions has contributed to the country's appeal to attract businesses. A survey by The Union of Chambers and Commodity Exchanges of Turkey found that more than 6,000 global companies established operations in Turkey during the first half of 2019. This was approximately a 6% increase compared to 2018 (Bilgener Group, 2019a). The growth in global companies in Turkey may be due to the improved ease of doing business in Turkey.

According to the World Bank's Ease of Doing Business 2020 report, Turkey is ranked 33rd among 190 economies in the ease of doing business (World Bank, 2019a). The report measures the ease of doing business by comparing the regulatory environment in 190 countries based on a list of factors such as dealing with construction permits, getting electricity, registering property, getting credit, protecting minority investors, paying taxes, trading across borders, enforcing contacts, and resolving insolvency. Turkey made significant improvements compared to the 2017 report when it was ranked 69th on the list (Bilgener Group, 2019b).

Factors that contributed to Turkey's ease of doing business included (1) the reduction of time to obtain a tax assessment simultaneously reducing mortar charges to transfer of property; (2) value-added tax (VAT) was exempted from some capital investments; (3) the elimination of notarisation of legal books of companies; (4) paid-in minimum capital requirement, which has facilitated starting a business for entrepreneurs; (5) facilitating the criteria for obtaining construction permits by removing some manual application processes and making the building regulation transparent by publishing pre-application online; (6) simplifying the process to pay taxes by improving the online portal for filing and payment of taxes; (7) reducing the cost and time for trading internationally, which includes the functionalities of the national trade single window, enhancing the risk management system and lowering customs brokers' fees, and (8) facilitating the enforcement of contracts by publishing judgements rendered at all levels in commercial cases (Doshmanli et al., 2018; Salamzadeh, 2018; Tekin et al., 2021).

The increased number of global companies in Turkey may also be attributed to the opportunities offered by the country in terms of quality of life, work–life balance, financial return and family life. According to the Hong Kong and Shanghai Banking Corporation (HSBC) Expat Explorer Guide, Turkey was ranked as seventh best country in the world for international workers by expats residing in Turkey. Turkey ranked ahead of key international locations including Germany (8th), the United Arab Emirates (UAE) (9th), the United States of America (USA) (23rd), and the United Kingdom (UK) (27th) (HSBC, 2019). Turkey was described as a place that, "oozes expat appeal, particularly for businesspeople looking to take advantage of its growing economy. With sunny skies and a low cost of living, the country is also an ideal retirement destination. And its culture lives up to the cliché 'something for everyone' with a fascinating blend of Eastern and Western traditions" (HSBC, 2020). Exhibit 15.1 shows restaurants under the Galata Bridge on the Golden Horn in Istanbul.

Exhibit 15.1 Restaurants under the Galata Bridge in Istanbul; artwork © 2021 by Çolpan Karan Galperin

Turkey's unique geographical location, cultural diversity, increased ease of doing business and favourable rankings by expatriates provide a dynamic and competitive context for doing business. This chapter provides an overview of the historical and current business context and its impact on business. Future implications for doing business are then discussed.

Historical Context

Turkey's history begins more than 4,000 years ago when Turks lived in Central Asia around 2,000 BC. Some Turks left Central Asia and established various states and empires independent from each other in Asia and Europe. The empires included The Great Hun Empire (established during the 3rd century BC), the Göktürk Empire (552–740), the Uygur Empire (741–840), the Avar Empire (6th–9th century AD), the Hazar Empire (5th– 10th century AD), the Great Seljuk Empire (1040–1157) and many others (Turkish Cultural Foundation, 2020b).

In particular, Anatolia, the western part of Turkey, is one of the oldest and inhabited regions in the world. The Hittites, the earliest empire in the area, controlled the area from the 18th to 13th century BC. The Phrygians, an Indo-European people, then invaded the land and controlled the region until they were conquered by the Cimmerians in the 7th century BC, who were later defeated by the Lycians. During this time, the Greeks also settled along the west coast of Anatolia and used the ports to ship goods produced in the area. Around 546 BC, the Persians invaded the area from the east and controlled Anatolia for the next two centuries until Alexander the Great conquered the area in 334 BC (Education Encyclopedia, 2020).

In 129 BC, the Roman Republic conquered Anatolia and established the province of Asia (or Asia Minor), with its capital in Ephesus. Under the Romans, there was greater trade and prosperity to Anatolia, which facilitated the spread of a new religion. St. Paul, an Anatolian born in the city of Tarsus, a town west of Adana on Turkey's Mediterranean coast, became one of the greatest of preachers for Christianity. His journeys in his Anatolian homeland were crucial to the foundation of the Christian Church (Brosnahan, 2019).

It was only in 324 CE, when the Roman emperor Constantine I, also known as Constantine the Great, moved the Roman Empire's capital to the ancient city of Byzance and renamed the city Constantinople, which is now known as Istanbul. With the Roman Empire divided into two segments – the East and the West, Constantinople became the capital of the Eastern Roman or Byzantine Empire (Education Encyclopedia, 2020). With the rise of Islam, there was a further separation of the peninsula between the Byzantine Christian world and the Islamic Middle East. The Seljoukites, a group of Central Asiatic Turks, then conquered Baghdad in 1055 CE and established themselves in Anatolia. They created a highly developed Muslim culture in their great capital of Konya, in central Turkey, which became a Middle Eastern and Anatolian Empire. While this empire was divided by Mongol invasions, small Turkish states still remained on the border of Anatolia. It was one of these states that became the Ottoman Empire.

In 1453, the Ottomans conquered Constantinople during the reign of Sultan Mehmet II and renamed the capital city to Istanbul. This marked the fall of the Byzantine Empire and the beginning of the New Age (Turkish Cultural Foundation, 2020b). The Ottoman Empire was multinational and multicultural. The Ottoman Empire reached its peak under Suleiman the Magnificent, who ruled between 1520 and 1566 (Dana, 2000). Since the empire was largely decentralised, non-Muslim ethnic groups, such as Armenians, Greek Orthodox and Jews, were able to conduct trade with the West, providing revenue to the empire.

Over the years, several sultans expanded the Ottoman Empire by wagering wars on neighbouring territories, including what is known as Greece, Bulgaria, Yugoslavia, Albania and Romania in the Balkans; the islands in the Eastern Mediterranean and the Middle East. The borders of the Empire were expanded from Crimea to Yemen in the north, Sudan in the south, from Iran and the Caspian Sea in the east to Vienna in the northwest, and Spain in the southwest.

It was only in the 18th and 19th centuries that the Ottoman Empire saw its decline when European countries started fighting for control. In 1914, the Ottoman Empire entered World War I and fought with the allied powers. Due to its defeat from the war in 1918, the Ottoman Empire was compelled to sign the Armistice of Mudros on October 30, 1918. Under the terms of this Armistice, the territories of the Ottoman Empire became occupied by Britain, France, Russia and Greece, which marked the actual end of the Ottoman Empire (Turkish Cultural Foundation, 2020b).

The ruins of the Ottoman Empire drove a national resistance and liberation movement under the leadership of Mustafa Kemal, an Ottoman military commander. In the pursuit of Turkish self-determination and national independence, Kemal mobilised Anatolia and united several resistance groups into a structured army. This movement grew in cohesion, and the Turks were successful in fighting for national liberalisation. On July 24, 1923, the Lausanne Peace Treaty was signed with France, Greece, Italy, the United Kingdom and others; this created the international borders of a Turkish state and guaranteed its complete independence. The republic proclaimed on October 29, 1923, marked self-rule of the Turkish people the first time in centuries. Mustafa Kemal (Exhibit 15.2) was elected as the first president of the Republic of Turkey (Turkish Cultural Foundation, 2020b).

In 1924, Mustafa Kemal expelled the royal family – descendants of Osman I, the Anatolian ruler who had established the monarchy in 1299. The men of the monarchy were given 24-hour notice to leave; the women were allowed a week. Born in 1912, Ertogroul Osman, Imperial Prince (Şehzade) of the Ottoman Empire was the 43rd head of the Imperial House of Osman from 1994 until his death. He was the last surviving grandson of an Ottoman emperor. As a child, Ertogroul Osman played at his grandfather's home, the 285-room Dolmabahçe Palace (see Exhibit 1.2, in Chapter 1). Because of his exile, he spent most of his life in Manhattan,

Exhibit 15.2   Kemal Atatürk; photo © 2021 by Léo-Paul Dana

New York and died at 97, during a visit to Istanbul with his second wife Princess Zeynep of Afghanistan.

Kemal became known as Atatürk or "Father of Turks". Under his leadership, a wide range of political, social, legal, economic and cultural reforms were introduced. Namely, a new political system was introduced based on principles of parliamentary democracy and human rights, secular education system was established, the Arabic alphabet was changed into the Latin alphabet and new civil and criminal codes were adapted from European models. Turkish women also received equal rights, which included the right to vote and be elected to public office. These changes put Turkey ahead of many Western nations in terms of women's rights (Turkish Cultural Foundation, 2020b).

The new Turkey established by Atatürk was an evolution, unparalleled at its time, and even today, it can be considered as transporting a predominantly Muslim nation in line with Western civilisation and universal values (Britannica, 2020, p.1). The reforms introduced by Atatürk still impact modern Turkey's business environment and practices today. These reforms set the stage for the country's economic and social development.

In 1947, US President Harry S. Truman asked Congress to appropriate aid to Turkey to protect itself from communist threats. This came to be known as the Truman Doctrine.

Since 2000, Turkey's performance in economic and social performance has been remarkable. Due to increased employment and incomes, Turkey is now considered an upper-middle-income country. Overall, Turkey has kept a long-term perspective by implementing reforms. Government programmes have also been developed to assist groups in need and underprivileged regions (Tekin et al., 2021; World Bank, 2020a).

Between 2002 and 2015, poverty decreased more than 50%, and extreme poverty was even further reduced. Turkey significantly urbanised, strong macroeconomic and fiscal policy frameworks were implemented. The country also increased foreign trade and finance, coordinated many laws and regulations with the European Union (EU) standards, and invested access to public services. Compared to other countries, Turkey also recovered favourably from the global crisis of 2008–2009 (World Bank, 2020a).

Currently, Turkey is the 18th largest economy in the world, with a gross domestic product (GDP) of around US\$ 770 billion (World Bank, 2019b). From 2000 to 2018, per capita GDP in Turkey more than doubled from US\$ 4,200 to US\$ 9,505. Turkey is also a member of the Organisation for Economic Co-operation and Development (OECD) and the G20, and an increasingly important donor of Official Development

Assistance. However, due to the rising economic uncertainties, it has been more challenging for the country to maintain these accomplishments given the increasing inflation and unemployment, increased challenges in the corporate and financial sectors and geopolitical tensions in the region (World Bank, 2020a). In the past five years, the country has also experienced terror attacks, a coup attempt followed by a squelching of dissenters, a currency crisis, and diplomatic disagreements with Europe and America (The Economist, 2020). As with other countries around the globe, the COVID-19 pandemic has also furthered reduced economic and social gains (Kawamorita et al., 2020). The World Bank reported that Turkey's GDP decreased 10% in the second quarter year-on-year. Turkey's GDP for 2020 is reported as 761.8 billion US$ (World Bank, 2020a).

Context for Enterprise and Implications for Doing Business

Despite the current environment, Turkey continues to attract foreign and domestic investment since its foundation for development remains strong. The 2018–2021 Country Partnership Framework (CPF), which is aligned with Turkey's 10th Development Plan, provides a good overview of the context for enterprise (World Bank Group, 2017). The CPF outlines key development goals in three areas: (1) growth, (2) inclusion and (3) sustainability.

- **Growth:** In the area of growth, Turkey's priorities are to (a) address macro-fiscal risks, (b) develop financial markets, (c) improve the quality of regulatory and accountability institutions, (d) improve competition policy, (e) improve corporate governance (e.g., business and investment climate, productivity growth), (f) improve technology absorption and innovation, (g) address geopolitical tensions in the east and southeast and (h) move away from small mixed-crop agriculture.
- **Inclusion:** In the area of inclusion, Turkey's priorities are to (a) address regional differences and lack of convergence in the area of healthy life, mobility, and healthcare industries; (b) raise female labour force participation and (c) increase educational achievements (basic and occupational skills and development)
- **Sustainability:** In the area of sustainability, Turkey's priorities are to (a) link energy consumption to GDP growth, (b) manage urban development, (c) address water scarcity and (d) improve land management.

More recently, the Turkish government introduced its second New Economic Programme (NEP) on September 30, 2019. The second plan addresses the increasing economic uncertainty and highlights macroeconomic issues, such as the 3.6 million Syrian refugees living in Turkey. In conjunction with the World Bank Group and the EU's Facility for Refugees in Turkey (FRiT), Turkey is implementing programmes in the areas of social support and adaptation, labour markets and the economy and education (Salamzadeh et al., 2016). The CPF, along with Turkey's development plan, has signalled to investors that Turkey is interested in conducting business.

When considering doing business in Turkey, there are a number of factors to consider, namely

- **Length of time to start a business:** It typically takes less than a week (six days) to start a business in Turkey. Nevertheless, there are several procedures that may make it more difficult for overseas firms. For example, after executing and notarising the articles of association, companies must deposit a percentage of capital to an account of the Competition Authority. The deposit must be made prior to making a deposit of the initial capital into a bank, filling the incorporation notice form, certifying the legal books by a notary and communicating with the tax office on Commercial Registry's notification (TMF, 2019).
- **Obtaining a construction permit:** There are many procedures in place in order to get a construction permit in Turkey (TMF, 2019). As noted earlier, while Turkey made significant improvements in its ranking in the 2020 World Bank's Ease of Doing Business, Turkey still ranked 53 out of 186 countries in the category of dealing with construction permits, outperforming other countries such as Canada (64) and Switzerland (71) (World Bank, 2020b).
- **Registering a property:** It takes less than a week to register a property. The registration process is fairly streamlined in order to obtain registration for a commercial residence (TMF, 2019).
- **Understanding the culture:** It is recommended that investors become familiar with Turkish business meeting etiquette and culture before conducting business. Since meetings are important for Turkish businesspeople, it is advisable to schedule a meeting one or two weeks in advance to avoid Turkish holidays. Given Turkey is largely an Islamic country, it may be necessary to schedule meetings around the five daily prayer times (European Commission, 2019).

As discussed earlier, Turkey is a large country that is rich in cultural diversity. When conducting business in Turkey, it is important to be aware of the differences between the east and west. In general, it will be easier to conduct business in Istanbul because it's a large city that regularly conducts business with Europeans and its large expatriate communities. In Anatolia, Western Asian peninsula, people are more religious, conservative, and family oriented (Payne, 2019). Despite the differences between the east and west, one must remember that Turks have a strong identity and culture. Central parts of the Turkish culture are hospitality and entertainment. Businesspeople should expect a lot of food, tea, and coffee – whether it is a formal business meeting or negotiating for a carpet at the Grand Bazaar.

Bazaars play an important role (Dana et al., 2008) in Turkey's business activities (Exhibits 15.3 and 15.4). The Grand Bazaar (Exhibit 15.3), also known as Kapali Çarşi, has been described as the "beating heart of Istanbul for five centuries" and is viewed as a living museum with 557 years of history (Anadolu Agency, 2018, p. 1). Istanbul's Grand Bazaar is one of the Turkey's most significant cultural attractions and considered one of the first shopping malls in the world. The Grand Bazaar was built in 1461 as one of the most prominent projects of the Ottoman Empire's economy and as a means for Sultan Mehmed II to provide income to fund the construction in the Hagia Sophia Mosque. The bazaar occupies 40,000 square metres of space, covers 60 covered streets, and accommodates more than 2,500 shops that sell a diverse range of goods including carpets, bags, textile good, gold and silver jewellery, antiques and souvenirs. There are also restaurants in the Grand Bazaar that serve hot and cold home cooking, and Turkish coffee.

With a recorded number of 91.25 million visitors in 2013, the Grand Bazaar is considered one of the most popular destinations worldwide (Istanbulview, 2020). Other bazaars in Istanbul include the Istiklal Caddesi Bazaar, the Egyptian Spice Bazaar, and the Sahaflar Çarşisi (Book Bazaar). While Grand Bazaar is no longer the commercial centre of Istanbul, these bazaars show the importance of new venture creation as an important part of the Turkish culture (Dana, 2000). More recently, new malls with modern stores, boutiques, food markets and restaurants have become common places to shop.

Exhibit 15.3 The Grand Bazaar, Istanbul; artwork © 2021 by Çolpan Karan Galperin

Exhibit 15.4   A sidewalk shoe shiner in Istanbul; photo © 2021 by Léo-Paul Dana

Towards the Future

According to a report by PriceWaterhouseCoopers (PwC), it was noted that Turkey has the opportunity to increase a skilled labour force to sustain long-term economic growth. It is expected that Turkey will be able to get closer to its European peers by 2050 (Büyüksarıkulak and Kahramanoğlu, 2019; Pricewaterhouse Coopers, 2015). More recent projections suggest that Turkey will become the 12th largest economy in the world by 2030, with its overall GDP rising to US\$ 2.7 trillion (Deggin, 2020). Turkey's transformation in the last three decades has placed the country in a good position for the future. Turkey's free economy and integration with the European market have facilitated a high degree of expertise and competitiveness in production, export and investment (Deloitte, 2014).

Various leading sectors hold much promise for exports and investments in the future. Turkey has been positioning itself in the global value chain by leveraging its logistical advantage, lower labour costs and flexible production capabilities. Turkey's large population size (83 million), relatively young population (average age of 31) (Salamzadeh, 2014), growing entrepreneurial class and favourable location between Europe, Asia and Africa has made the country a central manufacturing and distribution hub (International Trade Administration US Department of Commerce, 2020a). Turkey's leading sub-sectors include innovative materials/technical textiles, additive manufacturing (automobile, aerospace, and defence) and industrial automation, big data and analytics, robotics and augmented and virtual reality. In the last decade, Turkey's manufacturing share of GDP has been 16.5%, but the country plans to increase it to 21% by 2023 (International Trade Administration US Department of Commerce, 2020a). It is also expected that mineral exports will increase as the demand in Asia grows (Deggin, 2020).

In addition to Turkey's strategy to invest in manufacturing, the agricultural sector holds much potential for the future. Turkey's agricultural economy is one of the top ten in the world (International Trade Administration US Department of Commerce, 2020b). Around half of the land in the country is used for agriculture, with about 25% of the population employed in the agricultural industry. Turkey is a major producer of wheat, sugar beets, milk, poultry, cotton, tomatoes and other fruits and vegetables, and is the largest producer in the world for apricots and hazelnuts. Turkey imports oilseeds (e.g., soybeans, grain products) as inputs in order to manufacture animal feed for its meat and rapidly growing poultry sector. Although the country grows cotton, Turkey also imports additional cotton as an input for its advanced textile sector (Exhibit 15.5 shows the harvest time in a place near Kapadokya). Turkey's retail food sector has also been steadily growing and expected to further increase in the future due to its rising numbers of modern retail chains, traditional small grocery stores and new deep discount stores. Turkey's young and growing population will also provide many opportunities for new product innovations.

In conclusion, Turkey's steady economy, growing market and entrepreneurial class have contributed to the increase in foreign and domestic investment (Zulfiu et al., 2015). As the most eastern country in Europe and perhaps the most western country in the Middle West, the unique location of Turkey along with its rich heritage and culture have provided investors with many opportunities to do business. In addition, the improved ease of doing business and recognition as one of the top ten countries in the world for expats have contributed to the increase in global companies in the country. A transcontinental continent situated on the Anatolian peninsula in West Asia and southeastern Europe in western Turkey is certainly an intriguing and fascinating place to conduct business.

Exhibit 15.5   Harvest time near Kapadokya; photo © 2021 by Çolpan Karan Galperin

References

Anadolu Agency (2018), "The Grand Bazaar: The Beating Heart of Istanbul for Five Centuries," Daily Sabah, (Retrieved from https://www.dailysabah.com/feature/2018/09/05/the-grand-bazaar-the-beating-heart-of-istanbul-for-five-centuries, accessed 5 September 2020)

Bilgener Group (2019a), "More Than 6,000 Global Companies have Been Established in Turkey in the First Half on 2019. Doing Business in Turkey," (Retrieved from https://doingbusinessinturkey.com/more-than-6-000-companies-have-been-established-in-turkey-in-the-first-half-of-2019/)

Bilgener Group (2019b), "Turkey Ranked 33rd in the World Bank's 2020 Ease of Doing Business Report," (Retrieved from https://doingbusinessinturkey.com/turkey-ranked-33rd-in-the-world-banks-2020-ease-of-doing-businessreport/#:~:text=Turkey%20Ranked%2033rd%20in%20the%20World%20Bank's%202020%20Ease%20of%20Doing%20Business%20Report,-November%

204%2C%202019&text=Turkey%20is%20ranked%2033rd%20amo ng,2017%20version%20of%20the%20report)

Britannica (2020), "Cultural Life," (Retrieved from https://www.britannica. com/place/Turkey)

Brosnahan, Tom (2019), "The Romans in Turkey," (Retrieved from https:// turkeytravelplanner.com/details/History/Romans.html#:~:text=In% 20129%20BC%20the%20Roman,spread%20of%20a%20new%20re ligion)

Büyüksarıkulak, Ahmet Mesut, and Ali Kahramanoğlu (2019), "The Prosperity Index and its Relationship with Economic Growth: Case of Turkey," *Journal of Entrepreneurship, Business and Economics* 7 (2), pp. 1–30.

Dana, Léo-Paul (2000), *Economies of the Eastern Mediterranean: Economic Miracle in the Making,* London, Singapore & Hong Kong: World Scientific.

Dana, Léo-Paul, Hamid Etemad, and Richard W. Wright (2008), "Toward a Paradigm of Symbiotic Entrepreneurship," *International Journal of Entrepreneurship and Small Business* 5 (2), pp. 109–126.

Deggin, Cameron (2020), "Turkey's Star to Rise as Emerging Markets Set to Dominate 2030 Economy," Property Turkey, (Retrieved from https://www.propertyturkey.com/blog-turkey/turkeys-star-to-rise-as-emerging-markets-set-to-dominate-2030-economy#:~:text= exports%20or%20manufacturing.-,Turkey,growth%20over%20the% 20next%20decade, accessed 5 May 2020)

Deloitte (2014), "How to do Business in Turkey," (Retrieved from https:// www2.deloitte.com/tr/en/pages/tax/articles/how-to-do-business-in-turkey.html)

Doshmanli, Masoumeh, Yashar Salamzadeh, and Aidin Salamzadeh (2018), "Development of SMEs in an Emerging Economy: Does Corporate Social Responsibility Matter?" *International Journal of Management and Enterprise Development* 17 (2), pp. 168–191.

The Economist (2020), "Life is Tough for Turkish Businesses," (Retrieved from https://www.economist.com/business/2020/06/13/life-is-tough-for-turkish-businesses, accessed 13 June 2020)

Education Encyclopedia (2020), "Turkey: History and Background," (Retrieved from https://education.stateuniversity.com/pages/1560/ Turkey-HISTORY-BACKGROUND.html)

European Commission (2019), "Passport to Trade: Meeting Etiquette in Turkey," (Retrieved from https://businessculture.org/southern-europe/business-culture-in-turkey/meeting-etiquette-in-turkey/)

HSBC (2019), "Expat Country Guide: Your Guide to Turkey," (Retrieved from https://www.expatexplorer.hsbc.com/country-guides/turkey/moving)

HSBC (2020), "A Bridge Between East and West," (Retrieved from https://www.expatexplorer.hsbc.com/country-guides/turkey)

International Trade Administration US Department of Commerce (2020a), "Advanced Manufacturing," (Retrieved from https://www.trade.gov/knowledge-product/turkey-advanced-manufacturing, accessed 7 October 2020)

International Trade Administration US Department of Commerce (2020b), "Agriculture," (Retrieved from https://www.trade.gov/knowledge-product/turkey-agriculture, accessed 7 October 2020)

Istanbulview (2020), "Istanbul Grand Bazaar Ranked World's Most Popular Tourist Destination," (Retrieved from https://www.istanbulview.com/istanbul-grand-bazaar-ranked-worlds-most-popular-attraction/)

Kawamorita, Hiroko, Aidin Salamzadeh, Kursat Demiryurek, and Mahyar Ghajarzadeh (2020), "Entrepreneurial Universities in Times of Crisis: Case of COVID-19 Pandemic," *Journal of Entrepreneurship, Business and Economics* 8 (1), pp. 77–88.

Payne, Neil (2019), "How to do Business in Turkey," Entrepreneur Handbook, (Retrieved from https://entrepreneurhandbook.co.uk/doing-business-in-turkey/, accessed 1 September 2019)

PricewaterhouseCoopers (2015), "Doing Business in Turkey. PwC Turkey," (Retrieved from https://www.pwc.com.tr/en/publications/arastirmalar/pdf/doing-business-in-turkey.pdf)

Salamzadeh, Aidin (2014), "Youth Entrepreneurship in Developing Countries: Do Young People Know Their Potentials?" in Hiroko Kawamorita Kesim, ed., *International Conference on Youth and Our Cultural Heritage,* Samsun, Turkey: Ondokuz Mayis University, pp. 15–18.

Salamzadeh, Aidin (2018), "Start-Up Boom in an Emerging Market: A Niche Market Approach," in Datis Khajeheian, Mike Friedrichsen, and Wilfried Mödinger, eds., *Competitiveness in Emerging Markets,* Cham: Springer, pp. 233–243.

Salamzadeh, Aidin, Hiroko Kawamorita, and Yashar Salamzadeh (2016), "Entrepreneurial Universities and Branding: A Conceptual Model Proposal," *World Review of Science, Technology and Sustainable Development* 12 (4), pp. 300–315.

Tekin, Erol, Veland Ramadani, and Léo-Paul Dana (2021), "Entrepreneurship in Turkey and Other Balkan Countries: Are there Opportunities for Mutual Co-Operation through Internationalisation?" *Review of International Business and Strategy* 31 (2), pp. 297–314, https://doi.org/10.1108/RIBS-10-2020-0133

TMF (2019), "Top 10 Challenges of Doing Business in Turkey," (Retrieved from https://www.tmf-group.com/en/news-insights/business-culture/top-challenges-turkey/)

Turkish Cultural Foundation (2020a), (Retrieved from http://www.turkishculture.org/lifestyles/turkish-culture-portal/various-aspects-of-502.htm)

Turkish Cultural Foundation (2020b), "A Brief Outline of History," (Retrieved from http://www.turkishculture.org/general-1067.htm)

World Bank (2019a), "Doing Business 2020: Comparing Business Regulation in 190 Economies. Group Bank Group," (Retrieved from https://www.doingbusiness.org/en/reports/global-reports/doing-business-2020)

World Bank (2019b), "The World Bank in Turkey: Country Snapshot," (Retrieved from http://pubdocs.worldbank.org/en/288681571384697671/Turkey-Snapshot-Oct-2019.pdf)

World Bank (2020a), "The World Bank in Turkey: Overview," (Retrieved from https://www.worldbank.org/en/country/turkey/overview#2)

World Bank (2020b), "Ease of Doing Business," (Retrieved from https://www.doingbusiness.org/en/rankings)

World Bank Group (2017), *Turkey – Country Partnership Framework for the Period FY18–FY21 (English),* Washington, DC: World Bank Group, (Retrieved from http://documents.worldbank.org/curated/en/585411504231252220/Turkey-Country-partnership-framework-for-the-period-FY18-FY21)

Zulfiu, Vedat, Veland Ramadani, and Léo-Paul Dana (2015), "Muslim Entrepreneurs in Secular Turkey: Distributors as a Source of Innovation in a Supply Chain," *International Journal of Entrepreneurship and Small Business* 26 (1), pp. 78–95.

Successor to the Kingdom of Iraq under British Administration

Chapter 16

The Context for Business in Iraq

Aidin Salamzadeh, Ali Ahmadi & Ali Safar Kamel

Abstract: Located at the heart of the Middle East, Iraq is an oil-producing country with economic potential. Although its economy relies highly on selling oil and gas products, the country has a fascinating history of traditional bazaars. In recent years, Iraq has changed dramatically due to increased foreign direct investments, especially in Kurdish regions. New technology-based firms are growing in terms of quantity and quality during the past decade. This chapter reviews the historical background of the country and also discussed the context of business in Iraq. Finally, the authors provide a series of directions for the future of Iraq.

Keywords: business, context, bazaar, market, Iraq

Introduction

With an approximate area of 435,052 square kilometres, Iraq neighbours Iran to the east, and Syria, Jordan and Saudi Arabia to the west. To the south, Iraq shares borders with Kuwait and has a narrow access to the Persian Gulf through the city of Basrah. On the north, it neighbours Turkey (Exhibit 16.1). In order to get a better understanding of Iraq, readers need to know about the two rivers that rise from the Turkish highlands, flowing through the country and into the Persian Gulf (Al-Shahri et al., 2004), Tigris and Euphrates. Iraq has a largely mountainous area near the Iranian border side, merging with the Zagros mountains (Zeder and Hesse, 2000).

The official language in Iraq is Arabic and Kurdish based on the regions in the country, and the official religion is Islam throughout the

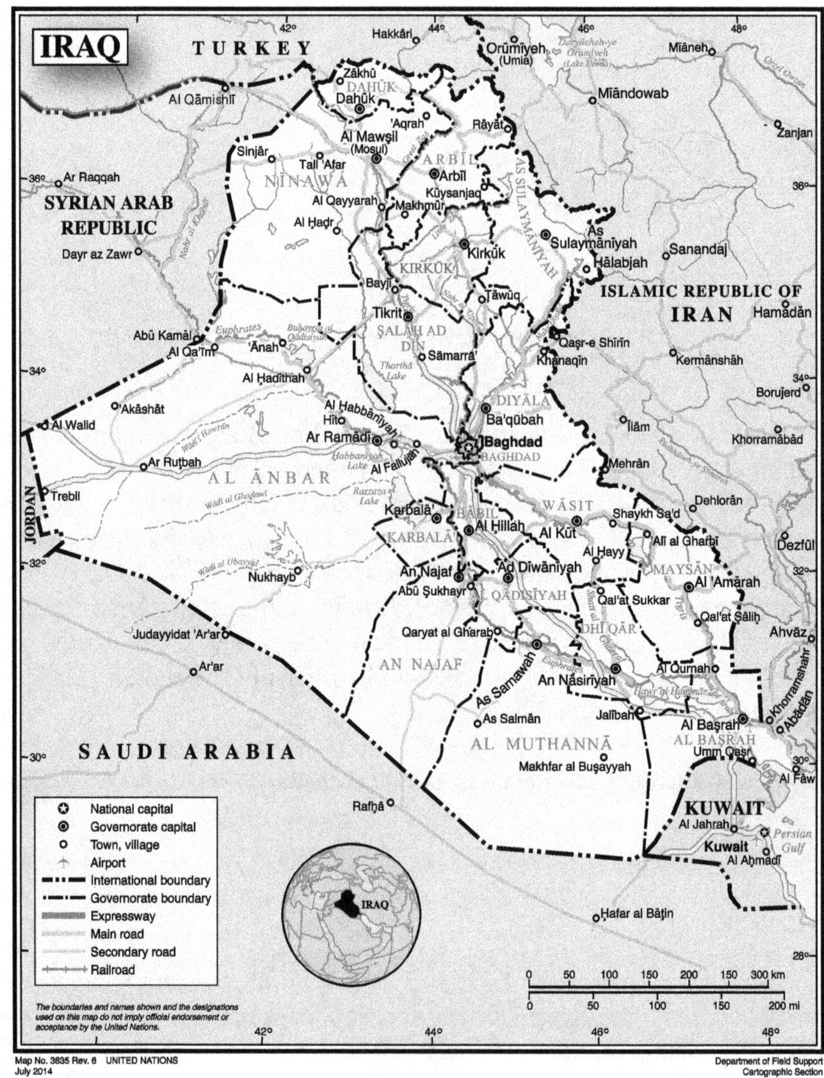

Exhibit 16.1 Map 3835 of Iraq; courtesy of the United Nations

whole country (Britannica, 2021a). Iraq was formerly the home to many ethnic groups such as the ancient Babylonians, Assyrians and Sumerians (Foster and Foster, 2021), but through the conquest of Arabs since the 7th century, now Arabs are the majority with two-thirds of the population, followed by Kurds, mainly in the northeast, with one fourth. There are also small minority communities of Azerbaijanis, Bahais, Christians, Mandaeans, Turkmens and Yazidis. In 2020, five Jews remained in Iraq (Shashoua, 2020). Known as the "healer of the poor", orthopaedic surgeon Dr Thafer Fouad Eliyahu died in March 2021. His mother – one of the first female doctors in Iraq – had her own clinic in Baghdad during the mid-20th century. He worked at Al-Wasita Hospital in Baghdad and also ran his own clinic, where he treated people for free. His death flooded Iraqi social media as he was the last Jewish doctor in Iraq. Thereafter, only three Jews remained in Iraq.[1]

Exact and renewed demographic data are not available for Iraq, and after the war with the United States in 2003, most figures are estimates. Nevertheless, in 2018, US officials stated that the Iraq population was 40,194,216 (Amouzegar et al., 2021). Thirty-nine per cent of people in Iraq are 14 years old or less, thus making the country's demographics very young. Most of the country (almost 70%) live in cities. Density is higher in the north, central and eastern Iraq. Major cities in Iraq are Baghdad with 6.6 million, Mosul with 1.5 million and Basrah with 1.3 million people. There are 18 regions called governorates that make the general government of Iraq except for the Kurdistan region, which is administrated autonomously by the Kurdistan Regional Government or KRG (EASO, 2020). Kurdistan owns around one-third of Iraq's total oil reserves. The primary non-oil industries in the Kurdistan Region include agriculture and tourism. Historically, conflicts and sanctions have hindered agricultural development in this region, but roughly 13% of Kurdistan's land is arable. Therefore, agriculture is the second-largest industry following oil. Besides, as a safe, peaceful and attractive touristic destination, its tourism industry has also improved. There are several exciting places to visit in Iraq, such as Qalat Erbil (Exhibit 16.2).

---

[1] Jews have lived here since 586 BC and until World War II inter-ethnic relations were fine. Supported by Nazi Germany, in 1941 Rashid Ali Ali Al-Gaylani conducted a coup, seizing control of the Kingdom of Iraq; the British responded with the Anglo-Iraqi War. Some leaders blamed Jews for British imperialism and immediately after the British victory in the Anglo-Iraqi War, violent dispossession known as Farhud took place against Jews in Iraq. Jews in Baghdad were violently robbed, beaten and/or raped while others were hung in an event called the Farhud (see Black, 2010). There were 150,000 Jews living in Iraq in 1947. Between 1950 and 1952, approximately 125,000 Iraqi Jews immigrated to Israel; Hillel (1987) recounts the massive emigration of Jews from Iraq. Among the emigrants is Abe Karem, profiled in *The Economist* as the father of the drone. In 1963, the Ba'ath Party froze property belonging to Jews and subsequent years saw increasing restrictions on Jews.

Unfortunately, the relationship between the central government and the Kurdistan region is not well enough. Then, budget restrictions are proposed generally to this region, which is the leading touristic destination of Iraq.

Iraq's flag, which is shown in Exhibit 16.3, contains bright red, white and black colours with a green-rendered *Takbir* in the middle. The Iraqi flag faced a handful of changes throughout the years. Prior to the current

Exhibit 16.2 Qalat Erbil; photo © 2021 by Ali Safar Kamel

Exhibit 16.3 Flag of Iraq

flag, it had three stars in the middle, with a *Takbir* handwritten by the former Baathi dictator of Iraq, Saddam Hussein (Britannica, 2021a).

This chapter is structured as follows. First, the historical context of Iraq is reviewed. Then, the authors discussed the context for enterprise and implications for doing business in Iraq. Then, some directions for future research and practice are proposed.

Historical Context

The rich oil reserves of Iraq were first found in 1927 in Kirkuk, and it had a tremendous effect on the country ever since (Hanish, 2010). The first export destinations were British-controlled Tripoli and French-controlled Haifa through primitive pipelines from Kirkuk via the international player called "The Iraq Petroleum Company (IPC)". IPC, facing no competition in Iraq, exported the oil to Mediterranean countries with meagre fee margins for the Iraqi government (Fitzgerald, 1991).

Through the 1950s, the pipelines were developed, and IPC subsidiaries discovered even new oil fields in the south. As the oil exports surged, the flow of wealth into the country fed the industry for even more growth, and the importance of domination over the industry grew more and more critical. To confront the control of a small number of companies over the oil fields in the oil-rich regions, in 1960, the Organisation of the Petroleum Exporting Countries (OPEC) was formed by a coalition of Iraq, Iran, Saudi Arabia, Kuwait and Venezuela (Issawi, 1978).

Using the power of OPEC and significant oil policies, Iraq gradually beat the IPC and saw the most important benefits of oil revenues during the 1970s when the oil prices spiked. However, much like any other OPEC country, Iraq grew more and more reliant on oil income and high government spending until a point when 95% of all country's revenue was from oil. The oil production started a plummetting trend with the Iran–Iraq war (1980), the Persian Gulf war (1991) and the 2003 war on terror (Vogler, 2017). As of 2018, Iraq has the fifth-largest crude oil reserves in the OPEC countries after Venezuela, Saudi Arabia and Iran (OPEC, 2020).

In 1990, Saddam Hussein declared war on Kuwait, and the consequences triggered the start of the Persian Gulf War (Alkandari, 2019). International sanctions were imposed on Iraq by the United Nations Security Council. Despite all the pressure, the Baathist regime intended to push with its agenda, acquire Kuwait's oil reserves and cancel the national debt to the Kuwaiti government. Provoked by the threat to the

Saudi Arabia oil reserves that could disrupt the international oil market, the US and NATO forces defeated Iraqi forces and demanded full compliance in divesting all weapons of mass destruction and long-range missiles. In the aftermath of the war, Kurds in the north started a rebellion to which Saddam brutally responded. The United States, the United Kingdom and other allies against Iraq continued a no-fly zone programme over Kurd areas with constant air patrols (Britannica, 2021c; CRS, 2017).

In 2003, in a relatively quick attack, lasting about a month, the US and the Great Britain forces attacked Iraq, defeating the Iraqi military and Baathist paramilitary forces, disbanding the Baathist party and occupying Iraq in the second wave (Britannica, 2021b).

In 2014, the Salafi Jihadist group, The Islamic State of Iraq in Syria and Levant (ISIL), gradually invaded Iraq and took 30% of the territories by force. After another international coalition of troops from the region and the west, the ISIL gave up the claimed lands, and the conflict ended in 2017. UN stated that ISIL actions constituted war crimes, crimes against humanity and even genocide in the three and a half years in those lands. The return of the coalition forces and military interventions instituted a dislocation crisis and significant human rights concerns (EASO, 2020).

With the help of international organisations and a stable government, modern Iraq is moving forwards in innovation and technology foundations. Along with the high proportion of youngsters in the country, there is a bright prospect for a more developed and technology-driven industry in Iraq. Businesses in technology such as Sandoog, Miswag, Brsima, Shiffer, Erbil Delivery, BazaryOnline, FastPay and Talabatey prove that the Iraqi economy can have a more prominent technology sector run by younger generations in the private sector. The presence of these companies is creating an environment for innovative tech startups that create opportunities and jobs for youngsters in the near future (IOM, 2019).

Context for Enterprise and Implications for Doing Business

The oil and gas resources are the main drivers of the economy, which create most of the countries national income. Nevertheless, other economic sectors are not well developed despite the income generated from selling oil and gas resources (Khajeheian et al., 2018). This situation has led to high unemployment rates during the past decades, as even the oil and gas sector did not create enough employment opportunities for the people. Most graduates do not have any hope to find appropriate jobs (Al-Rubay, 2021).

Before the US occupation, the country's economy relied mainly on the government's central plans that state-owned companies implemented, and the government did not allow foreigners to own companies in Iraq. Hopefully, after 2003, a new wave of privatisation began, and the government opened the doors to foreign investors (Mustafa, 2021). However, the country faced several problems due to its external debts. Many Iraqis displaced and moved to other countries as refugees due to the socio-political state of the country (Gangamma, 2018).

Hopefully, the government devised various policies to recover the economy. Nevertheless, the situation has become more complex due to the coronavirus pandemic and volatilities of oil and gas prices in the last few years. All these issues made Iraq's economy more fragile and sensitive to global trends. On the one hand, previous plans are restricted due to the new limitations. On the other hand, the government has limited access to funds to provide stimulus packages for economic players. Therefore, Iraq is experiencing a challenging situation similar to what the country experienced in 2003. Iraq's GDP sharply decreased up to 10.4% in 2020. This decrease included both oil and non-oil economy. Other than the oil sector, sectors such as the tourism sector were also challenged dramatically due to the shocks caused by the pandemic and subsequent lockdowns (Kawamorita et al., 2020).

The government devised a national plan to face the crisis that includes a set of medium-term sustainable development goals. In this plan, they also considered the private sector players at the centre of their attention as these players could creatively contribute to improving the economy. The plan aims at (i) improving the business environment and its fiscal stability, (ii) ensuring appropriate economic governance, (iii) helping the financial sector players, (iv) supporting agriculture, gas and electricity sectors and (v) providing social protection and labour (Abdulsattar and Jones, 2021). Table 16.1 provides an overview of the major specifications of Iraq.

According to the Doing Business index (2020), Iraq is among the vulnerable countries as it stands in 172nd place. In terms of dealing with construction permits, the country is ranked 103rd globally, which is its best rank among the others. Protecting minority investors (111th) and registering property (121st) are the following average ranks. Besides, all the other indexes are worse than this (Paying taxes (131st), Getting electricity (131st), Enforcing contacts (147th), Starting a business (154th), Resolving insolvency (168th), Trading across borders (181st), Getting credit (186th). These numbers show that starting and running a business in Iraq is a

Table 16.1. Some Statistics

	1990	2000	2010	2018
Population, total (millions)	17.42	23.50	29.74	38.43
Population growth (annual %)	2.5	3.0	2.6	2.3
Surface area (sq. km) (thousands)	438.3	438.3	435.2	435.1
GNI, Atlas method (current US$) (billions)	123.12	37.50	136.16	186.02
GNI per capita, Atlas method (current US$)	7,070	1,600	4,580	4,840
GNI, PPP (current international $) (billions)	47.18	258.21	382.58	403.82
GNI per capita, PPP (current international $)	2,640	10,990	12,860	10,510
People				
Income share held by lowest 20%			8.8	
Life expectancy at birth, total (years)	66	69	69	70
Primary completion rate, total (% of relevant age group)	59	56	67	
School enrollment, primary (% gross)	108.9	97.0	108.7	
School enrollment, secondary (% gross)	47	38	54	
Economy				
GDP (current US$) (billions)	180.41	48.36	138.52	212.27
GDP growth (annual %)	57.8	16.9	6.4	−1.2
Inflation, GDP deflator (annual %)	73.6	24.6	16.6	12.6
Agriculture, forestry, and fishing, value added (% of GDP)	8	5	5	2

(*continued*)

Table 16.1. Some Statistics (*continued*)

	1990	2000	2010	2018
Industry (including construction), value added (% of GDP)	72	85	56	56
Exports of goods and services (% of GDP)	8	76	39	44
Imports of goods and services (% of GDP)	7	50	34	27
Gross capital formation (% of GDP)	44	29	16	19
Revenue, excluding grants (% of GDP)				41.8
Net lending (+) / net borrowing (−) (% of GDP)				10.1
States and markets				
Time required to start a business (days)			31	27
Domestic credit provided by financial sector (% of GDP)				
Tax revenue (% of GDP)				2.1
Military expenditure (% of GDP)			2.7	2.9
Mobile cellular subscriptions (per 100 people)	0.0	0.0	78.2	95.0
Individuals using the Internet (% of population)	0.0	0.1	2.5	75.0
High-technology exports (% of manufactured exports)				
Statistical capacity score (Overall average)			41	38

Source: The World Bank – World Development Indicators database

challenging task. Lack of enough access to credit, low international trade rate and resolving insolvency are among the most challenging issues for those interested in establishing or who are already running their businesses in Iraq.

Starting a business is a challenge as online businesses are not legally defined and legalised, and entrepreneurs could not register their websites or online businesses. As they are not legally registered, they are marginally protected and supported by the government. Then, they need to follow a traditional brick-and-mortar business model and register a physical office. It makes the process more complex for young entrepreneurs and technology-based startups. Besides, the lack of sufficient access to skilled workers who could act entrepreneurially or become team members of new technology-based startups has made such efforts time-consuming and costly. In addition, launching a business is costly, and as the entrepreneurial ecosystem is not mature, a limited number of entrepreneurs could find financing to start their businesses. Also, most emerging business models are not applicable, as cash on delivery is the primary way of buying products online. Finally, due to the sanctions and the lack of required infrastructure, e-payment options are not available (Salamzadeh, 2018).

Despite the existing challenges and opportunities, Iraq has a long history of bazaars. Persians have had a word for the marketplace since 2500 years ago, and the word "bazaar" has even penetrated other languages as the location to exchange commodities and goods (Rezaei et al., 2019). The traditional physical Persian bazaar has a unique architectural design and mainly involves trading food, worn merchandise and crafts. Bazaar is a model of commercial space that works for economic and social, and cultural exchanges domestically and internationally (Dana and Wright, 2015). As the historic location of these marketplaces and their unique design inspire a tourism attraction and intrinsic value for the community, bazaars are considered national heritage and of significant importance. Bazaars are usually designed in diverse forms of open or closed, indoors and outdoors, with subparts and mostly decorated with arches. The bazaar works as a network of social interactions, gradually crafted through the centuries of contact between people, governments and merchants. Individuals privately own bazaars, but the whole concept responds as a social entity to the political, economic and social environment (Yadollahi, 2017).

The Safavid dynasty in Iran, which consisted of almost the eastern half of Iraq, is known for local marketplaces in that shape and order (Dādfar, 2010). Local bazaars are common in Iraq, and they are called bazaar, despite the Arabic word *souq* for the concept of marketplaces (Mohammadi, 2014). One of the most famous bazaars in Iraq is the Qaysari Bazaar in Centre Erbil, the Kurdistan region (Exhibit 16.4). Erbil is an exceptional city because of its geographic position on a strategic route between Iran, Turkey, Syria and the rest of Iraq. In addition, the Erbil Citadel is an ancient monument and one of the oldest habitable places (UNESCO, 2021). To the south gate of the Erbil Citadel lies the Qaysari Bazaar, one of the most important markets in east Iraq and Erbil, is of paramount significance due to the city's geographic advantages (Mati and de Boer, 2011). Another fascinating bazaar is Nishtiman Bazaar in Erbil (Exhibit 16.5).

Bazaars have been revolutionised in the 21st century and with the expansion of the Internet in Iraq (Zilinskas and Mauger, 2015). Among the very first internet bazaars was the online shopping website of Reem, which dominates the market. Commodities are now more diverse in bazaars in contrast to the previous forms that only included local merchandise. Internet bazaars are now defined by their topics and the type of commodities they supply, not their location on the map (Jameel and Ahmad, 2018).

Exhibit 16.4 Qaysari Bazaar in Erbil, Iraq; photo courtesy of Andre Klimke, Unsplash.com

Exhibit 16.5 Nishtiman Bazaar in Erbil; photo © 2021 by Ali Safar Kamel, used with permission

Towards the Future

The economic situation of Iraq was susceptible during the past decade, as the country experienced many socio-political changes and market volatilities in international oil markets. Therefore, Iraq needs to design a sustainable macroeconomic framework based on which the country could survive. Nevertheless, one should not overlook the existing opportunities in Iraqi markets that made various countries compete to win them. The economic development of Iraq is subject to several issues, including but not limited to rebuilding its fiscal policies, cutting extra spending, diversifying the revenue streams that would be less dependent on oil prices, devising relevant monetary policies and improving the business environment. Besides, the country must take specific actions to manage its deficits, international debts and motivate foreign investors to increase foreign direct investments.

In addition to the priorities mentioned earlier, Iraqi government officials are required to manage the coronavirus pandemic crisis. Otherwise, its huge impacts might worsen the current situation. The oil prices could be critical for facing these challenges, especially in the short term. Nevertheless, by improving the non-oil markets, such as the entrepreneurial ones, they might manage future crises more effectively. It is noteworthy that there is massive pressure on the healthcare system to respond to the pandemic. Another priority is to alleviate poverty through both oil and non-oil markets. By improving the non-oil markets, the government could create more jobs and improve the total entrepreneurial activity rate. People at the bottom of the pyramid have limited access to national resources, but there are several opportunities to improve the creative economy.

References

Abdulsattar, Ban O., and Ian M. Jones (2021), "The Pandemic of COVID-19: Current Scheme of Iraq (24 February–8 August 2020)," *Rafidain Journal of Science* 30 (1), pp. 11–17.

Al-Rubay, Rajaa Khudhair (2021), "The Economic and Social Implications of Unemployment on The Aggregate Demand and The Labor Market In Iraq," *Turkish Journal of Computer and Mathematics Education* 12 (10), pp. 3389–3402.

Al-Shahri, Mohammad Zafir, Stuart Brown, Adrian Ezzat, and Oussama Khatib (2004), "Palliative Care Initiative for the Eastern Mediterranean Region: A Proposal," *Annals of Saudi Medicine* 24 (6), pp. 465–468.

Alkandari, Ali (2019), "The Development of Kuwaiti Islamists' Political Ideology: The Administration of the Kuwaiti Supreme Committee and the Free Kuwait Campaign During the Second Gulf Crisis 1990–91," *Middle Eastern Studies* 55 (5), pp. 786–797.

Amouzegar, Atefeh, Ali K. Abu-Alfa, Mona N. Alrukhaimi, Aminu K. Bello, Mohammad A. Ghnaimat, David W. Johnson, Vivekanand Jha, et al. (2021), "International Society of Nephrology Global Kidney Health Atlas: Structures, Organisation, and Services for the Management of Kidney Failure in the Middle East," *Kidney International Supplements* 11 (2), pp. e47–e56.

Black, Edwin (2010), *The Farhud: Roots of the Arab-Nazi Alliance in the Holocaust,* Washington: Dialog Press.

Britannica (2021a), "Iraq," (Retrieved from https://www.britannica.com/place/Iraq, accessed 30 June 2021)

Britannica (2021b), "Iraq War," (Retrieved from https://www.britannica.com/event/Iraq-War, accessed 30 June 2021)

Britannica (2021c), "Persian Gulf War," (Retrieved from https://www.britannica.com/event/Persian-Gulf-War, accessed 30 June 2021)

Congressional Research Service (2017), "Iraq: Background and US Policy," (Retrieved from https://www.everycrsreport.com/reports/R45025.html, accessed 30 June 2021)

Dādfar, Sajjad (2010), "A Look at the Relationship Between the Bazaar and the Shia Clergy in Iraq," *Historical Sciences Studies* 1 (2), pp. 71–86.

Dana, Léo-Paul, and Richard W. Wright (2015), "Bazaar Economies, Modern Networks and Entrepreneurship," in Sir Cary L Cooper, ed., *Wiley Encyclopedia of Management,* 3rd edition, John Wiley & Sons, Volume 3, Michael Morris and Don Kuratko, volume editors, pp. 13–18.

Doing Business (2020), "Ease of Doing Business in Iraq," (Retrieved from https://www.doingbusiness.org/en/data/exploreeconomies/iraq#, accessed 30 June 2021)

European Asylum Support Office (2020), "EASO Country of Origin Information Report – IRAQ," (Retrieved from https://easo.europa.eu/information-analysis/country-origin-information/country-reports, accessed 30 June 2021)

Fitzgerald, Edward Peter (1991), "The Iraq Petroleum Company, Standard Oil of California, and the Contest for Eastern Arabia, 1930–1933," *The International History Review,* 13 (3), pp. 441–465.

Foster, Benjamin R., and Karen Polinger Foster (2021), *Civilisations of Ancient Iraq,* Princeton, NJ: Princeton University Press.

Gangamma, Rashmi (2018), "A Phenomenological Study of Family Experiences of Resettled Iraqi Refugees," *Journal of Marital and Family Therapy* 44 (2), pp. 323–335.

Hanish, Shak (2010), "The Kirkuk Problem and Article 140 of the Iraqi Constitution," *Digest of Middle East Studies* 19 (1), pp. 15–25.

Hillel, Shlomo (1987), *Operation Babylon,* New York: Doubleday.

International Organization for Migration (2019), "Technology and Innovation in Iraq," (Retrieved from https://www.humanitarianresponse.info/sites/www.humanitarianresponse.info/files/2019/09/Technology-%26-Market-assessment-in-Iraq.pdf, accessed 30 June 2021)

Issawi, Charles (1978), "The 1973 Oil Crisis and After," *Journal of Post Keynesian Economics* 1 (2), pp. 3–26.

Jameel, Alaa S., and Mohammed Abdul-Aziz Ahmad (2018), "Determine Some Factors That Affect to Adoption of e-Commerce Among Small and Medium Enterprises in Erbil," *Polytechnic Journal* 8 (1), pp. 1–12.

Kawamorita, Hiroko, Aidin Salamzadeh, Kursat Demiryurek, and Mahyar Ghajarzadeh (2020), "Entrepreneurial Universities in Times of Crisis: Case of COVID-19 Pandemic," *Journal of Entrepreneurship, Business and Economics* 8 (1), pp. 77–88.

Khajeheian, Datis, Mike Friedrichsen, and Wilfred Mödinger, eds. (2018), *Competitiveness in Emerging Markets,* Berlin, Germany: Springer pp. 3–11.

Mati, Evan, and Hugo de Boer (2011), "Ethnobotany and Trade of Medicinal Plants in the Qaysari Market, Kurdish Autonomous Region, Iraq," *Journal of Ethnopharmacology* 133 (2), pp. 490–510.

Mohammadi, Rojan (2014), *Moving a Market: Impacts of Heritage Nomination on a Local Community. A Case Study of Delal Khaneh in Iraqi Kurdistan.* Master's thesis, University of Waterloo, Waterloo, Ontario, Canada.

Mustafa, Razzaq (2021), "The Obstacles Facing the Privatisation of Manufacturing Industries and Economic Reform in Kurdistan Region/Iraq," *Qalaai Zanist Scientific Journal* 6 (1), pp. 870–901.

Organization of the Petroleum Exporting Countries (2020), "Opec Annual Statistical Bulletin 2020," (Retrieved from https://asb.opec.org/, accessed 30 June 2021)

Rezaei, Shahamak, Birte Hansen, Veland Ramadani, and Léo-Paul Dana (2019), "The Resurgence of Bazaar Entrepreneurship: 'Ravabet-Networking' and the Case of the Persian Carpet Trade," in Veland Ramadani, Léo-Paul Dana, Vanessa Ratten, and Abdylmenaf Bexheti, eds., *Informal Ethnic Entrepreneurship,* Cham: Springer, pp. 63–82.

Salamzadeh, Aidin (2018), "Start-Up Boom in an Emerging Market: A Niche Market Approach," in Datis Khajeheian, Mike Friedrichsen, and Wilfred Mödinger, eds., *Competitiveness in Emerging Markets,* Cham: Springer, pp. 233–243.

Shashoua, Lisette (2020), "Escaping Iraq," *The Scribe,* Autumn, pp. 28–29.

United Nations Educational, Scientific and Cultural Organization (2021), "Erbil Citadel," (Retrieved from https://whc.unesco.org/en/list/1437/, accessed 30 June 2021)

Vogler, Gary (2017), *Iraq and the Politics of Oil: An Insider's Perspective,* University Press of Kansas, Lawrence, Kansas, United States.

Yadollahi, Solmaz (2017), "The Iranian Bazaar as a Public Place: A Reintegrative Approach and a Method Applied Towards the Case Study of the Tabriz Bazaar," (Retrieved from https://opus4.kobv.de/opus4-btu/frontdoor/index/index/docId/4294, accessed 30 June 2021)

Zeder, Melinda A., and Brian Hesse (2000), "The Initial Domestication of Goats (Capra Hircus) in the Zagros Mountains 10,000 Years Ago," *Science* 287 (5461), pp. 2254–2257.

Zilinskas, Raymond A., and Philippe Mauger (2015), "E-commerce and Biological Weapons Nonproliferation: Online Marketplaces Challenge Export Controls to Reduce the Risk That Rogue States or Terrorists Could Acquire the Capacity to Produce Biological Weapons," *EMBO Reports* 16 (11), pp. 1415–1420.

Successors to the French Mandate for Syria and the Lebanon

Chapter 17

The Context for Business in Lebanon

Miriam R. Aziz, Diala Kabbara & Charbel Salloum

Abstract: The Lebanese Republic – Lebanon – is located in the Levant region of Western Asia. Its capital is Beirut, once known as the Paris of the Middle East, and its currency is the Lebanese pound. Lebanon is recognised for its religious sects, rich cultures, cuisine, which is extended around the globe and the hospitality of its people. Lebanon is a multilingual country, where Arabic is the main language spoken. Christian Maronites believe the word Arab is related to Islam and prefer to be known as descendants to the Phoenicians and do not like to be grouped as Arabs. A free trade model characterises the Lebanese economy, where the government has limited to nil intervention in the private sector. Lebanon is also known for its entrepreneurial awareness and involvement, as well as the development of family businesses. Lebanon has a vibrant market economy with expertise in marketing, educated and talented Lebanese individuals, and an advanced consumer base.

Keywords: Lebanon, economy, markets

Introduction

Lebanon, officially known as the Lebanese Republic, is located in the Levant region of Western Asia, nowadays known as the Middle East. Its name is said to be derived from *leben* – Aramaic for whiteness (Dana, 2000). Its capital is Beirut (Exhibit 17.1) and its currency is the Lebanese pound/lira.

Exhibit 17.1 Beirut; photo © 2021 by Christian Atalah used with permission

Lebanon is bounded from the west by the Mediterranean Sea and bordered to the north and east by Syria, and the south by Israel (see Exhibit 17.2). Although Arabic is the main language spoken in Lebanon, many Lebanese – especially Christian Maronites who believe the word "Arab" is related to Islam (Ramadani et al., 2017) – prefer to be known as descendants of the Phoenicians and do not like to be grouped as Arabs.

The country is known for its diverse religious sects, rich culture, cuisine, which is well spread all across the globe, and the hospitality and warmth of its people. Culture differs from one region to another via living, food, Lebanese accents and so forth. Lebanon is popular as a multilingual vacation destination for other Middle Eastern countries (Lebanon, 2020).

After the civil war that ended in 1990, Lebanon went through different stages to re-attain its presence in the Middle East, economically, socially and environmentally. The nation is still trying to build back what

Exhibit 17.2   Guard tower at the southern border and Lebanese flag on water tower; photo © 2021 by Léo-Paul Dana

has been lost during the days of the war. It still suffers from the control of warlords, who came into power after 1990, and put their hands on most governmental bodies; they exercise their dominion by employing people who support them and applaud their corruption – consequently, leading to absolute exhaustion and exploitation of the government resources, and to the current economic deficit, mass poverty, hunger and currency devaluation.

The private sector is the primary driver of growth in a country and is seen as capable of reversing the effects of years of unprofessional institution management, contributing to the flourishing of the private sector and the creation of jobs. There are efforts to "heal" from the war, which the Lebanese government directed by introducing some initiatives as the Beirut Stock Exchange's reactivation in 1996 and the launch of the economic zones. The presence of family businesses is very dominant in the country (Al-Midfa, 2017; Gopak, 2017; Gore, 2017). Yet, Lebanon still has a poor infrastructure (Ministry of Economic, Trade and Industry, 2015); the need for proper roads, highways and bridges is essential, as well as public transportation between the five major coastal cities: Beirut, Byblos, Sidon, Tripoli and Tyre.

Historical Context

Lebanon appeared in recorded history around 3,000 BC as a group of coastal cities. Exhibit 17.3 features Byblos, known in Arabic as *Jubayl*. Approximately 7,000 years ago, it was the great Phoenician port of Gebal. Today it is one of the major five coastal cities (see Exhibit 17.4) in modern Lebanon, and among the oldest cities to exist.

Exhibit 17.3 Along Lebanon's Mediterranean coast; photo © 2021 by Christian Atalah
used with permission

Lebanon was inhabited by the Canaanites, a Semitic people, called Phoenicians by the Greeks; due to the purple dye they sold; these people referred to themselves as "men of Sidon" according to their city of origin. Location allowed the Phoenicians to take advantage of the sea; they engaged in navigation and trade. Tyre and Sidon were significant maritime and trade centres. Gubla (now known as Byblos or *Jubayl*) and Berytus

Exhibit 17.4 Coastal home; photo © 2021 by Christian Atalah used with permission

(Beirut) were trade and religious centres. Byblos was the first city to trade with Egypt in exporting olive oil and wine while importing gold and other products from the Nile Valley; Byblos excelled in the production of textiles, carving ivory and working with metals land making glass.

Having invented the alphabet, the Phoenicians were capable in trade and commerce, they developed excellent communication skills. Masters of the sea, they sailed everywhere around the Mediterranean, from Cyprus to

Rhodes, to Crete and beyond, and they established trade routes to Europe and Western Asia. These trade routes flourished until Assyrians invaded the coastal areas.

Among important traders were the Jews. Meron (2022) examined the Jewish community in Lebanon during the past years of Ottoman rule. As detailed by Dana (2000), after the fall of the Ottoman Empire, Lebanon enjoyed a period of rapid industrialisation. Unlike its neighbours, where the state was the major economic player, it was the private enterprise that developed Lebanon. The nation came to be known as the Switzerland of the Middle East. Its capital, Beirut – with the largest gold market between Tangiers and Bombay – was nicknamed the Paris of the Middle East.

In 1920, France, which governed Lebanon as a League of Nations mandate, developed the State of Greater Lebanon. Lebanon became a republic in 1926 and obtained its independence 17 years later, in 1943. Meron (2019) investigated Jewish entrepreneurs working under colonial rule in Beirut towards the end of the first decade of the French mandate and found that patterns of entrepreneurial activity were influenced by mandatory economic policies that created different opportunities in regional trade and services (Lebanon, 2020).

In 1945, Lebanon's flag carrier was created – Middle East Airlines. It merged with Air Liban in 1963. During Lebanon's civil war (1975–1990), Beirut International Airport was closed, and the airline survived by leasing aircraft to others.

In 2014, the Magen Abraham synagogue built in 1926 – one of over a dozen in this country – re-opened after renovations. During the televised re-opening, Lebanese politicians declared support for a community they said they cherished as much as the other 17 sects that comprise the Lebanese government (https://www.arabnews.com/JewsOfLebanon, accessed 31 January 2021).

Lebanon made world news again in August 2020, when a blast at Beirut Port rocked the city (see Exhibit 17.5). The explosion, caused by ammonium nitrate stored at the port, injured 5,000 people and killed 220. The port was partially destroyed.

Context for Enterprise and Implications for Doing Business

The Lebanese are descendants of Phoenicians, Greeks, Armenians and Arabs; Lebanon is composed of a heterogeneous society with numerous religious, ethnic and kinship groups. The long-term ties and local

Exhibit 17.5 Beirut Port after explosion; photo © 2021 by Christian Atalah used
with permission

communalism cause to occur earlier in the present territorial and political entity and persist with remarkable perseverance. Having Arabic as the official language of the country, French is the second most spoken language, in addition to Armenian and English. Syriac, a rare language that dates back to the time of Jesus, is used in Maronite churches following the Eastern rites. Exhibit 17.6 features Our Lady of Lebanon.

Exhibit 17.6 Our Lady of Lebanon; photo © 2021 by Christian Atalah used with permission

Religion acts as the driving force, the engine, the base, on which any social, economic, political or governmental structure is built. It is the main component of the dynamics of individuals and communities coming together. Although the past decade witnessed the massive change that was brought about by the new generations; distinguished by their openness to others and indifference towards religious affiliation, religion, nevertheless, remains the strong ingredient within the Lebanese society, affecting people's lives and decisions in many ways, and acting as a barrier to transition towards a civil government. The main religious factions are Muslim Shiites, Muslim Sunnis, Christian Maronites, Christian Greek Orthodox and the Druze, a religious minority, who play an influential role in society. In 2020, there were also 29 Jews (https://www.arabnews.com/JewsOfLebanon) in Lebanon, descendants of many generations of Jews who lived here (Schulze, 2001; Zeïdan, 2021) and who will hopefully be recognised by the new wave of friendship between Jews and Muslims.

Jews are the oldest religious community in the country. Zeïdan (2021) noted that in 47 BC, Roman Emperor Julius Caesar ordered Jews of Sidon to pay taxes to Jerusalem, indicating that there were already Jews here at the time. Jews later settled in Tripoli in 1098, in Tyre in 1173, in Baalbek in 1250, in Hasbaiyya in 1310, in Deir Al-Qamar in 1710 and in Beirut in 1800 (Zeïdan, 2021). Christian historian Nagi Zeïdan said about the Jews, "They taught us honesty and trust. You know how valuable that is in a country like ours" (see: https://www.arabnews.com/JewsOfLebanon). Most Lebanese Jews have left Lebanon; Kossaify (2020) noted, "The Lebanese Jewish diaspora's love for Beirut never died; it lives on in their hearts".

The Lebanese economy is characterised by a free trade model, where the government has limited to nil intervention in the private sector. The Lebanese market is a welcoming market for business endeavours, since it encourages investments and free trade with a minimal taxed system. Tourism, banking sector and agriculture are the three main drivers of the economic wheel in Lebanon. Tourism and hospitality are basically imprinted within the Lebanese culture as they are part of the local traditions. Lebanese are very well known for their hospitality, and they have managed to build a big part of their economy upon this strength (Issa and Altinay, 2006). Moreover, the Lebanese economy is built on a big disproportion between exports and imports, as the latter constitutes a big chunk of the dynamics, a simple comparison of the 2018 figures can give us an idea; $3.6B of exports versus $21B of imports.

Exports are generally influenced by the internal stability and security of the country, we can clearly note the difference of when everything is in order how exports rise, as to when chaos strikes and the economy freezes. One note worth mentioning is that whenever the exports of a country are high or exceed well its imports, it means that the country has a solid economic base, relying on the flow of foreign liquidity, which helps maintain the economic cycle and be well preserved against any challenge. However, public debt is the major problem in Lebanon due to clustering the public finances because of the large debt-service charges (Saad, 2012). Additionally, the public debts in Lebanon are to be public debts and are considered as unsustainable. The Lebanese government pinpoints that the increase in wages does not have any influence on the gross domestic product (GDP); in contrast, it will be examined as a failure because of the high level of public indebtedness, which will danger the fixed exchange rate (Badra, 2016).

According to Lebanon's Central Administration Statistics (CAS) and the International Labour Organisation, the unemployment rate during 2019–2020 displayed an increasingly high rate of 11.4%, reaching 23.3% for youth. A weak social security system and poor strategies to deal with youth unemployment magnified the gravity of the situation.

In early October 2019, the economic crash took its toll, which was of course the result of years of bad financial management; the Lebanese Pound had been frozen against the US dollar (USD) for the past 30 years, at a rate of $1 = LBP 1.515 – this strategy caused an inflexible and unhealthy accumulation of monetary reserves, loans were generously offered to the public and money frozen over a long period against high interest rates, which caused a slow economic cycle where people would rather put their money in a bank and get interest rates in return, instead of investing and stimulating the economic wheel (Araji et al., 2019). All of the above, in addition to numerous other erroneous schemes and public corruption involving government officials and the central bank governor, led to the collapse of a fragile structure. Small businesses got affected at first, feeling the weight of the crisis. Salaries were cut down as part of the adaptation plan, as a first reactive move. Then companies started reducing their working force, letting go of up to 90% of their employees, to be able to sustain their businesses and extend their lives as much as possible. Cutting cost was necessary for survival. People were no longer able to transfer money abroad because of the shortage of USD in the market and the currency devaluation.

As the crisis developed within months, many companies' owners and managers reduced salaries and working hours for employees, to address the firing action for staff to cut costs. However, other companies, as the hospitality and tourism sector have "fired" many employees, and the restaurant also cut their costs by being based more on online services (Executive Magazine, 2020). In Lebanon, there is no presence of unemployment benefits and fragile social security profiting as the developed countries. However, an unemployment crisis has serious and crucial implications, which have a continuous impact on the economy and the country's social structure. Furthermore, the conversions of currencies, that is, between the Lebanese lira and the USD have accounted for inflation in the country, leading to an increase in the goods and services, and the salaries did not improve. For that reason, the Ministry of Labour should begin the development and improvements within itself and claim the need for a restart, to have the hope of coming up with solutions and embracing the crisis (Executive Magazine, 2020).

Lebanon's leading industries include the manufacture of food products, cement, bricks and ceramics and textiles. The construction industry has given energy to the economy after the civil war, although it experienced downturns due to recurrent damage to the infrastructure in the early 21st century and the regional instability (Lebanon, 2020). Lebanon's main exporting destinations are the Middle Eastern countries; products such as textiles, non-precious metals and fruits and vegetables are exported. Imports are taking a good part in the economy through importing consumer goods, machinery, transport equipment, petroleum products and food from Europe, China and the United States. Therefore, some items like foreign remittances and government loans have covered somewhat a large trade deficit (Lebanon, 2020).

Many industries lack proper investments and refinement, hence opportunities are there for the grab in almost any industry we can think of: agriculture, metal production, commerce, construction, education, financial services, health services, oil and gas production, telecommunications, technology, public service, textiles, transport (civil aviation, railways, roads, public transportation), equipment manufacturing and utilities (water, gas, electricity). A need to develop and invest in all of the above is strongly present, opportunities are numerous. However, challenges remain many as well; first, governmental bureaucracy and outdated regulations make it slightly hard to launch – laws have not been made to go with the advancement of our current times, some date back a 100 years. In addition, the Ottoman-descendant organisational composition of governmental institutions encourages bribery and corruption. No file can move forward unless extra money is paid or some sort of power is exercised by highly valued/influential individuals (Araji et al., 2019).

To be able to revitalise the economy and counter the government impairment and handicap, microfinance institutions are a must to support micro-entrepreneurs, looking to invest in socially responsible industries, including recycling, up-cycling, community development, hospital and health-care centres, crafts creation and sustainability, art, cultural heritage, eco-friendly tourism and so on. By empowering micro-entrepreneurs, the economic wheel would be able to move again independently from the public sector.

In parallel, extensive judicial reforms and news laws must be enacted to go with the development and technological advancement of our times. This will open the way for foreign investments, which would encourage international businesses to venture into the Lebanese market.

Political violence is described to be associated with poor governance. Therefore, political instability is examined as a factor that handicaps the economy of the country. For example, in Lebanon, political instability influences economic developments, leading to fear, unemployment, disturbances and disabilities. The sectarian violence display in Lebanon in terms of political and religious divisions is to be the factor of disruption of trade, tourism and investment that will be affecting the social and economic costs, with a significant overflow outside the conflict regions (Herrala and Turk-Ariss, 2016; as cited in Herrala and Turk-Ariss, 2016). A country like Lebanon facing political unstable situation challenges diverse problems, as cash flow, funding, supply, foreign investors, hostility views, unstable demand, public image, infrastructure quality, safety and security issues, which lead to a negative impact on the society due to the connection of the plurality of factors. High-political uncertainty plays a major role in negatively influencing the economy. Investors and entrepreneurs display a risk-averse behaviour when it comes to operating in Lebanon (Clements and Georgiou, 1998). Lebanese citizens protested several times to separate politics from religion, and still, there is no point to be achieved. Too, Lebanese citizens are defined to survive against the odds, but Lebanon remains a deeply troubled country. Also, Lebanon's political system has proven with time its instability through providing the basic services for citizens and topped with corruption through corrupted performance by the elites (politicians). Further, Lebanon's religious elites have a great impact on individual's decision-making about political views. Likewise, they can shape communities' goals and interests by controlling and redefining the relationship between religion and the state (Danzell, 2011; Hoffman and Nugent, 2017).

Lebanon is known for its entrepreneurial awareness and involvement, as well as the development of family businesses. The entrepreneurship concept started in two ways: on the one hand, by the Lebanese individuals living in the country, and on the other hand, through Lebanese entrepreneurs abroad, whom they were part in the contribution of the economy and growth, reconstruction, innovation and utilisation of opportunities after the civil war (Stel, 2013). Moreover, Lebanese entrepreneurs are generally based on family business perceptions, excelled in opening, managing and organising new ventures abroad and in Lebanon. For example, Fattal Group is an organisation that started as entrepreneurship through family members and became a big company in the country and export some of its brand abroad. Additionally, in a free market economy, as in Lebanon, the profits and losses are explored as a "judge" for the business to claim the ventures' survival or failure. Some factors also played an influential role in creating a business or idea and entrepreneurial framework and its sustainability in the market, such as social, cultural, political and economic factors. Besides, informed policy decisions help develop the best environment for an entrepreneur to establish, grow and succeed with its venture (Ismail et al., 2018). The point of being a self-employed entrepreneur is not quite easy; therefore, to be a successful entrepreneur, the immigrant involved in it should be patient, strong during uncertain situations and have the will of achievements through setting goals, making profits and enthusiasm of accepting risks. Moreover, the immigrant should overcome the challenges coming from the foreign country's culture, as the art of communicating proficiently, knowing the mother tongue, the slang and body language, because they are essential factors to move forward and get partially or totally socialised with natives. Along, becoming an entrepreneur in a foreign country should also be through knowing the cultural unfamiliarity, learning the practices of the country and exploiting, planning and operating the unfamiliar tax codes, labour and business laws (Omar, 2011).

Lebanese entrepreneurs are mainly known for being die-hard individualists. This individualism drives them to the trade and services sectors, where the operation is by individuals in general or small partnerships are accepted and widespread (Ahmed and Julian, 2012; Sayigh, 1962). Moreover, in Lebanon, family and small businesses dominate the country's economy; for instance, family loyalty in this country is very important in any form of business and goes beyond everything. Furthermore, Lebanon is determined by social and financial support for entrepreneurial individuals that include a central bank providing funds for the early-stage entrepreneurs and a developing ecosystem of incubators and accelerators (Ismail et al., 2018). However, Lebanese adults prefer to own a business for innovation, self-employment, creativity, independence, earning money and lack of job opportunities present in the country. The facilitation to get involved in entrepreneurship was through the central bank through circular 331, which is a form of equity investment giving the authorisation to the commercial banks to invest in a direct (venture capital funds, accelerators and incubators) or indirect way in startups or via the government that has come up with funding facility by giving loans through the World Bank but managed by Kafalat SAL under the name Innovation in small- and medium-sized enterprises (SMEs) (Ismail et al., 2018; Kawamorita et al., 2020; Salamzadeh, 2018; Salamzadeh and Kawamorita, 2017). Lebanese entrepreneurs are characterised as individuals who quickly spot profitable business opportunities while maintaining successful businesses. Besides, Lebanese entrepreneurs are seen as intelligent, clever and organised individuals applying management skills (Mambula, 2010). Some businesses grew and became large enterprises in the Lebanese territory with importing abroad, whereas others remained SMEs with being locally successful. Hence, entrepreneurship in Lebanon is acknowledged as a premium driver of the family business; along, the latter are forming 85% of the private sector, in the means of accounting for the majority of jobs (Ahmed and Julian, 2012). For instance, the majority of businesses' structure is acknowledged as small and family-owned enterprises, in which they will be facing the challenges of updating and improving their management, human resources and the equality of the services offered to customers. Entrepreneurs play a major role in Lebanon's economic and social systems; as a matter of fact, the majority of production is in control by the private sector, which is the critical point and energy of Lebanese development (Ahmed and Julian, 2012; UNDP 2002). Entrepreneurs should be more flexible in Lebanon to quickly adapt to the unstable market due to the disturbances happening in the economic and political sectors and the unclear future. Therefore, their involvement in digital platforms as the World Wide Web will help them have access to more up-to-date technologies and innovative products and services, as well as helping in the development and improvement of the corporate image, attracting new customers and integrating other advertising tools (Ahmed and Julian, 2012). SMEs' presence and development are significant in the country, certainly for economic recovery and sustainable growth. Moreover, competitiveness is playing a major role nowadays, although it is not just related to price, quality is taking a significant influence on demand because customers prefer good quality and a better price. The idea falls into Lebanese entrepreneurs having the capability to develop added-value products and services that will respond to the market signals and grabbing opportunities present in the market, and taking advantage of quality (UNDP, 2002; Ahmed and Julian, 2012).

City markets turn to be good places for the aim of having some insights within a particular community. To try some local street foods, look for a random bargain, or just to take in the atmosphere; therefore, markets offer unique opportunities to experience a new culture. It is too present in Lebanon's vibrant capital, Beirut lacks a vast regional bazaar and introduces good lively outdoor markets. Remarkably, the most popular markets are Souk El Tayeb, Souk El Ahad, Bourj Hammoud, Beirut Souks and Souk El Ard. First, Souk El Tayeb is directly translated to the "good market", an open-air market for farmers in downtown Beirut, specialising in Lebanon's organic produce. This market was created in 2004, to bring communities together to share food and local traditions, and promote the culture of small-scale agricultural production in Lebanon. Every Saturday on "Trablos" street, farmers from all over the country bring their fresh produce, juices, jams and labneh yogurt to the market to sell. Further, the same organisation of Souk El Tayeb runs a restaurant and a social business called *Tawlet* (table) on Rue Naher, where profit is generated to support the farmers, cooks, producers and different chefs presenting different cultural viewpoints each week. Second, Souk El Ahad (Sunday Market), a busily market with shouting vendors situated under a highway bridge close to Corniche al-Nahr in the east of Beirut. It opens on Saturdays and Sundays, attracting crowds of locals, searching for second-hand things, performing for up to 20 years. Individuals can find and buy an electric mix of trinkets, jewellery, antiques, clothes and electronics through indoor and outdoor sections. Therefore, to get a good search, getting up early is better, because the stalls are set at 7 am and packed at 1 pm. Third, the Bourj Hammoud Marash Market to experience the ethnic diversity that crowds Beirut. It is situated in the east of Achrafieh, a populated and industrious neighbourhood, and home to a large Armenian population. The fundamental things found are related to food, where there are lines of stalls full of herbs and spices, street food and the city's changing demographic signs. Moreover, Syrian vendors selling anything from bric-a-brac to artisan crafts, alimentary products and brassware run many stalls. Fourth, Beirut Souks is situated in the city's cosmopolitan centre, a combination of Souk al Tawileh (bustling with tailors) and Souk al Franj (popular fruit, flowers and vegetable market) through being restructured to reopen in 2009. It displays new-found modern appeal and numerous luxury brand stores.

Finally, Souk El Ard (literally the earth market) opens every Tuesday morning to early afternoon in Hamra district, providing a significant outlet for small-scale farmers and producers to maintain traditional agricultural methods and offers the locals of the city access to healthy and quality foods (Ricca, 2017).

Towards the Future

The Lebanese are descendants of the Phoenicians, who were great seafarers. Then came the Greek influence, after it the crusaders and then Ottoman Empire followed who was heavily present for 400 years – resulting in an exquisite mix clearly present everywhere around the country; ancient Phoenician cities include Anjar, Baalbeck, Byblos, Sidon and Tyre. Christina monasteries, dating back 1,000 years, are found in Wadi Qadisha in the north, a 30-minute drive from the Sacred "Cedars of God" forest. Villages have a unique touch to them, with a unique architecture distinguished by stone-built arches and a pyramid-shaped brick housetops. In almost every village as well as city, there is a church and a mosque; people with different religious affiliations live harmoniously together (outside the political influence of course). The Lebanese are known for their cuisine and high sense of hospitality, the Lebanese cuisine is rich and diverse, herbs, olive oil, fresh yogurt, flat local bread called "khubz" dominate the taste buds. Lebanese are warm and welcoming, and this is part of their cultural heritage. Family is essential and is a major pillar of the societal structure, families remain together and children usually leave their parental house only to start their own families themselves.

Lebanon is a vibrant market economy with expertise in marketing, educated and talented Lebanese individuals and an advanced consumer base (Sarkis et al., 2009). However, a full reformation is needed: a cleansing of the old, rusted, outdated, obsolete, dirty system, and the introduction of a new, energetic, visionary, young, practical, open-minded, upgraded administration. One that will ensure the creation of new institutions, policies, laws – it will invest in infrastructure and public transportation, it will stimulate the economic wheel and be open towards neighbouring countries, which will in turn invigorate trade and eliminate economic and political instability. An administration that will seek first to respect its citizens, and build its values on acceptance, openness, brotherhood, solid societal bonds, collective good, social benevolence and goodwill (Schellen, 2020).

Unless such an administration comes with an agenda in hand to genuinely work for the betterment of humans living in that part of the world and apply these reforms, nothing will change, neither in the future nor in the farther future. That tiny piece of land in the Western Asia will remain a battle ground where foreign states like Iran, Qatar, Saudi Arabia, the United Arab Emirates (UAE) and the United Kingdom try to impose their dominion for their own motives.

References

Ahmed, Zafar U., and Craig C. Julian (2012), "International Entrepreneurship in Lebanon," *Global Business Review* 13 (1), pp. 25–38.

Al-Midfa, Najla (2017), "The (Right) Formula To Cultivate Entrepreneurial Talent. Entrepreneur Middle East," Starting a Business, (Retrieved from https://www.entrepreneur.com/article/304821, accessed 2 February 2021)

Araji, Salim, Vladimir Hlasny, Layal Mansour Ichrakieh, and Vito Intini (2019), "Targeting Debt in Lebanon: A Structural Macro-Econometric Model," *Middle East Development Journal* 11 (1), pp. 75–104.

Badra, Nasser (2016), "Myopic Consumption and Wage Increase: The Case of Lebanon," *Arab Economic and Business Journal* 11 (2), pp. 146–152.

Clements, Mike A., and Andrew Georgiou (1998), "The Impact of Political Instability on a Fragile Tourism Product," *Tourism Management* 19 (3), pp. 283–288.

Dana, Léo-Paul (2000), *Economies of the Eastern Mediterranean Region: Economic Miracles in the Making,* Singapore, London, Singapore & Hong Kong: World Scientific.

Danzell, Orlandrew E. (2011), "Political Parties: When Do They Turn to Terror?" *Journal of Conflict Resolution* 55 (1), pp. 85–105.

Executive Magazine. (2020), Lebanon Faces Growing Unemployment. (Retrieved from https://www.executive-magazine.com/opinion/leaders/lebanon-faces-growing-unemployment)

Gopak, Arthur (2017), "Entrepreneruship Trends in 2017: Overview of the Top 3 Largest Startup Ecosystems. What is Happening Inside the Startup Ecosystems of Europe, the US and China?" (Retrieved from https://www.alphagamma.eu/entrepreneurship/entrepreneurship-trends-2017/)

Gore, Elizabeth (2017), "Here are the Top Entrepreneurship Trends for 2017," (Retrieved from https://www.inc.com/elizabeth-gore/top-entrepreneurship-trends-for-2017.html)

Herrala, R., and Rima Turk-Ariss. (2016), "Capital accumulation in a politically unstable region," *Journal of International Money and Finance* 64 (1), pp. 1–15.

Hoffman, Michael T., and Elizabeth R. Nugent (2017), "Communal Religious Practice and Support for Armed Parties: Evidence from Lebanon," *Journal of Conflict Resolution,* 61 (4), pp. 869–902.

Ismail, Ayman, Thomas Schøtt, Abbass Bazargan, Basheer Salaytah, Hamed Al Kubaisi, Majdi Hassen, Penny Kew et al. (2018), "The MENA Region National Entrepreneurial Framework Conditions," in Nezameddin Faghih and Mohammed Reza Zali, eds., *Entrepreneurship Education and Research in the Middle East and North Africa (MENA),* Cham: Springer, pp. 73–102.

Issa, Ina Aurelia, and Levent Altinay (2006), "Impacts of Political Instability on Tourism Planning and Development: The Case of Lebanon," *Tourism Economics* 12 (3), pp. 361–381.

Kossaify, Ephrem (2020), "An Age-Old Connection," (Retrieved from https://www.arabnews.com/JewsOfLebanon)

Lebanon (2020), in *Encyclopædia Britannica,* (Retrieved from https://academic-eb-com.ezproxy.usek.edu.lb/levels/collegiate/article/Lebanon/108463)

Mambula, Charles I. (2010), "Characteristics of Migrant Entrepreneurs as Agents of Direct Investment in Sub-Saharan Africa: An Observation of the Lebanese in Nigeria," *World Journal of Entrepreneurship Management and Sustainability Development* 6 (3), pp. 193–212.

Meron, Orly C. (2019), "Haifa and Beirut in a Comparative Perspective: Jewish Entrepreneurship between the British and the French Mandates," *Iyunim Bitkumat Israel* 32, pp. 245–295.

Meron, Orly C. (2022), "The Economy," in Yaron Harel, ed., *Lebanon: Jewish Communities in the East in the Nineteenth and Twentieth Centuries,* Jerusalem: Ben Zvi Institute & Ministry of Education.

Ministry of Economy (2015), "Trade and Industry," *Nuclear Engineering International* 60 (731), p. 6.

Omar, Husam (2011), "Arab American Entrepreneurs in San Antonio, Texas: Motivation for Entry Into Self-Employment," *Education, Business and Society* 4 (1), pp. 33–42.

Ramadani, Veland, Léo-Paul Dana, Shqipe Gërguri-Rashiti, and Vanessa Ratten, eds. (2017), "An Introduction to Entrepreneurship and

Management in an Islamic Context," in *Entrepreneurship and Management in an Islamic Context,* Cham: Springer, pp. 1–5.

Ricca, Andrew (2017), "The Best Markets in Beirut," Lebanon, (Retrieved from https://theculturetrip.com/middle-east/lebanon/articles/the-5-best-markets-in-beirut/)

Saad, Wadad (2012), "Causality Between Economic Growth, Export, and External Debt Servicing: The Case of Lebanon," *International Journal of Economics and Finance* 4 (11), pp. 134–143.

Salamzadeh, Aidin (2018), "Start-Up Boom in an Emerging Market: A Niche Market Approach," in Datis Khajeheian, Mike Friedrichsen, and Wilfried Mödinger, eds., *Competitiveness in Emerging Markets,* Cham: Springer, pp. 233–243.

Salamzadeh, Aidin, and Hiroko Kawamorita (2017), "The Enterprising Communities and Startup Ecosystem in Iran," *Journal of Enterprising Communities: People and Places in the Global Economy* 11 (4), pp. 456–479.

Sarkis, Joseph, Josiane Fahed-Sreih, David Pistrui, Wilfred Huang, and Harold Welsch (2009), "Family Contributions to Entrepreneurial Development in Lebanon," *International Journal of Organizational Analysis* 17 (3), pp. 248–261.

Sayigh, Yusif A. (1962), *Entrepreneurs of Lebanon: The Role of the Business Leader in a Developing Economy,* Cambridge, MA: Harvard Business Press.

Schellen, Thomas (2020), "Full Interview with Investment Expert Romen Mathieu," (Retrieved from https://www.executive-magazine.com/special-report/full-interview-with-investment-expert-romen-mathieu, accessed 3 November 2020)

Schulze, Kirsten (2001), *The Jews of Lebanon: Between Coexistence and Conflict,* Brighton, UK: Sussex Academic Press.

United Nations Development Programme (UNDP) (2002), *Globalisation — Towards a Lebanese Agenda: Lebanon 2001–2002,* New York: UNDP: National Human Development Report.

US Library of Congress (n.d.), "Ancient Times, The Phoenicians," (Retrieved from http://countrystudies.us/lebanon/4.htm, accessed 15 March 2022)

Zeïdan, Nagi Gergi (2021), *Juifs du Liban: D'Abraham à nos jours, histoire d'une communauté disparu,* Versailles France: VA Editions.

Chapter 18

The Context for Business in Syria

Ekaterina Vorobeva

Abstract: Since its start in 2011, civil war in Syria dramatically affected the economic life of the country and the entire region. Due to the ongoing conflict, the environment for business conduct has worsened in Syria, and business activities have considerably shrunk. Nevertheless, with its diverse self-sufficient economy, numerous natural resources and abundant human capital, Syria appears to be prepared for economic shocks better than any other Middle Eastern states (Lyme, 2012). Although prospects for democratisation in post-war Syria remain dim, the country would face the urgent need to reinvent itself both economically and politically.

Keywords: Aleppo, bazaar, civil war, French mandate

Introduction

The Syrian Arab Republic is a low-income country located in Western Asia and sharing borders with Turkey, Jordan, Iraq, Israel and Lebanon (see Exhibit 18.1). The state's capital, Damascus, is a political centre and a business hub with a population of around 1.6 million residents. Similar in size, Aleppo is another big city, old trading and industrial centre making up 75% of industrial output of the state (Lyme, 2012; World Population Review, 2021). To the west, the country has access to the Mediterranean Sea with its main ports of Latakia and Tartus. Airports have been constructed in Damascus, Aleppo, Latakia, Palmyra and other cities but due to the ongoing military conflict most flights are suspended. Regarding the population, Haddad (2012) mentions that Syrian society consists of multiple minorities. Indeed, while Arabs constitute the largest ethnic group and Sunnis the biggest religious one, 17-million Syrian population is extremely diverse (World Population Review, 2021). Although there are fewer than five Jews in Syria today, there were 15,000 Jews in 1947. Jews were employed primarily as merchants and businessmen. However, following discrimination and violence against the Jews, starting in the 19th century and culminating in 1948, Jews emigrated from Syria, mainly to Israel (Doueck, 2017). Religious groups are represented by Alawites, Christians, Druze, Mandeans, Shiites and Yazidis, while Kurds, Turkmens, Assyrians and Armenians make Syrian society multicultural (Izady, n.d.). Although having grown in the past years, the poverty rate was relatively low; around 10% of the population spent less than $2 a day to cover living

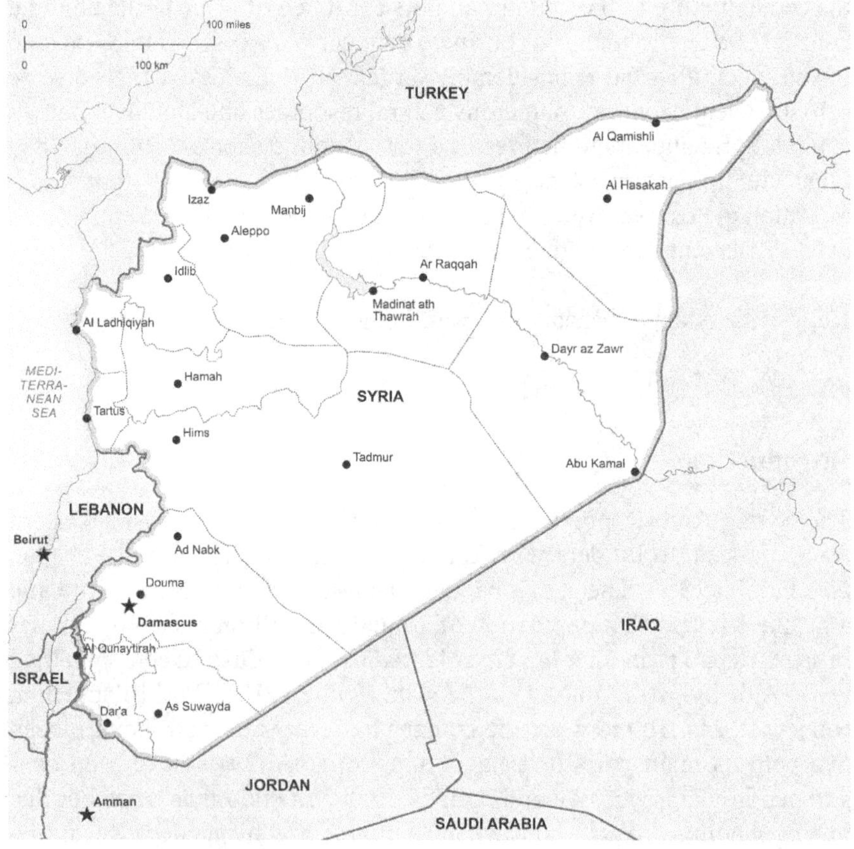

Exhibit 18.1 Map of Syria; courtesy of Pixabay

expenses while the average number for the region accounts for 20% (Goulden, 2011).

Historical Context

Throughout time, various civilisations inhabited the territory of Syria, among whom were the Assyrians, the Babylonians, the Phoenicians and the Persians. The earliest civilisation in Syria is believed to be the Kingdom of Ebla, which was actively involved in trading with Sumer, Akkad and Egypt around 3000–2300 BC. A thriving Jewish presence in Syria, mainly in Aleppo and Damascus, was traced to the time of King David, about 1000 BC. There was also a large immigration of Sephardi Jews from Spain, after their expulsion in 1492 (Doueck, 2017).

In 330 BC, Alexander the Great conquered Syria and made it the Coele-Syria province of his empire. The Roman Empire reached the territory in 64 BC, and later on Syria became a part of the Byzantine Empire. By 640 AD, Arab Muslims had conquered Syria, and rulers of Umayyad dynasty pronounced Damascus a capital of the state. In fact, Damascus is believed to be one of the oldest cities continuously inhabited over the course of history (Dana, 2000). During this time, Arabic became the dominant language. In 1096, Crusaders reached the region and established the Principality of Antioch, which was later conquered by the Mameluke Sultanate in 1268.

After the long Mameluke rule, in 1516, Syria was conquered by the Ottoman Empire. That was the beginning of prosperous times and the establishment of new trading ties with other parts of the world. As explained by Dana (2000), Syria thrived under Ottoman rule. Venetian entrepreneurs, and other Europeans, established offices in Aleppo, an important market town and node along the desert trade routes between Persia and the West. However, the opening of the Suez Canal caused a decline in caravan trade, and Aleppo subsequently declined in economic importance. By the early 20th century, Damascus was linked to Beirut and to Medina by rail. Nevertheless, local entrepreneurs, including Jacob Safra, continued to prosper, by financing camel caravans. Jacob's son Edmond later established the Republic National Bank of New York.

During World War I, the British promised the Syrians their independence, under the rule of Sherif Hussein Mecca of Saudi Arabia; Britain also pledged Syria as a French sphere of influence, as per the secret Sykes-Picot agreement between France and the United Kingdom. In 1919, the

Banque de Syrie was established as a French company affiliate of the Ottoman Bank. Most of its shares were owned by French shareholders, and the balance by the Ottoman Bank. The *Banque de Syrie* issued the new Syrian currency, which was covered by French government bonds and by a French credit account, opened for the Levant, at the French treasury. The Syrian pound could only be redeemed in Paris.

Victorious in the war, Emir Faisal was proclaimed king in 1920. He was the son of Hussein, Sherif of Mecca, and brother of King Abdullah of Iraq. However, no monarchy was established. Instead, the French exiled him. The League of Nations gave France a mandate over the Levant, and by decree from Paris, in 1920, the *Banque de Syrie* notes became the compulsory unit of contract in Syria. A series of treaties between 1920 and 1923 subdivided the territories taken from the Ottomans, formally creating and defining the Levant states, Lebanon and Syria (Dana, 2000).

Syria remained under a French mandate until 1946 when the country finally gained independence. The *Banque de Syrie et du Liban* became the official bank of the Levant states under French mandate; according to the convention, the *Banque de Syrie et du Liban* was granted the exclusive right to issue currency – redeemable in Paris or Marseilles – until 1939 (Dana, 2000).

With independence the state lived through political instability, until 1963, when the Arab Socialist Ba'ath Party gained the power. Later on, Hafez al-Assad was elected as the President of Syria and stayed in power until his death in 2000 when his son, Bashar al-Assad, came to power.

The recent dramatic events in Syria, the Arab Spring, and the beginning of the civil war, could partly be seen as a result of political economy of the last decades. During the 1960s, the state became the major economic actor; all big enterprises in Syria passed nationalisation including the financial sector (Dana, 2000). Under the so-called "Arab socialism" established by Hafez al-Assad in Syria, state-building got prioritised over economic development (Abboud, 2008; Goulden, 2011).

In June 1967, Israeli Prime Minister Eshkol publicly declared to Damascus that Israel had no desire to wage war against Syria; nevertheless, in June 1967, Syria attacked civilian targets in Israel, thus entering the 6-Day War.

Despite crucial improvements in the standards of living, infrastructure and services for regular citizens, the Ba'athist statist model could not last long, and throughout the 1980s and 1990s the government had to introduce market mechanisms into the existing system.

In July 1991, Syrian forces backed Lebanon, forcing the Palestinian Liberation organisation to retreat from its positions in southern Lebanon. The *Jordan Times* cover story on 7 December, 1999 reported a demand, in Syria, for Israeli technology. In 2000, Bashar al-Assad came to power as president of Syria.

The year 2005 became an important turning point when liberalisation of the market was announced in the Social Market Economy policy (Haddad, 2011a). New laws, privatisation of enterprises, creation of VAT and elimination of price subsidies were introduced (Lyme, 2012). A few private banks have been opened since 2004. In 2005, many bilateral trading agreements were signed, and the country joined the Greater Arab Free Trade Area, which gave Syrian products easier access to the immense 280 million markets (Anderson, 2018). Moreover, the membership in the Trade Area attracted foreign investments from China, Russia and Iran that considered Syria's location beneficial for conducting trade in the region (Anderson, 2018). Development of international business connections revitalised economic life of the state; for example, Aleppo became a resale place for commodities from China and earned the name "little China" (Anderson, 2018). In 2007, the Syrian Investment Agency was established. Investors were given an opportunity to obtain loans from foreign banks (Lyme, 2012). The Damascus Stock Exchange was founded in 2009.

Despite all these positive changes, private sector stayed underdeveloped with the public sector remaining the largest employer (Lyme, 2012; Haddad, 2011a). Public enterprises were extremely unprofitable, with less than 10% of them making profits in 2010 (Haddad, 2011a). Ineffective public administration and corruption impeded the further development of entrepreneurship (Lyme, 2012). Caught between two fires, trying to secure the power as well as to revitalise the stagnant economy with the help of the private sector, the government has decided to distribute economic opportunities arising from market liberalisation predominantly among trusted actors who would not threaten the regime through newly acquired influence (Abboud, 2008). Thus, mutual dependency between the state and the big business has been formed: businesspersons had no interest in overthrowing the regime that provided them with exclusive benefits. Abboud (2008, p. 160) called this change "a shift from authoritarian populism to neoliberal authoritarianism". Thus, privatisation became beneficial to so-called "new rentier bourgeoisie" who had access to exclusionary networks uniting state officials and selected entrepreneurs (Haddad, 2011a, 2011b). Using their connections, some actors managed to take advantage of market opening-up, accumulate significant wealth, and become oligarchs (Lyme, 2012). Indeed, significant economic growth was detected only in the sectors of banking and tourism, captured by economic elite (Abboud, 2008). Just before the Arab Spring and the start of the civil war, the Five-Year Plan for 2011–2015 confirmed the state's ambition to continue the process of integration into the global economy; since the civil war broke out, the Syrian economy has been continuously deteriorating due to destruction, armed conflicts, flight of capital and people, and international sanctions.

Context for Enterprise and Implications for Doing Business

The economy of Syria could be called relatively well diversified with developed sectors of manufacturing, agriculture, mining, tourism and energy (Lyme, 2012). The Syrian Arab Republic is a resource-rich state; oil, gas, phosphates and other natural resources are considered as key assets (Lyme, 2012). Oil production has been the centre of Syrian economy constituting around 10% of the Syrian GDP in 2010 (Lyme, 2012; Haddad, 2011a). The country becomes an important transit centre for energy products in the region (Haddad, 2011a). Moreover, human capital represents another national asset; educated manpower is available and relatively cheap (Haddad, 2011b). More up-to-date statistics are missing, but in 2004, literacy rate accounted for 81% (The World Bank, 2020b). Agriculture is another crucial sector, employing around 30% of the local labour force (Lyme, 2012). Among the crops there are wheat, cotton and sugar beet (Lyme, 2012). Nevertheless, both poor water resources and frequent droughts dramatically impact agriculture especially in the north eastern part of the republic (Lyme, 2012). To outline the scale of the problem, in the area of Salamiyyeh, around 60% of all wells dried up (Haddad, 2011a). Manufacturing is diversified and encompasses food products, textiles, leather and chemicals. A particular success was achieved in pharmaceuticals where local enterprises covered 95% of the local demand and exported their products to 55 countries around the globe (Haddad, 2011a). Finally, one of the recently developed sectors, tourism, became crucially important in the years prior to the civil war, and in 2010 made a significant contribution to the Syrian GDP, around 11%–12% (Lyme, 2012). In 2009 year alone, Syria was visited by 6.1 million tourists (Haddad, 2011a); a popular site is the Roman theatre in Bosra (Exhibit 18.2). In the prewar period, main trading partners of Syria were the European Union, Iran,

Exhibit 18.2   Roman theatre in Bosra, on UNESCO list of world heritage in danger;
photo courtesy of Pixabay

Iraq, Lebanon, Turkey and China (Azizi and Issaev, 2019; Lyme, 2012). Important exports have included petroleum products, minerals, cotton fibre/clothing and foodstuffs (see Exhibit 18.3).

Small- and medium-sized enterprises (SMEs) in Syria in particular are not extensively studied (Ibeh and Kasem, 2011). The same is true of one-man micro-enterprises (see Exhibit 18.4). Moreover, the armed conflict posed many obstacles to conduct research, thus, most available findings are dated back to the pre-war period. Nevertheless, some up-to-date information about doing business in Syria is still available. For instance, the report of the World Bank *Doing Business 2020* ranked Syria 176 out of 190 global economies, which constitutes a significant decrease in business attractiveness of the state compared to 2010 when it was ranked 143 (The World Bank, 2010; The World Bank, 2020a). At the moment, main obstacles to business conduct proved to be access to construction permits, to credit and to transnational trade (The World Bank, 2020a).

Prior to the conflict, most enterprises in Syria were small and medium size, overwhelming majority of which were family-run (Abboud, 2008). The research suggests that religious and regional differences in the way of business conduct can be observed in Syria (Anderson, 2018; Hejase

Exhibit 18.3   Apricot paste exported to Canada; photo © 2021 by Léo-Paul Dana

Exhibit 18.4   Ambulant trader; photo © 2021 by Emilian Robert Vicol used
with permission

et al., 2013). For example, Hejase et al. (2013) claim that Muslim workers of banking sector proved to be more committed to ethical conduct of business in the sector with high level of unethical practices. Introducing regional divide, Anderson (2018) maintains that Aleppo traders distinguish themselves from Damascene colleagues; originating from a wholesale centre of Syria, Aleppo traders measure success by the volume of their sales while traders of Damascus do that by the size of their profit margins. At the Aleppo bazaar, traders sell manufactured goods (Exhibit 18.5) as well as foodstuffs (Exhibit 18.6).

In the context of the ongoing conflict, some regions can be easier to do business than others; Anderson (2018) mentions that entrepreneurs operating on the territory controlled by the regime seem to be more often exposed to bribes and higher tariffs. Finally, even the war can present new economic opportunities; it rose demand for certain products such as engines, spare parts and food for soldiers (Anderson, 2018).

With the beginning of the Syrian civil war, the economy has experienced a rapid downturn; increasing inflation, relocation of capital, declining production, destruction, inflation, devaluation of the Syrian pound and loss in population are just a few economic outcomes of the

Exhibit 18.5 Selling manufactured goods at Aleppo bazaar; photo © 2021 by Iyad Al Ghafari used with permission

Exhibit 18.6 Trader of dry goods; photo © 2021 by Iyad Al Ghafari used with permission

military conflict (Lyme, 2012). The country lost its status as lower-middle-income country and moved to a low-income group. The civil war affected all sectors but especially tourism and transport (Lyme, 2012). Lyme (2012) states that only from tourism alone the state lost around 1 billion dollars. In 2012, the Syrian GDP reached its record low of –26% (CEIC, n.d.). Syrian debts to other countries grew; at the moment, Syria owes around 6 billion dollars to Iran (Azizi and Issaev, 2019). By 2017, economic activity in Syria has shrunk by 60% in comparison with 2010 (The World Bank, 2021). While the number of Syrian refugees is estimated at 6.6 million worldwide, 13.4 million Syrian residents found themselves in need for humanitarian aid due to destructions and growing poverty (UNHCR, 2021). For example, in May 2012, prices for most items rose by 50% (Lyme, 2012). With growing unemployment which reached 25% in 2012, domestic consumption dropped, so do imports to Syria (Lyme, 2012). Banks stopped granting any loans, thus, preventing business activities (Lyme, 2012). Many enterprises had to shut down; only during the first year of political instability 30% of SMEs got closed (Lyme, 2012). Due to the growing insecurity, by 2012, several hundred plants in industrial centre Aleppo had suspended their activities leaving thousands of people without jobs (Lyme, 2012).

Economic sanctions imposed on Syria by the United States, the European Union and others cost Syria $4 billion during the first year alone (Lyme, 2012). Under the pressure of the sanctions, main international oil companies left the country or stopped operations (Lyme, 2012). Shipping companies refused to transfer Syrian oil abroad which resulted in significant financial losses for the state without its own tankers (Lyme, 2012). The sanctions put on main banks, such as the Central Bank of Syria and Real Estate Bank, prevented international transactions and hampered income from export (Lyme, 2012). Thus, many enterprises, even those not affiliated with the regime, faced significant obstacles to international trade.

Despite the overall dramatic effects that the sanctions had on the Syrian economy, the local elite had found a way to adapt to the situation by, for example, opening accounts in Russian banks (Lyme, 2012). Moreover, those who managed to accumulate wealth before the crisis gained new opportunities during the upheaval by involving in increasingly growing informal economy. In fact, Lyme (2012) argues that particularly informal economy kept afloat some of the Syrian enterprises. Exploiting the black market opportunities by selling shortage products varying from diesel to weapons, entrepreneurs earned the name *tijar al-azma*, "traders of the crisis" (Lyme, 2012). After the doors to the Western market had closed, the government tried to redirect its exports towards Iraq and Iran whose importance as trading partners substantially grew during the past years.

Towards the Future

The Syrian civil war may be described as one of the worst humanitarian disasters of the last decades – comparable to Rwanda genocide of 1994 (Heydemann, 2013). Nevertheless, although making any predictions about the future of Syria is difficult nowadays, Heydemann (2013) is sceptic about democratisation after the civil war ends; he states (2013, p. 59) that "countries emerging from ethno-sectarian civil wars are widely understood to be among the least likely to democratise once conflict ends". As the regime of Bashar al-Assad has strengthened connections to other authoritarian leaders, such as of Russia and China, the country continues moving away from the Western democracies (Heydemann, 2013). Thus,

Heydemann (2013) concludes that the regime in Syria might become even more resistant to democratisation after the end of the civil war.

However, what can be said for sure, the country does and will face numerous challenges of post-war reconstruction (Abboud, 2008). In fact, many states have already expressed interest in assisting Syria to reconstruct its destroyed infrastructure. For example, Russia and Syria plan to involve in 30 common projects in industry, education and healthcare (Azizi and Issaev, 2019). Iran has also signed investment agreements on the construction of power plants and housing, development of agriculture and mining. Moreover, Haddad (2012) links the current events to the failure of the private-sector-led policy which means the state will have to redefine its approach to entrepreneurship. Several reforms have been proposed by researchers: creation of an independent economic team overlooking entrepreneurial activities, reinforcement of the judicial branch to protect businesspersons' rights, elimination of corruption and favouritism, reduction of bureaucratic procedures and reinvention of the education system that should meet demands of the modern market (Haddad, 2011a; Salhani and Khnouf, 2017).

References

Abboud, Samer. N. (2008), "Economic Transformation and Diffusion of Authoritarian Power in Syria," in Larbi Sadiki, and Heiko Wimmonen, eds., *Unmaking Power: Negotiating the Democratic Void in the Arab Middle East,* London: Routledge, pp. 159–177.

Anderson, Paul (2018), "Aleppo in Asia: Mercantile Networks between Syria, China and Post-Soviet Eurasia since 1970," *History and Anthropology* 29, pp. 67–83.

Azizi, Hamidreza, and Leonid Issaev (2019), *Russian and Iranian Economic Interests in Syria (Pre-2010 and Intra-war Period),* Discussion Paper (8). GCSP, OMRAN, (Retrieved from https://dam.gcsp.ch/files/2y10nlGNuebJ3zh4kU5wS7N66uuFm35TYDmJjO9jyzKVQYbDoO7vybkfq, accessed 28 March 2021)

CEIC (n.d.), "Syria Real GDP Growth," (Retrieved from https://www.ceicdata.com/en/indicator/syria/real-gdp-growth, accessed 30 March 2021)

Dana, Léo-Paul (2000), *Economies of the Eastern Mediterranean Region: Economic Miracles in the Making,* London, Singapore & Hong Kong: World Scientific.

Doueck, Gina (2017), "The Syrian Jewish Community, Then and Now," *Institute for Jewish Ideas and Ideals* 29, pp. 58–69.

Goulden, Robert (2011), "Housing, Inequality, and Economic Change in Syria," *British Journal of Middle Eastern Studies* 38 (2), pp. 187–202.

Haddad, Bassam (2011a), "The Political Economy of Syria: Realities and Challenges," *Middle East Policy,* 18 (2), pp. 46–61.

Haddad, Bassam (2011b), *Business Networks in Syria: The Political Economy of Authoritarian Resilience,* Palo Alto, CA: Stanford University Press

Haddad, Bassam (2012), "Chapter 11. Syria, the Arab Uprisings, and the Political Economy of Authoritarian Resilience," in Clement Henry and Jang Ji-Hyang, eds., *The Arab Spring, The Asan Institute for Policy Studies,* London: Palgrave Macmillan, pp. 212–226.

Hejase, Hussin Jose, Bassam Hamdar, and Raslan Mohammad (2013), "Business Ethics and Religion in the Financial Business Sector: Case of Syria," *Journal of Business & Management, COES&RJ-JBM* 1 (2), pp. 72–111.

Heydemann, Steven (2013), "Tracking the 'Arab Spring': Syria and the Future of Authoritarianism," *Journal of Democracy* 24 (4), pp. 59–73.

Ibeh, Kevin, and Laila Kasem (2011), "The Network Perspective and the Internationalization of Small and Medium Sized Software Firms from Syria," *Industrial Marketing Management* 40 (3), pp. 358–367.

Izady, Michael (n.d.), *Atlas of the Islamic World and Vicinity,* New York: Columbia University, Gulf 2000 Project: 2006–present, (Retrieved from https://gulf2000.columbia.edu/maps.shtml, accessed 27 March 2021)

Lyme, Rune Friberg (2012), *Sanctioning Assad's Syria: Mapping the Economic, Socioeconomic and Political Repercussions of the International Sanctions Imposed on Syria since March 2011,* DIIS Report 13, (Retrieved from https://www.diis.dk/files/media/publicat ions/import/extra/rp2012-13_sanctioning_assads_syria_web_1.pdf, accessed 29 March 2021)

Salhani, Alaa, and Victoria Khnouf (2017), "University-Business Research Collaboration in Syria: An Empirical Assessment and Suggested Conceptual Model," in Jorge Marx Gómez, Marie K. Aboujaoude, Khalil Feghali, and Tariq Mahmoud, eds., *Modernizing Academic Teaching and Research in Business and Economics,* Springer, Cham, Switzerland, pp. 165–180.

UNHCR (2021), "Syria Emergency," (Retrieved from https://www.unhcr.org/syria-emergency.html, accessed 29 March 2021)

World Bank (2010), "Doing Business 2010," (Retrieved from file:/// C:/Users/575G/Downloads/DB10-FullReport.pdf, accessed 30 March 2021)

World Bank (2020a), "Doing Business 2020. Economic Profile: Syrian Arab Republic," (Retrieved from https://www.doingbusiness.org/ content/dam/doingBusiness/country/s/syria/SYR.pdf, accessed 30 March 2021)

World Bank (2020b), "Literacy Rate, Adult Total (% of People Ages 15 and Above) – Syrian Arab Republic," (Retrieved from https://data. worldbank.org/indicator/SE.ADT.LITR.ZS?locations=SY, accessed 30 March 2021)

World Bank (2021), "The World Bank in Syrian Arab Republic," (Retrieved from https://www.worldbank.org/en/country/syria/overview, accessed 1 April 2021)

World Population Review (2021), "Population of Cities in Syria (2021)," (Retrieved from https://worldpopulationreview.com/countries/cities/ syria, accessed 29 March 2021)

Section XI

Successors to the British Mandate for Palestine

Chapter 19

The Context for Business in Jordan

Saad Zighan

Abstract: Jordan is a small country with fewer natural resources than neighbouring countries. The financial crisis, regional turbulences, along with increasing food, power and oil prices have all put substantial pressure on Jordan's economy. Furthermore, Jordan has been faced with rising unemployment rates that have worsened with the influx of Syrian refugees. Jordan has made important progress in promoting the country's economic infrastructure, aided by openness to foreign trade and investments. Still, government services and finance are the main contributors to Jordan's gross domestic product (GDP) and neither of these can be considered engine of economic growth. An enhancement of the macroeconomic and fiscal stability of Jordan through increased government revenues and the development of a diversified and competitive national economy are required.

Keywords: Jordan, Palestine, Palestinian refugees, Syrian refugees

Introduction

Following the Arab Revolt and the demise of the Ottoman Empire, Transjordan was established under British Mandate in 1921, becoming the Hashemite Kingdom of Jordan in 1946 (Dana, 2000; Zighan and Dwaikat, forthcoming). The monarchy has common borders with Syria to the north, Palestine (the West Bank) and Israel to the west, Iraq to the east and Saudi Arabia to the south. Jordan also has shores along the Gulf of Aqaba. The area of Jordan is 89,213 square kilometres, the water area of which is

Exhibit 19.1   Amman; photo © 2021 by Léo-Paul Dana

329 square kilometres, while the total length of the Jordanian border is 1,635 kilometres. Cities in Jordan are called governorates and the kingdom is divided into 12 governorates. Amman (see Exhibit 19.1) is the capital and is known as the Capital Governorate.

This chapter explores the context for business in Jordan. It draws a timeline of business environment development in Jordan, from the ancient era to modern times. This historical narrative highlights the evolution of life in Jordan and the successive civilisations that have inhabited it, leading to the establishment of the current state and its emergence under Hashemite rule.

Historical Context

Jordan is considered an area of historical importance and has been home to many civilisations, which have each left their own traces and hallmarks (Abu-Khafajah et al., 2015). According to Rasul and Stewart (2018), from at least 5,000 years ago, the land of Jordan has been strategically important for four main reasons – its water, fertile land, varied climate and strategic geographical position linking the continents of the ancient world and forming trade routes for silks, spices and incense between the various parts of the world.

Throughout history, Jordan has witnessed developments in various aspects of life (mainly in agriculture) and gradually developed an integrated relationship between sedentary and pastoral lifestyles, that is, between the first villagers, who knew how to benefit from the construction of small dams on the foothills of the mountains, and the Bedouins, who knew how to raise livestock and sheep. The Bedouin, the villagers and the town dwellers have had a symbiotic relationship that was mutually beneficial, for example, the Bedouin traded animal products for manufactured or imported goods (Gubser, 1991). Relations also developed between various societies, who traded in craft products. These cooperative relationships helped in the development of the region and the small villages gradually developed into cities, which consolidated their power, allowing them to remain in control for centuries (Assyria, Egypt, Nabataea Rome, Byzantium and Islam) and changed the cultural landscape of Jordan in major ways (Sawyer and Clines, 1983). In every historical era of Jordan, there was an enterprising society that has shaped its business environment (Maffi, 2009).

The Hellenistic era was characterised by the Greek civilisation, which spread Greek culture and language through the establishment of cities in the Greek style. Principally, this took the form of the Union of Ten Cities (the Decapolis), which was a federative economic and cultural union. This led to a mix between Western Greek civilisations and Eastern civilisations (Keilholz, 2014).

The Nabateans (69 BC – 106 AD), an ancient Arab kingdom, established one of the most prominent civilisations in the region and took Petra (see Exhibit 19.2) as their capital, which was a strategic stop on the Incense Road, located at the crossroads of convoys coming from Yemen and linking them to the Levant, Egypt and the Mediterranean. The Nabataeans were able to take advantage of Jordan's location to pass the arteries of trade. Nabataeans built irrigation canals and were interested in agriculture and the exploitation of the land (Grattan et al., 2007).

In 324 AD, the Roman period began, and Jordan witnessed many construction works, as cities were built during the Roman era and continued to flourish. As a result, the population of the region increased significantly. This era was marked by stability and peace, and several important developments took place in the area's infrastructure (Al Karaimeh, 2019).

Exhibit 19.2 Petra the capital of Nabatean Kingdom; photo © 2021 by Saad Zighan

In the Islamic era, Jordan witnessed changes in some cities, such as Jerash, whose urban features reflected the new religion. Mosques were built and both economic and commercial developments flourished. Islamic civilisation contributed to the consolidation of the role of science and learning as an essential part of the Islamic religion and contributed to spreading the culture of creativity and discovery (Kirk, 2016). Muslim scholars have made innumerable discoveries and wrote countless books about chemistry, philosophy, physics, medicine, surgery, geometry, astrology and numerous other scientific fields. The Islamic religion also strengthened the role of women in society (see Ramadani et al., 2017). The history of Transjordan continued with the Muslim empires. The Ottoman period spanned four centuries, during which Ottoman strength both grew and waned, and Jordan's history in the Ottoman period was marked by a period of general stagnation (Corbett, 2015). The Ottoman Empire built the telegraphic network and the Hejaz railroad line running 1,320 kilometre from Damascus through Jordan to the holy sites in the Hejaz; this was established to serve religious, political, military and economic objectives (Landau, 2016).

The Arab Revolt began in Najd and ended in 1918 with the withdrawal of the Ottomans from Arab countries. Thus, the contemporary era of Jordan history began. With the demise of the Ottoman Empire and the end of the World War I, the Emirate of Transjordan was established due to British colonisation. The Emirate of Transjordan remained under the British Mandate until it gained independence in 1945 and changed its name to the Hashemite Kingdom of Jordan. During that period, the British worked mainly on a policy of Bedouin resettlement (see Dana, 2000).

The Arab–Israeli War of 1948 was a victory for Jordan. Bank wrote, "when Israel declared independence in May 1948, the Jordanian Arab legion occupied areas of Palestine adjacent to the Jordan that had been allocated to the Arabs in the United Nations Partition Plan of November 1947. Abdullah's forces were the most successful of the Arab armies (2020)".

The 1950s was a period of political tumult throughout the Arab world. Bank explained, "On April 24, 1950, Abdullah unilaterally annexed the portion of Palestine called the West Bank, the territory west of the Jordan River. The 1948 Arab-Israeli war had also resulted in a massive Palestinian refugee influx into Jordan…By the early 1950s, then, Jordan's demography was transformed completely. Prior to the war, Jordan counted no more than 380,000 mostly tribal residents in its territory on the east bank of the Jordan River; now, it accommodated the 450,000 Palestinians living in the West Bank, and an additional 350,000 refugees who had entered from both sides of the kingdom…Abdullah alone among the Arab rulers extended full citizenship rights to the Palestinians living in the Hashemite-controlled territories east and west of the Jordan River…As King Abdullah was leaving the al-Aqsa Mosque in Jerusalem on July 20, 1951, he was assassinated by a Palestinian nationalist (Bank, 2020)". The West Bank of the Jordan River remained under Jordanian rule until 1967.

After Jordan succeeded in overcoming extremism in the 1950s, Jordan's contemporary history entered a period of hope and confidence during the 1960s. These years were promising – the Jordanian economy began to take off, and the industrial backbone of the modern economy in Jordan was developed (i.e., the potash, phosphate and cement industries), oil refineries were built, the kingdom was connected to a highway network and a new educational system was introduced. Moreover, before the 1967 war, the rates of economic growth in Jordan were higher than in most other developing countries (Ashton, 2008). In the contemporary history of Jordan, internal politics were primarily aimed at promoting national unity among the Jordanian population, and this desired unity is the ultimate guarantee of Jordan's survival and security. Jordan's contemporary history has achieved an organised, pluralistic political structure that could serve as a model for the region, since it resumed its commitment to parliamentary policy in 1989.

In 1994, the *Wadi Araba Treaty* was signed resulting in opening a border and allowing business between Jordan and Israel (see Exhibit 19.3). "The treaty guaranteed Jordan the restoration of its occupied land (approximately 380 square kilometres), as well as an equitable share of water from the Yarmouk and Jordan rivers (see: http://www.kinghussein. gov.jo/peacetreaty.html)". Contemporary Jordan has also adopted several

Exhibit 19.3　Jordan–Israel border; photo © 2021 by Léo-Paul Dana

comprehensive reforms, most notably the re-introduction of political parties to parliament, the drafting of the national pact and the expansion of press freedoms (Robins, 2019).

Context for Enterprise and Implications for Doing Business

According to a Department of Statistics report (2019), the population of Jordan at the beginning of 2020 was about 10.5 million. The distribution of the population by sex is also relatively balanced, with a 52.9% male and 47.1% female distribution in 2018. People between 0 and 14 years of age represented 34.4% of the population, between 15 and 64 years represented 61.9% of the population, and those over 65 years of age represented 3.7% of the population. The annual growth rate of the population between 2017 and 2019 was around 2.4%. About 75% of the country's population is concentrated in Amman, Zarqa and Irbid.

This increase in population is mainly due to forced migrations from other countries of the area and the search for asylum in the kingdom. In addition to the indigenous people, the population in Jordan consists of immigrants from many different countries. Those immigrants contribute to the diversification of Jordanian culture. They have contributed with new ideas and tools for building, agriculture and herding. Handicrafts and various skills have emerged, ranging from the production of carpets (still knotted or woven by hand on traditional looms), to objects made from metal, weapons and jewellery, and pottery (Arinat, 2016).

Exhibit 19.4 shows a tent used as a classroom. Human capital in Jordan plays an important role in supporting the national economy. Jordan has witnessed unprecedented levels of growth in several areas, especially in the services, construction and financial sectors. The main contributor to this rapid economic and social development was the massive flow of finances from Jordanian citizens who provide skilled labour to the oil-rich Gulf states (Khader and Badran, 2014). Jordan took advantage of its human capabilities and worked to improve its efficiency and effectiveness by investing in learning and education by all available means (Zighan and Ahmed, 2020).

In 1962, the first national university was established – the University of Jordan. Today, Jordan has many universities and training institutes. In 1991, one of the first universities in the Arab world was opened for girls only in Jordan, which at the time was called the Al-Banat (Girls) Jordanian University. Jordan has the same number of universities as Egypt, despite

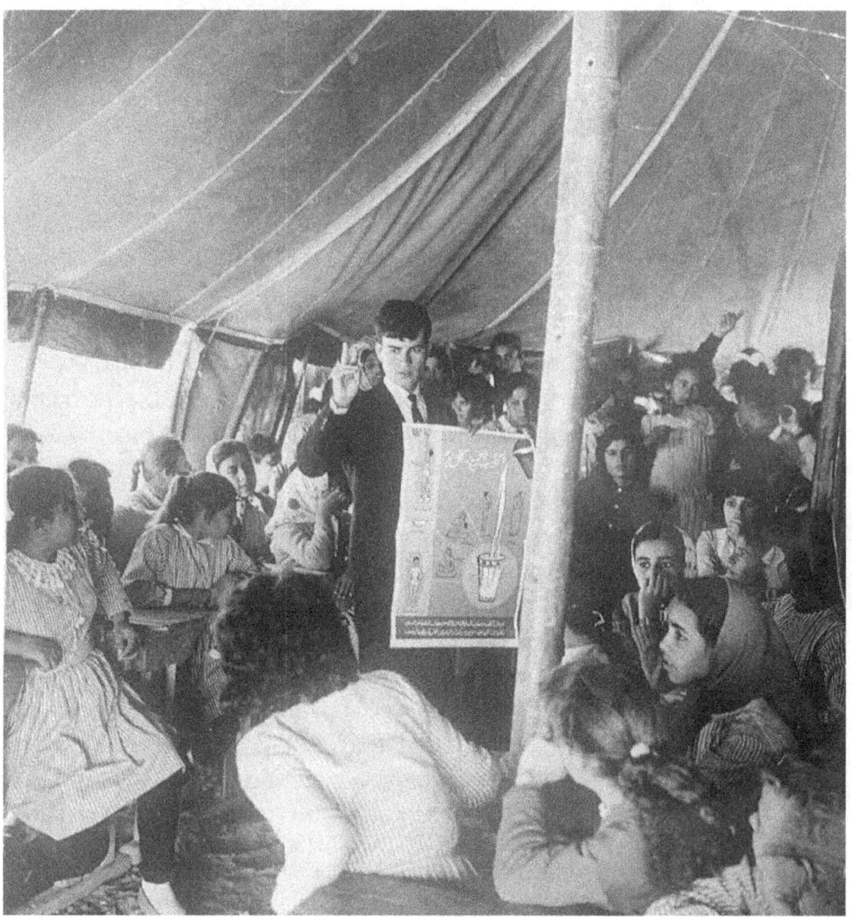

Exhibit 19.4 Using tents as school classrooms; photo © 2021 by Saad Zighan

the fact that Egypt is 10 times the size of Jordan in terms of area and population. Jordan, therefore, has a high literacy rate (98.2%), which is above the average for countries in the region (Assaad et al., 2018). However, Jordan has more than enough reasons not to fall into complacency. According to the Report on the Human Development Index (2018), prepared by the United Nations (UN), Jordan ranked 95th among 189 countries. The education sector in Jordan should be refocused on providing students with unique skills and competencies to enhance employability and supply neighbouring MENA countries with high-calibre intellectual and professional expertise (Zighan and Ahmed, 2020).

The Jordanian economy is a market-oriented economy. Over the past three decades, it has undergone significant reforms, beginning with the liberalisation and reforms started by His Majesty King Hussein, which focused primarily on economic diversification and the stimulation of higher value-added economic activities. During the first decade of the 2000s, His Majesty King Abdullah II employed another set of reforms to attract foreign investment, which resulted in an average growth rate of 8% to the country's gross domestic product (GDP), between 2004 and 2008 (Alhajahmad and Lockhart, 2017; PKF Group, 2011). However, the global financial crises, regional turbulences, power crises, security costs, and a decline in remittances have all put substantial pressure on Jordan's economic growth (The Economic Policy Council, 2017). The growth rate of Jordan's GDP between 2000 and 2009 was 6.5%, however from 2010 to 2019, its average growth was a mere 2%. Furthermore, Jordan's public debt has reached JD 29.508 billion at the end of July 2019, comprising 94.4% of its estimated GDP. Moreover, Jordan's economic growth rate has been declining as a result of the effects of the global economic slowdown and the current regional crisis (see Exhibit 19.5). The repercussions of the Syrian syndrome have harmed the Jordanian economy due to the closure of trade routes with Iraq and Syria, due to security reasons (Alhajahmad and Lockhart, 2017).

Exhibit 19.5 Zaatari refugee camp in Jordan; photo © 2021 by Saad Zighan

The Jordanian economy is ranked 70th globally (The Global Competitiveness Report, 2019). The kingdom's economy depends mainly on the services sector, trade and tourism and on some extractive industries, such as fertilisers and medicines. Phosphate mines are located in the south of the kingdom, making Jordan the third largest exporter of this material in the world. Other essential resources extracted include potash, salts, natural gas and limestone. Broken down by sector, participation in GDP is as follows: agricultural sector contributes 5.9%, the industrial sector contributes 29% (distributed between the manufacturing industry at 20%, electricity and water at 3.7%, mining at 2.2% and construction at 3.1%) and the remainder, the service sector, contributes 65.1% (see Bank, 2020).

According to the latest data published in the *Monthly Statistical Bulletin* of the Jordanian Statistics Department, service sector jobs constitute more than 85% of the workforce, industry constitutes 10.8% and the agricultural sector sits at around 1.5%. Furthermore, according to official data, the public sector employs approximately 40% of the country's workforce. Jordan's economy faces five constraints: energy, water, farmland, asylum, and market volatility. It also suffers from many economic difficulties, perhaps the most prominent of which is the low rate of economic growth that recently decreased to a record rate of 1.8%, which is less than the natural growth rates of the population. Therefore, Jordan is witnessing a decline in the living standards of its citizens, increasing unemployment rates, widespread poverty, an escalation of the budget deficit and a steady and unprecedented rise in public debt (Nowrasteh et al., 2020).

The agricultural sector (see Exhibit 19.6) is inherently limited given that Jordan is mostly desert and lacks water. However, a robust agricultural investment plan capitalising on new agricultural technology, such as hydroponic systems, would significantly improve the efficiency of this sector in Jordan (Mikadze and Alhajahmad, 2017).

Jordan is the gateway to the Middle East for medical investments and hospital resorts, including medical tourism, spas, biomedical research, production, the sale of medical equipment and the production of natural skincare products that are used as a treatment for a number of skin diseases, with materials extracted from the Dead Sea. Although there are many tourist destinations in Jordan, there is a need to increase investments in this sector (Shdeifat et al., 2007).

Finally, the manufacturing sector, which is made up of small- and medium-sized enterprises (SMEs), constitutes the bulk of the Jordanian economy. However, the stability of these companies has become a cause

Exhibit 19.6 Agriculture in Jordan; photo © 2021 by Saad Zighan

for concern, as they suffer from intense competition, high production costs and high energy prices, which affect the competitiveness of domestic products in favour of foreign goods (Zighan and Dwaikat, forthcoming).

The ecosystem in Jordan is relatively developed, as it does not lack innovative and creative ideas, but the ability to support and set up start-up projects that investors may consider viable and sustainable is still limited. Many innovative ideas and start-ups have emerged, and Jordan has taken an excellent attitude towards entrepreneurship, especially in terms of high-tech projects (Bank, 2020). Many institutions have emerged supporting entrepreneurial activities and start-ups projects, such as Oasis 500, Beyond Capital Jordan and Endeavour. Jordan's ecosystem has had an impressive track record in graduating globally recognised entrepreneurs who have built hugely successful start-ups (Badran and Badran, 2020). In addition, in 2018, the "Work from Home" campaign was launched, which facilitated licensing and doing businesses from home. It is worth mentioning that more than 80% of work from homeowners are women, which represents a significant opportunity to increase the rate of participation of women in Jordan's economy. Nevertheless, the rate of start-ups has decreased significantly due to obstacles in the business environment and access to finance. The rate of new business creation has lagged behind many other regional economies. The Global Entrepreneurship Index (2018) ranked Jordan 64 out of 132 countries and 10th in the MENA region.

Towards the Future

Jordan is a small country with fewer natural resources than its neighbouring countries. Jordan enjoys political and social stability, a modern financial system and strong infrastructure. The country is pending a series of projects in infrastructure, water and energy, which are most relevant in the regional environment, although they are facing financing problems. Jordan aspires to deepen its role as a regional centre for education, health and other business services – such as engineering, new technologies or renewable energy, among others – although without neglecting the tourist attraction of the country, with Petra in the lead. Despite these assets, Jordan still has a long way to go towards creating a healthy business environment.

The Jordanian economy is currently dominated by government services and finance. Neither of these are the engine of economic growth in the years ahead, as the government remains under the pressure of further fiscal tightening. Thus, it is important that Jordan invests in the agriculture sector, with modern production technology, thereby producing different products with high technical specifications and quality standards that can be offered in local and international markets. Moreover, Jordan is blessed with very attractive weather, environment, natural wonders and historical sites. The tourism sector can play a major role in its economic growth. Although recent data shows an uptake in the numbers of tourist arrivals to Jordan, sustaining this trend requires further investments in marketing Jordan in both targeted countries and new regions, along with maintaining and upgrading tourist sites and the relevant infrastructure. Besides, Jordan's health sector has seen numerous pioneering firsts on the regional level. It has developed a professional and high-quality cadre of doctors and healthcare practitioners and a set of well-performing healthcare facilities. However, global competition, institutional gaps in quality assurance and an inability to develop a strategic clustering of the sector have inhibited its ability to continue to attract regional and international medical tourists. An action plan to position Jordan as a competitively priced hub of high-quality medical tourism will therefore yield fruitful results.

Further, investments in the education sector are imperative. For instance, one of Jordan's strong differentiators is the country's talent, entrepreneurial drive and imagination. Being a country of limited natural resources, Jordan's main strength lies in its human capital, and the entrepreneurial drive and imagination among the country's population is being highlighted as one of the country's major strengths. Good human capital is particularly found among professionals who have a number of years of work experience. However, skills are a two-edged sword in Jordan. While Jordanian Information and communications technology (ICT) specialists are increasingly being hired in other countries in the region, for instance, in Qatar, Dubai and Saudi Arabia, there are still barriers to overcome with regards to higher education modernisation, particularly in terms of curriculum relevance to the industry, and modes of cooperation between university and industry (see Zighan and Ahmed, 2020). These barriers can be addressed, however, and a modernisation process can be set fully in motion within a relatively short period (Badran and Badran, 2020). Moreover, the world is looking at the Fourth Digital Revolution, which combines multiple technologies that are leading to an unprecedented paradigm shift in the economy, business, society and among individuals. This means that increasingly, sectors are disrupted and increasingly digitised (Schwab, 2017). According to a report from the Ministry of Information and Communications Technology (2016), this offers a mammoth opportunity for Jordan's economic development. Yet, it also poses threats if timely actions are not taken. The progressively digitised world entails that Jordan should exploit the advantages of the digital revolution. The true differentiator of Jordan lies in the combination of three main areas:

- Producing specialised ICT talent
- Leveraging high-level strategic partnerships with global high-tech and technological enterprises
- Creating and integrating digital solutions for content platforms for the Arab market

Moreover, SMEs form the backbone of the Jordanian economy, and start-ups also contribute to Jordanian economic development. This forms an important base for expanding productive capacities, increasing exports and generating job opportunities in various geographical locations (Zighan and Dwaikat, forthcoming). Nevertheless, Jordan's entrepreneurship landscape is not up to its potential. Along with insufficient innovation performance, weak growth rates result from a lack of policies and programmes that support institutions and small and medium enterprises, which leaves a negative impact on state revenues and the economic situation in general, along with low levels of employment and income.

To enhance the effectiveness of SMEs in Jordan, it is important to integrate entrepreneurship education and training programmes in the school and university curricula, and to focus on stimulating creativity and innovation, which is the basis of entrepreneurship. It is imperative to motivate inventors, support them financially and facilitate their access to the necessary financial resources for their projects, which requires increased coordination between different organisations in Jordan, with a view to ensure an efficient allocation of resources. Activities could include making the registration of a business more straightforward, by minimising the costs and time required to register, streamline and minimise the methods for obtaining credit, so that entrepreneurs will have a source for their start-up capital (Zighan and Ahmed, 2020). Finally, it is also important to develop a unified and comprehensive roadmap to enhance the business environment and Jordan's competitiveness through minimising changes in policies and legislation. Therefore, a new and integrated financing programme should be developed that provides concessional financing, technical support and training, according to clear and transparent criteria, which will enable young people to establish small and medium productive projects and provide job opportunities. These programmes should also include youth counselling and networking with technical experts and the economic system. According to Palalić et al. (2018), protecting and supporting competitiveness and increasing the growth rates of small and medium enterprises is an urgent necessity when addressing the problems, demands and needs of these institutions. It is important to stimulate the work of small and medium enterprises to tackle poverty and unemployment, provide healthcare and education and find a balance between the family's public spending and the rate of income to achieve economic reform. For Jordan, it is an important and strategic matter, and projects in rural areas face basic challenges related to a lack of infrastructure when compared to urban areas. It is therefore important to strike a balance in the cost of production and the possibility of marketing by setting up a working group composed of the government, the private sector and chambers of commerce and industry in the kingdom. This should be accomplished by implementing policies and procedures addressing the sector's challenges and problems in an institutional, systematic and sustainable manner that aims to protect and burrow investment in small and medium enterprises. This requires designing sound economic policies for a sustainable market economy, building an attractive environment for investment and private sector development, directing investment policy to encourage foreign direct investment (FDI)–SME linkages and to enable innovation spillovers, increasing public funding for R&D in light of available resources and develop innovative finance instruments, encouraging capital market development and microfinance as alternatives to bank finance and developing a plan to promote entrepreneurship among unemployed Jordanians.

References

Abu-Khafajah, Shatha, Rama Al Rabady, Shaher Rababeh, and Fadael Al-Rahman Al-Tammoni (2015), "Hands-On Heritage! Establishing Soft Authority Over Heritage through Architectural Experiment: A Case Study from Jordan," *Public Archaeology* 14 (3), pp. 191–213.

Al Karaimeh, Sufyan (2019), "Maintaining Desert Cultivation: Roman, Byzantine, and Early Islamic Water-Strategies at Udhruh Region, Jordan," *Journal of Arid Environments* 166, pp. 108–115.

Alhajahmad, Shaddin, and Dorsey Lockhart (2017), *Jordan's Recent Economic Performance: Implications for Future Growth, Investment, Refugee Policy and Refugees,* Amman: WANA.

Arinat, Mahmoud (2016), "The Status of Handicrafts in Jordan: Challenges and Prospects," *Dirasat, Human and Social Sciences* 43 (5), pp. 2273–2284.

Ashton, Nigel (2008), *King Hussein of Jordan: A Political Life,* New Haven, Connecticut: Yale University Press.

Assaad, Ragui, Caroline Krafft, and Djavad Salehi-Isfahani (2018), "Does the Type of Higher Education Affect Labor Market Outcomes? Evidence from Egypt and Jordan," *Higher Education* 75 (6), pp. 945–995.

Badran, Adnan, and Serene Badran (2020), "Can Universities in the Arab Region Become the Engines for Knowledge and Innovation?" in Adnan Badran, Elias Baydoun, and John R. Hillman, eds. *Higher Education in the Arab World,* Cham: Springer, pp. 73–93.

Bank, André (2020), "Hashemite Kingdom of Jordan," in Sean Yom, ed., *Government and Politics of the Middle East and North Africa: Development, Democracy, and Dictatorship,* Oxon, UK: Routledge, pp. 377–408.

Corbett, Elena (2015), *Competitive Archaeology in Jordan: Narrating Identity from the Ottomans to the Hashemites,* Austin, TX: University of Texas Press.

Dana, Léo-Paul (2000), *Economies of the Eastern Mediterranean Region: Economic Miracles in the Making,* London, Singapore & Hong Kong: World Scientific.

Department of Statistics (2019), Jordan in Figures. Jordan. http://dosweb.dos.gov.jo/

Global Competitiveness Report (2019), *World Economic Forum,* Cologny, Switzerland: The World Economic Forum.

Global Entrepreneurship Monitor Jordan National Report (2017/2018), Jordan Enterprise Development Corporation and Centre for Strategic Studies, Amman, Jordan.

Grattan, John P., David D. Gilbertson, and Christopher O. Hunt (2007), "The Local and Global Dimensions of Metalliferous Pollution Derived from a Reconstruction of an Eight Thousand Year Record of Copper Smelting and Mining at a Desert-Mountain Frontier in Southern Jordan," *Journal of Archaeological Science* 34 (1), pp. 83–110.

Gubser, Peter (1991), *Historical Dictionary of the Hashemite Kingdom of Jordan* (No. 4), Oceania, and the Middle East: Historical Dictionaries of Asia Metuchen, N.J. : Scarecrow Press..

Human Development Index (2018). Human Development Indices and Indicators by the United Nations Development Programme. New York, USA, http://hdr.undp.org/sites/default/files/2018_human_development_statistical_update.pdf

Keilholz, Patrick (2014), "The Ancient Cisterns of Hellenistic Gadara/ Umm Qais (Jordan), in Patrik Klingborg and Martin Finné, eds., *Antike und Moderne Wasserspeicherung: Internationaler Workshop vom,* Vol. 11, Italy: VMC, p. 2011

Khader, Bichara, and Adnan Badran, eds. (2014), *The Economic Development of Jordan (RLE Economy of Middle East),* London: Routledge.

Kirk, George E. (2016), *A Short History of the Middle East: From the Rise of Islam to Modern Times,* London: Routledge.

Landau, Jacob M. (2016), *The Hejaz Railway and the Muslim Pilgrimage: A Case of Ottoman Political Propaganda,* London: Routledge.

Maffi, Irene (2009), "The Emergence of Cultural Heritage in Jordan: The Itinerary of a Colonial Invention," *Journal of Social Archaeology* 9 (1), pp. 5–34.

Mikadze, Maria, and Shaddin Alhajahmad (2017), *Investment and Business in Jordan to Create Employment: Opportunities and Challenges,* Amman, Jordan: WANA.

Ministry of Information and Communications Technology (2016), Reach 2025 From Vision to Action. Ministry of Information and Communications Technology and ICT Association of Jordan, (Retrieved from https://www.jordanict.com/2016/about-sector/infor mation-and-communications-technology-association-jordan-intj#:~:t ext=int%40j%2C%20The%20Information%20and,the%20Kingdom' s%20ICTES%20related%20activities)

Nowrasteh, Alex, Andrew C. Forrester, and Cole Blondin (2020), "How Mass Immigration Affects Countries with Weak Economic Institutions: A Natural Experiment in Jordan," *The World Bank Economic Review* 34 (2), pp. 533–549.

Palalić, Ramo, Léo-Paul Dana, and Veland Ramadani, eds. (2018), *Entrepreneurship in Former Yugoslavia: Diversity, Institutional Constraints and Prospects,* Cham: Springer.

PKF Group (2011), *Doing Business in Jordan,* London: PKF Accountants & Business Advisers.

Ramadani, Veland, Léo-Paul Dana, Shqipe Gërguri-Rashiti, and Vanessa Ratten, eds. (2017), *Entrepreneurship and Management in an Islamic Context*, Cham: Springer.

Rasul, Najeeb M., and Ian C. Stewart, eds. (2018), *Geological Setting, Palaeoenvironment and Archaeology of the Red Sea,* Cham: Springer.

Robins, Philip (2019), *A History of Jordan,* Cambridge: Cambridge University Press.

Sawyer, John F., and David J. Clines. eds, (1983), *Midian, Moab, and Edom: The History and Archaeology of Late Bronze and Iron Age Jordan and North-West Arabia,* A&C Black, Vol. 24.

Schwab, Klaus (2017), *The Fourth Industrial Revolution,* New York: Penguin Random House.

Shdeifat, Omar, Despo Kassinos, and Ihab Amarin (2007), *Development of Methods and Tools for the Establishment of Good Environmental Performance in the Tourist Accommodation Sector in Jordan,* Irbid: Jordan University of Science and Technology. The Economic Policy Council (2017), Jordan Economic Growth Plan 2018–2022, Amman: The Economic Policy Council.

Zighan, Saad, and Ahmed Elqasem (2020), "Lean Thinking and Higher Education Management: Revaluing the Business School Programme Management," *International Journal of Productivity and Performance Management* 70 (3), pp. 675–703.

Zighan, Saad, and Nidal Dwaikat (forthcoming), "Exploring Organisational Agility in SMEs," *International Journal of Entrepreneurship and Small Business*.

Chapter 20

The Context for Business in Israel

Osnat Akirav, Léo-Paul Dana, A. Allan Degen, Bella L. Galperin &
Meron Medzini

Abstract: Jews have continuously lived in Western Asia, where they have had their national ancestral homeland on the Land of Israel, before either Christianity or Islam was established. Jesus was among them. Some nations are secular in that they have a separation between church and state, and others – including Armenia and Georgia – have declared themselves to be Christian states; yet others are Islamic states, for example, the Islamic Republic of Iran. There is only one Jewish state, and that is Israel, the subject of this chapter.

Keywords: Bedouin, Druze, Jews, m-commerce, start-up nation, technology

Silicon Valley really has only one rival outside the United States – Israel.

Wall Street knows it.

– Newsweek

Introduction

Israel covers slightly over 20,000 km^2. Its neighbours are Egypt,[1] Jordan, Lebanon, Syria and the Palestinian Authority territories.

---

[1] For a discussion of the context of business in Egypt, see Dana (2000).

The Land of Israel is the historical homeland of the Jewish people and the State of Israel is the nation-state of the Jewish people, in which it realises its natural, cultural, religious and historical right to self-determination. That said, it has a heterogeneous population; the country is home to Bahais, Christians, Druze, Jews, Muslims, Samaritans and others. Christians (Exhibit 20.1) come on pilgrimage from Ethiopia and beyond.

The Druze practice a secret religion, based on *Epistles of Wisdom*, which was written during the 11th century (Firro, 2005). They have their own flag (Exhibit 20.2). Savta Gamila (Exhibit 20.3), a Druze industrialist who manufacturs soap (Exhibit 20.4) employs 50 women in Israel and 60 disabled people at her packaging plant in the Netherlands; she has been a leader in the emancipation of women in the Druze community (Akirav, 2019).

Arabic and Hebrew are widespread languages in Israel; Amharic, English, French, Spanish and Russian are also common. Exhibit 20.5 shows three languages on a sign at a bank. Exhibit 20.6 shows an Arabic-only sign in Israel. Exhibit 20.7 features Nahef, a typical Israeli village in which the primary language spoken is Arabic.

Exhibit 20.1   Ethiopian Orthodox pilgrims; photo © 2021 by Léo-Paul Dana

Exhibit 20.2 Druze flag flown in Israel; photo © 2021 by Léo-Paul Dana

Exhibit 20.3 Druze industrialist Savta Gamila, with visitors; photo © 2021 by Léo-Paul Dana

Exhibit 20.4 Soap for sale; photo © 2021 by Léo-Paul Dana

Exhibit 20.5 Arabic, English and Hebrew; photo © 2021 by Léo-Paul Dana

Exhibit 20.6 Arabic-only sign in Israel; photo © 2021 by Léo-Paul Dana

Exhibit 20.7 In Nahef, the primary language spoken is Arabic; photo © 2021 by Léo-Paul Dana

From its independence in 1948 until the 1970s, Israel was governed by the Labour Party with socialist policies. During the past 50 years, its economy shifted from a focus on agriculture (Exhibit 20.8) to high value-added technology-based products and services. Israel has reached the position of third worldwide in terms of the number of university degrees per capita.

It was the first nation to launch m-commerce, allowing Israelis to use mobile phones to activate fuel dispensers and to pay for petrol at service stations. The level of venture capital is second only to the United States (Hartz, 2018). This country has more start-ups per capita than any other country in the world (Coleman, 2018). Some successful examples that have gained attention globally include Fiverr, StoreDot and Wix (Bussgang and Stern, 2015). In 2017, Intel paid $15 billion to buy out an Israeli start-up, Mobileye.

According to the Organisation for Economic Co-operation and Development (OECD), in 2019, Israel had the highest ratio of research and development (R&D) expenditure to gross domestic product (GDP) (https://stats.oecd.org/). According to the 2020 Bloomberg Innovation Index, Israel was ranked sixth among the 50 most innovative countries (Johnson, 2020), up from 10th place in 2018 (Jamrisko and Lu, 2018).

Exhibit 20.8 Banana plants; photo © 2021 by Léo-Paul Dana

Prudent fiscal and monetary policies, the liberalisation of trade, deregulation, privatisation and the removal of exchange controls boosted the economy that became characterised by per capita GDP at par with western European economies, and growth rates as high as Asia's Tigers. Israel has been responsible for many innovations, for example, the invention of the USB stick by Dov Moran in 1998 and the development of WAZE by Ehud Shabtai in 2008. According to the Central Bureau of Statistics, the state of Israel invests twice the OECD average in R&D and – outside the undeclared sector – almost 1 in 10 jobs is in communications or the high-tech sector. There is also a brain drain as successful Israelis often use their talents and networks elsewhere; Gurau et al. (2020) focus on Israelis in China's industrial markets.

Historical Context

> The Land of Israel was the birthplace of the Jewish people. Here their spiritual, religious and national identity was shaped…Here they wrote and gave the Bible to the world...
>
> –Declaration of the Establishment of the State of Israel
> published in the *Official Gazette,* May 14, 1948

In Biblical times, the Jewish kingdoms of Judaea and Israel (Samaria) were founded here and the tribe of Zebulun specialised in commerce. Foreign trade accelerated economic development, especially under King Solomon. In 586 BC, Jewish sovereignty ended when the Babylonians captured Judea and Samaria and exiled the inhabitants. King Cyrus of Persia later permitted Jews to return to Judea. The country then came under the rule of Alexander the Great's descendants and was ruled by the Greeks until a Jewish rebellion headed by the Hasmonean family created an independent Jewish state – but that ended in 63 BC with the Roman occupation. The Romans ruled the country through a series of proxy kings; the most famous was Herod, during whose reign Jesus preached his sermons. A rebellion in 70 AD ended the autonomous existence of Judea, launching centuries of exile until the re-establishment of Israel in 1948. During its occupation by foreign troops, Jerusalem came to be known as *Aelia Capitolina* and the Jewish kingdom of Judaea was renamed *Syria Palaestina*.

The Jewish community that remained in the country after 70 AD lived predominantly in the cities of Jerusalem, Hebron, Tiberius and Safed (Exhibit 20.9). This land later fell under the influence of the Byzantine

Empire. Then came Muslim conquest in the 8th century, which lasted until 1089, when the Crusaders arrived, established a Christian state, and exterminated many Muslims and Jews. In Jerusalem, the Crusaders transformed the Dome of the Rock (Exhibit 20.10) – an Islamic shrine – into a church and Al-Asqa Mosque into a royal residence. Saladin defeated the Crusaders in 1281, and the country was then run by the Egyptian Mamelukes, who ruled it from 1291 until the arrival of the Ottomans.

Ben-Zvi (1966) noted that the Jewish community, already vibrant during the 15th century, was enthusiastic about the arrival of Ottoman rule in 1517. He noted that sultans "refrained completely from meddling in the lives of their Jews" (1966, p. 229). On Ottoman-era maps, the area making up the modern State of Israel is divided into the Ottoman : (i) Mutasarrifate of Jerusalem — also referred to as Jerusalem Sanjak (Yazbak, 2017); and (ii) Syria Vilayet that was subdivided into prefectures, including the Acre Sanjak (Late Ottoman Galilee, successor to the Safed Sanjak) and the Nablus Sanjak, among others. In 1888, these were transferred to the Beirut Vilayet.

In exchange for guaranteeing a substantial increase in the yearly tax revenues, Sultan Suleiman the Magnificent granted a long-term lease on the Tiberias region, to Dona Gracia (Mendes) Nasi; in 1558 she thus

Exhibit 20.9   Safed; photo © 2021 by Léo-Paul Dana

Exhibit 20.10   Gold-covered Dome of the Rock and the walled city; photo © 2021 by Léo-Paul Dana

obtained ruling authority over the region. With the help of the sultan, she began to rebuild the area's abandoned towns to make them available to refugees from Spain, so they could settle there, if they wished. Her aim was to turn Tiberias into a major new centre of Jewish settlement, trade and learning. This venture was one of the earliest attempts at a modern Zionist movement.

As of 1840 the majority of the population of Jerusalem was comprised of Jews. Jerusalem is a walled city, with seven gates open as well as others that have been sealed shut. Exhibit 20.11 features the Golden Gate, closed since medieval times, and Exhibit 20.12 shows Lion's Gate. From the early days, Jews emerged from the walled Old City of Jerusalem, establishing new neighbourhoods.

Haifa, situated northwest of Jerusalem, was a rapidly developing port on the Mediterranean Sea. In 1869, Templers (rooted in Lutheranism) established a German Colony in Haifa. Between 1876 and 1908, Ottoman Sultan Abdul Hamid II initiated reforms and encouraged the migration of Muslims to the Acre Sanjak, and in 1878, he exempted migrants from land taxes for 12 years. This encouraged Muslims from North Africa and the Caucasus Mountains as well as from Bosnia to settle in Haifa.

Exhibit 20.11   Golden Gate, shut since medieval times; photo © 2021 by Léo-Paul Dana

Exhibit 20.12   Lion's Gate; photo © 2021 by Léo-Paul Dana

The Bedouins – tribal groups whose traditional lifestyle was nomadic pastoralism – raised camels[2] (Exhibit 20.13), goats (Exhibit 20.14) and sheep (Exhibit 20.15) for a livelihood. As explained by Degen et al. (2019),

Exhibit 20.13 Herd of camels; photo © 2021 by Léo-Paul Dana

Exhibit 20.14 Bedouin with a mixed flock of goats and sheep; photo © 2021 by Léo-Paul Dana

---

[2] Degen et al. (2019) found that since transportation and ploughing were replaced by motorised vehicles there is much less need to maintain camels, and that younger Bedouin believe that they are less identified with camels than with sheep and goats; all, however, expressed their desire to maintain camels for traditional reasons.

Exhibit 20.15 Awassi cross ram with ewes; photo © 2021 by Léo-Paul Dana

Exhibit 20.16 Into the 1970s, camels were used for ploughing; photo © 2021 by A. Allan Degen

camels were used as pack animals, for transportation, and for ploughing (Exhibit 20.16). Tribal rulers, powerful leaders at the time, charged caravans for passage across the desert. There were two principal communities of Bedouins in the region. Those in Syria Vilayet and later the Beirut Vilayet were of Syrian ancestry. Bedouins in the south (Exhibit 20.17) had their origins in tribes that came from Saudi Arabia. The two groups were

Exhibit 20.17 Bedouin elders in the Negev Desert; photo © 2021 by Léo-Paul Dana

not related; they spoke dissimilar dialects. Those in the Negev Desert did not register their lands; this exempted them from paying taxes and serving in the army. By the late 19th century, the traditional pastoral economy of the Bedouins had evolved into a mixed agricultural and pastoral economy. As the Ottomans began building the railroad to Egypt, many Bedouins were attracted to wage labour.

Meanwhile in Europe, "A whole series of special taxes were invented and enforced against Jews...meat cost a third more to the Jews...a percentage tax was levied upon all rents received by Jews and on profits... printing presses owned by Jews paid annually...the Jewish head of a family had to pay a special tax...Jewish youths were stripped of practically all safeguards and legal reservations..." (Harold, 1892, pp. 28–29). Following large-scale pogroms against Jews in the Russian Empire in 1882, numerous Jews felt anti-Semitism was so rife that there was no future for them in that empire. A student group, the *Bilu'im*, arrived in the Syria Vilayet and established villages on land they purchased from local Arabs. Among these are Rishon Lezion, Rosh Pina, Rehovot and Nes Ziona. They were financially supported by Baron Edmond James de Rothschild – known in Hebrew as Binyamin *hanadiv* (literally the generous one) – who also sent inspectors to manage their farms.

Harms and Ferry noted that at the time, "Jews already resided in Palestine, some of whom had been there as long as any of the native Arabs" (2012, p. 60). The old Jewish communities were known as the Old Yishuv. During the 19th century many Jews here were self-employed artisans and peddlers. Harms and Ferry elaborated that these Jews "were Arabic-speaking Ottoman citizens who were integrated into the culture and, for all intents and purposes, had decent relations with the native Christians and Muslims (2012, p. 61)." A few of them became middlemen facilitating trade between Arab growers and European industrialists. For a detailed discussion of the Old Yishuv, see Meron (2022).

Baron Edmond James de Rothschild purchased much land from Ottoman landlords and he established the Carmel Winery in Rishon Lezion in 1882. This was the first major Jewish enterprise in the country.

Another baron interested in this part of the world was Baron Amadeus Marie Paul de Piellat, a member of a Catholic religious order. In 1887, he built *Hôpital Français Saint Louis* (Exhibit 20.18) in Jerusalem.

In 1891, in Zichron Yaakov – a community named after Binyamin's father Jakob (*Yaakov* in Hebrew), also known as James (Exhibit 20.19) – Binyamin's Pool was inaugurated, pioneering steam technology to pipe water to water fountains (Exhibit 20.20). In 1892, a branch of Carmel Winery opened (Exhibit 20.21) in Zichron Yaacov.

In 1894 a Viennese journalist, Theodore Herzl, who came from a Hungarian Jewish family, covered the trial of a French Jewish officer, Alfred Dreyfus, accused of betraying military secrets to Germany and sentenced

Exhibit 20.18 *Hôpital Français Saint Louis*; photo © 2021 by Léo-Paul Dana

Exhibit 20.19 Jakob (*Yaakov*) Mayer de Rothschild; photo © 2021 by Léo-Paul Dana

Exhibit 20.20   Binyamin's Pool at Zichron Yaakov; photo © 2021 by Léo-Paul Dana

to a long prison term on the Devil's Island. Affected deeply, Herzl began to ponder the fate of the Jews. Very much under the influence of nationalism in the various parts of the Austro-Hungarian empire, he argued that the Jews had an ancestral homeland from which they were driven out centuries ago. In 1897, he called for a Zionist Congress in Basle that proclaimed that Zionism's goal was a recognised Jewish state. He established the World Zionist Organisation as its governing structure that would authorise him to negotiate with the Ottoman Empire for a concession of land for the purpose of a Jewish state. He also sought the support of the major European powers. In 1901, the World Zionist Organisation created the Jewish National Fund (JNF) to raise funds to purchase land under Ottoman rule and later administered by the British (Exhibit 20.22). Financial assistance came from Jewish philanthropists, including Sir Moses Montefiore. In his novel, *Altneuland* (Herzl, 1902) Herzl envisioned the return of Jews to the land of their origin, still under Ottoman rule.

Exhibit 20.21   One of six underground cellars at Carmel Winery in Zichron Yaakov; photo © 2021 by Léo-Paul Dana

In 1903, the British proposed the creation of a Jewish state in Uganda, but Jews wanted a return to the historical land where they had their roots – not imperialist colonialisation. In 1908, the World Zionist Organisation established an office in Jaffa (Exhibit 20.23) to help newcomers. Among the new immigrants were future founders of Israel, including David Ben Gurion. With Albert Einstein's support, the Technion was established in 1912; it is now the leading university in engineering in Israel (Beyar et al., 2017).

Zionist aspirations were achieved during the first World War when under the command of General Sir Edmund Allenby, the British captured Ottoman territories: They took Beersheba on 31 October 1917, and on 2 November the British Foreign Secretary – Arthur James Balfour – signed the document that came to be known as the Balfour Declaration. (See: https://avalon.law.yale.edu/20th_century/balfour.asp.) A major power, now on the verge of capturing a substantial area of land from the retreating Ottoman Empire, committed itself to sponsor the creation of a national Jewish homeland. The British proceeded to take Gaza on 7 November and Jaffa on 16 November. Finally, the British occupied Jerusalem on 11 December 1917.

Exhibit 20.22   JNF "blue box" to collect funds to purchase land and re-create a country, made in British Mandatory Palestine; photo © 2021 by Léo-Paul Dana

Exhibit 20.23   Aerial view of Jaffa; photo © 2021 by Léo-Paul Dana

The Treaty of Versailles set up a system of mandates, for the administration of former possessions of Germany and of the Ottoman Empire, and to prepare them for future independence. Based on this promise, in 1920 the newly created League of Nations, awarded the mandate over a 120,466 km^2 area from the Mediteranean Sea to Iraq (henceforth Mandatory Palestine), to the British, with the understanding that the mandatory government would implement the Balfour Declaration. On 25 April 1920, the San Remo Conference confirmed the Balfour Declaration's pledge, concerning the establishment of a Jewish national home in Palestine. At this conference, the mandate for Palestine – including the Golan Heights – was presented to the United Kingdom; the basis for the British regime in Palestine was the Balfour Declaration. The mandate was ratified by the Council of the League of Nations on 24 June 1922. France backed the idea of a Jewish homeland in Palestine, and the United States followed suit. Herzl's (1896) book was soon widely read in French (1926).

Yazbak and Weiss wrote, "Haifa became the administrative capital of northern Palestine. The region's largest factories were built in Haifa during the first decade of British rule, Le Grand Moulin, Shemen for soup production, Nesher for cement, al-Hajj Tahir Qaraman's factory for cigarettes and tobacco, as well as many others" (2011, p. 8). A prominent

Exhibit 20.24 Cigarette factory of Karaman, Dick & Salti Ltd., Haifa; photo © 2021 by Léo-Paul Dana

entrepreneur here was Hajj Tahir Karaman (also spelled Qaraman). Here, Tahir Karaman, Hasan Dick and Farah Naser Salti established the largest cigarette factory (Exhibit 20.24) of British Mandatory Palestine, providing jobs to 50 employees (Karkabi and Roitenberg, 2011); the firm produced the Mabrouk brand of cigarettes. Also, Karaman established the Eastern Rice Marketing Company and a factory to produce edible salt; his family was also involved in other firms including the lime furnace and quarry at Mount Carmel (Karkabi and Roitenberg, 2011). Karaman became Deputy Mayor of Haifa in 1935.

Although the League of Nations recognised the legality of the Balfour Declaration, the British were not pressed to conform to it. In 1920, the Mandate for Palestine covered 120,466 km^2. In 1922, most of this (89,213 km^2) was cut off to form the Emirate of Transjordan[3] and Jewish settlement was prohibited there. In 1923, the United Kingdom ceded the Golan Heights to the French Mandate of Syria.

Jerusalem was increasingly developed in British Mandatory Palestine and the city's business sector grew (Exhibit 20.25). In 1924, the High

Exhibit 20.25   Businesses in Jerusalem; photo © 2021 by Léo-Paul Dana

---

[3] Severed from British Mandatory Palestine, Transjordan later became the Hashemite Kingdom of Jordan, the subject of Chapter 19 of this volume.

Commissioner for Palestine opened King George V Avenue, which became a major artery.

In 1930, a British Commission recommended that immigration be curtailed to fit the country's absorptive capacity. Nevertheless, during the mandate, the Jews managed slowly to create their own administrative, educational, medical and financial institutions, trade unions, industrial bases and, above all, advanced agriculture. In 1932, 1934 and 1936, the Levant Fair was held in Tel Aviv (Exhibit 20.26) to promote trade.

The British kept a tight hold on the economy. They went as far as disallowing Bedouin Arabs from collecting salt from Sodom. Meanwhile, camel trade dwindled with the arrival of the automobile. Formerly wealthy people became impoverished. Many went to work for wages in Jewish agricultural settlements. By now, Jews had established institutions including banks and trade unions, economic arrangements ranging from small business to socialist communities and several forms of settlements including *moshavim* (the singular of which is *moshav*), and communal *kibbutzim* (the singular of which is *kibbutz*).

The original ideology of the *kibbutz* involves a communal sharing of work (as per one's ability), profit (as per one's needs), child-rearing and leisure time, on communal grounds. Meals and child-care are provided.

Exhibit 20.26 Tel Aviv; photo © 2021 by Léo-Paul Dana

The *kibbutz* economy was formerly based on agriculture. Today, these establishments have been supplemented by urban *kibbutzim*, most of which provide services (e.g., education) and have reformed their communal structure. Only few *kibbutzim* still adhere to strict communal sharing. *Kibbutzim* now have highly developed facilities, producing a wide variety of products, including plastics, irrigation systems, metal products and even computer components; 60% of the output is exported.

In 1939, the United Kingdom was strategically concerned about retaining, and even strengthening, its friendship with Arabs as it would be a valuable asset to have them as allies on the eve of a war. The MacDonald White Paper of 1939 confirmed the pro-Arab policy of the British, by restricting Jewish immigration and land purchase.

World War II resulted in the extermination of six million European Jews. Following the war, the Jews of British Mandatory Palestine, whose population was 600,000, engaged in anti-British acts eventually forcing the British government to abandon the mandate. In April 1947, having given up India, the United Kingdom asked the United Nations (UN) to propose a solution for the future of Palestine. That body adopted Resolution 181 to partition the country into two states, terminate the mandate and internationalise Jerusalem. Nine percent of the area of the land received by the British as Mandatory Palestine was allotted to the Jews, while the rest would yield the Arabs two states, namely Jordan and Palestine. While the Jews accepted, the Palestinian Arabs and the neighbouring Arabs states rejected the resolution and vowed to undo it by war – that broke out on 30 November 1947, as Egypt, Iraq, Jordan, Lebanon and Syria united to fight against the possibility of a Jewish state. Azzam Pasha, Secretary-General of the Arab League, exclaimed: "This will be a war of extermination and momentous massacre." Egypt occupied the Gaza Strip and Jordan occupied East Jerusalem and the West Bank of the Jordan River. The Israelis were able to withstand the war because they had a well-organised army, a working economy, a robust financial system, reserves of food, a highly motivated population and first-class civilian leadership embodied in its founding father David Ben-Gurion. Thus, British Mandatory Palestine was carved up, but not according to Resolution 181. On 14 May 1948, the State of Israel was declared. War raged on and one of its consequences was the creation of a Palestinian refugee problem.

As a result of hostility against Jews in Arab countries (Browne, 1948), there also came to be Jewish refugees. Between 1948 and 1951, approximately 850,000 Jews were forced to leave Arab countries in which they had lived for millennia, and became Jewish refugees. Many arrived in Israel to escape religious persecution in their countries of origin. Among the newcomers, many identified themselves as Arabic-speaking Jews rather than as Israelis. Julius (2018) argued that the Jewish exodus from Muslim lands and the flight of Palestinian refugees constitute an unfinished population exchange, with Jewish rights yet to be addressed.

In 1949, armistice agreements between Israel and Egypt, Lebanon, Jordan and Syria ended the war, but failed to promote peace; Arab nations violated the agreements, blocked Israeli shipping from using the Suez Canal and the Straits of Tiran, proclaiming an economic boycott of Israel, and launching cross-border raids. Incidents became common and the situation rapidly deteriorated towards another war. Israel's economy survived this massive challenge with the help of world Jewry and German reparations. At the time, the state regulated many sectors, and taxes were high, as military expenditures put a high toll on the economy. The socialist policies of the labour-led government were not conducive to private business.

In 1956, Egypt nationalised the Suez Canal, the result of which was a new conflict – France and the United Kingdom angered by Egypt. It was the start of a second war with Israel, during which Israel captured and occupied the entire Sinai Desert. As a result of American pressure, the Sinai Desert was returned to Egypt in 1957.

In 1957, Israel's flag carrier El Al introduced Bristol 175 Britannia turbo-props (Exhibit 20.27), significantly reducing travel time between Tel Aviv and New York, via London. This aircraft could cross the Atlantic Ocean without fuelling in Newfoundland and it broke speed records. By departing from the great circle route (the shortest distance route) in search

Exhibit 20.27 Bristol 175 Britannia; photo courtesy of Marvin G. Goldman

of better wind conditions, El Al was able to fly between London and New York faster than British Overseas Airways Corporation (predecessor to British Airways), using the same type of aircraft (Goldman, 2008).

Israel's thriving economy, expanding international ties, growing tourism and the completion of its nuclear facility in Dimona alarmed neighbouring states. During the 1960s they created a unified command, absorbed massive quantities of Soviet weapons and sought to halt Israel's waterworks. In January 1965 the newly created Palestine Liberation Organisation (PLO) launched its first military operation against Israel. Also in 1965, a new harbour was built at Eilat.

A third war brewed in 1967, with the re-establishment of the Arab High Command, a joint effort of Iraq, Syria and the United Arab Republic (UAR) – as Egypt was called at the time. On 19 May – at the request of the UAR's President Nasser – the UN began withdrawing its peace-keeping forces from the Gaza Strip, a stretch of land which the UN had allocated to the Palestinians, but which was controlled by Egypt since 1948. Despite the accord confirming that the Gulf of Aqaba was an international waterway, on 22 May 1967, the UAR blocked the Straits of Tiran, preventing all Israeli cargo from reaching or leaving Eilat, Israel's only port on the Red Sea. That day, Israeli Prime Minister Eshkol publicly declared to Cairo and Damascus that Israel had no desire to wage war against them. On 5 June Eshkol sent a communication to Jordan's King Hussein, "We shall not initiate any action whatsoever against Jordan. However, should Jordan open hostilities we shall react with all our might" (Mann, 1973, p. 185). Israel's General Moshe Dayan (Exhibit 20.28) had already declared that a threat of invasion from Jordan would be "a move which would oblige the Israel Army to capture the West Bank of the river Jordan" (Dayan, 1966, p. 36). That which came to be known as the Six-Day War broke out on 5 June 1967. Israel occupied the Gaza Strip, the Golan Heights and the West Bank. On 5 June, Israeli forces cut off the Gaza Strip from Egypt; later that day, Jordan opened a second front, with fighting in Jerusalem. On 6 June the Israelis penetrated the West Bank; that same day, the UN Security Council approved a cease-fire resolution. On 7 June, on the Egyptian front Israeli troops occupied Sharm el Sheikh, thereby putting to an end the blockade of the Gulf of Aqaba. The Israelis reached the Suez Canal on 8 June 1967, and this ended the war with Egypt. During the next two days, Israel took control of the Golan Heights, from which the Syrians had been shelling Israeli civilian targets. Israel annexed eastern Jerusalem, thus reuniting the city (Exhibit 20.29).

Exhibit 20.28   General Moshe Dayan; photo © 2021 by Léo-Paul Dana

Exhibit 20.29   Jerusalem reunited; photo © 2021 by Léo-Paul Dana

Israeli offers to withdraw from the Sinai Desert and the Golan Heights in return for full peace were rebuffed by Egypt and Syria. Israel's new doctrine was to remain in the newly acquired territories until its neighbours would negotiate with it directly for a peace treaty that would include normalisation of relations, open borders, freedom of navigation in international waterways and demilitarised zones.

Various attempts to bring about a resolution of the crisis failed. With the failure of diplomacy, Egypt's new president Anwar Sadat felt he had to engage Israel in a war that would start a political process. His gamble paid off.

Meanwhile, as a result of the Six-Day War, Israel's economy boomed and there was massive immigration from the United States and Europe. The Gaza Strip, the Golan Heights and the West Bank were integrated into the Israeli economy. East Jerusalem (Exhibit 20.30) became increasingly heterogenous, but integration was costly and discontent was on the rise. In May 1973, biophysicist Ephraim Katzir became the president of Israel. Exhibit 20.31 shows him shaking hands with a young graduate.

The state of ceasefire between Israel and its Arab neighbours came to an abrupt end when Syria and Egypt launched an attack on Israeli forces in the Sinai Desert and the Golan Heights on the most sacred Jewish Holy Day, Yom Kippur. At first (6–9 October 1973) Israel was caught by surprise and unprepared, thus suffering many casualties and the loss of weapons.

Exhibit 20.30 In East Jerusalem; photo © 2021 by Léo-Paul Dana

Exhibit 20.31 Ephraim Katzir on left; photo © 2021 by Léo-Paul Dana

The tide turned on the Golan Heights on 10 October and in Sinai on 15 October when Israeli forces crossed the Suez Canal and reached some 101 km from Cairo. At this point, the Soviet Union intervened and demanded an immediate ceasefire that was accepted on 22 October 1973 (Security Council Resolution 338).

The war cost Israel 2,600 lives, and 1.5 years of its national product. Israel was forced to accept the proposals of US Secretary of State Henry Kissinger; Israeli forces withdrew from their previous positions. Prime Minister Yitzhak Rabin, whose policy was to oversee the rehabilitation of the Israeli economy, accepted an agreement with Egypt on further withdrawal in Sinai. During these turbulent times, taxes were high in order to pay for a high national defence budget. With the Labour Party in power, the state was deeply involved in the heavily regulated economy characterised by powerful unions.

Led by Menachem Begin (Exhibit 20.32), the Likud Party was elected in 1977, and the Camp David Accords established the framework for peace with Egypt. A principal aide to the prime minister was Reuben Hecht, an industrialist with a family background in shipping; he had created Dagon Batey-Mamguroth Le-Israel Ltd. He was owner/operator of grain silos, including the Dagon silo (Exhibit 20.33) with a capacity of 100,000 tons at Haifa port.

On 26 March 1979, Prime Minister Menachem Begin signed a peace treaty with Egypt's President Sadat. Under the terms of this accord, Israel returned the entire Sinai Desert to Egypt. Borders (Exhibit 20.34) have since been open for business and leisure travel. Despite the peace treaty with Egypt, the Israeli economy was bleak. Inflation increased from 43% in 1977 to 445% in 1984.

In 1982 Israel found itself engaged in another war, this time against the PLO in Lebanon. Its forces reached Beirut and destroyed PLO infrastructure; the organisation relocated to Tunisia.

By 1984, Israel was on the verge of an economic collapse. The over-protected economy was in need of massive restructuring, so the government launched a comprehensive economic stabilisation programme. This emergency measure included a wage freeze, cuts in public spending and pegging of the national currency to the US dollar. In September 1985, a new currency was introduced; one thousand sheqels became one new sheqel (NIS).

During the first Gulf War, Israel yielded to American demands and did not respond to 39 scud missile attacks that came from western Iraq. During the early 1990s, many Jews arrived from the former Soviet Union; they were mostly well-trained educated people who contributed enormously to Israel's growing hi-tech industries and its medical services. Israel also absorbed 30,000 immigrants from Ethiopia.

Israel began privatising government-held companies in 1991. The first firm to be privatised was the nation's domestic airline, Arkia. In an attempt to increase self-employment among minorities in Israel, the American Jewish Joint Distribution Committee (JDC) initiated a special entrepreneurship

Exhibit 20.32 Menachem Begin; photo © 2021 by Léo-Paul Dana

Exhibit 20.33   Dagon silo, Haifa; photo © 2021 by Léo-Paul Dana

Exhibit 20.34   Border between Egypt and Israel; photo © 2021 by Léo-Paul Dana

and small business programme. The "First Entrepreneurship Course in the Arab Sector" was launched in June 1993. As well, the JDC launched an entrepreneurship course for single mothers.

In September 1993, Israel and the PLO signed their first accord. In 1994, it was agreed to allow free movement of goods and services between Israel, the Gaza Strip and the West Bank. In 1994, Israel and Jordan signed a peace agreement; at the Casablanca Conference, the Arab boycott of Israel crumbled. Fast-growing markets opened up to Israel, while foreign investment rushed in.

As less was being spent on defence, more capital was available for R&D in technology. During the 1990s, Israel became characterised by a high degree of high-tech activity (Almor and Heilbrunn, 2013). According to Frucht-Eren (1996), Israeli researchers were responsible for major contributions, including the discovery of a bacterium that is toxic only to mosquito larvae, and adopted by the World Health Organisation to control malaria; the first demonstration of the effectiveness of deprenyl in treating Parkinson's disease; the first demonstration of the clinical diagnosis of amniocentesis, used to identify abnormalities in a foetus; affinity chromatography; an instrument to scan and sort cells, to detect cancer at an early stage; a strategy to fight parasitic weeds, which has already saved crops in Africa and the Middle East; an encoding technology for protecting computer-generated data, used in smart-cards; crystallisation of the ribosome; and revelation of the three-dimensional structure of the enzyme responsible for nerve impulses. As well, Israeli researchers developed: a new method of transplanting bone marrow from non-compatible donors; a paediatric heart surgery technique; lithium substitutes for psychiatric use; a protein to treat chronic hepatitis and herpes; a medical procedure to treat earthquake victims crushed under rubble; a method to heal shattered bones; and a drug to control multiple sclerosis.

Formerly agricultural cooperatives, *kibbutzim* diversified to produce computer chips and software (Dana, 1999). Heilbrunn (2008) found a significant increase in innovative activity among *kibbutzim*. At *Kibbutz Sde Eliyahu*, farmers use barn owls for pest control of organic produce, a safer solution than pesticides for crops. This project has brought together Israelis, Jordanians and Palestinians supported by the Ministry of Agriculture and the Ministry of Co-operation.

By 2000, *Wired* had ranked Israel as the fourth most influential high-tech hub in the world, after Silicon Valley, Boston and Stockholm-Kista. According to Carmel and de Fontenai (2001), at the dawn of the millennium, Israel had 135 scientists, technicians and engineers in engineering and life sciences per 10,000 employees – compared to 80 per 10,000 in the United States. Coupled with high expenditures on R&D, this transformed Israel into a highly advanced country, with a technology-driven economy, a mere 2% of which is derived from agriculture – although agriculture still provides much to the local market (Exhibit 20.35).

In 2005, a Likud-led coalition headed by Ariel Sharon unilaterally decided to remove all Israeli presence in the Gaza Strip. In 2008, Innovation Africa was founded as a non-profit social enterprise to bring Israeli agricultural, solar, and water innovations to villages in Africa.

As of 2009, under the leadership of Benjamin Netanyahu, Israel focused on building an ecosystem to propel itself into a start-up hub. The Israel Innovation Authority, formerly known as the Office of Chief Scientist, became a central governmental agency responsible for fostering innovation; in 2013, it worked with Nielsen and Partam Hi-Tech, an Israeli venture capital fund, to create the Nielsen Innovate Fund.

As Israel's economy flourished, Fraiberg (2017, p. 353) examined this nation's start-ups as a result of innovation systems or "constellations of resources" (e.g., technologies, knowledge workers, regulations, policies) that increase economic growth. Exports grew, including military

Exhibit 20.35 Making juice from locally-grown oranges; photo © 2021 by
Léo-Paul Dana

hardware, hi-tech products, pharmaceuticals and electronics. Ousset-Krief (2018) reported that Israel had become the world's second innovation hub after Silicon Valley.

Israel's international standing improved substantially and ties with the United States were cemented during President Donald Trump's administration. In November 2019, a team of students from Israel's Technion University won a gold medal in Boston for developing technology to create honey without bees.

In 2020, COVID-19 hit Israel severely. In July that year, Israel Aerospace Industries and Rafael signed an agreement with the Emirati Group 42, to cooperate towards a technology to combat COVID-19. The following month, President Donald Trump announced a deal he had brokered between Israel and the United Arab Emirates (UAE), culminating in an agreement calling for Israel and the UAE to establish mutual diplomatic relations and the inauguration of flights between Tel Aviv and Abu Dhabi. The deal immediately drew support from Bahrain, Egypt and Oman. In September, Israel signed the Abraham Accords signalling peace and cooperation with Bahrain and the UAE. Economic consequences were seen as unlimited. Israel and the UAE agreed to allow 28 direct flights weekly between Tel Aviv and the UAE. This was in addition to unlimited flights to and from Eilat-Ramon Airport. The Migal Galilee Research Institute – a regional R&D centre of the Israeli Science and Technology Ministry – was among the first in Israel to cooperate with the UAE.

In October 2020, Israel announced normalisation of relations with Sudan. In December, an Israeli delegation met with King Mohammed VI of Morocco and full diplomatic relations with Morocco became official. Despite the diplomatic relations with neighbouring countries, there has been tension in the area. More recently, open hostilities between Israel and Hamas in the Gaza Strip emerged in May 2021, which culminated into airstrikes and rocket attacks. After nearly two weeks of fighting, there was a cease-fire.

In June 2021, Naftali Bennett took over as the country's new prime minister. He succeeded Benjamin Netanyahu, who had served as prime minister of Israel from 1996 to 1999 and from 2009 to 2021.

Context for Enterprise and Implications for Doing Business

As do all countries in Western Asia, Israel has its share of bazaars. Among others, these include the Thursday Bedouin Market in Beersheva, the Carmel Market in Tel Aviv, *Mahane Yehuda* operating since the 19th century in Jerusalem and the Talpiot Market in Haifa. Lesser-known markets off the tourist trails include the Ramla market that has been operating since Ottoman times; it is complemented by a travelling market that sets up on Wednesdays in front of the Grand Mosque.

North of Tel Aviv, Rosh Haayin has a large community of Yemenite descent. Deviating from the traditional bazaar where prices are negotiated, the vendors at the Friday Rosh Haayin Market have fixed prices.

While the traditional bazaar as an institution is alive and well in Israel, this country has been focusing on high-tech innovation. Israel has an unusual combination of high growth and a stable economic infrastructure. The state traditionally did relatively little to encourage enterprise or economic growth; rather, private initiatives did so (Dana, 1999).

During the first decades following independence, enterprises were hindered by bureaucratic red tape, punitive tax rates and required payments to the national insurance scheme, *Bituah Leumi.* In 1987, reforms were instituted to help small businesses and corporate tax rates fell from 61% to 45%, but Israel still had neither a venture capitalist network nor loan funds for small firms (Katzenstein, 1991). Bijaoui and Regev (2015) found most entrepreneurs in Israel were ready to cooperate with an open incubator. Beyar et al. (2017) summarised, "The explosive growth in start-up companies is fairly recent in Israel's history. Education, science, and industry have been important elements of Israeli culture even before Israel's birth as a nation, yet the explosive growth is only evident in the past two decades, therefore time is also an important factor. It is difficult to delineate and isolate specific factors and their impact on the growth and success of the life science industry in Israel. Clearly, a combination of factors is key in generating an entrepreneurial culture: hunger for innovation, lack of natural resources, educational and technological infrastructure, infusion of new immigrants who are trained engineers and scientists, efficient government support through incubators and other mechanisms, and the availability of private investments" (p. 2567).

Foreign investors are attracted to Israel's highly educated and motivated workforce and the industrial parks wherein technology is highly concentrated. Incubators such as the Nielsen Innovate Fund have been important in supporting the entrepreneurial eco-system in Israel (Yin, 2017).

The Ministry of Economic Affairs supports numerous technological incubators, including the Meytav Technological Incubator that focuses on the life science sector. It is in Kiryat Shmona, which has an airport (Exhibit 20.36) 2 km away; however, airline service was discontinued as improvements in motorway infrastructure have made driving a very viable alternative to flying.

Exhibit 20.36   Airport at Kiryat Shmona; photo © 2021 by Léo-Paul Dana

The government has a very positive attitude towards foreign investment; foreigners can participate in all sectors of the economy, other than those concerning national defence. The Investment Promotion Centre is a full-service, "one-stop shop" providing information and contacts for firms considering expansion in Israel. To enhance matters, Israel offers tax holidays, tax allowances, tax reductions and accelerated rates of depreciation.

With approximately 200 venture capital firms in Israel, finance is no longer a problematic issue. Furthermore, special financial incentives are offered to industries that contribute to employment and to exports. From its capital in Jerusalem (Exhibit 20.37), the state offers a variety of grants. Among these are grants for developing innovative products (50% of approved expenditures) and for new ventures (66% of approved expenditures). Assistance is available to train employees and to reduce the cost of rent. Besides, the government provides market research grants and subsidies towards the preparation of business plans. The Marketing Encouragement Fund, for instance, provides financial support to enterprises seeking to enlarge their international marketing efforts. Bi-national funds are also

Exhibit 20.37   Jerusalem; photo © 2021 by Léo-Paul Dana

available in Israel, including the Singapore Israel Industrial Research and Development Fund. Complementing the many grants, loans are also readily available. There are several loan funds in Israel, including government, philanthropic and private funds, some described by Dana (1999).

Israel's free port zones are also attractive; firms can benefit from freeport zones in Haifa and Ashdod on the Mediterranean Sea, and Eilat on the Red Sea. Goods imported into Eilat for local use are VAT-exempt. Israel was the first country in the world to have free trade agreements with the European Union and with the three North American Free Trade Agreement (NAFTA) members.

Women in Israel – regardless of religion – were the first in the Middle East to obtain the right to vote. Subsequently, the role of women in Israel changed more rapidly than was the case in neighbouring countries. The *kibbutz* movement contributed to this, as men and women participated equally on a rotational basis in various jobs. Defence considerations also emancipated the women in Israel. Since boys and girls were sent to the army, both men and women gained various skills, that is, assets that have been used in the non-military economy. Women in Israel have on average more academic degrees than do men.

While mainstream women in Israel experienced emancipation, Bedouin men continued to expect their women to fulfil traditional roles; for instance, Bedouin women are expected to bear many children, care for them and even to arrange marriages. Bedouin women are responsible for the upkeep of the home, including baking bread (Exhibit 20.38), cooking, cleaning and sewing – and they also take care of livestock kept near the

Exhibit 20.38 Making bread; photo © 2021 by Léo-Paul Dana

home, and help in harvesting dates and olives. However, many Bedouin women are attending schools of higher education, comprising approximately 75% of the Bedouin students in Israeli universities and colleges (El-Meccawi and Degen, 2016).

Catarivas (1957) argued that the word impossible was not relevant among Hebrew-speakers. This was in the context that Israelis were already doing that which seemed impossible. More than half of Israel is desert, but much was being grown, even in arid conditions. More recently, Israeli innovations improved the quality of life. Drip irrigation was an Israeli invention, Israel built the world's largest water desalination plant, and much agriculture in this country thrives on irrigated water purified by ultra-violet light. While Water-Gen extracts water from the air, Israel also developed technology that allows potatoes to be irrigated with salt water. Israel is the only country in the world with a net gain in its number of trees. Israeli technology allows blind people to see virtually (Dana, 2018); Israel leads the world in medical patents. The PillCam (camera in a pill that is swallowed) for endoscopy was invented in Israel; entrepreneur Gavriel Meron was the founder and CEO of Given Imaging (now Medtronic) the company behind this innovation. Israel was also the first to deliver insulin in a pill. In Haifa, MeMed is a point-of-care medical device that has regulatory approval, which determines within minutes if an infection is bacterial or viral. This innovation will greatly reduce the inappropriate use of antibiotics and thus lower the risk of antibiotic-resistant microbes. As the late Lord Rabbi Jonathan Sacks suggested, one can change the world not by the idea of power but by the power of ideas and that's what Judaism is about; Israelis are people whose heroes are teachers, whose citadels are houses of study and whose passion is learning.

Towards the Future

During its first 50 years of independence, the State of Israel transformed itself from a poor, agriculturally based country into a world leader in innovation and technology development. Reflecting confidence in this country, annual investments by foreign nationals in Israel rose from $4.6 billion in 2009 to $21.8 billion in 2018 (see: https://investinisrael. gov.il/HowWeHelp/downloads/The%20economic%20impact%20of%20 Foreign%20Investments%20in%20Israel.pdf).

During its 50th year of existence, Israel exported software amounting to $1.5 billion. Since then, international agencies have upgraded the financial and business rankings of Israel. While financial investments are being prompted by opportunities in local capital markets, industrial investments are being attracted to the high level of technological skills available in Israel. Among successful investors are Apple, AT&T, IBM, Intel, IBM, Motorola, Microsoft and Phillips.

Israel has an impressive number of engineers per capita. While the United States has 8 engineers per 1,000 workers, Japan has 7.5 and Israel has 14 qualified engineers per 1,000 workers. While the nation is host to important foreign investors, local new ventures are highly visible in its export-oriented high-tech industry. Israel's economy is being led by scientific and industrial R&D. In 2019, high-tech products and services accounted for 45.6% of Israeli exports.

A favourable environment for enterprise – coupled with a highly educated workforce and free trade agreements – has been beneficial for the economy; yet, economic development in Israel has been hindered by the need for heavy defence expenditures. Israel could not fully benefit from its potential. Peace with all neighbours would allow efforts to be more focused on the economy. Diplomatic relations with neighbours can open up new markets. When Israelis sub-contract to enterprises in other countries, this is beneficial in at least two ways. Firstly, this creates employment in host countries, enhancing the buying power of people who can then be better positioned to purchase Israeli products. As well, producing in low-cost environments would allow for Israeli products to become increasingly competitive in world markets; lower costs would lead to lower prices, which, in turn, would lead to more demand, allowing for greater opportunities of scale, and further cost reductions.

Entrepreneurial ecosystems are defined as the interacting elements that foster new firm creation in a specific context (Neck et al., 2004) and research on entrepreneurial ecosystems contributes to our understanding of entrepreneurship (Neck et al., 2004), while literature focuses on gaining an understanding of components within these systems (Cohen, 2006). Likewise, the Global Startup Ecosystem Ranking provides a framework to understand entrepreneurship (Compass, 2017) and, the entrepreneurship ecosystem in Tel Aviv ranked sixth in the world in 2020.

Much literature profiles successful ecosystems (Feld, 2012; Saxenian, 1994); while this is valuable, it is important to also recognise the dark side. The Wheel of Life in Israel, a broad-based index, outlines Israeli's performance relative to other nations along five dimensions: (i) innovation; (ii) science and technology; (iii) economy; (iv) society, government and education; and (v) environment and energy (Maital, 2014). With respect to innovation, Israel scored high on most measures. While Israel is a world leader in wastewater treatments (ranking fourth), the country lags in renewable energy (ranking 45th). Exhibit 20.39 shows the coal-burning Orot Rabin electricity-generating plant that is being converted to use natural gas.

Despite successes, Israel has been unable to fully benefit from its creativity and innovations. This is in line with the Aristotelean perspective that suggests happiness and success are a function of maintaining the virtues at the mean between the two extremes of deficiency and excess (Nussbaum,

Exhibit 20.39 Coal-burning electricity-generating plant outside Hadera;
photo © 2021 by Léo-Paul Dana

1995, 2004). Grant and Schwartz (2011) further argue that that once positive activities reach inflection points, their effects turn negative.

Calling Israel the "start-up nation", Senor and Singer (2009) suggest that mandatory military service contributes to Israeli entrepreneurial culture because military personnel have minimal guidance from the top to solve problems and, therefore, must improvise. Additionally, the Israeli immigration policy and national culture, which values risk-taking, may contribute to its start-up success. Indeed, the term "start-up nation" is appropriate.

According to Giora Shalgi, a researcher from the Samuel Neaman Institute, Israel should be more appropriately named the "exit nation" since creativity and innovation are transported abroad before Israelis benefit. Perhaps that was the case at the time, but no longer so. Israel is facing the future as a "scale up nation" (Stub 2021).

References

Akirav, Osnat (2019), "The Lioness from Peki'in," *International Journal of Entrepreneurship and Small Business* 37 (2), pp. 232–249.

Almor, Tamar, and Sibylle Heilbrunn (2013), "Entrepreneurship in Israel: Theory and Practice," *American Journal of Entrepreneurship* 6 (2), pp. 16–36.

Ben-Zvi, Izhak (1966), "Under Ottoman Rule 1517–1917," in David Ben-Gurion, ed., *The Jews in Their Land,* London: Aldous House.

Beyar, Rafael, Benny Zeevi, and Gideon Rechavi (2017), "Israel: A Start-up Life Science Nation," *Lancet* 389, pp. 2563–2569.

Bijaoui, Ilan, and David Regev (2015), "Entrepreneurship and Viral Development in Rural Western Negev in Israel," *Journal of Research in Marketing and Entrepreneurship* 17 (1), pp. 54–66.

Browne, Mallory (1948), "Jews in Grave Danger in all Muslim Lands: Nine Hundred Thousand in Africa and Asia Face Wrath of Their Foes," *New York Times,* 16 May, Section E, p. 4.

Bussgang, Jeffrey, and Omri Stern (2015), "How Israeli Start-ups Can Scale," *Harvard Business Review,* September 10, (Retrieved from https://hbr.org/2015/09/how-israeli-startups-can-scale, accessed 18 June 2021)

Carmel, Erran, and Catherine de Fontenai (2001), "Israel's Silicon Wadi: The Forces behind Cluster Formation," (SIEPR Discussion Paper No. 000–40), Stanford Institute for Economic Policy Research, (Retrieved from https://siepr.stanford.edu/publications/working-paper/israels-silicon-wadi-forces-behind-cluster-formation, accessed 18 June 2021)

Catarivas, David (1957), *Israel,* Paris: Editions du Seuil.

Cohen, Boyd (2006), "Sustainable Valley Entrepreneurial Ecosystems," *Business Strategy and the Environment* 15 (1), pp. 1–14.

Coleman, Alison (2018), "Tel Aviv Tech Startups to Watch in 2018," *Forbes,* March 6, (Retrieved from https://www.forbes.com/sites/alisoncoleman/2018/03/06/the-tel-aviv-tech-startups-to-watch-in-2018/#54270ee26011, accessed 3 January 2021)

Compass (2017), *The Global Start-Up Ecosystem Ranking 2017,* (Retrieved from https://startupgenome.com/reports/global-startup-ecosystem-report-2017 accessed 23 September 2021)

Dana, Léo-Paul (1999), "Small Business in Israel," *Journal of Small Business Management* 37 (4), pp. 73–79.

Dana, Léo-Paul (2000), *Economies of the Eastern Mediterranean Region: Economic Miracles in the Making,* Singapore, London & Hong Kong: World Scientific.

Dana, Léo-Paul (2018), "Computers for the Blind," in Robert D. Hisrich and Veland Ramadani, eds., *Entrepreneurial Marketing: A Practical Management Approach,* Cheltenham: Edward Elgar, pp. 97–98.

Dayan, Moshe (1966), *Diary of the Sinai Campaign,* London: Wiedenfield & Nicolson.

Degen, A. Allan, Shaher El-Meccawi, and Michael Kam (2019), "The Changing Role of Camels Among the Bedouin of the Negev," *Human Ecology* 47 (2), pp. 193–204.

El-Meccawi, Shaher, and A. Allan Degen (2016), "Higher Education among Bedouin of the Negev: Tel Sheva as a Case Study," *Nomadic Peoples* 20 (1), pp. 88–107.

Feld, Brad (2012), *Startup Communities: Building an Entrepreneurial Ecosystem in your City,* Hoboken, NJ: John Wiley & Sons.

Firro, Kais M. (2005), "Druze Maqamat (Shrines) in Israel: From Ancient to Newly-Invented Tradition," *British Journal of Middle Eastern Studies* 32 (2), pp. 217–239.

Fraiberg, Steven (2017), "Start-up Nation: Studying Transnational Entrepreneurial Practices in Israel's Start-up Ecosystem," *Journal of Business and Technical Communication* 31, pp. 350–388.

Frucht-Eren, Leora (1996), *Israel: A Scientific Profile,* London: The British Council.

Goldman, Marvin G. (2008), *El Al: Israel's Flying Star,* Sandpoint, Idaho: Airways International.

Grant, Adam M., and Barry Schwartz (2011), "Too Much of a Good Thing: The Challenge and Opportunity of the Inverted U," *Perspectives on Psychological Science* 6 (1), pp. 61–76.

Gurau, Calin, Léo-Paul Dana, and Erez Katz-Volovelsky (2020), "Spanning Transnational Boundaries in Industrial Markets," *Industrial Marketing Management* 89, pp. 389–401.

Harms, Gregory, and Todd M. Ferry (2012), *The Palestine-Israel Conflict: A Basic Introduction,* 3rd edition, Ann Arbor: Pluto Press.

Harold, Frederick (1892), *The New Exodus,* London: C.P. Putnam's Sons.

Hartz, Brian (2018), "From Israel, with Innovation," *Business Observer,* February 16, (Retrieved from https://www.fiba.io/press/2197/, accessed 23 September 2021)

Heilbrunn, Sibylle (2008), "Factors Influencing Entrepreneurial Intensity in Communities," *Journal of Enterprising Communities: People and Places in the Global Economy* 2 (1), pp. 37–51.

Herzl, Theodore (1896), *The Jewish State: An Attempt to Solve the Jewish Question,* Leipzig & Vienna: Verlags-Buchhandlung.

Herzl, Theodore (1902), *Altneuland,* Leipzig: Hermann Seemann Nachfolger.

Herzl, Théodore (1926), *L'Etat Juif: Essai d'une Solution de la Question Juive,* Paris: Lipschutz.

Jamrisko, Michelle, and Wei Lu (2018), "The U.S. Drops Out of the Top 10 in Innovation Ranking," *Bloomberg,* January 22, (Retrieved from https://www.bloomberg.com/news/articles/2018-01-22/south-korea-tops-global-innovation-ranking-again-as-u-s-falls, accessed 5 January 2021)

Johnson, Holly (2020), "The World's Most Innovative Countries in 2020," *CEO Magazine,* March, (Retrieved from https://www.theceomagazine. com/business/innovation-technology/most-innovative-countries-2020/)

Julius, Lyn (2018), *Uprooted: How 3000 Years of Jewish Civilization in the Arab World Vanished Overnight,* Elstree, United Kingdom: Vallentine Mitchell.

Karkabi, Waleed, and Adi Roitenberg (2011), "Arab-Jewish Architectural Partnership in Haifa during the Mandate Period: Qaraman and Gerstel Meet on the 'Seam Line'," in Mahmoud Yazbak and Yfaat Weiss, eds., *Haifa Before & After 1948. Narratives of a Mixed City,* Dordrecht: Institute for Historical Justice and Reconciliation and Republic of Letters Publishing, pp. 43–68.

Katzenstein, Liora (1991), "The Ten Commandments for the Beginning Entrepreneurs," in John C. Oliga, ed., *Proceedings of the ENDEC World Conference on Entrepreneurship and Innovative Change,* Singapore: Nanyang Technological University, pp. 142–143.

Maital, Shlomo (2014), "Start-up Nation's Dark Side," *The Jerusalem Report*, 22 September, pp. 36–39.

Mann, Peggy (1973), *Golda,* New York: Washington Square Press.

Meron, Orly C. (2022), "The Economy of the Sephardic Old Yishuv in Eretz Yisrael, 1830–1917," in Yaron Ben-Naeh and Michal Held Delaroza, eds., *The Sephardim in Erets Israel: Jewish Communities of the East in the 19th and 20th Centuries,* Jerusalem: Ben Zvi Institute and The Ministry of Education.

Neck, Heidi M., Gary D. Meyer, Boyd Cohen, and Andrew C. Corbett (2004), "An Entrepreneurial System View of New Venture Creation," *Journal of Small Business Management* 42 (2), pp. 190–208.

Nussbaum, Martha Craven (1995), *Poetic Justice,* Boston: Beacon Press.

Nussbaum, Martha Craven (2004), "Positive Psychology and Ancient Greek Virtue Ethics," paper presented at The Philosophical History of the Virtues Conference, University of Pennsylvania, Philadelphia, September.

Ousset-Krief, Annie (2018), "Israel a la Pointe des Decouvertes Scientifiques," *Magazine LVS*, pp. 26–27.

Saxenian, Anna Lee (1994), *Regional Advantage: Culture and Competition in Silicon Valley and Route 128,* Cambridge, Massachusetts: Harvard University.

Senor, Dan, and Saul Singer (2009), *Start-up Nation: The Story of Israel's Economic Miracle.* New York: Twelve.

Stub, Zev (2021), "With Huge Tech Growth, Israel's Start-up Nation Becomes Scale-up Nation," *The Jerusalem Post,* 8 February, https://www.jpost.com/jpost-tech/with-huge-tech-growth-israels-start-up-nation-becomes-scale-up-nation-658247 accessed 18 June 2021.

Yazbak, Mahmoud (2017), "The Birth of the Jerusalem Sanjak 1864–1914: Administrative and Social Impacts," *Filistin Ara tirmalari Dergisi* 2, pp. 32–57.

Yazbak, Mahmoud, and Yfaat Weiss, eds. (2011), *Haifa Before & After 1948. Narratives of a Mixed City,* Dordrecht: Institute for Historical Justice and Reconciliation and Republic of Letters Publishing.

Yin, David (2017), "What Makes Israel's Innovation Ecosystem So Successful," *Forbes Asia,* (Retrieved from https://www.forbes.com/sites/davidyin/2017/01/09/what-makes-israels-innovation-ecosystem-so-successful/?sh=595e9ab270e4, accessed 31 December 2020)

Chapter 21

The Context for Business in Palestine

Aliaa El Shoubaki & Léo-Paul Dana

Abstract: For centuries, Palestinian lands were part of the Ottoman Empire. With the defeat of the Ottomans during World War I, the British occupied this region. The Principal Allied Powers subsequently gave the British full powers of legislation and of administration over Mandatory Palestine to create a national home for the Jewish people. In 1922, the land in question was divided. The eastern part, most of British Mandatory Palestine, was made into a new country, Jordan. In 1923, the United Kingdom ceded the Golan Heights to the French mandate. War broke out in 1947, leading to the occupation of Gaza by Egypt. In 1950, Abdullah annexed the portion of Palestine called the West Bank. In 1967, the Gaza Strip and the West Bank came under Israeli occupation. In 1993, the Oslo Accord with Israel gave Palestinians rule over the Gaza Strip and in Jericho, on the West Bank. The Palestinian Authority became the administrative body empowered to govern the Palestinian population and began its administration in May 1994. This chapter is about Palestinian territories, recognised by some countries as the State of Palestine.

Keywords: Gaza Strip, West Bank, Palestine, Palestinians

Introduction

The term Palestine was first used to describe a district of Syria, between Egypt and Phoenicia (today's Lebanon). As a political entity, the term was first used by the British and this included all the land that is now Jordan.

Palestine's location and heritage made it desired by many, as far as recorded history can go. After four centuries of Ottoman rule, during World War I vast areas of the Ottoman Empire came under British control. In 1920, the Mandate for Palestine covered 120,466 km^2. In 1922, most of this (89,213 km^2) was cut off to form the Emirate of Transjordan, today's Kingdom of Jordan (see Chapter 19). In 1948, the State of Israel (see Chapter 20) was founded in the spirit of the Balfour Declaration of 1917 and a United Nations (UN) resolution from 1947. Following the Camp David Accords signed in 1978, the Oslo Agreement ratified in Washington, DC, in 1993 and the Oslo II Accord ratified in Taba, Egypt, in 1995, a Palestinian Authority was established in the territories of the West Bank of the River Jordan (that had been annexed by Jordan in 1950), and also in the Gaza Strip (occupied by Egypt from 1949 to 1967). Today there are about 10 million self-declared Palestinians, most of them outside of Palestine, with significant communities in neighbouring countries and in North America. Arabic is their main language. On a global level, Palestinians are highly educated and financially savvy. Palestinian women are entre-preneurial. Compared to people in several Arab countries, Palestinians are significantly higher than average in terms of the Human Capital Index, Human Development Index (HDI), social stability and innovation.

Enshassi et al. (2007) examined labour productivity in the Gaza Strip; Enshassi et al. (2009) focused on factors affecting construction projects in the Gaza Strip. Sabella et al. (2015) studied management practices in Palestinian hospitals. Setti (2017) compared entrepreneurial intentions of Palestinian youth elsewhere. However, there is little written about the con-text for business in either the Gaza Strip or the West Bank. This chapter will attempt to bring information about the context for business there.

The Palestinian economy is dominated by services where tourism is especially attractive and knowledge-intensive services are bourgeoning. The industrial sector has promising prospects with the potential of avail-able trade agreements.

Historical Context[1]

The official Palestinian narrative traces their origins to the Canaanites, who settled this land prior to the Israelite conquest 4,500 years ago, but the

---

[1] Data is from UN agencies or Palestinian government and research agencies, unless another reference is mentioned.

hard evidence suggests that *Palestina* is the name given by Roman emperor Adrianus to the annihilated territory of Judea; others trace it to the Late Bronze Age, to the geographic region between the Mediterranean Sea and the Jordan River, in addition to other neighbouring lands (Masalha, 2020). For centuries, this region was an important trade hub for international commerce. Its geopolitical location and cultural and historical heritage of Palestine made it the envy of many.

This part of the world has experienced the Bronze Age, the Iron Age, Egyptian, Israelite, Assyrian, Hellenistic, Roman, Byzantine, Crusader, Umayyad, Abbasid, Fatimid, Ayyubid, Mamluk and Ottoman periods. Ancient biblical cities that are now under Palestinian jurisdiction include Jericho, considered the oldest town in the world (established in approximately 9600 BC) conquered from the Canaanites by Joshua and the children of Israel), and Hebron (from 4500 BC) home to the Tomb of Patriarchs: Abraham, Isaac and Jacob and the matriarchs, Sarah, Rebecca and Leah thereof, and subsequently King David's capital before Jerusalem. Exhibit 21.1 features a settlement south of Hebron, within the Hebron Governorate.

Exhibit 21.1 Outside Yatta, Hebron Governorate, West Bank; photo © 2021 by
A. Allan Degen

For Christians, the most significant biblical city under Palestinian jurisdiction is Bethlehem (Exhibit 21.2), on the West Bank. Established in approximately 1400 BC, it was the home of Jesse, father of King David of Israel, and birthplace of Jesus. Whereas pork meat is rarely sold in neighbouring countries, pork is available here (see Exhibit 21.3) since a significant part of the local population is Christian.

The coastal land between Egypt and Israel, along the Mediterranean coast, is referred to as the Gaza Strip, named after its principal city and port, Gaza. It is believed that Gaza was founded 4,000 years ago, by frank-incense traders from Yemen. The walled city overlooked fertile land, which produced almonds, barley, olives and vegetables. While Gaza prospered with trade, its wealth made it the envy of many, and this prompted continuous invasions. Gaza was ruled by Egyptians, Persians, Babylonians, Greeks, Seleucids, Syrians, Assyrians, Judaeans, Romans, Sejuk Turks, Muslim Arabs and Crusaders. With the spread of Islam, camel caravans from North Africa passed through Gaza, on their way to Mecca for *haj* – pilgrimage. In contrast to the two-humped Bactrian camel, the Arabian camel (the dromedary) has one hump, as shown in Exhibit 21.4.

The Gazan traders provided provisions for thousands of pilgrims who stocked up on almonds, apples, barley, corn, dates, figs, lemons, olives,

Exhibit 21.2 Bethlehem; photo © 2021 by Léo-Paul Dana

Exhibit 21.3 Pork for sale; photo © 2021 by Léo-Paul Dana

oranges, vegetables, watermelons and wheat. Exhibit 21.5 features an old olive tree.

Led by Richard the Lion-Hearted, the Crusaders destroyed Gaza's city walls and built a church, which was later refurbished to become a mosque. Following Crusader rule, Gaza was governed by the Egyptian Mamelukes and then by the Ottoman Empire, the United Kingdom, Egypt, the United Arab Republic (UAR) and Israel.

For centuries, until World War I, Gaza was an important shipping hub for international commerce. As the Ottoman Empire weakened, the prominence of Gaza faded. The British occupied Gaza on 7 November 1917.

Formerly Ottoman lands from the Mediterranean Sea to the Persian Gulf came under British control in 1920 as prescribed by the Sykes–Picot Agreement, a treaty between the United Kingdom and France partitioning and allotting mandates over the territories of the expected-to-collapse Ottoman empire. The map of the Middle East that was re-drawn then caused much of the current political tensions in the region.

Exhibit 21.4   Dromedary (Arabian camel) *Camelus dromedarius;*
photo © 2021 by Léo-Paul Dana

In 1920, the League of Nations met in Italy and signed an agreement that the land from the Mediterranean Sea to the Iraqi border be put aside for a Jewish state. In light of the Arab opposition to the Balfour Declaration – the British commitment to establish a national home for the Jewish people in their ancestral homeland – the British decided to reduce the planned borders of the future Jewish state only to the area between the Mediterranean Sea and the Jordan River. Thus, the area of British Mandatory Palestine was greatly reduced by carving out Transjordan, covering the mandate's area east of the Jordan River. In 1946, this became the Hashemite Kingdom of Jordan (see Chapter 19).

A narrow western strip of British Mandatory Palestine, Judaea & Samaria, west of the Jordan River, remained under British mandate with British military presence until 1948. Metzer (1998) studied the economy of British Mandatory Palestine, home to Christian and Muslim Palestinians descending primarily from: (i) Muslim invaders from when

Exhibit 21.5 Old olive tree; photo © 2021 by Léo-Paul Dana

the Byzantines were conquered by Muslims during the 7th century (see Gil, 1992); (ii) subsequent Arab immigrants; and (iii) local converts to Islam. British Mandatory Palestine was also home to Arabic-speaking indigenous Jews whose families had lived here since Roman times, also Arabic-speaking Jews with origins in various Muslim countries, some Ladino-speaking Sephardic migrants from the European Ottoman provinces, and finally Yiddish-speaking Ashkenazi migrants who failed to integrate well with the local population. There were also Bahai, Druze, Karaite and Samaritan minorities.

Since the late 19th century, following the Ottoman land reforms including official land ownership registration, many Arabs sold land to Jews; this is the focus of Stein (1984) who wrote, "The suggestion in 1937 that Palestine be partitioned into separate Jewish and Arab states expanded Zionist land-purchase objectives…an analysis of Jewish land acquisition and Arab land sales makes it seem quite evident that a formidable Jewish national territory was necessary and was already present in Palestine in 1939."

During the British mandate, some European Jews survived persecution by the Nazis by escaping to British Mandatory Palestine, and joining the Arabic-speaking indigenous Jewish community established here for millennia. Inter-ethnic conflict rose as the newcomers did not speak Arabic and did not integrate into the local population. After World War II, survivors of Nazi concentration camps also arrived.

In 1947, what remained of British Mandatory Palestine (after most of the original British Mandatory Palestine became Jordan) was further partitioned by a United Nations proposal to create two new entities – a second Arab state and a Jewish state. According to the United Nations partition plan of 29 November, biblical Judaea, Samaria and the Gaza region (known as the Gaza Strip as of 1949) would become a Palestinian state upon the termination of the British mandate no later than 1 August 1948 (Ben-Dror, 2016). While the Jews accepted the United Nations partition plan, the Arabs rejected it and started hostilities. Following the declaration of the establishment of the State of Israel in May 1948, the armies of five Arab nations invaded the Jewish state. The Palestinian pound was withdrawn from circulation by the end of 1948.

Although provisions had been made for a Palestinian state, in 1949 the Gaza Strip was occupied by Egypt and this land remained annexed to Egypt's successor, the United Arab Republic (UAR) until 1967. In 1950, Jordan annexed Judaea and Samaria – collectively known as the West Bank.

Christians, Muslims and Jews including hundreds of thousands of Jewish repatriated refugees mainly from Arab new nation-states, who were persecuted and compelled to abandon their livelihoods and assets,

within the boundaries of Israel were given Israeli nationality. Those in the Gaza Strip found themselves ruled by Egypt, and those in the West Bank by Jordan. Hundreds of thousands of Palestinians sought refugee in other countries. The first Palestinian exodus became known as the *Nakba*. The new state's bureaucracy decreed the Custodian of Absentee Property allowing to seize the property and assets of the Palestinians who left, to freeze and transfer the Palestinian bank accounts to the custodian's account (Mitter, 2014).

The Palestine Liberation Organisation (PLO) was established in 1964, with the goal to achieve Palestinian self-determination and diaspora return, by force if necessary. Also in 1964, the Hotel Jerusalem Intercontinental (see Exhibit 21.6) was opened in Jerusalem. This is where the PLO held its first Palestine National Council in May 1964. The hotel is now known as the Seven Arches Hotel.

Until 1967, agriculture (Exhibit 21.7) was the backbone of the Palestinian economy, whether under Egyptian or Jordanian rule. Pastoralism was an important activity. Being annexed to Jordan, the economy of the West Bank was integrated to that of Jordan, with the Jordanian dinar being legal tender. While Pepsi products were not available in Israel, they were available in the West Bank (see Exhibit 21.8). The ceasefire

Exhibit 21.6 Venue of the first Palestine National Council; photo © 2021 by Léo-Paul Dana

Exhibit 21.7   Hand-harvesting wheat, West Bank; photo © 2021 by A. Allan Degen

Exhibit 21.8   Pepsi-Cola; photo © 2021 by Léo-Paul Dana

boundary between the West Bank and Israel was closed and Jerusalem was a city divided by the Green Line.

> *Before 1967…we had the land but did not utilise it. No factories, little trade and no tourism.*
>
> –Dr. Mohammad A. Sarsour
> General Manager, Beit El-Mal Holdings

In 1967, as an aftermath of the Six-Day War, Gaza and the West Bank fell under Israeli occupation. Palestinians from these territories were allowed to seek employment in Israel. Those in Jerusalem were given Israeli citizenship, regardless of religion. The Palestinian economy was integrated into that of Israel. From 1967 until the 1990s, one-third of the labour force commuted to Israel for employment. Israel is visible in Exhibit 21.9, photographed from the West Bank; distance is not an issue. Between 1968 and 1970, under Israeli administration, per capita Gross National Product (GNP) in the Gaza Strip rose by 46%.

After 1967, the economy of the Palestinian people shifted away from agriculture, as Palestinians found wages in Israel more attractive than farming in the Gaza Strip or the West Bank. Both Israeli and Jordanian currencies flowed freely in the West Bank. Under Israeli rule, Palestinians spread out beyond the geographic scope of their ancestral lands and into the Sinai Desert. The sprawling town of Rafah came to include a southern suburb, known as Mukhayim Canada, technically in the Sinai. Its residents typically went to work in Israel, and their children to school in the Gaza Strip. This was so until 25 August 1982, when Israel completed its hand-over of the Sinai to Egypt, a requisite for peace with Egypt; the international border then cut through Rafah, as coils of razor wire sliced the city in two, leaving the 4,500 Palestinians of Mukhayim Canada on the Egyptian

Exhibit 21.9 Close neighbours; photo © 2021 by Léo-Paul Dana

side of the border. This day came to be known as *youm iswid* – "black day". Thereafter, Mukhayim Canada remained cut off from the Gaza Strip by *El Silik* – the wire. Unable to physically get to work in Israel, 70% of adult men in Mukhayim Canada were idle, and the Egyptians did not allow them to seek employment in Egypt. Only later, Israel provided land and the Government of Canada provided financial support for some families to relocate in the Gaza Strip. Nevertheless, there remained Palestinian refugees in various countries.

In 1987, Palestinians protested against Israeli occupation in sustained series of terror attacks that became known as the first *Intifiada*. In 1988, Jordan's King Hussein ceded all territorial claims to the West Bank, to the PLO. In November, that year, Yasser Arafat[2] unilaterally declared the establishment of the State of Palestine, covering the Gaza Strip and the West Bank, though it was under Israeli jurisdiction at that time.

During the Gulf War of 1990, Palestinian support for Iraq led to a deterioration of relations between the Palestinians and the West. In July 1991, the Lebanese Army – backed by Syrian forces – forced the PLO to retreat from its positions in southern Lebanon.

In 1993, the Oslo Accord with Israel gave Palestinians rule over the Gaza Strip and in Jericho, on the West Bank. The Palestinian Authority became the administrative body empowered to govern the Palestinian population and began its administration in May 1994.

On 13 September 1993, the PLO signed a peace agreement with Israel. In accordance with the Israel–PLO Declaration of Principle, Israel's Prime Minister, Yitzhak Rabin allowed Palestinians self-rule in the Gaza Strip and in Jericho on the West Bank. In accordance with the Oslo Accord of 1993, the Palestinian Authority became the administrative body empowered to govern Palestinian population centres. Palestinian leadership subsequently moved from Tunisia to the Middle East, and the Palestinian Authority began its administration in May 1994.

In March 1995, the Development & Planning Department, in Gaza, established the Small and Micro Enterprise Training Programme, providing training courses in a variety of subjects. Initially, courses ranged from 15 to 24 hours in duration. Later, longer courses were introduced. In consideration of the cost involved in bringing in trainers from abroad, it was decided that most courses be taught by local trainers. Over time, the range of topics was enlarged. Over time, the range of courses was increased.

---

[2] Born in Cairo, in 1929, Mohammed Yasser Abdel Rahman Abdel Raouf Arafat al-Qudwa al-Husseini, commonly known as Yasser Arafat and locally as Abu Ammar, was a Palestinian political leader. He chaired the Palestine Liberation Organisation (PLO) from 1969 to 2004 and served as President of the Palestinian National Authority (PNA) from 1994 to 2004.

Each course attracts a symbolic participation fee. Most participants were business owners. Palestinians nevertheless expressed concern that their educational background did not reflect the needs of enterprises, either in the Gaza Strip or on the West Bank. It was pointed out, for instance, that the universities in the Gaza Strip – El-Azhar University, Islamic University, Open University and the College of Education – were not enterprise-based. For this reason, recent efforts have been focused on training individuals for enterprise, especially self-employment.

Negotiations, formalised in the Paris Protocol, established contractually the economic arrangements and relations between the Palestinian and Israeli people. In September 1995, the peace agreement expanded with the withdrawal of Israeli troops from more areas in the West Bank. This came to be known as the Oslo II Accord (see Exhibit 21.10). That same month, Yasser Arafat sent greetings of *Shana Tova* to "our cousins the Jews and the Israeli people".

Until 1996, banks in the Gaza Strip and on the West Bank focused on short-term loans. To fill the need for longer-term investments, the World Bank accepted to enter a joint venture with existing banks, to create the

The Government of the State of Israel and the Palestine Liberation Organisation (hereafter the PLO) the representative of the Palestinian people;
Within the framework of the Middle East peace process...
Reaffirming their determination to put an end to decades of confrontation...
While recognising mutual legitimate and political rights ...
Recognising that the peace process and the new era it has created ... are irreversible ...
Recognising that the aim of Israel-Palestinian negotiations ... is ...
heading to a permanent settlement ...
Desirous of putting into effect the
Declaration of Principles on Interim Self-Government Arrangements
Signed at Washington DC, on September 13, 1993 ...
Hereby agree as follows:

CHAPTER 1: *Transfer of Authority.* Israel shall transfer powers and responsibilities ... from the Israeli Military Government and its Civil Administration to the Palestinian Council.

CHAPTER 2: *Land.* The two sides view the West Bank and the Gaza Strip as a single territorial unity, the integrity and status of which will be preserved.
Signed in Washington DC, September 28, 1995

Exhibit 21.10   Excerpt from the Oslo II Accord

Arab Palestinian Bank for Investment, based in Ramallah, with a liaison office in Gaza. This was a joint project involving the Arab Bank (based in Jordan), the International Finance Corporation (subsidiary of the World Bank), the German Investment and Development Company (DEG) and the Enterprise Investment Company. Among its first concerns was a US$23 million project to develop handicraft work.

In 1996, a business centre was established in Ramallah to promote private enterprise development among Palestinians. This was an initiative of the European Union, in association with the Palestinian Authority. With the objective of establishing sustainable export-oriented industrial sectors, cost-sharing support was offered to Palestinian firms to develop their products to internationally competitive standards.

In September 1996, the Expatriates Affairs Department of the Ministry of Planning and International Co-operation sponsored a convention for Palestinians living abroad. The emphasis was on encouraging Palestinians working abroad to invest in the Gaza Strip and in the West Bank. A representative of the Ministry of Labour announced that investors will be allowed to settle in the territories; it was felt that Palestinians should not simply invest money but also time and effort in managing local firms. A representative of the Ministry of Economy & Trade undertook to facilitate importing.

In October 1998, Israel and the Palestinian Authority signed the Wye Accord. In accordance with the conditions of this agreement, the Palestine National Council voted to remove anti-Israel clauses from the PLO's charter.

In 2000, another major Palestinian uprising took place, known as the Second *Intifada*. The Palestinian economy experienced severe structural shocks. In October 2000, the Windmill Hotel owned by a prominent Gazan entrepreneur – Basil Eleiwa – was burned down by Islamic extremists, because it was serving alcoholic beverages.

According to a unilateral disengagement plan, Israel completely withdrew from the Gaza Strip in 2005. Since 2007, two Palestinian territories, namely the Gaza Strip and the West Bank, have been ruled by rival factions. The Gaza Strip has been governed by Hamas, an Islamist party. The West Bank has been governed by the Fatah wing of the PLO. Repeated attempts to reconcile the two have failed. There has actually been divergence since then. For example, until 2012, motor vehicle registration plates had the same form in the Gaza Strip as in the West Bank (Exhibit 21.11), but that year authorities of the Gaza Strip opted to have their own design.

Exhibit 21.11   West Bank registration plate; photo © 2021 by Léo-Paul Dana

Sabella et al. (2014) examined the post-Oslo Accords relationship between entrepreneurship and economic growth in the West Bank. Using data spanning 16 (post-Oslo) years, these authors illustrated that contrary to a reservoir of research, entrepreneurship appeared to have no significant impact on economic growth. They explained that by the fact entrepreneurial activity is expected to decrease as a result of growth in the economy, new jobs are created. Sabella and Analoui (2015) subsequently focused on managerial training and development for Palestinians.

In 2016, the European Union and the United Nations Development Programme (UNDP) launched a €2.4 million programme to boost private-sector development in Gaza. In June 2019, Palestinian businessman Ashraf Jabari, co-founder of the Judaea and Samaria Chamber of Commerce and Industry, attended an economic workshop in Bahrain. Realising that peace has positive effects on the economy as well as society, Jabari expressed support for President Trump's peace plan.

Context for Enterprise and Implications for Doing Business[3]

> For 27 years we blamed our poor economy on the Israeli occupation. But in the same time our economy improved. Individual income increased, housing projects everywhere, and unemployment decreased…Yet we are good of blaming our problems on other people. So if not to blame it on the West, who to blame it on?
>
> –Dr. Mohammad A. Sarsour
> Quoted in *Palestine Business Report*
> Vol. 1, N 10, October 1996, p. 18.

Public service today is provided by three groups: the Palestinian National Authority (PNA), the United Nations Relief and Works Agency for Palestine Refugees in the Near East (UNRWA)[4] and a handful of non-governmental organisations (NGOs). Aid agencies play a crucial role for Palestinians: the political instability and limited self-rule inhibit institutional capacity and economic competitiveness. Easing import/export restrictions, circulation control (of people and goods), infrastructure demolition and fiscal resources' leakage can enhance Palestinian Gross Domestic Product (GDP) in the range of 10%–20%. Adverse conditions result in volatile GDP growth and tax revenues, one in three people unemployed, and poverty level is near 30%. Humanitarian aid mitigates the pressure on the Palestinian government by providing critical services to Palestinians; however, that too is volatile. The aid budget dropped from 30% of GDP in 2008 to 3.5% of GDP in 2019.

Human capital among Palestinians is high, with a literacy rate in Gaza exceeding 97.4%. Women's literacy rate in Palestine is even higher relatively: it is at 95.9%, compared to 66% and 56% in Arab and conflict countries, respectively. Human Capital Index – capturing health and education expected by age 18 – in Palestine is higher than its peers including Jordan and Egypt. HDI – an indicator reflecting health, education and standard of living – is 0.708, again placing Palestine higher than the average Arabic-speaking states. In terms of tertiary education, 18.6% have a bachelor's

---

[3] Figures are from 2019 and are either from UN reports or Palestinian statistics and research agencies, unless another reference is mentioned.

[4] UNRWA is a UN agency established in 1949 to provide relief to all the Palestinian refugees resulting from the establishment of Israel in 1948. It is the only UN agency dedicated to helping refugees from one specific country. UNRWA is funded mostly from voluntary contributions by UN member states, a yearly total ranging between US$1 billion and US$1.3 billion during the past five years. UNRWA plays a government-like role in providing education, infrastructure and health services to Palestinians.

degree or above and 5.5 have an associate diploma, the rates for women are higher than men. Palestine hosts internationally ranked universities, such as Bir Zeit University and An Najah National University, contributing to scientific research. Universities coped with the corona pandemic and proved to have adequate e-learning capacities. Palestinians are largely connected: around 84% own a smartphone and nearly 52% have the Internet at home. Throughout the different financial administrations since the early 20th century, Palestinians proved capable and financially savvy.

Education supply needs to match employment demands better. Vocational education increases economic capability (Hilal and McGrath, 2016). Suboptimal market-matched education and hostile political conditions make it harder for women to work (Hilal and McGrath, 2016). Most women work in sectors with relatively safe environments such as agriculture, social work and education. Another reason is large families: the average number of births per woman is 3.64 and was higher in the previous years. Hence, it makes economic sense when one parent forfeits market-work for household-work. Many aid programmes focus on integrating women into the workforce and vocational training. These programmes provide micro-credit loans and training. Examples include the United Nations Children's Emergency Fund (UNICEF) providing life skills and entrepreneurship skills programmes for adolescents to prepare them for their future employment; UNRWA running a handful of vocational training centres.

Palestinian diaspora is an important source of capital. The Expatriates Affairs Department, part of the Ministry of Foreign Affairs, ensures maintaining the diaspora linked to Palestine. Remittance inflows can represent about a quarter of the GDP. While most of the capital goes to the families and their consumption, the rest goes into investments. The Palestinian government invested in infrastructure and introduced tax exemptions for investors – investment promotion law – to attract Palestinian expatriates and foreign investors. Several conglomerates emerged to encourage expatriate's capital such as the Palestine Development and Investment Company (PADICO) or the Arab Palestinian Investment Company (APIC). These later act as a node for state investments contributing to the development of telecommunications, industrial zones and other critical infrastructure. The political situation hardens job conditions and leads many Palestinians abroad, hence, the large diaspora and the brain drain (Mataria et al., 2008). Germany International Cooperation (GIZ) has a programme helping Palestinians abroad return to their roots. Programmes shape candidates for available jobs or starting a business; courses focus on civil engineering skilled trades, business start-up training or also IT skills. Other initiatives enable the flow of skills from expatriates: UNDP Transfer of Knowledge through Expatriate Nationals (TOKTEN) is a local assistance programme, Palestinian Scientists and Technologists Abroad (PALESTA) is an online network, and partnerships between the Palestine ICT Incubator (PICTI) and the Palestine Investment Promotion Agency (PIPA) enable networking events.

Several institutions provide accurate information for business needs. Established in 1993, the Palestinian Central Bureau of Statistics (PCBS) provides statistics on trade, price indexing, social and economic data in line with international recommendations specified in the *United Nations Manual for Industrial Statistics*. Other sources for data include the Palestine Economic Policy Research Institute (MAS), the Federation of Palestinian Chambers of Commerce, Industry and Agriculture, the Palestine Trade Centre (PALTRADE)[5] and supranational agencies such as the UN and the World Bank.

The financial sector is fully functional. It includes all the usual sub-sectors: banks, a securities market, insurance companies, payments system, housing finance companies, microfinance institutions and leasing companies. The Palestine Exchange (PEX) includes stocks from nearly 50 companies and a primary stock index *Al Quds*. Palestine's stock exchange comes second in the region in terms of investor protection. Two regulatory bodies regulate and supervise the financial sector: the Palestinian Monetary Authority for the banking sector and the Capital Market Authority for the non-banking sector. The formal financial sector started with the signing of the Oslo Accords and the Paris Protocol and the transfer of the authority to administer monetary and financial affairs to the Palestinians. The development of the sector remains limited since Palestine does not have a national currency, nor a central bank. Instead, the currencies of Egypt, Israel and Jordan are used, each with a different purpose. While some say that diversification may reduce risk, Sabri (2009) suggested that this reduced the efficiency of the Palestinian economy, and Mitter (2014) considers this as the core of Palestinian's financial vulnerability. However, if the closure regime is reduced, the financial sector can manage the subsequent economic growth (Sabri, 2009).

---

[5] For a detailed "Doing Business in Palestine" guide, refer to the last PALTRADE report from 2014.

The demand for microfinance is particularly high. Between 2007 and 2017, the total microloan portfolio grew by 212% in terms of total value and almost doubled in terms of the average size of microloan – reaching US$2,600 in 2017 – according to the Palestinian Network for Small and Microfinance, *Sharakeh*. Many microcredit institutions target women in the scope of women empowerment, a top priority for microcredit programmes offered by NGOs. Essentially providing capital to start a business, microfinance proved positive on the economy, but the rate of penetration is only 2% of the population (Karsh et al., 2019).

Micro-firms are dominant followed by small enterprises and so on. Micro, Small and Medium Enterprises (MSMEs) are mostly family businesses – owned and run by families. While family firms often resonate with lack of professionalism and succession problems, Palestinian family businesses are most successful (Sabri, 2010). The upside is they are embedded in the community and develop a capital of trust benefitting business owners, customers and other stakeholders. More than half of new businesses are funded by individual and family savings. MSMEs receive support from the government and other bodies (many already mentioned previously).[6] However, the GIZ estimates the unmet demand for finance reaches US$ 900 million per year, for new businesses. The market has little knowledge and confidence in financial products and their providers, and there are little innovative alternatives to bank loans (e.g., more options in leasing, factoring and insurance).

Many financial technology services (fintechs) would be interested to enter the Palestinian market and would increase its financial inclusion. One of the GIZ's programmes provides a programme for educating SMEs on alternative financing options and collaborates with the relevant authorities to build the infrastructure for these products to exist in the Palestinian market. In 2020, The Palestine Monetary Authority first authorised the use of electronic and mobile payment services. Another example is the Korean Palestine Startup Support Programme (PASS). This programme focuses on training in non-regular coding education, support in establishing ICT social enterprises, provision of funding schemes and enabling women entrepreneurship. Palestine has one of the world's largest proportions of start-ups led by women (Wamda, 2018).

The Palestinian economy is dominated by services (circa 60% of GDP), industry and manufacturing (13%) and agriculture (5%). There are several many motivating trade agreements (namely free trade agreements

---

[6] For a detailed review, refer to Sabri (2010).

with the United States and Canada, and advantageous agreements with the Arab World, EU, Turkey and Russia), but the political situation inhibits their full exploitation.

The service sector employs about 60% of the workforce. It includes subsectors such as telecommunications, transportation, distribution, banks, hotels and restaurants (i.e., traditional services). Promising subsectors include tourism and knowledge-based services.

Tourism employs only 4% of the workforce but caters to all tastes. Palestine hosts a myriad of religious, historical, archaeological sites and natural landscapes. It is home to some of the oldest cities continually inhabited, holy sites for monotheist religions and sites at the heart of human history. Examples include the Church of the Nativity (see Exhibit 21.12); for a discussion of tourism here, see Isaac (2010). The local food is also an important tourist attraction given that much of it has become a global vegan staple such as falafel, hummus and zaatar. The number of tourists has been growing steadily in the past years. Recent endeavours of the Ministry of Tourism and Antiquity, in cooperation with the private sector, aim to develop socially responsible tourism packages. In reaction to the COVID crisis, collaborations between public, private and development agencies, implemented an e-learning platform – Jahzeen.ps – to upscale the skills of the workforce skills for post-COVID tourism. The website of the ministry of tourism is well developed and easy to navigate.

Knowledge-intensive services are bourgeoning. In marketing, communication, graphic design and IT, many people offer their services on a freelance mode, working remotely and online. Few online businesses use state-of-the-art business models. The Palestinian tech scene is in its infancy. Incubators include GazaSkyGeeks, Flow and Bader; venture capital funds include the Ibtikar Fund, Sadara and Siraj. Examples for successful digital start-ups include: Bareedee – a package delivery service following the uber model with its deliverers, that won awards in Amman, and pitched in San Francisco; and RedCrow providing customised automated intelligence on security in the Middle East and North Africa (MENA) region using big data technology and mining Arabic content.

The industrial sector represents 13% of GDP. It includes extractive, processing and handicrafts branches. The marble and stone industry provides limestone exported to several countries in the world, representing 4% of world production. The competitiveness of this limestone stems from its quality and historical connotation.

Exhibit 21.12   Church of the Nativity; photo © 2021 by Léo-Paul Dana

Agro-industries and food processing are also important for local markets (Exhibit 21.13), and they represent one-fourth of exports. This sector includes flowers, olive products, figs (Exhibit 21.14), pomegranates (Exhibit 21.15) and tomatoes (Exhibit 21.16), some of which are exported (Exhibit 21.17).

The fishing sector has a large potential. The textile and garment industry exports 30% of its output. What remains in the domestic market covers 20% of the demand. Products include footwear, knitwear and tailored wear of competitive quality. Palestinian handicrafts go hand in hand with tourism. It consists of souvenirs, furniture, embordered textiles and materials such as clay, glass, bamboo, wood, and mother of pearl. Then,

Exhibit 21.13   Local produce; photo © 2021 by Léo-Paul Dana

the chemical, metal products and engineering industry cover most of the needs of the domestic market. Finally, unrealised oil and natural gas are estimated in the tens of billions of dollars.

A representative 2019 survey[7] sums up the environment of business in Palestine in comparison to the MENA region. Participation of women in employment, top management and ownership are lower. Companies see a decline in growth in terms of employment and sales. The physical infrastructure lags behind; for example, it takes double and half the time to obtain an electrical connection in Palestine compared to the average of Arab countries; and, the reliability of water supply is lower. In terms of exporting, Palestine's main trading partner is Israel. In terms of sources of financing, firms rely primarily on their internal resources and make

---

[7] This survey administered by the World Bank covers a representative sample of private firms in non-agricultural, formal, private economy in services and manufacturing, and with more than five employees.

Exhibit 21.14 Young fig tree; photo © 2021 by Léo-Paul Dana

little use of loans. This indicates that financial intermediation is inefficient. Competition from the informal sector is bigger. Business owners and managers in the West Bank and Gaza highlight several business environment constraints, considerably more than their peers in MENA: political instability and access to finance. However, Palestine's competitiveness lies in social stability and innovation. Innovation is considerably higher both in terms of research and development (R&D) spending and novelty products/services to the market.

Initially designed as an interim plan, the Paris Protocol remains in vigour (Samhouri, 2016). Israel controls Palestinian logistics, borders and import/export activity with policies tightened and loosened depending on

Exhibit 21.15   Pomegranates; photo © 2021 by Léo-Paul Dana

Exhibit 21.16   Tomatoes; photo © 2021 by Léo-Paul Dana

Exhibit 21.17   Produce of the Gaza Strip; photo © 2021 by Léo-Paul Dana

the political situation. Linking the West Bank and Gaza through a convoy system was never implemented. The two territories are separated yet complementary, the West Bank has water resources and fertile lands, and Gaza has access to the sea and natural gas resources. All airports are defunct. Yasser Arafat International Airport, in Gaza, operated from 1998 until 2000.

At the time of writing, 5,000 Palestinian wage-earners cross daily from Gaza to work in Israel, contributing to the economy of Gaza. Another 25,000 Palestinians commute to Egypt to work. In addition to these day workers, 35,000 Palestinians spend their week working in Israel and return home for weekends. Other Palestinians work in the Persian Gulf.

Towards the Future

Palestine offers many opportunities for business. It is an untapped market with a business environment – on some levels, better than other countries. Strong economic capabilities include human capital, geographic location, functional institutions and social stability. A cast of programmes and initiatives aim to facilitate the exploration of market opportunities. Better vocational training and fewer political constraints will unleash economic productivity, trade and industrial potential.

ICT and social responsibility are keywords when it comes to business opportunities. The online and remote mode is adequate for an educated and connected (to the Internet) population. There are opportunities in innovative financial services, ICT sub-contracting (e.g., IT services, graphic design) and vocational education. This is in line with Abu Naseret al. (2017) who emphasised the importance of technical education in Palestine and appealed to decision-makers in technical colleges to promote interest in leadership and to put their own courses in all technical education programmes in these colleges.

Social responsibility is the other keyword because humanitarian conditions in Palestine present an issue. As such, Palestine is a good place to implement bottom-up ideas and social businesses. Targeting the Palestinian market checks the social responsibility box that many firms are after.

Peace with Israel is likely to greatly benefit the Palestinian people and their economy. The son of Palestinian refugees, Mudar Zahran, addressed an audience at Oxford, stating, "We never had a problem with the Jews in Palestine before the colonial British had other ideas about how they should separate us, and then the United Nations….decided to separate the land. Jews are our brothers and sisters and neighbours. They have always been".

References

Abu-Naser, Samy S., Suliman A. El Talla, Youssef M. Abu Amuna, and Mazen J. Al Shobaki (2017), "Technical Education and its Role in Promoting Entrepreneurship in the Gaza Strip," Second Scientific Conference on Sustainability and Enhancing the Creative Environment of the Technical Sector Palestine Technical College, 6–7 December.

Ben-Dror, Elad (2016). *Ralph Bunche and the Arab-Israeli Conflict: Mediation and the UN 1947–1949*. Oxon: Routledge.

Enshassi, Adnan, Sherif Mohamed, Zaid Abu Mustafa, and Peter Eduard Mayer, (2007), "Factors Affecting Labour Productivity in Building Projects in the Gaza Strip," *Journal of Civil Engineering and Management* 13(4), pp. 245–254.

Enshassi, Adnan, Sherif Mohamed, and Saleh Abushaban (2009), "Factors Affecting the Performance of Construction Projects in the Gaza Strip," *Journal of Civil Engineering and Management* 15 (3), pp. 269–280.

Gil, Moshe (1992), *A History of Palestine, 634-1099,* Cambridge: Cambridge University Press.

Hilal, Randa, and Simon McGrath (2016), "The Role of Vocational Education and Training in Palestine in Addressing Inequality and Promoting Human Development," *Journal of International and Comparative Education* 5(2), pp. 87–102.

Isaac, Rami Khalil (2010), "Alternative Tourism: New Forms of Tourism in Bethlehem for the Palestinian Tourism Industry," *Current Issues in Tourism* 13 (1), pp. 21–36.

Karsh, Abu, M. Sharif, and Anan Deek (2019), "Microfinance Institutions: Its Role in Palestine Economic Development," *International Business Research* 12 (2), pp. 165–173.

Masalha, Nur (2020), *Palestine: A Four Thousand Year History*, London: Zed.

Mataria, Awad, I. Abu-Hantash, and Wajeeh Amer (2008), *The 'Brain Drain' of the Palestinian Society: With an Exploratory Study of the Health and Higher Education Sectors,* Jerusalem & Ramallah: Palestine Economic Policy Research Institute (MAS).

Metzer, Jacob (1998), *The Divided Economy of Mandatory Palestine,* Cambridge: Cambridge University Press.

Mitter, Sreemati (2014), *A History of Money in Palestine: From the 1900s to the Present.* Doctoral dissertation, Harvard University, Cambridge, Massachusetts: Harvard University.

Sabella, Anton Robert, and Farhad Analoui (2015), "Managerial Training and Development in Telecommunication Organizations in Palestine," *Journal of Management Development* 34 (6), pp. 685–703.

Sabella, Anton Robert, Wojdan A. Farraj, Maisa Burbar, and Dana Qaimary (2014), "Entrepreneurship and Economic Growth in West Bank, Palestine," *Journal of Developmental Entrepreneurship* 19 (1), https://doi.org/10.1142/S1084946714500034

Sabella, Anton Robert, Rami Kashou, Omar Omran (2015), "Assessing Quality of Management Practices in Palestinian Hospitals," *International Journal of Organizational Analysis* 23 (2), pp. 213–232.

Sabri, Nidal Rashid (2009), "Palestine," in Léo-Paul Dana, Mary Han, Vanessa Ratten, and Isabell M. Welpe, eds., *Handbook of Research on Asian Entrepreneurship,* Cheltenham: Edward Elgar, pp. 238–247.

Sabri, Nidal Rashid (2010), *MSMEs in Palestine: Challenges and Potential,* Ramallah: Palestine Economic Policy Research Institute (MAS).

Samhouri, Mohammed (2016), "Revisiting the Paris Protocol: Israeli-Palestinian Economic Relations, 1994–2014." *The Middle East Journal* 70 (4), pp. 579–607.

Setti, Zakia (2017), "Entrepreneurial Intentions among Youth in MENA Countries: Effects of Gender, Education, Occupation and Income," *International Journal of Entrepreneurship and Small Business* 30 (3), pp. 308–324.

Stein, Kenneth W. (1984), *The Land Question in Palestine, 1917–1939,* Chapel Hill and London: University of North Carolina Press.

Wamda (2018), "Entrepreneurship in Palestine: More Than Just a Job," (Retrieved from https://www.wamda.com/2018/11/entrepreneurship-palestine-just-job, accessed 5 February 2021)

Section XII

Successor to the Rashidun Caliphate

Chapter 22

The Context for Business in Saudi Arabia

Wassim J. Aloulou & Mohammad Alarifi

Abstract: This chapter aims to understand the context of business in the Kingdom of Saudi Arabia (KSA). It provides a historical overview of the KSA and examines enterprise development and implications for doing business in the country. The chapter highlights the deep transformation that the country has undertaken in all business sectors since the announcement of the vision of the kingdom of 2030. The chapter concludes with a look towards the future of the KSA as it progresses to achieve its objectives for the next decade.

Keywords: The Kingdom of Saudi Arabia, historical view, doing business, context for enterprise, Saudi Vision 2030

Introduction

The Kingdom of Saudi Arabia (hereafter KSA) is a country in the Middle East and located in the Southwest of Asia. It is extended from the Red Sea in the west to the Arabian Gulf in the east. Its borders are with Jordan, Iraq and Kuwait to the north, Yemen and Oman to the south, the Persian Gulf, the United Arab Emirates, Qatar and Bahrain to the east, and the Red Sea on the west (Exhibit 22.1). The KSA takes around four-fifths of the Arab Peninsula, with a total area of around 2,000,000 km^2. Its capital city is Riyadh with over 7.5 million people, and Jeddah is the second largest city, with 3,976,400 citizens (Khan and Khan, 2020).

KSA is divided into 13 administrative regions (emirates). Each has a certain number of governorates. Each emirate is ruled by a member of the royal family. This administrative division is shown in Exhibit 22.1, and the regions

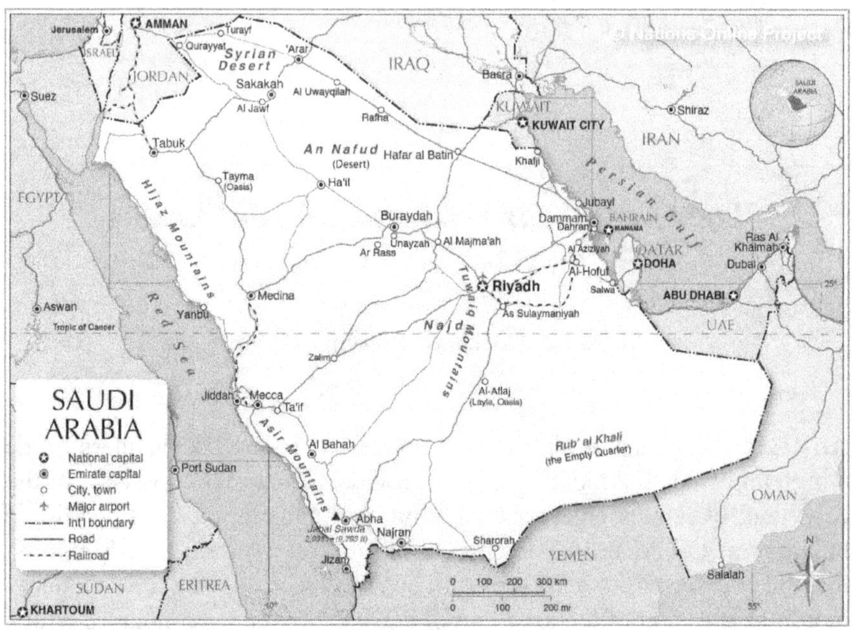

Exhibit 22.1   Map of Saudi Arabia; courtesy of Nations Online Project.

are mapped out as follows: (1) Riyadh, (2) Makkah Al-Mokarramah (Mecca), (3) Al-Madinah Al-Monawarah (Medina), (4) Al-Qassem (5) Eastern Province, (6) Asser, (7) Tabouk, (8) Hail, (9) Northern Borders, (10) Jazan, (11) Najran, (12) Al-Baaha, and (13) Al-Jowf.[1]

The flag of KSA (Exhibit 22.2) has the following meaning: First, the green colour symbolises richness and prosperity. Second, the sword represents strength and protection. Third, the Arabic words are the "Shahada", and they are meant to symbolise the Islamic origin of the state. As a word of Tawheed, the Shahadah "there is no god except Allah, and Mohammed is his messenger" is the Islamic statement of faith. And by Saudi law, the flag of the KSA that carries the name of God and the Islamic testimony cannot be lowered.[2]

The KSA is a monarchy, with a constitution based on the Quran and Sharia (Islamic) Law. It is home to the two Holy mosques of Islam (located in Mecca and in Medina, and Muslims from all over the world visit to

---

[1] https://www.stats.gov.sa/: General Authority for Statistics.

[2] According to Article 13 of the Saudi flag law: *"It is not permissible to lower the Kingdom's flag or the King's flag that carries Al Shahada"*.

Exhibit 22.2 Flag of Saudia Arabia

perform their pilgrimage as the fifth pillar of Islam alongside Shahadah, Salat, Zakat and Sawm. The King of Saudi Arabia is entitled The Servant of the Two Holy Mosques. All these facts underscore how important the Islamic religion and rulings are in Saudi Arabia for the Saudi population. Faith has an undisputed influence on everyone's day-to-day activities in Saudi Arabia.

This chapter will be discussing the historical context of Saudi Arabia and its impact on business in the country, the context for Saudi enterprises and the implications for doing business, and the look towards the future.

Historical Context

Islam is a religion, which started in Mecca, Saudi Arabia, at the beginning of the 7th century by the prophet Muhammad. The word Islam means "submission to the will of God." People who believe in Islam are called Muslims. Masjids are places where Muslims go to perform prayers. There are three most famous Masjids, which are the Islamic holy places. The first one is Masjid Alharam, which is located in Mecca, which has the Kaaba al-Musharrafah ("House of God 'Allah'") that is faced by Muslims, whenever they are in the world and when they perform prayers. Al-Aqsa Masjid is in Jerusalem, and the Prophet Muhammad's Masjid is in Medina. The Quran al Kareem is the holiest book in the central religious text of Islam. The start of the Islamic calendar was when Prophet Muhammad (peace be upon him) moved from Mecca to Medina with his supporters in 622. This journey is known as the Hijra.

The start of Islam was around the year 610 when Prophet Muhammad received a message from God (Allah) through the Angel Gabriel. In 622, Prophet Muhammad (peace be upon him) moved to Yathrib, which is today called Medina. A few years later, some battles happened between the supporters of the Prophet Muhammad and the pagans of Mecca. In 628, Medina was totally under control by the Muslims, and the Prophet had united the tribes, so successfully he and his supporters re-entered Mecca in a peaceful way without bloodshed.[3]

For a long time, the country was considered as an ancient trade centre and at the crossroads of the ancient world with the development of caravan routes transporting different kinds of goods (agricultural, dates, aromatics, Spices, etc.). With the emergence of the Islamic empire, trade has flourished in the area of the two holy cities of Mecca and Medina during the periods of Hajj (annual five-day pilgrimage) and Umrah (minor pilgrimage). Additionally, the two cities remained the spiritual heart of the Islamic world and continued to attract pilgrims from many countries for many centuries. Trading activities during Hajj and Umrah bring to the KSA higher revenues each year originated from the pilgrims' spending.

At the beginning of the 20th century, the Ottoman empire was partitioned and lost control of several parts of their territory. The empire was dissolved, and the United Arab State of Saudi Arabia emerged. The Unification of Saudi-ruled Arabia was accomplished through many stages. The most remarkable stage was the battle of Riyadh. In 1902, King Abdulaziz decided to retake Riyadh from Al-Rashid family, who had taken over Riyadh earlier. King Abdulaziz, with only 40 supporters, arranged to go to Riyadh to retake the city garrison, which was Masmak Fortress. This occasion was the start of the modern Saudi state.[4]

After the success in capturing Riyadh as headquarters, from 1924 to 1925, King Abdulaziz united warring tribes into one nation through capturing all of the Hijaz, including Mecca and Medina. This led to the establishment of the KSA on September 23, 1932, an Islamic country that considers The Quran al Kareem as its constitution and uses Arabic as the main language.[5]

---

[3] Source: https://www.saudiembassy.net.
[4] Source: https://www.saudiembassy.net/history.
[5] Source: https://www.saudiembassy.net/history.

The stability of the KSA led to the discovery of oil in 1938. In 1933, a Concession Agreement was signed between Saudi Arabia and the Standard Oil Company of California (SOCAL), which was the start of the company, Saudi Aramco. To manage that agreement, a subsidiary company, called the California Arabian Standard Oil Company (CASOC) was established. After that, there was a survey of the Saudi desert for oil. In 1935, drilling started. After years of hard work, there was not a real success, so in 1937, SOCAL executives decided to look for advice from their chief geologist, Max Steineke. Max Steineke, who has a long experience in fieldwork, recommended them to continue drilling. In 1938, Saudi Arabia succeeded in making an oil discovery. The success of Saudi Arabia and Saudi Aramco company was clear when commercial quantities of oil were discovered at the aptly named "Prosperity Well" in Dammam.[6] The Saudi oil industry was established, and mass production of oil began.

From the late 1940s, the company made a rapid increase in oil production, and the country became very famous for its energy and natural resources in reaching milestones from one decade to another. The Saudi government showed its interest in Aramco by making huge investments in it. Throughout the 1990s, the company started to extend its ties and partnerships across the world by making several international investments. The company is witnessing the advantages of technological and innovation advancements. And Saudi Arabia became the world's largest exporter of petroleum and a leader in OPEC. Oil exports account for more than 85% of government revenue. Further, Kalu et al. (2020) found that "the growth of the Saudi economy as a positive function of renewable energy use and an insignificant function of fossil fuel consumption" (p. 29).

Saudi traditions are rooted in Islamic teaching and Arab customs, and the country is characterised by a high degree of cultural homogeneity based on such Arab and Muslim heritage (Anishchenkova, 2020):

- *Muslim heritage:* The culture of Saudi Arabia is extensively influenced by the religion of Islam that governs every aspect of a Muslim's life. This Islamic culture is based on ethics, respect, solidarity and generosity, since the Islam religion is seen as a system of ethics. The Saudi culture follows Islam's guidance on the values of hard work, dedication, moderation, discipline, equity and excellence. The Islamic socio-economic system aims to guarantee individual liberty, freedom

---

[6] Source: https://www.saudiaramco.com: the official website of the leading producer of energy and chemicals in Saudi Arabia.

of choice, private property and enterprise, the profit motive and possibilities of unlimited efforts and reward.

- *Arab Heritage:* Saudi Arabian social and cultural norms are often associated with the social codes of Bedouin tribes. Bedouin culture played and continues to play a very important role in the construction of the Saudi national identity. Such a culture is based on social interaction between tribal members and solidarity within the groups prioritising family over any other relationships throughout life. Saudi Arabia's culture is particularly collectivist since that the most important social unit is the group, a close family, extended family or extended relationships, to which loyalty and respect are due. Thus, Saudi people prefer doing business relationships with those they know and trust.

Context for Enterprise and Implications for Doing Business

The population of Saudi Arabia in 2019 was 34,218,169 (nationals and non-nationals). The percentage of young Saudis aged 15–34 from the total population is 36.7%.[7] The birth rate in Saudi Arabia is about 1.6% and it is well above the world average. More than 30% of the Saudi population are expatriates (more than 10 million), especially from Syria, India, Pakistan, Egypt, Yemen, Bangladesh, Philippines, and so on. Most of them come for work. This foreign labour has boosted for years the different sectors of the Saudi economy. Saudi Arabia and other countries of the Gulf Cooperation Council (GCC) have become the largest markets for foreign job seekers. However, the number of expatriates started to diminish since 2013 with the implementation of the programme of Saudisation – *Nitaqat* – to increase the employment of Saudi nationals in the private sector in a few years in private sectors after government measures towards Saudisation in technical (engineering, accounting, IT-related) jobs and also in industrial sectors. New Saudisation labour initiatives have been launched in this case to encourage Saudi entrepreneurship and start-ups.[8]

Saudi Arabia is the largest economy in the Middle East and the richest Arab country in the region. Its GDP is about US\$ 680 billion in 2020 and US\$ 792.97 billion in 2019. Its growth rate is about 0.33% in 2019, and certainly affected by the pandemic global crisis in 2020. In terms of the Human Development Index, the Kingdom ranks second in the Arab World,

---

[7] https://www.stats.gov.sa/: General Authority for Statistics.

[8] http://www.arabnews.com/tags/saudization/: See "Saudization" rubric.

36th among 189 countries and 40th (with an index of 0.854) globally among countries with very high human development. It achieved 10th place among the G20 countries (United Nations Development Programme, 2020).

According to the World Bank Group's Doing Business 2020 report (World Bank, 2020), Saudi Arabia accelerated business climate reforms, joined ranks of 10 most improved and placed 62nd globally in ease of doing business rankings with an overall score of 71.6 out of 100. The Government (Exhibit 22.3) has implemented and carried out a record number of business reforms in the past year, earning the country a spot in this year's top 10 global business climate improvers. It made the greatest paces in the areas of starting a business (starting costs of about only 5.4% of income per capita with no required minimum capital), of the protection of minority investors and of registering property by reducing the number of days and rendering the process entirely free. Additionally, new reforms in the area of getting electricity make it almost twice as fast for a business to obtain a permanent electricity connection in Saudi Arabia as it was a year ago. In addition, the process can be done in only two procedures, making it one of only six economies around the world where it can be done in a few steps.

The KSA has made progress in the Global Competitiveness Report 2020 to be the only country from the Middle East region, which is progressing in its rank to jump from 39th place in 2018 to 26th place in 2019 before climbing to 24th place in the 2020 edition of the Global Competitiveness Report published by the World Economic Forum (WEF, 2020) and ranked eighth among the G20 countries in 2020.

According to the IMD World Digital Competitiveness Index (2020), KSA has been ranked among the top 10 countries in the world in digital skills. The top three Digital Risers in the G20 are Saudi Arabia, France and Indonesia. Governments around the world are now investing heavily in digital economy initiatives with the goal of enhancing value creation and national prosperity and reducing the impacts of the COVID-19 pandemic. The World Economic Forum (WEF) attributed the KSA progress to four factors: adoption of information and communication technology, flexible work arrangements, the national digital skills and the legal digital framework. The investments in King Abdullah Financial District, represent a concrete example related to these aspects above. The strength and development of electronic administration is another example of a heavy investment spent to serve and interact with citizens and residents. The country has improved its United Nations E-Government Development Index (EGDI) rankings from 52 to 43 from 193 countries, considered as a very high EGDI (United Nations Department of Economic and Social Affairs, 2020).

Exhibit 22.3　The Palace of Government from the eastern side in Riyadh; photo © 2021 by Mohammad Alarifi

Saudi Arabia's Economic Freedom score is 62.4, making its economy the 83rd freest in the 2020 Index. The country is ranked 9th among 14 countries in the MENA region, and its overall score is nearly equal to the regional and world averages. Its overall score has increased by 1.7 points due to higher property rights and judicial effectiveness scores. The index of Economic Freedom is based on the rule of law, government size, regulatory efficiency and open market dimensions.

According to the Global Gender Gap Report (World Economic Forum, 2020), Saudi Arabia is ranked 146th out of 153 countries for gender parity with a score of 0.599. Saudi women do not have equal rights to men in the Kingdom.

Table 22.1 shows the most important indicators and rankings of KSA from the different perspectives of official reports and sources measuring its economic performance and considering it as an emergent high-income country in transition from a factor-driven to an efficiency-driven economy.

As a developing country, the KSA witnessed significant restructuration of its entire economy. A series of restructuration is done up to now: Saudi Arabia Vision 2030 (Exhibit 22.4) as National Reform Plan, with 12

Table 22.1. Vital Statistics

Population (% Saudi) in 2019[a]	34,218,169 (68.8%)
Population growth rate[e]	1.6%
GDP US\$ (Growth rate)[b]	792.967 Billion (0.331%)
Score in HDI index (and ranking)[c]	0.854 (40/189)
Ranking in "Ease of Doing Business" 2020[b]	62nd/190 (71.6 /10)
WEF Global Competitiveness 2019[d]	36th/141 (70.0/100)
Ranking Digital competitiveness 2020 (score)[f]	34th/63 (67.910/100)
Unemployment rate[h]	5.86%
Global Innovation Index 2020[g]	66th/131 (30.94/100)
Economic Freedom Rank and Index[i]	83th – 62.4/100
Global Gender Gap Index 2020[d]	146th/153 (0.599/1)

[a] General Authority for Statistics' official website and SAMA (2020)
[b] World Bank (2020)
[c] UNDP (2020)
[d] World Economic Forum (2020)
[e] World Factbook (2020)
[f] IMD Digital World Competitiveness ranking 2020
[g] Dutta et al. (2020)
[h] Statistica (2020)
[i] Heritage Foundation (2020).

programmes such as the National Transformation Plan NTP 2020 among other programmes that were developed to help fulfil the Saudi Vision (Saudi Council of Economic and Development Affairs, 2016).

Three themes are the basis of the Saudi Vision 2030:

- "A vibrant society with strong roots, fulfilling lives and strong foundations" to promote the Saudi cultural heritage, the religious tourism, provide a healthy and balanced lifestyle, empower the society with the basic essentials of life and build a health care system.
- "Thriving economy with rewarding opportunities and investment in the long term and open for business for leveraging the unique position of the KSA"
- "Ambitious nation effectively governed to increase the KSA's ranking in the Government Effectiveness Index from 80 to 20 and to raise the E-Government Survey Index ranking from 36 to among the top five nations; and responsibly enabled to raise household savings from 6% to 10%, to raise the non-profit sector's contribution to the GDP from less than 1% to 5% and to rally 1 million volunteers per year".

Exhibit 22.4	Logo of 2030 KSA Vision

Source: http://vision2030.gov.sa/

The commitment of the KSA to the 2030 agenda for sustainable development and the achievement of the SDGs is reaffirmed and significant improvements in key aspects of human development were recorded (Kingdom of Saudi Arabia, 2018). Accordingly, the Saudi Arabia Vision 2030 aims to increase women's participation in the workforce from 22% to 30% and reduce the unemployment rate from 12.6% to 7%. It gives a significant emphasis to the Saudi woman and to her leading role as a catalyst for change in both social and developmental areas and as a major growth driver for the country's diversification policy.

According to the 2019–2020 Global Entrepreneurship Monitor (Saudi National report), the KSA ranks amongst the top 20 within the 54 economies on the overall National Entrepreneurial Context Index (3rd with regard to support and relevance of government policies, the 10th in the government taxes and bureaucracy, and the 13th in internal market dynamics). The Saudi government has provided different facilities towards supporting entrepreneurship. Its entrepreneurship ecosystem has been significantly growing in a number of institutions over the past years (Aloulou, 2021b; Aloulou and Al Othman, 2021). Regarding societal values about entrepreneurship, almost 70% of Saudi adults consider starting a business to be a good career choice, and about 79% believe that entrepreneurs are well regarded and enjoy high status within society.

These numbers, along with the government's vision of 2030, may indicate high expectations of increasing entrepreneurs in the country. In addition, the percentage of women entrepreneurs might have considerable incensement due to recent policies in the country regarding women.

As a result, there might be an improvement in entrepreneurial activities in the country in the future. A political and social stability registered since decades is another important factor in the attraction of investments and the growth of entrepreneurship. All this may also help in developing the economy and decreasing the unemployment rate, which was 5.7% in Q4 of 2019, through creating new jobs in the market and helping young citizens to find jobs. Unfortunately, this rate has increased to 15.4% in Q2/2020 due to the effects of the COVID-19 pandemic on the Saudi economy.[9]

The traditional shopping area in Saudi Arabia is generally located in the centre of each city and is made up of small shops, situated along a street or clustered according to the type of merchandise handled (Anishchenkova, 2020;

---

[9] https://www.stats.gov.sa/: General Authority for Statistics.

Leonidou, 1995). In the bazaar/*souq* economy, the competition is keen, and the prices are negotiated through a bargaining process between seller and buyer (Dana, 2000; Dana and Wright, 2015). In the main regions of the KSA, especially Riyadh (centre), Jeddah, Mecca and Medina (West) and Dammam (East), there are different kinds of traditional and popular markets or *souqs* for furniture, household utensils and other goods (e.g., Al Owais Souq, Ad Dirah's Gold Souq, Al-Muqailia Souq in Riyadh; and Souq Al Zal, Qabel Trail, Souq Al-Balad, Souq Al-Bado, Souq Al-Nada in Jeddah). Some of these are shown in Exhibit 22.5. The old town of Jeddah has many khans (small shops) such as Khan Al-Honood (Indians), Khan Al-Qasaba, Khan Al-Dalaleen (auctioneers) and Khan Al-Attareen (perfume makers/sellers).[10] These places still attract tourists visiting Saudi Arabia.

With increasing urbanisation in the KSA, which started in the 1970s, along with the traditional bazaar, appear a new type of shopping inside new pleasantly decorated places regrouping stores, supermarkets and boutiques (Anishchenkova, 2020; Leonidou, 1995). In addition to the shopping, malls perform the function of entertaining their visitors (especially women and children). In many cities of the KSA, the culture of malls is well spread. Different concepts are found for shopping high-end accessories, luxury brands, exquisite jewellery, trendy fashions, electronics and cheap souvenirs (dates, oud perfume, women colourful dressing abaya, etc.).

E-commerce has been flourishing in the KSA since 2016 with the announcement of the Saudi Vision 2030. Since this date, the country is supporting e-commerce as part of the transformation undertaken to transit to the new economy. According to Statista.com, revenue in the Saudi e-commerce market across all product categories was US$ 6.13 billion in 2017 and it is projected to reach US$ 7,051 million in 2021. It is expected to show an annual growth rate of 5.4%, resulting in a projected market volume of US$ 8,697 million by 2025. Total revenue generated by the fashion market stood at US$ 1,628.3 million followed by electronic and media at US$ 1,580.1 million.[11]

With an expected number of online shoppers at 19 million e-shoppers by 2020, KSA is expected to be the top e-commerce market in the Middle East. Currently, the country ranks 46th on the UNCTAD E-commerce Index worldwide (UNCTAD, 2019). The internet penetration is about 90%

---

[10] https://www.jeddah.gov.sa/english/jeddahcity/Markets/index.php
[11] https://www.statista.com/outlook/110/243/ecommerce/saudi-arabia.

Exhibit 22.5 Market scene; photo © 2021 by Mohammad Alarifi

and user penetration is more than 95% and counts for more than 25.6 million users of e-commerce in 2020.

The cross-border trade within a regional context (with the GCC countries) is provided with known websites and digital platforms based in this context (noon.com, souq.com recently purchased by Amazon, Amazon Global, AliExpress, etc.). Such e-markets facilitate quick communication between buyers and sellers, information about the products, their options and promotions, and comparison of prices.

Towards the Future

The KSA has witnessed an incredible transformation in the span of a single generation (Saudi Arabian Ministry of Foreign Affairs, 2017). Since the adoption of Vision 2030 as a road map for KSA's future, a key focus in achieving this vision is to create an environment that unlocks business opportunities, extends the economic base and creates jobs for all Saudis (men and women). This will include the following:

- the continuity to improve the business environment ecosystem and boost entrepreneurship and innovation (Aloulou, 2021b; Aloulou and Al Othman, 2021; Ashri, 2019; Dana et al., 2021; Merani, 2019);
- taking the advantage of modern and emerging technologies to achieve the digital transformation, shape new digital entrepreneurial start-ups and build the digital economy, society and nation (Aloulou, 2019; Aloulou, 2021a);
- the diversification and remodelling of its economy away from the dependence on traditional hydrocarbon-based industries (McKinsey & Company, 2015; Porter, 2012);
- the development of tourism sector by investing in mega-projects and in Saudi heritage (entertainment city near Riyadh at Qiddiya, northern megacity of NEOM, world-class exclusive wellness destination of Amaala and UNESCO-listed cultural birth of the kingdom in Diriyah);
- helping private sector to boost Saudisation of jobs for male and female citizens, and economically empowering women, helping them to access employment and enabling them to strengthen their future and contribute to the development of society and economy (Aloulou, 2018);
- the transfer of technology and the investment in technology: Tech investment is the way of the future in KSA and local companies

by shaping the Saudi Arabia innovation ecosystem (Arabnet, 2017; InnovationENABLED, 2016; OC & C Strategy Consultants, 2018); and

- building a country's capacity of optimistic resilience in the most challenging situations (such as COVID-19 pandemic started in March 2020) from resilient sectors (education, healthcare, etc.) (Invest Saudia, 2020).

This chapter has illustrated how the KSA has started its deep transformation towards modernisation and competitiveness from a historical and business perspective since its unification in 1932. Last year, KSA celebrated its 90th national day. It has also been noted throughout this chapter that KSA is an emerging economy with diversified potentialities, especially with its growing young population and with a challenging transformation plan such as Saudi Vision 2030.

References

Aloulou, Wassim J. (2018), "Enhancing Women's Economic Empowerment Through Entrepreneurship in Saudi Arabia." in Ebtihaj Al-A'ali, Minwir Al-Shammari, and Hatem Masri, eds., *Arab Women and Their Evolving Roles in the Global Business Landscape*, Hershey, PA: IGI Global. pp. 120–151. doi:10.4018/978-1-5225-3710-6.ch006.

Aloulou, Wassim J. (2019), "Entrepreneurship and innovation in the digitalization era: Exploring uncharted territories," in Karim Mezghani, Wassim Aloulou (2019), *Business Transformations in the Era of Digitalization*. Premier Reference Source, Hershey, PA: IGI Global Publisher, (chapter 11, 179-203). http://doi.org/10.4018/978-1-5225-7262-6.ch011.

Aloulou, Wassim J. (2020), "Instilling Fintech culture in a digitalized world: Defining, issuing and opening up," in Amira Sghari, Karim Mezghani, *Influence of Fintech on Management Transformation*, Hershey, PA: IGI Global Publisher, chapter 4, pp. 74–101. http://doi.org/10.4018/978-1-7998-7110-1.ch004.

Aloulou, Wassim J. (2021), "Mapping incubation mechanisms in Saudi Arabia: State-of-the-art and challenges for the future," in Sarfraz A. Mian, Magnus Klofsten, Wadid Lamine, *International Handbook of Research on Business and Technology Incubation*, Edward Elgar, Chapter 20, 351–366, http://doi.org/10.4337/9781788974783.00029.

Aloulou, Wassim J., and Nouf Al Othman (2021), "Entrepreneurship in Saudi Arabia," in Léo-Paul Dana, Ramo Palalić, and Veland Ramadani, eds., *Entrepreneurship in the Gulf Cooperation Council Region. Evolution and Future Perspectives*, Singapore: World Scientific.

Anishchenkova, Valerie (2020), *Modern Saudi Arabia* (Nations), Santa Barbara, California: ABC-CLIO.

Arabnet (2017), *KSA Innovation Economy Tech Startups (Report, in collaboration with the Saudi Ministry of Communication and Information Technology),* (Retrieved from https://www.arabnet.me/ContentFiles/4195PDFFile1.pdf, accessed 23 December 2018)

Ashri, Osama M. (2019), *On the Fast Track: Saudi Arabia's Entrepreneurship Ecosystem,* (Retrieved from https://www.entrepreneur.com/article/336766, accessed 23 September 2019)

Dana, Léo-Paul (2000), "Economic Sectors in Egypt and Their Managerial Implications," *Journal of African Business* 1 (1), pp. 65–81.

Dana, Léo-Paul, Ramo Palalić, and Veland Ramadani, eds., (2021), *Entrepreneurship in the Gulf Cooperation Council Region. Evolution and Future Perspectives,* Singapore: World Scientific.

Dana, Léo-Paul, and Richard W. Wright (2015), "Bazaar Economies, Modern Networks and Entrepreneurship," in Sir Cary L Cooper, ed., Wiley Encyclopedia of Management, 3rd edition, John Wiley and Sons, Volume 3, Michael Morris and Don Kuratko, volume editors. pp. 13–pp. 18.

Dutta, Soumitra., Bruno Lanvin, and Sacha Wunsch-Vincent (2020), *Global Innovation Index 2020. Who Will Finance Innovation?* (13th edition), Cornell University, INSEAD, and the World Intellectual Property Organization, Ithaca, Fontainebleau, and Geneva. (Retrieved from https://www.globalinnovationindex.org/Download.aspx?file=/userfiles/file/reportpdf/gii-full-report-2020.pdf, accessed 20 October 2020)

GEM (2020), Kingdom of Saudi Arabia National Report 2019-2020, Global Entrepreneurship Monitor, BGCEL at MBSC, Jeddah (Retrieved from https://www.gemconsortium.org/report/50534)

Institute for Management Development (2020). IMD World Digital Competitiveness Ranking 2020. IMD World Competitiveness Center. (Retrieved from: https://www.imd.org/globalassets/wcc/docs/release-2020/digital/digital_2020.pdf, accessed 28 December 2020).

Innovation ENABLED (2016), *Shaping the Saudi Arabia Innovation Ecosystem, RTI International and RPD Innovations* (Retrieved from https://www.rti.org/sites/default/files/innovation_enabled_workshop_report_med.pdf, accessed 1 June 2020)

Invest Saudia (2020), Investment Highlights. *Special Report*, Opening Remarks at the Extraordinary G20 Leaders' Summit, Spring, Riyadh, (Retrieved from http://www.investsaudi.sa, accessed 20 June 2020)

Kalu, Ebere Ume, Florence U. Nwafor, Augustine C. Arize, Léo-Paul Dana, John Malindretos, and Josaphat U. Onwumere (2020), "Green or Gas in OPEC Member Countries: A Linear and Asymmetric Investigation of Energy–Growth Nexus," *OPEC Energy Review* 44 (4), pp. 451–485, https://doi.org/10.1111/opec.12190.

Khan, Muhammad Khurram, and Muhammad Babar Khan, eds. (2020), *Research, Innovation and Entrepreneurship in Saudi Arabia: Vision 2030*, Routledge, New York, NY.

Kingdom of Saudi Arabia (2018), *Towards Saudi Arabia's Sustainable Tomorrow (First Voluntary National Review 2018-1439)*, (Retrieved from https://sustainabledevelopment.un.org/content/documents/20230SDGs_English_Report972018_FINAL.pdf, accessed 15 May 2020)

Leonidou, Leonidas C. (1995), "The Saudi Distribution System: Structure, Operation and Behaviour," *Marketing Intelligence and Planning* 13 (11), pp. 27–35.

McKinsey & Company (2015), *Saudi Arabia Beyond Oil: The Investment and Productivity Transformation, McKinsey Global Institute Report* (Retrieved from http://www.mckinsey.com/, accessed 20 December 2015)

Merani, Megha (2019), *Driven by Growth: Saudi Arabia sees a Rise in Support for Startups and Entrepreneurs,* (Retrieved from https://www.entrepreneur.com/article/339873, accessed 30 September 2019)

Miller, Terry, Anthony B. Kim, James M. Roberts, and Patrick Tyrrell (2020), *2020 Index of Economic Freedom*, The Heritage Foundation, Washington DC. (Retrieved from https://www.heritage.org/index/pdf/2020/book/index_2020.pdf)

OC&C Strategy Consultants (2018), *Tech Entrepreneurship Ecosystem in Kingdom of Saudi Arabia,* (Retrieved from https://s3-eu-west-1.amazonaws.com/wamda-prod/resource-url/2018_KSA_Report_Digital_Version_OC%26C_Updated.pdf, accessed 10 December 2018)

Porter, Michael (2012), Entrepreneurship and Competitiveness: Implications for Saudi Arabia, Riyadh: Global Competitiveness Forum.

Saudi Arabian Ministry of Foreign Affairs (2017), *Saudi Arabia and Political, Economic & Social Development 2017,* (Retrieved from https://www.saudiembassy.net/sites/default/files/WhitePaper_Development_May2017.pdf, accessed 12 January 2021)

Saudi Arabian Monetary Authority (2020), *56th Annual Report,* (Retrieved from https://www.sama.gov.sa/en-US/EconomicReports/AnnualReport/Annual_Report_56th-EN.pdf)

Saudi Council of Economic and Development Affairs (2016) *Saudi Vision 2030,* (Retrieved from http://vision2030.gov.sa/download/file/fid/417, accessed 2 June 2016)

Statistica (2020), Global No.1 Business Data Platform, (Retrieved from https://www.statista.com/, accessed 13 January 2021)

United Nations Conference on Trade and Development (2019), *UNCTAD B2C E-Commerce Index 2019,* UNCTAD Technical Notes on ICT for Development N°14, (Retrieved from https://unctad.org/system/files/official-document/tn_unctad_ict4d14_en.pdf, accessed 13 January 2021)

United Nations Department of Economic and Social Affairs (2020), UNCTAD B2C E-Commerce Index 2019, UNCTAD Technical Notes on ICT for Development N°14, (Retrieved from https://publicadministration.un.org/egovkb/Portals/egovkb/Documents/un/2020-Survey/2020%20UN%20E-Government%20Survey%20(Full%20Report).pdf, accessed 22 March 2021)

United Nations Development Programme (2020), *Human Development Report 2020. The next frontier. Human Development and the Anthropocene,* (Retrieved from http://hdr.undp.org/en/2020-report/download)

World Bank (2020), *Doing Business* 2020. *Comparing Business Regulation in 190 Economies (Economy Profile Saudi Arabia, Country Report),* (Retrieved from https://www.doingbusiness.org/content/dam/doingBusiness/country/s/saudi-arabia/SAU.pdf, accessed 22 October 2020)

World Economic Forum (2020), *The Global Competitiveness Report. Special Edition, How Countries are Performing on the Road to Recovery,* (Klaus Schwab, and Saadia Zahidi), (Retrieved from http://www3.weforum.org/docs/WEF_TheGlobalCompetitivenessReport2020.pdf, accessed 25 December 2020)

World Factbook (2020), Saudi Country Profile, (Retrieved from https://www.cia.gov/the-world-factbook/countries/saudi-arabia/, accessed 15 December 2020)

Successors to Trucial Sheikhdoms

Chapter 23

The Context for Business in the United Arab Emirates

Luan Eshtrefi

Abstract: This chapter examines how the United Arab Emirates (UAE) supports and thrives on international business. The UAE can easily be considered a leader of the Western Asian region in attracting foreign direct investment and supporting international business growth. Moreover, the UAE can be categorised as one of the most economically liberal countries of the Western Asian region. The chapter provides a historical overview of the UAE and examines enterprise development and implications for doing business in the UAE by comparing the UAE to other countries in the region. The chapter ends by looking towards the future of the UAE as it advances to shape its role as a benchmark country for international business development in the decades to come.

Keywords: The United Arab Emirates, international business, Western Asia, Gulf Cooperation Council

Introduction

The United Arab Emirates (UAE) is a prominent geostrategic and economic player of the Western Asian region, including the Middle East and especially the Gulf countries. The UAE is also one of the wealthiest countries in the world in terms of relative economic size based on population.

The UAE is located in Southwest Asia, in the east of the Arabian Peninsula, bordered on the north and northwest by the Arabian Gulf and to the east by the Indian Ocean. The country shares a maritime border with Qatar on the northwest, while there are land borders with Saudi Arabia in the south and west and with the Sultanate of Oman in the southeast. Its location on the Persian Gulf and even near the Strait of Hurmuz provides much significance given that most of the world's crude oil has historically passed through this area.

The UAE area is more than 70,000 km^2 of land, including a few islands in the Arab Gulf, and more than 27,000 km^2 of territorial water. The capital city Abu Dhabi (also an emirate) accounts for more than 80% of the country's total landmass (UAE Government Official Portal, 2020).

Roughly three-quarters of the UAE land area are desert; however, there are wide varieties of landscapes including towering red sand dunes, a natural oasis dotted with palm trees, mountains and flat coastal plains (NMC, 2016). The mountains represent an insignificant landmass of 3% of the total area, while the territorial waters of the UAE include more than 200 islands of different sizes and geological origins (NMC, 2016). Given its proximity to the equator, the UAE has very hot summers and warm to mild winters, with mostly sunny days all year round, such as many of its Gulf neighbours.

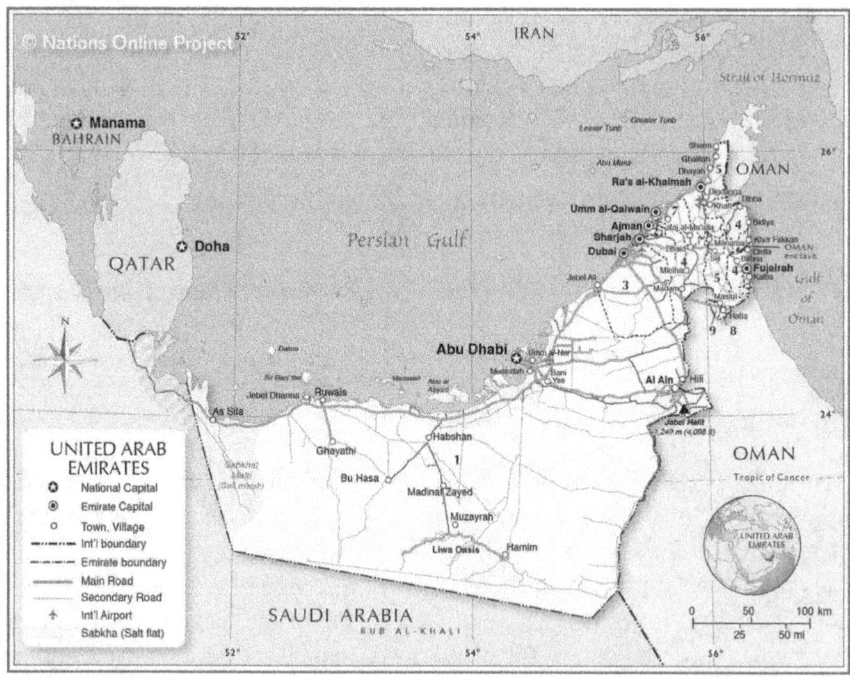

Exhibit 23.1 Map of the United Arab Emirates; courtesy of Nations Online Project

According to Federal Competitiveness and Statistics Authority, the UAE's total population (nationals and expatriate residents) was more than 9.36 million in 2018; as seen from Table 23.1 there has been significant population growth from 2010 to 2018 in the UAE (FCSA, 2020). Like other small and wealthy Gulf nations, most of the population in the UAE comes from expatriate residents with a ratio of around 10 expatriates to 1 Emirati as estimated in 2019 (FSCA, 2020). This is a testament to the international feel of the country given such a high ex-pat portion of the population.

Accordingly, given the significance of the ex-pat population, it can easily be said that English is the majority language that has been unofficially adopted and used for communication, including the private and public sectors. Many public universities in the country also offer English-only instruction to Emirati students and thus have created an environment where most citizens and residents enjoy an international perspective to business, education and communication in general. In fact, all major road signs are in two languages, Arabic and English, even though Arabic is the official language of the country.

A major increase in population arose in the mid-2000s given the economic boom of the UAE and the acceptance of a foreign workforce in multiple industries.

Table 23.1   UAE Population 2010–2018

Year	Population
2010	8,264,070
2011	8,394,019
2012	8,526,425
2013	8,661,345
2014	8,798,841
2015	8,938,974
2016	9,121,167
2017	9,304,277
2018	9,366,829

Source: (Federal Competitive and Statistics Authority, 2020)

The UAE flag is similar in both regional colours and design, however, noting some changes to differentiate its flag from its Gulf region neighbours. Each of the four colours (red, green, white and black) have their own symbolic meanings.

The UAE is unique from other Gulf nations in that it is a federation of seven territories or emirates: Abu Dhabi, also the capital city, Dubai, with the largest population in the UAE, Sharjah (Exhibit 23.2), which is adjacent to Dubai and a cultural centre of the Emirates, Ajman, Fujairah, Umm Al Quwain and Ras Al Khaimah (UAE Government Official Portal, 2020). These seven Emirates form one united federal country, which only gained independence from the United Kingdom in the early 1970s.

Islam is the official religion of the UAE and practised by Muslims; however, given that many expatriate residents come from other faiths, other religions are also allowed and practised in the UAE. In terms of government organisation, the UAE is considered a constitutional federation that was established in December 1971, after the unification of the Emirates into one federal state (FSCA, 2020).

Unique to the UAE from other distinct Gulf countries are some important initiatives to showcase the international character of the country and the role of tolerance of the Emirati minority towards the foreign/expatriate (residents) majority of the population. In 2019, the UAE implemented the

Exhibit 23.2 The Vibrant Downtown Area of Sharjah, UAE; photo © 2021 by Luan Eshtrefi

"Year of Tolerance" illustrating the UAE as a global location of tolerance, highlighting tolerance as a universal concept and a sustainable institutional endeavor focused on showcasing the values of tolerance, dialogue, coexistence and openness to different cultures.

Throughout 2019, with various initiatives, conferences, marketing campaigns and educational awareness, the UAE showcased its uniqueness to embrace its foreign residents as the building block of its economy and society. The Year of Tolerance mission, vision and broad objectives are illustrated in Table 23.2.

Its political system is different from many Western Asian countries as the UAE has no political parties and is ruled by the Supreme Council, the highest constitutional authority of the UAE, which consists of each of the rulers of the seven Emirates. Table 23.3 illustrates the eight current members of the Supreme Council.

The UAE President and Head of State is H.H. Sheikh Kalifa but has not been seen publicly for many years, while his younger brother, Crown Prince H.H. Mohammed bin Zayed Al Nahyan, has taken on his brother's role in the Supreme Council until any further new public announcements. As the Crown Prince, it is assumed that H.H. Mohammed bin Zayed Al

Table 23.2 Mission, Vision, and Objectives of the UAE Year of Tolerance

Mission	Objectives	Vision
To highlight the impact of tolerance and to expand the scope and opportunities for communication and dialogue.	• To establish values of tolerance, communication and coexistence in society. • Introducing the UAE model of tolerance to the world to become part of community virtues. • Enabling tolerance in society through policies and legislation. • Openness to other human cultures.	Devoting efforts to building a tolerant society that believes in the importance of human communication.

Source: (Year of Tolerance, 2020)

Table 23.3 Members of the Supreme Council of the UAE

- H. H. Sheikh Khalifa bin Zayed Al Nahyan, President of the UAE and Ruler of Abu Dhabi
- H. H. Sheikh Mohammed bin Rashid Al Maktoum, Vice President and Prime Minister of the UAE and Ruler of Dubai
- H. H. Sheikh Sultan bin Mohammed Al Qasimi, Ruler of Sharjah
- H. H. Sheikh Humaid bin Rashid Al Nuami, Ruler of Ajman
- H. H. Sheikh Saud bin Rashid Al Mualla, Ruler of Umm Al Quwain
- H. H. Sheikh Saud bin Saqr Al Qasimi, Ruler of Ras Al Khaimah
- H. H. Sheikh Hamad bin Mohammed Al Sharqi, Ruler of Fujairah

Source: (UAE Government Official Portal, 2020)

Nahyan will be chosen as the next President of the UAE. The Head of Government of the UAE, who is coincidently the Vice President and Prime Minister of the UAE, is the ruler of Dubai, H.H. Sheikh Mohammed bin Rashid Al Maktoum.

Sheikh Maktoum has been the "face" of the UAE and is considered the visionary leader of the country given his bold public relations. For example, Sheikh Maktoum can be seen driving on the roads of Dubai and speaking with ordinary citizens and residents of the Emirate of Dubai. Just recently, adding to his public health initiatives, Sheikh Maktoum made a public relations event when he was vaccinated with a Chinese version of the COVID-19 vaccine, showcasing his leadership to push the UAE people to take the vaccine in order to eradicate the pandemic (Aljazeera, 2020). Given that tourism plays a significant role in the UAE, the eradication of the pandemic is key to the Emirati economy.

The chapter now examines how the UAE is considered as the benchmark host country in Western Asia for local (Exhibit 23.3) and international companies to thrive and grow. Various comparisons are made between the regional economies and a closer examination on multiple business indices follow.

Historical Context

Economically, the historical significance of the UAE bazaar has influenced its growth. The Arabic version of the bazaar is the *souq*, an Arabic word for market, but much more than that, it was considered a gathering place or meeting place for all locals. Some have even brought attention to

Exhibit 23.3 Local firm; photo © 2021 by Anne Behar

the significance of the bazaar to social influences and the importance of *souqs* in creating social and business relationships (Dana, 2000). Bazaars have existed in the area now know as UAE, for many centuries before the UAE existed. Dubai had multiple markets for different sectors, for example, textiles or spices and other bazaars showcasing a market for other goods. Much influence on what was traded at these bazaars came from South Asian countries, specifically India (Vora, 2013).

The traditional *souq* and the current economic development of the UAE provide for a mixture of international business growth today. In the past two decades, the UAE has developed into one of the most international business-friendly environments in Western Asia. Dubai, for example, is seen as the financial centre of the Middle East, welcoming international companies to expand into the region by setting up regional headquarters in Dubai. More recently, Abu Dhabi has become a high-tech Emirate, which coincidentally also competes with its sister Emirate, Dubai, for attracting new and innovative foreign companies.

Politically, the UAE's modern history is influenced and dominated by the United Kingdom given its geopolitical impact in the region and subsequently the Emirati independence from the United Kingdom only decades ago. The exploration and production of crude oil in Abu Dhabi, Dubai and Sharjah in the early 1960s placed the UAE in prominent global economic affairs (National Archives, 2020). This and other reasons lead to the desire for the separate Emirates to unify into one nation as the British announced intentions to withdraw from the Gulf region in the early 1970s (National Archives, 2020). The rulers of Dubai and Abu Dhabi merged their sovereignty into one union and later the other five Emirates joined the union, creating the *Dawlat Al Imarat Al Arabiyya Al Muttahida* or the UAE in December 1971 (National Archives, 2020).

The UAE is one of the youngest nations in the Middle East and, as mentioned earlier, comprises of mostly expatriates and a minority of Emiratis. This, therefore, makes the UAE unique in driving its international character compared to the other Western Asian countries. This portion of the chapter examines how the UAE became such a benchmark nation in the Western Asian region in terms of its economic significance.

The following examination focuses on some macroeconomic indicators of the UAE and compares them with he regional players in the Gulf, namely with the five other Gulf Cooperation Council (GCC) member-states. The GCC is a regional trading block of six Persian Gulf countries and has deepened trade integration. As one might see, the UAE stands out in many ways.

In the past decade, the UAE has seen significant economic growth, especially from 2011 to 2015 with an average of over 5% of annual growth in GDP; moreover, the size of the Emirati economy in 2019 was over $421 billion compared to around $350 billion in 2011 (World Bank, 2020c).

As more foreign direct investment (FDI) entered the UAE economy, topping nearly $14 billion in 2019, the time required to start a new business was drastically reduced from an average of over 13 days to less than 4 days (World Bank, 2020c). This is a true testament to the Emirati focus on attracting FDI by creating incentives to do so.

Examining the amount of trade relative to the size of its economy, and compared to its neighbours, the UAE far exceeded Oman, Kuwait, Qatar, and Saudi Arabia in the past decade. It has also outpaced Bahrain since 2014 when the UAE traded more than 175% of GDP while leading the GCCs since then and trading at more than 160% of GDP in 2019 (World Development Indicators, 2020). This information proves that trade is a highly significant factor in the GDP calculation, especially for the UAE.

In terms of attracting foreign investors, the UAE is again the benchmark nation in the region. In terms of net inflow of FDI, the UAE was far ahead of Oman, Bahrain, Kuwait and Qatar in the last decade. Moreover, the UAE became the benchmark attractor of FDI, exceeding even Saudi Arabia in 2013, with nearly $10 billion in total FDI (World Development Indicators, 2020). In 2019, the UAE attracted more than double the value of FDI than Saudi Arabia, widening the gap of FDI significantly between the UAE and the other countries in the region. This implies that foreign investors clearly found the UAE as a much more attractive investment of capital than any other country in the region.

Context for Enterprise and Implications for Doing Business

The UAE provides a safe and easy environment for international businesses to operate and thrive. Key metrics with specific data are provided below to illustrate how the UAE has and continues to attract international businesses (Tables 23.4, 23.5, 23.6 & 23.7).

It can easily be asserted that when international companies decide to do business in Western Asia, the one key dominator is setting up the regional headquarters in Dubai, Abu Dhabi or another Emirate of the UAE. The focus now turns to some of the key metrics to associate the assertions such as illustrating the following indexes for the UAE compared to other nations in the region: Freedom Index, Human Development Index (HDI), Corruption Perceptions Index (CPI), Doing Business Reports, Global Competitive Index (DCI) and the Worldwide Governance Indicator (WGI). The results are outstanding; the UAE tops its neighbours in almost all indexes and reports.

The UAE has an economic freedom score is 76.2 in 2020, making its economy the 18th freest in the 2020 Index (Index of Economic Freedom, 2020). Moreover, it is ranked first among all 14 countries in the Middle East and North Africa region, and its overall score is well above the regional and world averages (Index of Economic Freedom, 2020).

If we examine most of the GCCs, it is clear that, on average and historically, the UAE has scored significantly higher than other GCCs in economic freedom. This is especially true for the last five years of the index.

The HDI is a summary measure of average achievement in three key dimensions of human development: (i) a long and healthy life, (ii) being knowledgeable and (iii) have a decent standard of living (Human Development Index, 2020).

Table 23.4   UAE Macroeconomic Indicators 2011–2019

UAE Macroeconomic Indicators	2011	2012	2013	2014	2015	2016	2017	2018	2019
GDP (current Billion US$)	$350.67	$374.59	$390.11	$403.14	$358.14	$357.05	$385.61	$422.22	$421.14
GDP growth (annual %)	6.93	4.48	5.05	4.28	5.11	3.06	2.37	1.19	1.68
Inflation, GDP deflator (annual %)	13.17	2.24	−0.87	−0.91	−15.48	−3.27	5.50	8.21	−1.90
GNI per capita, PPP (current $)	$67,710.00	$69,160.00	$70,460.00	$73,740.00	$65,220.00	$64,340.00	$67,670.00	$68,780.00	$70,240.00
Exports of goods and services (% of GDP)	90.08	100.25	100.55	99.56	100.87	101.00	99.59	93.05	92.46
Imports of goods and services (% of GDP)	61.59	64.00	64.73	68.93	74.35	75.74	75.41	66.68	68.48

(*continued*)

Table 23.4. UAE Macroeconomic Indicators 2011–2019 (*continued*)

UAE Macroeconomic Indicators	2011	2012	2013	2014	2015	2016	2017	2018	2019
Time required to start a business (days)	13.2	8.2	8.2	8.3	8.3	8.3	8.3	3.8	3.8
FDI, net inflows (BoP, current Billion US$)	$7.15	$9.57	$9.76	$11.07	$8.55	$9.60	$10.35	$10.39	$13.79
Life expectancy at birth, total (years)	76.5	76.7	76.9	77.1	77.3	77.5	77.6	77.8	N/A

Source: (World Bank, 2020c)

Table 23.5 Human Development Index Data (2010–2018), GCCs

Human Development Index (HDI)										
HDI Rank (2018)	Country	2010	2011	2012	2013	2014	2015	2016	2017	2018
45	Bahrain	0.796	0.798	0.8	0.807	0.81	0.834	0.839	0.839	0.838
57	Kuwait	0.794	0.796	0.8	0.798	0.8	0.807	0.809	0.809	0.808
47	Oman	0.793	0.795	0.804	0.811	0.815	0.827	0.834	0.833	0.834
41	Qatar	0.834	0.845	0.85	0.857	0.854	0.851	0.847	0.848	0.848
36	KSA	0.81	0.824	0.837	0.846	0.853	0.857	0.857	0.856	0.857
35	UAE	0.821	0.826	0.832	0.839	0.847	0.86	0.863	0.864	0.866

Source: (Human Development Index, 2020)

Table 23.6 Corruption Perceptions Index (CPI) of GCCs 2012–2019

Country	CPI score 2019	CPI score 2018	CPI score 2017	CPI score 2016	CPI score 2015	CPI score 2014	CPI score 2013	CPI score 2012
UAE	71	70	71	66	70	70	69	68
Qatar	62	62	63	61	71	69	68	68
KSA	53	49	49	46	52	49	46	44
Oman	52	52	44	45	45	45	47	47
Bahrain	42	36	36	43	51	49	48	51
Kuwait	40	41	39	41	49	44	43	44

Source: (Corruptions Perceptions Index, 2020)

In the past nine years reporting, the HDI scores of all six GCC nations illustrate once again that the UAE is the benchmark nation, topping the index. Both historically on average and most recently in 2018, the UAE has the top HDI score. In a global context, the UAE ranks 35 of the 189 countries measured, making the UAE a top 20% player in this index.

Moreover, the UAE overtakes its neighbours in terms of the CPI. The CPI scores and ranks countries based on how corrupt a country's public sector is perceived to be by experts and business executives (Corruptions Perceptions Index, 2020). A quick examination of the data shows that the UAE scored 71 out of 100 in 2019, far better than its neighbours, as shown in Table 23.6. Over the past eight years, the UAE also scores the best in terms of least corruption perception as well.

More importantly, the UAE ranks 21 out of 198 countries surveyed in 2019 and is therefore perceived as having a very low corruption perception compared to all other countries in the world (Corruptions Perceptions Index, 2020).

The Doing Business Index (DBI) is an objective study that measures five areas of business, along with 11 parameters, which provide relevant information on business climate in a particular country, as surveyed by private industry and published by the World Bank.

From 2010 to 2020, the UAE has far outpaced other regional countries in the DBI, a measure of 190 economies and their business regulations and enforcement (World Bank, 2020a). Not only was the UAE a benchmark economy in the DBI in the past decade, but the UAE has also

Table 23.7   Doing Business Reports 2010–2020

Economy	EDB score 2020	EDB score 2019	EDB score 2018	EDB score 2017	EDB score 2016	EDB score 2015	EDB score 2014	EDB score 2013	EDB score 2012	EDB score 2011	EDB score 2010
Bahrain	76	70.1	69.1	68.7	66.6	67.7	66.6	66.6	66.2	66.3	66.3
Kuwait	67.4	62.6	61.8	60	60.7	60.5	61	61	60.7	59.8	60.3
Oman	70	68.8	68.6	68.1	66.3	66.7	66.7	68.5	67.4	65.7	65.6
Qatar	68.7	66.7	66	65.4	66.5	67.5	67.4	68.7	66.9	65.4	66.2
KSA	71.6	63.8	62.1	59.4	59.2	65.3	65.2	68	67	67.1	66.1
UAE	80.9	81.6	79.3	77.4	76.3	76.5	74.6	73.6	72.2	71.9	71.8

Source: (World Bank, 2020a)

Exhibit 23.4 Sheikh Zayed Road Towards Downtown, Dubai UAE; photo © 2021 by Luan Eshtrefi

had a progressively better score from year to year, such as 71.8 in 2010 and reaching 80.9 in 2020.

In terms of global ranking, in 2020, the UAE ranked 16 out of 190 national economies, providing stellar performance to top-ranked economies in the indicators and areas surveyed. This confirms the UAE's ability to maintain international businesses and FDI in the country, especially compared to regional neighbours.

Another index to illustrate the comparative value of the UAE economy relative to its neighbours is the GCI, published by the World Bank. The index is a yearly measurement determining progress in productivity (World Bank, 2020b). The GCI examines 12 areas: Institutions; infrastructure; ICT adoption; macroeconomic stability; health; skills; product market; labour market; financial system; market size; business dynamism; and innovation capability (World Bank, 2020b).

A closer examination of the GCCs clearly shows that on average, during 2007–2017, the UAE economy was the benchmark compared to its neighbours. This does exclude the years 2014 and 2015, where Qatar placed first place regionally; however, the UAE has topped the chart before and after this period.

In global terms, the UAE ranked 27 out of 140 countries in 2018 and jumped to 25 out of 140 countries examined in 2019 (World Economic Forum, 2020). This relatively high global ranking of the UAE necessarily implies its economic superiority not only regionally, but globally, even of many advanced economies in the world.

Looking at the map in, one can see that the UAE is the only country in the Middle East region that is green, noting that the UAE is considered to be in a high percentile rank for the WGI in the government effectiveness parameter.

The government effectiveness parameter of the WGI examines the perceptions of the quality of public services, civil service and degree of its independence from political pressures, and the quality of policy formulation and implementation (World Bank, 2020d).

The UAE has progressively improved on the government effectiveness parameter, moving from 79.43 percentile to as high as 88.94 percentile (World Bank, 2020d). No other country in the region comes close to the high rank of the UAE in this parameter of the WGI.

Lastly, the UAE has been the leader in attracting foreign capital and international business given its commitment to, and expansion of, economic free zones. Today, the UAE has more than 40 free zones, allowing 100% foreign ownership of business in-country (Invest in UAE, 2020). This has replaced the former local content requirement of a need to have a local Emirati company or citizen sponsor an international company that wanted to operate the Emirati economy.

More than half of the free zones in the UAE are in Abu Dhabi, and especially in Dubai. An independent free zone authority (FZA) governs each free zone company and is responsible for issuing operating licenses and assisting companies with establishing their business (English Business Council, 2020). Furthermore, the procedures for establishing free zone international businesses are efficient and these businesses receive much support from the relevant FZA.

Towards the Future

Dubai Expo 2020 (see Exhibit 23.5) was a major win for the UAE allowing it to showcase characteristics of business strength and aptitude. Given that this world event was scheduled to have taken place in 2020 and the

Exhibit 23.5 Promoting Expo; photo © 2021 by Léo-Paul Dana

significant impact of the COVID pandemic, the UAE has adopted, with the approval of more than two-thirds of the country participants, to postpone the global event to begin in October 2021 and to last until March 2022 (EXPO2020 Dubai, 2020). The UAE competed with various countries in order to host the next largest global exposition event and in November 2013, the UAE was announced as the site of the significant event (Nagraj, 2013). As stated in the official website of the event, more than 190 countries will participate in the Dubai Expo event, the largest ever event to take place in the Arab world, connecting businesses, multilateral organisations and educational establishments (EXPO2020 Dubai, 2020). The most significant of the Dubai Expo project is the economic value. The event was projected to boost the Emirati economy by more than $33 billion and support nearly 1 million jobs between the period of 2013 and 2031 (EXPO2020 Dubai, 2020). This is one of the most significant economic and construction projects of the UAE's history.

Space ambitions are another frontier for the UAE. The Emirati focus on space exploration and becoming the first Gulf country to fund such activities provides insight into the strategic plans of the country. The

UAE's mission is timed to coincide with the missions into Mars orbit with the nation's 50th independence anniversary. The significance here will be to illustrate the diversification of the Emirati economy from traditional activities, including oil, to innovation through engineering and science (Steenmans and Morisetti, 2020).

Other large construction projects in the UAE continue to provide for a significant portion of the UAE GDP. As of June 2019, the estimated value of active construction projects was over $3 trillion. The UAE has seen competition in which country will maintain the highest building in the world. Today, Dubai's Burj Khalifa in Dubai is the tallest building in the world; however, Saudi Arabia announced plans to shift the title to its territory. Soon after, the UAE announced it would bring back the title of tallest building back to the UAE with the announcement of The Tower at Dubai Creek Harbour, scheduled for completion towards the end of 2021. This structure will be the world's tallest manmade building, rising over 1.3 kilometres (HSBC, 2020).

Meanwhile, a highly significant and historical event has taken place to expand trade and business relationships for the UAE. Namely, the UAE has normalised relations with Israel since September 2020. The normalisation of relations between the two countries was brokered by the United States while Bahrain was included in the new accord. The new relationship between Israel and the UAE mostly signifies the economic potential between the two countries, but moreover, illustrates how the UAE is a regional powerhouse in broadening its geopolitical and economic influence in the region. Since normalising relations, the UAE and Israel have announced various business-related ties bringing the two economies closer than ever before.

Lastly, the COVID-19 pandemic has hit the UAE as it has much of the world. However, the UAE has handled the pandemic much more efficiently than other economies in the region. As of 18 November 2020, the UAE has a very low total death rate per million inhabitants at around 55, as opposed to the United Kingdom, for example, reporting more than 787 deaths per million (Statista, 2020). With innovative approaches to keep low levels of positive infection of the virus such as efficient contract tracing, digitalisation of multiple government agencies and innovation of the education sector, the UAE was able to reopen its borders to tourists in July 2020 (KPMG, 2020). This is a very significant development, given the high proportion of the Emirati economy to tourism.

This chapter has illustrated how its strategic location in the Middle East, its infrastructure, government initiatives and peace initiative have made the UAE a place where international businesses will continue to thrive. In October 2020, Etihad was the first Gulf-based airline company to operate a scheduled flight to Israel. This is only the beginning.

References

Aljazeera (2020), "UAE Prime Minister Receives Coronavirus Vaccine Shot," (Retrieved from https://www.aljazeera.com/news/2020/11/3/uae-pm-and-dubai-ruler-receives-coronavirus-vaccine, accessed 3 November 2020)

Corruptions Perceptions Index (2020), "Corruption Perceptions Index," (Retrieved from https://www.transparency.org/en/cpi/2019/resultsv, accessed 3 November 2020)

Dana, Léo-Paul (2000), *Economies of the Eastern Mediterranean: Economic Miracles in the Making,* London, Singapore & Hong Kong: World Scientific.

English Business Council (2020), "Doing Business in the UAE," (Retrieved from https://www.englishbusinesscouncil.com/doing-business-in-the-uae/, accessed 19 November 2020)

EXPO2020 Dubai (2020), "Expo's One-Year Postponement Confirmed," (Retrieved from https://www.expo2020dubai.com/en/whats-new, accessed 3 November 2020)

HSBC (2020), "International Business Guides: United Arab Emirates," (Retrieved from https://www.business.hsbc.com/business-guides/uae, accessed 18 November 2020)

Human Development Index (2020), "Human Development Index of the United Nations Development Programme," (Retrieved from http://hdr.undp.org/en/data#, accessed 3 November 2020)

Index of Economic Freedom (2020), "Index of Economic Freedom 1995–2020, UAE, KSA, Qatar, Oman, Kuwait," (Retrieved from https://www.heritage.org/index/visualize, accessed 3 November 2020)

Invest in UAE (2020), "The UAE: An Ideal Investment Destination and Partner," (Retrieved from https://visituae.economy.ae/investment/en/old-en/competitive-edge-of-the-uae.html, accessed 18 November 2020)

KPMG (2020), "COVID 19 Government Measures of the UAE," (Retrieved from https://home.kpmg/ae/en/home/insights/2020/08/covid-19-government-measures-uae.html, accessed 15 June 2021)

Nagraj, Aarti (2013), "The UAE is the First Middle Eastern Nation in History to be Granted the Expo Bid," *Gulf Business News,* (Retrieved from https://gulfbusiness.com/dubai-wins-expo-2020-bid/, accessed 15 June 2021)

National Archives (2020), "Ministry of Presidential Affairs: History of the UAE and the British Era," Abu Dhabi, (Retrieved from https://www.na.ae/en/archives/historicalperiods/britishprince.aspx, accessed 25 November 2020)

National Media Council (2016), *United Arab Emirates: An Introduction to Its Origins and Phases of Development in Various Spheres of Life,* Abu Dhabi: UAE Annual Book, REFLECTION.AE

Statista (2020), "Coronavirus (COVID-19) Deaths Worldwide per One Million Population as of November 18, 2020, by Country," (Retrieved from https://www.statista.com/statistics/1104709/coronavirus-deaths-worldwide-per-million-inhabitants/, accessed 18 November 2020)

Steenmans, Ine, and Neil Morisetti (2020), "UAE Mars Mission: Extraordinary Feat Shows How Space Exploration Can Benefit Small Nations," *Space.com,* (Retrieved from https://www.space.com/uae-mars-mission-extraordinary-feat-shows-how-space-exploration-can-benefit-small-nations.html, accessed 15 June 2021)

United Arab Emirates Government Official Portal (2020), "Fact Sheet and Statistics," (Retrieved from https://government.ae/en/about-the-uae/fact-sheet, accessed 30 October 2020)

United Arab Emirates Protocol Department Dubai (2021), "UAE and Dubai" (Available at https://www.protocol.dubai.ae/UAE-Dubai/UAE_Flag (accessed 20 June 2021)

Vora, Neha (2013), *Impossible Citizens: Dubai's Indian Diaspora,* Durham: Duke University Press.

World Bank (2020a), "Doing Business, Measuring Business Regulations," (Retrieved from https://www.doingbusiness.org/en/custom-query, accessed 4 November 2020)

World Bank (2020b), "Global Competitive Index GCCs," (Retrieved from https://govdata360.worldbank.org/indicators/gci?country=ARE&indicator=631&countries=BHR,KWT,SAU,OMN,QAT&viz=line_chart&years=2007,2017&indicators=944, accessed 5 November 2020)

World Bank (2020c), "World Development Indicators Databank," (Retrieved from https://databank.worldbank.org/reports.aspx?source=2&country=ARE#, accessed 5 November 2020)

World Bank (2020d), "Worldwide Governance Indicators," (Retrieved from http://info.worldbank.org/governance/wgi/Home/Reports, accessed 30 October 2020)

World Development Indicators (2020), "Databank World Development Indicators," (Retrieved from https://data.worldbank.org/indicator/NY.GDP.PCAP.CD?end=2019&locations=BH-KW-OM-QA-SA-AE&name_desc=false&start=2010&view=chart, accessed 12 November 2020)

World Economic Forum (2020), "The Global Competitive Report 2019," (Retrieved from http://www3.weforum.org/docs/WEF_The GlobalCompetitivenessReport2019.pdf, accessed 4 November 2020)

Zaki, Yousra (2019), "What do the Colours of the UAE Flag Mean?" *Gulf News,* (Retrieved from https://gulfnews.com/uae/what-do-the-colours-of-the-uae-flag-mean-1.1608733, accessed 15 June 2021)

Section XIV

A New Paradigm

Chapter 24

The New Economy with Aspects of the Bazaar

Léo-Paul Dana, Aidin Salamzadeh, Veland Ramadani & Ramo Palalić

Abstract: This chapter concludes this book about the contexts of Western Asia, a very diverse region with striking contrasts. It observes changes over time and emphasises the need for firms to adapt to changing contexts. Borders change and mindsets evolve. The chapter distinguishes between explicit and implicit assumptions that reflect cultural values. It reviews the characteristics of the bazaar and the firm-type economy. It then discusses the New Economy of high-tech booms and emphasises the similarity between the structured bazaar and the World Wide Web. After providing thoughts for the business sector, the chapter concludes with thoughts for policy-makers.

Keywords: Abraham Accords, bazaar, firm-type economy, hijacking, terrorism

Changing Contexts

The world is always changing. To survive and thrive, firms need to understand changing contexts and to be able to adapt. In 1831, *Assicurazioni Generali* was established in Trieste, because at the time Trieste was the most important seaport in the Austrian Empire. Trieste, now in Italy, no longer dominates Austria's trade; yet, the Generali Group managed to maintain its prominence and is among the Fortune Global 500 companies. Featuring the Lion of Saint Mark (Exhibit 24.1), the Generali Building in Jerusalem was designed by the chief architect of the Italian Fascist regime, Marcello Piacentini and opened in 1935 as the Jerusalem branch

Exhibit 24.1   Lion of Saint Mark; photo © 2021 by Léo-Paul Dana

of *Assicurazioni Generali;* the British Mandatory government nationalised that building in 1946.

Thirty years later, on 4 July 1976, the United States celebrated the bicentennial of its independence from the United Kingdom. That same day, hostages of a hijacked Air France plane celebrated their release; their saga began on 27 June, when Air France flight 139 – scheduled to fly from Athens to Paris – was rerouted to Entebbe by hijackers who demanded $5 million (US) and the release of 53 Palestinian and pro-Palestinian militants in five different countries. The hijackers threatened that if their demands were not met, they would kill passengers whom they held as hostages. The dictator of Uganda, Idi Amin supported the hijacking. Led by Yonatan Netanyahu, counter-terrorist hostage-rescue mission Operation Entebbe (Exhibit 24.2) rescued most of the hostages and the Air France Airbus returned to the skies. Yonatan Netanyahu was killed during the rescue mission; in 1996 his brother Benjamin became prime minister of Israel.

Today, we rejoice that hijacking is something of the past and governments have been cooperating to fight terrorism. Peace treaties have been

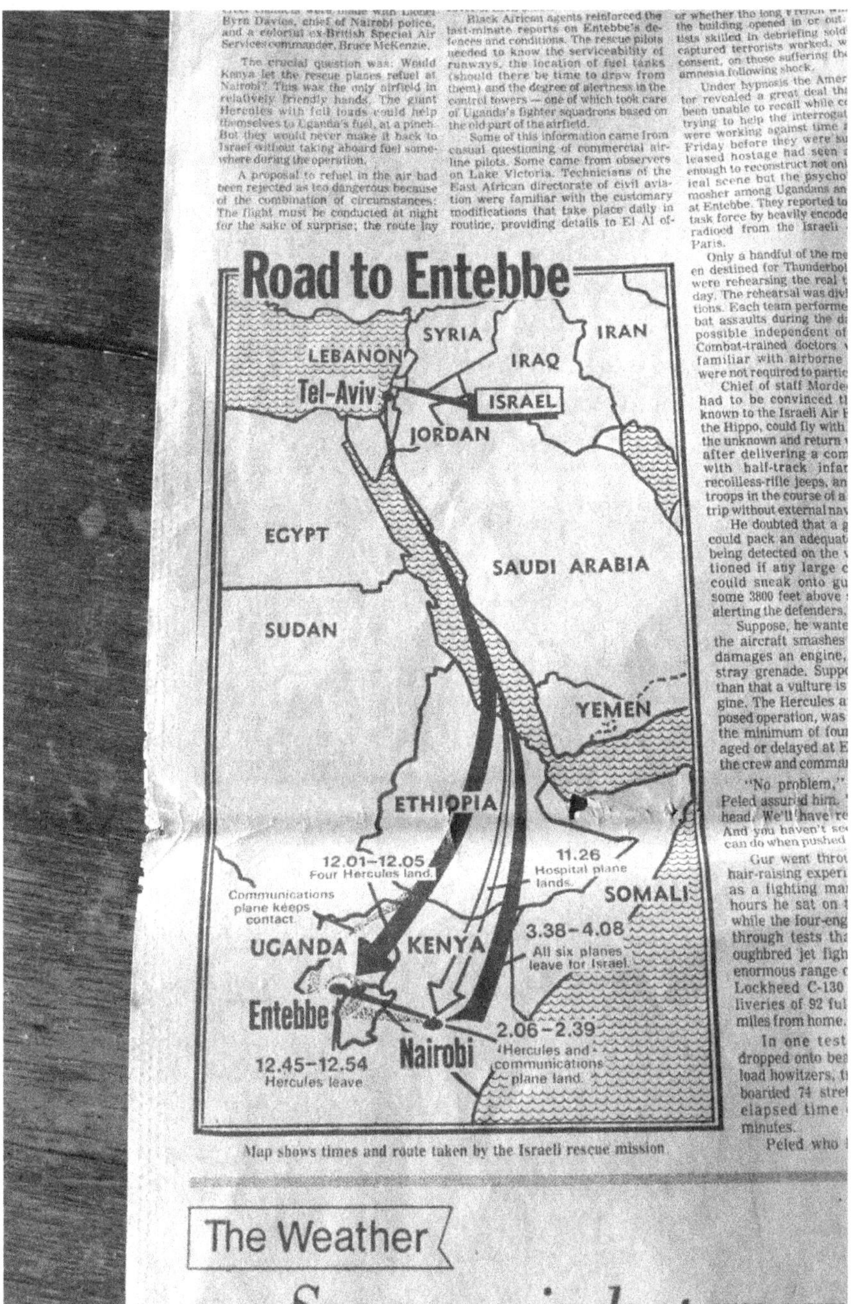

Exhibit 24.2 *The Montreal Star,* August 2, 1976; photo © 2021 by Léo-Paul Dana

signed and we see increased co-operation. A step in the right direction, in 2020 the Abraham Accords (see Exhibit 24.3) encouraged efforts to promote interfaith and intercultural dialogue to advance a culture of peace among the three Abrahamic religions and all humanity.

Of course, there are different ways to promote peace. In 1999, Argentina-born Israeli Daniel Barenboim and Palestinian Edward Said created the West–Eastern Divan Orchestra with the objective of promoting

The Abraham Accords Declaration:

We, the undersigned, recognize the importance of maintaining and strengthening peace in the Middle East and around the world based on mutual understanding and coexistence, as well as respect for human dignity and freedom, including religious freedom.

We encourage efforts to promote interfaith and intercultural dialogue to advance a culture of peace among the three Abrahamic religions and all humanity.

We believe that the best way to address challenges is through cooperation and dialogue and that developing friendly relations among States advances the interests of lasting peace in the Middle East and around the world.

We seek tolerance and respect for every person in order to make this world a place where all can enjoy a life of dignity and hope, no matter their race, faith or ethnicity.

We support science, art, medicine, and commerce to inspire humankind, maximize human potential and bring nations closer together.

We seek to end radicalization and conflict to provide all children a better future.

We pursue a vision of peace, security, and prosperity in the Middle East and around the world.

In this spirit, we warmly welcome and are encouraged by the progress already made in establishing diplomatic relations between Israel and its neighbors in the region under the principles of the Abraham Accords. We are encouraged by the ongoing efforts to consolidate and expand such friendly relations based on shared interests and a shared commitment to a better future.

Signed:

Exhibit 24.3 The Abraham Accords Declaration Signed by Israel, Bahrain, the United Sates and the United Arab Emirates

peace through music. The orchestra includes Iranian, Israeli, Jordanian, Lebanese, Palestinian and Syrian musicians of different faiths. In recognition of his efforts, Barenboim was offered a Palestinian Authority Passport.

Despite some common desires and the effects of globalisation, cultural differences remain strong. These shape the context for business and cultural diversity is increasingly being paid attention to by economists (Yong, 2019). The context of business is a critical issue that businesspersons, policymakers and researchers should pay plenty of attention to; otherwise, by failing to consider the contextual factors, businesspersons might fail, policymakers are likely to devise irrelevant policies, and researchers underestimating the impact of context could likely reach invalid or misleading findings (Dana, 2007; Dana and Ramadani, 2015).

Culture shapes managerial assumptions. In the West, context is often explicit and easy to understand. In Western Asia much is implicit, and it is easy for a foreigner to stumble. The objective of this book has been to introduce the reader to the contexts of Western Asia.

On the one hand, firms in each country take advantage of the capitalist markets that dominate the globe (Guerrero et al., 2015; Light and Dana, 2020); on the other, each country has its own features. While Israel is known for its life science research and associated industry (Beyar et al., 2017), other countries are rich from abundant oil reserves. Characteristics of Oman include the low crime rate and the high level of tolerance. Some shepherds in Western Asia face desert conditions (Exhibit 24.4), while others enjoy greener lands (Exhibit 24.5).

Among this book's principal contributions is its focus on two-faceted contexts in which values of the bazaar economy are interlinked into the firm-type economy (see Exhibit 24.6). While the bazaar economy is a way of life based on trust, negotiation and bargaining, the firm-type economy is an economic institution largely shaped by profit-seeking players (Geertz, 1978; Penrose, 1959). The firm-type economy exists in Western Asia as it does in the West where it dominated business during the 20th century.

Exhibit 24.4 Awassi sheep in desert; photo © 2021 by Léo-Paul Dana

Exhibit 24.5 Awassi sheep in greener pasture; photo © 2021 by Léo-Paul Dana

Exhibit 24.6 Prices are indicated; photo © 2021 by Léo-Paul Dana

Lawyers are very important in the firm-type economy as transactions are monitored. In the bazaar, it is more important to monitor the relationship between buyer and seller rather than monitor any one transaction. If the relationship is one of trust, there is less need to spend on monitoring transactions.

Principles of the Bazaar Economy

As discussed earlier, the word bazaar refers to a historical type of marketplace in which merchants and craftsmen sell their goods and services. Bazaar exchange has existed for thousands of years.

The bazaar concept is believed to have originated in Persia and spread from this region throughout Western Asia and beyond; in time, bazaars became an integral part of the economy (Geertz, 1978). As caravans travelled along the Silk Road, camels could be exchanged for fresher ones at roadside inns, caravanserai, where traders could rest (Thompson et al., 2018). As the population of urban centres near these markets grew, bazaars moved into city centres (Keshavarzian, 2007). One variant was such that city gates were the two entrances of a linear bazaar. Such an arrangement facilitated exchange as people walked throughout these passages, discussed with merchants and bargained until an agreement was reached.

Even before Islam, Persian bazaars developed with a complex structure. There were different walkways – *rasteh* – for various products. Clustering by-product facilitated the information search, somewhat like a search on google today. This structure was both exciting and challenging, as potential buyers had several choices, and their bargaining power was higher and information asymmetry was lower than was the case in other types of bazaars (Amini Badr et al., 2020). Such bazaars still exist across Iran (Rezaei et al., 2019). Geographical clustering in a bazaar, according to the specialisation of suppliers, has been richly documented by Passantino (1946), Long (1952), Geertz (1963), Dana (2000; 2002) and McMillan (2002).

After the emergence of Islam, bazaars continued to thrive – with added religious/spiritual features. Although a bazaar may appear to be a simple geographic clustering of individually competitive vendors, a high degree of collaboration exists here (Geertz, 1978; McMillan and Woodruff, 1999). Although a bazaar may appear to function similar to street markets in the West, there are important differences. Street markets elsewhere do have some similarities (Normohammadzad and Makky, 2018), but informal practices are quite different; for instance, when a bazaar trader faces challenges in his/her personal or professional life, others will help him/her and try to keep him/her from going out of business. This contrasts with the general capitalist axioms of Western markets and standard marketing techniques. It is just one example of informal institutions within bazaars.

Geertz (1963) explained that the bazaar holds a complex web of carefully managed relationships. Sellers cooperate for mutual gain. When a vendor does not have in stock a widget that is in demand by a potential client, the seller is likely to source it from a competitor with whom cooperation is profitable. Request for a product is communicated with great speed. Christian (1943) gave an account of his personal experience: "News spreads rapidly in a Shan States bazaar. Within the hour I was offered half a dozen old pistols (1943, p. 504)".

Axelrod (1984) explained how cooperation is more effective than predation. As noted by Webster (1992), building long-term relationships can be viewed as a social and economic process. In the bazaar, effective communication is essential, allowing a sale to be equated to building a social relationship, rather than to work. Once a mutually satisfactory transaction has taken place, the establishment of a long-term relationship makes future purchases more pleasurable, and profitable. Unlike Western relationship marketing, which is customer-centred, whereby a seller seeks long-term business relationships with clients (Evans and Laskin, 1994; Zineldin, 1998), the focus in the bazaar is on the relationship itself. In the bazaar, both the buyer and the seller seek a personal relationship. Friendships cross generational lines as children acquire cultural capital from their parents, maintaining close links with friends of their parents after taking over a family business (Ramadani et al., 2020).

The bazaar economy today continues to focus on social bonds and involves traders who give importance to their reputation and social status. Christians, Jews, Muslims, and Zoroastrians have sold and are selling their products in such bazaars, and the bazaar logic has become a linking pin to make them friends, even in countries with religious conflicts (Dana, 2010; Salamzadeh et al., 2013). As mentioned earlier, Jews are considered among the most honest sellers in the bazaars of Muslim countries.

Although general principles of bazaars are alike across Western Asia, there are also differences. For instance, while bazaars in Iran are walkways with an Oriental flavour, in Armenia, Azerbaijan and Georgia, Soviet influence remains. Whereas some bazaars specialise in food and other products for the local market, in destinations frequented by pilgrims, or other tourists, retailers sell souvenirs such as handicrafts.

Thoughts for the Business Sector

Writing about the West, Dana et al. noted that during the 19th and 20th centuries, business largely took place in "firm-type economy, in which industry and trade primarily evolved within a set of impersonally defined institutions, grouping people according to organization and specialization.... It is assumed that profit-maximizing transactions are based on rational decision-making ... Decision space is occupied by product attributes and by the services attached to them, often backed by formal warranties. Consequently, the relationship between the buyer and the individual salesperson is largely irrelevant to the transaction decision. The interaction between the buyer and the product (or service) is more important than that between the buyer and the seller. Competition takes place among sellers. Geographic location – a large shopping mall, for example – is often a competitive advantage. Prices are set by the producers or sellers, and are generally not subject to negotiation. The entire economic space is assumed to be rational and largely devoid of subjective personal considerations (2004, p. 20)".

The same authors elaborated that in the New Economy of high-tech booms: "No longer are 'all people created equal'. Relationships play a more important role in business decisions, and transactions have become less standard ... This relationship leads to increased brand awareness and loyalty, even though differentiation in the product or service is less evident than ever before. Airline seats are sold as a commodity, yet brand loyalty prevails. The transaction decision is concerned not just with product attributes, but also with relationships and preferential treatment. There is less competition among individual sellers, as formerly rival firms collaborate in global alliances. The unit of competition is no longer the individual firm, enveloping product attributes, but rather its position within a multi-polar network of relationships (Dana et al., 2004, p. 20)".

They further elaborated, "Flexible pricing ... which typified the bazaar – is re-emerging in certain sectors of the economy. As in the bazaar, a flexible pricing system creates a range of possible outcomes, with the price varying greatly, depending on the relationship between buyer and seller. The vendor may sell for less when investing in a relationship (creating brand loyalty to increase market share); and conversely, the buyer may be willing to pay more when the other considerations (such as frequent flyer status) gained from the relationship are more valued than the transaction's differential costs (Dana et al., 2004, p. 20)".

Indeed, our New Economy includes some aspects of the bazaar. In the bazaar, the focus is on personal relations, would-be competitors cooperate, reinforcing relationship networks and negotiated pricing is influenced by relationships with members of networks; brand loyalty is influenced by preferential treatment and is based on relationships. In the firm-type economy that developed with industrialisation of the West, the focus shifted to impersonal transactions, prices are set by the vendor, competition takes place between sellers, decision-making is influenced by strategic considerations and brand loyalty is a function of product differentiation and therefore not applicable to commodities. In the New Economy, we see a return to sliding prices and former competitors cooperate for mutual gain, thus reinforcing relationship networks. There is a focus on relationship marketing and decision-making is influenced by relationships with members of networks. Brand loyalty is influenced by preferential treatment; brand loyalty – based on relationships – exists even for commodities such as airline travel.

As observed by Dana et al., "The degree to which the structured bazaar resembles the World Wide Web is striking. As is the case with industrial clusters, the Internet functions much like the traditional bazaar: both facilitate exchanges between buyers and sellers whom in other situations might not have had an opportunity to conduct transactions ... Key features of the ... digital economy include: Knowledge dissemination ... Absorptive capacity ... Supply ... Efficiency ... Like the structured bazaar which allowed the physical concentration of vendors and therefore functioned efficiently, the Web also provides the concentration and clustering of vendors. Potential buyers and suppliers meet on-line, reducing search costs and minimizing any disparity caused by geographic dispersion. Therefore the Web reduces overall transaction costs, as all parties concerned converge on a limited number of key cyber locations – just as they converged once on the grand bazaars. As with the bazaar, the Web provides key functions: information search; updating; intermediation; and opportunity for cooperation (2004, p. 27)".

Dana et al. summarised how the New Economy includes characteristics of the bazaar, "A potential buyer easily finds several web pages (through search engines), thus learning about supplies and prices from several suppliers. This process allows the individual to form a reasonably informed opinion about the state of the market at that time. The search, as in the bazaar, is limited only by the buyer's time and effort ... the bazaar enhanced the efficiency of caravans by acting as clearing houses. As precursors of modern trade missions caravans manifested many features of modern alliances. In the absence of international law (and its enforcement), a system of mutual trust and interdependence developed ... So, too, in the absence of web-wide law and enforcement, trust is required, as clients rely on the supplier's reputation and reveal sensitive information to suppliers. In the bazaar, collective sanctions against the violators imposed heavy punishments. Interestingly, readily available information on the World Wide Web on misdeeds and misbehaviours is approaching the bazaar sanction systems (2004, p. 28)".

They also emphasised the return to flexible pricing, "In the bazaar, the customer first tested price levels informally, and only later began to bargain. Often it was the buyer who proposed a price, which was eventually raised ... In the firm-type economy, sellers compete with each other, usually on the basis of price. One firm asks a lower price than does another, in the hope of obtaining larger market share. The customer generally accepts or rejects the asking price, without bargaining. As was the case in the bazaar, the new economy invites the customer to initiate the bidding ... Also similar is the fact that not everyone pays the same. The final price may vary according to timing and circumstances (Dana et al., 2004, p. 29–30)".

In our world of high-tech booms, the essence of the New Economy paradigm is that preferential treatment, when reciprocated, reduces transaction costs and provides the key to survival and long-term profitability – not far from the bazaar model. Knowledge about the bazaar is indeed useful well beyond Western Asia.

Thoughts for Policy Makers

Alon, Ilan and Chase wrote, "International businesses should be concerned about religious freedom because it affects the general business environment, political relationships among countries, and consumer sentiment of companies doing business in countries that supress religious freedom (2005, p. 399)". Indeed, firms prefer stability than unrest. Governments are wise to promote tolerance.

The Abraham Accords are a significant step in attracting business. Among the initiatives that resulted there from was the establishment of the

Gulf-Israel Centre for Social Entrepreneurship, known as *Sharaka* – literally "partnership" in Arabic. The mission of this centre is to build bonds between young Israeli and Gulf leaders in order to strengthen peace, trust and cooperation between both societies.[1] This seems in line with advice from the late Rabbi Jonathan Sacks who stated that we can change the world – not by the idea of power but – by the power of ideas.

As summarised by Dana and Dana writing about the impact of political problems on business, "Taking sides is not maximizing the potential of either … If both peoples were tolerant to the religion, culture and values of the other side, it would be to the advantage of all (2000, p. 86)".

We can help each other by faith,
You by ours, us by yours.

References

Alon, Ilan, and Gregory Chase (2005), "Religious Freedom and Economic Prosperity," *Cato Journal* 25 (2), pp. 399–406.

Amini Badr, Fedra, Mostafa Mokhtabad Amrei, and Hamid Majedi (2020), "Analysis of the Presence of Light in Rasteh and Charsooq of the Grand (Qeysarriyeh) Bazaar of Isfahan," *Journal of Iranian Architecture & Urbanism* 11 (1), pp. 5–24.

Axelrod, Robert M. (1984), *The Evolution of Cooperation*, New York: Basic Books.

Beyar, Rafael, Benny Zeevi, and Gideon Rechavi (2017), "Israel: A Start-Up Life Science Nation," *The Lancet* 389, pp. 2563–2569.

Christian, John LeRoy (1943), "Burma: Where India and China Meet," *National Geographic* 84 (4), pp. 489–512.

Dana, Léo-Paul (2000), *Economies of the Eastern Mediterranean Region: Economic Miracles in the Making*, Singapore, London & Hong Kong: World Scientific.

Dana, Léo-Paul (2002), *When Economies Change Paths: Models of Transition in China, the Central Asian Republics, Myanmar, and the Nations of Former Indochine Française*, Singapore, London & Hong Kong: World Scientific.

Dana, Léo-Paul (2007), *Asian Models of Entrepreneurship from the Indian Union and the Kingdom of Nepal to the Japanese Archipelago:*

---

[1] For details see: https://sharakango.com

Context, Policy and Practice, Singapore, London & Hong Kong: World Scientific.

Dana, Léo-Paul, ed. (2010), *Entrepreneurship and Religion,* Cheltenham: Edward Elgar.

Dana, Léo-Paul, and Teresa Dana (2000), "Taking Sides on the Island of Cyprus," *Journal of Small Business Management* 38 (2), pp. 80–87.

Dana, Léo-Paul, Hamid Etemad, and Richard W. Wright (2004), "International Entrepreneurship in the New Economy," in Marian V. Jones and Pavlos Dimitratos, eds., *Emerging Paradigms in International Entrepreneurship,* Cheltenham: Edward Elgar, pp. 19–36.

Dana, Léo-Paul, and Veland Ramadani (2015), "Context and Uniqueness of Transition Economies," in Léo-Paul Dana and Veland Ramadani, eds., *Family Businesses in Transition Economies,* Cham: Springer, pp. 39–69.

Evans, Joel R., and Richard L. Laskin (1994), "The Relationship Marketing Process: A Conceptualisation and Application," *Industrial Marketing Management* 23 (5), pp. 432–452.

Geertz, Clifford (1963), *Peddlers and Princes: Social Development and Economic Change in Two Indonesian Towns,* Chicago: University of Chicago Press.

Geertz, Clifford (1978), "The Bazaar Economy: Information and Search in Peasant Marketing," *American Marketing Review* 68, pp. 28–32.

Guerrero, Maribel, David Urbano, and Aidin Salamzadeh (2015), "Entrepreneurial Transformation in the Middle East: Experiences From Tehran Universities," *Technics Technologies Education Management* 10 (4), pp. 533–537.

Keshavarzian, Arang (2007), *Bazaar and State in Iran: The Politics of the Tehran Marketplace,* Cambridge University Press.

Light, Ivan H., and Léo-Paul Dana (2020), *Entrepreneurs and Capitalism Since Luther: Rediscovering the Moral Economy,* Lanham: Lexington Books.

Long, George W. (1952), "Indochina Faces the Dragon," *National Geographic* 102 (3), pp. 287–328.

McMillan, John (2002), *Reinventing the Bazaar: A Natural History of Markets,* New York and London: W.W. Norton & Company.

McMillan, John, and Christopher Woodruff (1999), "Informal Relationships and Interfirm Credit in Vietnam," *Quarterly Journal of Economics* 114, pp. 1285–1320.

Normohammadzad, Hamid, and Saeed Makky (2018), "Redesigning Bazaar Physical Structure According to its Dealing Culture Structure-Case Study: Arab Bazaar in Ahvaz City," *Iran University of Science & Technology* 28(2), pp. 202–214.

Passantino, Joseph E. (1946), "Kunming, Southwestern Gateway to China," *National Geographic* 90 (2), pp. 137–168.

Penrose, Edith T. (1959), *The Theory of the Growth of the Firm,* Oxford: Blackwell.

Ramadani, Veland, Esra Memili, Ramo Palalić, and Erick P. C. Chang, eds. (2020), *Entrepreneurial Family Businesses,* Cham: Springer.

Rezaei, Shahamak, Birte Hansen, Veland Ramadani, and Léo-Paul Dana (2019), "The Resurgence of Bazaar Entrepreneurship: 'Ravabet-Networking' and the Case of the Persian Carpet Trade," in Veland Ramadani, Léo-Paul Dana, Vanessa Ratten, and Abdylmenaf Bexheti, eds., *Informal Ethnic Entrepreneurship,* Cham: Springer, pp. 63–82.

Salamzadeh, Aidin, Mohammad Ali Azimi, and David A. Kirby (2013), "Social Entrepreneurship Education in Higher Education: Insights From a Developing Country," *International Journal of Entrepreneurship and Small Business* 20 (1), pp. 17–34.

Thompson, Jamie, Ian W. F. Baxter, Ross Curran, Martin Joseph Gannon, Sean Lochrie, Babak Taheri, and Ozge Yalinay (2018), "Negotiation, Bargaining, and Discounts: Generating WoM and Local Tourism Development at the Tabriz Bazaar, Iran," *Current Issues in Tourism* 21 (11), pp. 1207–1214.

Webster, Frederick E. (1992), "The Changing Role of Marketing in the Corporation," *Journal of Marketing* 53, pp. 1–17.

Yong, Enn Lun (2019), "Understanding Cultural Diversity and Economic Prosperity in Europe: A Literature Review and Proposal of a Culture–Economy Framework," *Asian Journal of German and European Studies* 4 (5), pp. 1–34.

Zineldin, Mosad Amin (1998), "Towards an Ecological Collaborative Relationship Management," *European Journal of Marketing* 32 (11–12), pp. 1138–1164.

CPSIA information can be obtained
at www.ICGtesting.com
Printed in the USA
JSHW051556060722
27556JS00001BA/73

9 789811 229688